Theoretical Perspectives on Sexual Difference

Theoretical Perspectives on Sexual Difference

EDITED BY DEBORAH L. RHODE

YALE UNIVERSITY PRESS

NEW HAVEN AND LONDON

Published with assistance from the foundation established in memory of Philip Hamilton McMillan of the Class of 1894, Yale College.

Designed by Nancy Ovedovitz and set in New Baskerville type by Keystone Typesetting, Inc., Orwigsburg, Pennsylvania. Printed in the United States of America by Vail-Ballou Press, Binghamton, New York.

Library of Congress Cataloging-in-Publication Data

Theoretical perspectives on sexual difference / edited by Deborah L. Rhode.
     p.   cm.
  ISBN 0–300–04427–5 (cloth)
       0–300–05225–1 (pbk.)
   1. Feminism—Philosophy. 2. Sex differences. 3. Sex role. I. Rhode, Deborah L.
HQ1206.T45 1990
305.42'01—dc20   89–25083
                                                                                   CIP

3   5   7   9   10   8   6   4   2

For Lorraine

Contents

PART SIX
EPILOGUE

Acknowledgments

This volume is the outgrowth of a conference sponsored by Stanford's Institute for Research on Women and Gender in winter 1987. It owes debts of gratitude to many individuals including Stanford faculty participants Lawrence Friedman, Eleanor Maccoby, and Diane Middlebrook, and Institute staff Dee Gustavson and Marilyn Hershey. Marilyn Yalom, Deputy Director of the Institute, offered crucial guidance and support; Peter Chadwick, Cynthia Epstein, and Temma Kaplan made astute editorial suggestions; Ann Tillery painstakingly prepared the index; and Lorraine Macchello provided invaluable assistance in preparing the manuscript for publication. Finally, and most importantly, I am deeply grateful to all of the contributors to this volume. The insights we have exchanged across multiple disciplines have been of great value to those of us affiliated with the project and, we hope, to a broader audience.

Theoretical Perspectives on Sexual Difference

DEBORAH L. RHODE

No issue has been more central to the American women's movement than sexual difference. From a variety of disciplinary perspectives, these collected essays explore a common set of questions about the nature, origins, and consequences of that difference. Taken together, these perspectives lay the foundations for a more integrated approach to enduring concerns. What difference difference makes has fundamental implications for social theory and social change.

This work grows out of a conference sponsored by Stanford's Institute for Research on Women and Gender, which brought together scholars in anthropology, biology, history, law, literature, philosophy, political theory, psychology, and sociology. The objective was to encourage analysis that, by bridging disciplinary boundaries, would become more conscious of its own capacities and constraints. Since gender as a conceptual framework cuts across traditional academic territories, the rationale for such intellectual interchange is particularly strong. Although this point is often recognized in principle, it is difficult to realize in practice due to limitations of time, tradition, and academic structure. The premise of this collection is that scholars concerned with women and gender can do more to engage and expand their audience. We can become less parochial in vocabulary, more self-critical in methodology, and better informed in our reliance on other disciplines.

Our scholarship can also become more attentive to an enduring paradox in feminist traditions. In an important sense, the women's movement rests on the differences it seeks to challenge. From its beginning, the feminist campaign has sought to prevent sex-related differences from limiting individuals' aspirations and achievements. Yet by definition the movement also presupposes some recognition of women's common interests and concerns. In that respect, feminism assumes a shared experience it seeks in large measure to challenge.

What complicates the issue still further is the diversity of those experiences, a diversity that is gaining greater recognition within the women's movement. Over the last century, American feminists have centered theoretical and political attention on differences between men and women. Over the last decade, feminists have increasingly realized the importance of focusing also on differences among women, and on the way those differences mediate gender relations. A crucial contribution of recent theory has been its emphasis on diversity across class, race, ethnicity, age, and sexual orientation. A primary objective, to which many of the essays in this volume speak, is to understand how common biological characteristics are differently experienced by different groups of women in different social and historical circumstances.

A related project is to develop better strategies for building on both the commonalities and variations in women's experience. We need a richer understanding of how the difference that unites women as women—their difference from men—can become a force for united political action. And we need a clearer sense of how the differences that separate women as women—class, race, ethnicity, age, sexual orientation—can become the basis for alliance with other subordinate groups. Only by enlarging our theoretical perspectives on difference are we likely to reduce the social disadvantages it has imposed.

THEORIES ABOUT DIFFERENCE

A threshold issue involves this collection's reliance on the term *sex* rather than *gender*. For the last quarter century, many American feminists have sought to distinguish between those concepts. Under contemporary usage, *sex* has referred to biologically based distinctions between man and woman and *gender* has referred to their cultural constructions. Underlying this distinction has been the premise, implicit or explicit, that the most significant differences between the sexes have been a function of culture, not chromosomes.

By the late 1970s, however, a growing number of feminist theorists were pointing up difficulties with that conceptual framework. Their work has emphasized the interdependence of social and biological forces. Increasing attention has focused on the way cultural practices influence the evolution of physiological differences and the way that these differences in turn help structure social relations.[1] Yet the deconstruction of the sex/gender divide has given new force to long-standing problems. How to acknowledge without amplifying difference remains a dilemma of central importance to the women's movement.

This dilemma grows out of a historical tradition that ascribed overriding importance to biological explanations for differences in the sexes' social roles and status. Throughout this nation's first two centuries, the assumption was that women's nature was to nurture and that cultural institutions must inevitably reflect this fact. As Carl Degler's historical account of sociobiology and Susan Moller Okin's review of traditional political theory remind us, American feminism emerged in the mid-nineteenth century, when the sexes' "separate spheres" appeared physiologically grounded, as well as spiritually ordained and culturally desirable. Women's unique reproductive capacities and responsibilities were thought to preempt other pursuits. A common premise within the nineteenth- and early twentieth-century scientific community was that individuals had limited "vital forces" available for cognitive and reproductive tasks. Females who diverted their scarce biological reserves to intellectual endeavors could expect a host of maladies including, in some cases, permanent sterility. Rigorous educational or vocational pursuits could result only in deforming, defeminizing, or eventually depleting any group of women who sought to avoid their domestic destiny.[2]

Similar theories about the deadly "brain-womb" conflict emerged to explain women's allegedly inferior cognitive abilities. Such theories, together with generalizations about innate maternal instincts, provided biological grounding for traits traditionally associated with femininity. Conventional wisdom was that woman's nurturing role "inevitably affect[ed] all her thoughts and sentiments," and left her with a "less developed capacity for abstract justice" and a less "rational" approach toward political and professional affairs than her male counterparts.[3]

In response to such claims, feminists generally have taken two approaches, both of which remain critical in contemporary debates over difference. One strategy has been to deny the extent or essential nature of differences between men and women. A second approach has been to celebrate difference—to embrace characteristics historically associated with women and demand their equal social recognition. A third, more recent strategy attempts to dislodge difference—to challenge its centrality and its organizing premises and to recast the terms on which gender relations have traditionally been debated.

The first approach, that of denial, has been most influential in exposing fallacies in the "eternal feminine." One result has been a richer understanding of gender biases in conventional paradigms. From a variety of disciplinary perspectives, feminists have explored how data have been constructed, not simply collected, and how cultural influences have been misrepresented as biological imperatives. Clinical, laboratory, and field research has documented the extended history of exaggerated differences.[4] The strengths of this approach are reflected in many of the essays

that follow, including Ruth Hubbard's and John Dupré's critiques of sociobiology, Jane Collier's and Sylvia Yanagisako's review of standard anthropological models, and Nancy Chodorow's challenges to conventional psychoanalytic frameworks.

Of course, whatever else we may wish to say about difference between
the sexes, we cannot deny its existence. But we can deny its essentiality and
identify reasons for its significance that are not biologically determined.
An important strand of feminist scholarship has focused on forces that
give cultural meaning to physiology, such as processes of role socialization,
sex-based divisions of labor, and devaluation of nonmarket work. These
forces are central to much of the discussion that follows, including Kay
Deaux's and Brenda Major's exploration of situational influences on gender behavior, Barrie Thorne's review of the literature on child development, Catharine MacKinnon's analysis of male dominance, and Nancy
Chodorow's explanations of the reproduction of mothering.

Yet as the preceding discussion has suggested, efforts to distinguish
cultural and biological factors have their own limitations. Nature and nurture interrelate in ways that defy quantification. As Hubbard's and Dupré's
critiques of sociobiology make evident, cultural norms have shaped even
the most ostensibly "natural" differences between men and women. For
example, we cannot understand sex-based differentials of height, weight,
and physical strength without considering the influence of diet, dress,
division of labor, and so forth. Such biological and cultural factors can
never be wholly disentangled. As Hubbard notes, changes in sex-related
characteristics do not occur "one variable at a time," and the evolution of
behavioral patterns leaves no fossils.[5]

Debates over "real" differences risk entrapping us in age-old controversies that are insoluble in theory and often irrelevant in practice. Even
commentators like Carl Degler, who are in some measure sympathetic to
sociobiological approaches, warn us against the "naturalistic fallacy," which
assumes that nature rather than values determines human choice. Recent
developments in reproductive technology emphasize that the most central
physiological distinctions between the sexes are subject to considerable
human control. What forms that control should take are matters for normative judgment. As Herma Kay's essay makes clear, biological premises
are a misleading guide to policy prescriptions.

A final limitation of approaches that deny the extent or essentiality of
difference is that they risk reinforcing a value structure they seek to challenge. Affirmations of similarity between women and men may inadvertently universalize or validate norms of the dominant social group, norms
that have been inattentive to women's interests, experiences, and perspectives. Arguments about whether women are like or unlike men still proceed with men as the standard of comparison.

In recognition of this difficulty, a second strand of feminist work has sought to challenge not the significance of gender differences, but the value society has attached to them. This tradition has demanded recognition for the concerns and characteristics historically associated with women. The strengths of this framework emerge in the philosophical contributions of Alison Jaggar, Nel Noddings, and Susan Okin. Drawing on theorists including Carol Gilligan, Mary O'Brien, and Sara Ruddick, this approach has stressed the importance of caretaking relationships in explaining attributes historically linked with women. This tradition can provide an important counterweight to pressures from the dominant culture and can enhance women's sense of solidarity and self-respect. By insisting that values central to women's experience be *valued,* it can also identify directions necessary for social change.[6]

Yet if strategies that deny the extent or essentiality of difference have proven problematic, the same is true of strategies that celebrate it. Approaches that acknowledge traditional dualisms while attempting to reverse their social standing present difficulties on several levels. In part, those difficulties are empirical. Critics from a variety of disciplines have identified limitations in such influential works as Carol Gilligan's, which posits that women reason in "a different voice," a voice concerned less with abstract rights than with concrete relationships. Too often, such research has been constrained by the same factors that feminists have criticized in more traditional scholarship: universalization from small, unrepresentative samples; failure to consider differences in women's experience across culture, class, race, age, ethnicity, and sexual orientation; and inattention to the historical, social, and economic factors that mediate these experiences.[7] The importance of avoiding such homogenization of women's experience is apparent from many of the essays that follow, particularly Bell Hooks's and Julianne Malveaux's work on race, Karen Offen's analysis of European feminism, and Barrie Thorne's exploration of the relationships between class, race, and gender among children.

These dangers of homogenization are underscored by empirical research that casts doubt on how different women's "different voice" really is. Much contemporary scholarship on moral reasoning and related issues suggests less substantial sex-based variations than feminist celebrations of difference imply.[8] Although gender is an important part of what constructs and constrains human identity, its influence is heavily dependent on other cultural institutions, ideologies, and ideals.

In any event, the most critical issue is neither empirical nor methodological, but normative. The extent to which the sexes exhibit different values or reasoning styles is far less important than the consequences of stressing such differences in particular contexts. On a theoretical level, an emphasis on difference often risks oversimplifying and overclaiming. Males' association with abstract rationality and females' with interpersonal nurturance reflects long-standing dichotomies that have restricted opportunities for both sexes.

Moreover, the exaltation of women's "different voice" overlooks circumstances in which that voice speaks in more than one register. Women's disproportionate assumption of caretaking responsibilities has encouraged forms of psychological dependence and sex-role socialization that carry heavy costs. That this "down side of difference" has received inadequate attention should not be surprising. Much of what is theoretically and politically empowering about the feminist validation of difference comes from its insistence on the positive attributes of women's experience. But that emphasis exacts a price. History warns against the sentimentalities that often colored suffragist claims. Despite the assertions of some nineteenth- and early twentieth-century activists, woman's participation did not "purify politics."[9] It is equally unlikely that an "add women and stir" approach will of itself reshape the structure and substance of contemporary decision making. As the essays by Nancy Chodorow, Barrie Thorne, Kay Deaux, and Brenda Major emphasize, situational factors play a critical role in eliciting and suppressing gender-related characteristics. If we wish to secure greater influence for values associated with women, we need greater attention to the social circumstances that would encourage such influence.

For that reason, an increasing body of feminist work seeks less to deny or embrace difference than to alter the terms on which it traditionally has been conceptualized. This third strategy attempts to challenge the deep hold that dualisms continue to exercise on public consciousness and the way that gender draws on such analytic structures. The objective is to dislodge difference as the exclusive focus of gender-related questions.[10]

As long as we formulate such questions only in terms of male-female comparisons, we risk obscuring much of the relationship we seek to understand. For example, when psychologists measure sex-related difference, they typically find statistical frequencies rather than rigid dichotomies. Yet this work often ends up reinforcing oppositional categories. To take one of Barrie Thorne's illustrations, much existing research on children translates sex-based correlations into discourses on dualism. Even studies that reveal few sex-linked differences and carefully avoid reductionist accounts often result in popular reinterpretations that view the world in "pinks and blues" (e.g., girls display more verbal ability, boys play more aggressively).[11] Such comparative frameworks inevitably, if inadvertently, flatten analysis. They deflect focus from gender as a social relation and obscure the processes that amplify or mute its significance. To see women only in comparison with men also diverts attention from women's relations to each other and to power distributions that cut across sex-based categories.

So too, as this volume's legal essays emphasize, the focus on difference in policy debates has yielded results that are inconsistent, indeterminate, and often indefensible. Differences have all too often served as "inequality's post-hoc excuse for itself. They are the outcome presented as its origin."[12] For purposes of structuring social policy, we need to worry less about difference and more about patterns of disadvantage and dominance. Women ought not to have to seem just like men to gain equal respect, recognition, and economic security.

That will require not only less preoccupation with sexual difference, but also greater resistance to masculine/feminine associations with other oppositional categories such as nature/culture, public/private, or emotion/intellect. In addition, we need to exercise greater skepticism about those categories themselves, since, as Collier and Yanagisako note, they often function to assume what they should explain. Our objective should be a more integrated conceptual landscape, one that offers a richer sense of gender dynamics and human possibilities.

When the subject is gender, we may never escape some themes of difference. But we can refocus inquiry on the differing dimensions of difference. Informed by interdisciplinary perspectives, our work can yield deeper understandings of the process through which sex-linked attributes acquire social meaning. By becoming more self-conscious about our strategic choices—about when to deny, celebrate, or dislodge difference—we may come closer to minimizing the inequalities it has traditionally entailed.

DIFFERENCES ABOUT THEORY

These crosscutting perspectives can also enrich our thinking about theory in general and feminist theory in particular. The interchange that produced this volume has raised concerns along several dimensions. One set of issues has to do with the role of theory in its broadest sense. A related group of questions involves the specific contributions of feminism, and the difficulties of aligning its methodological and political commitments.

It is ironic that just at the moment when feminist theory is gaining influence in traditional disciplines, it is raising increasing doubts about its own claims to influence. Over the last two decades, the dramatic growth of women's studies has transformed the academic landscape. Theoretical structures constructed primarily by, for, and about men have been forced to take account of different experiences, data, and methodologies.[13] Yet the same feminist strategies that have challenged traditional paradigms have also raised questions about their own theoretical foundations.

Informed by postmodernist criticisms from various disciplines, recent feminist work has expressed growing ambivalence about the capacities of theory. In part this disquiet stems from contemporary critiques of objectivity and universality. Leading social theorists, including prominent feminists, have increasingly emphasized the impossibility of value-free forms of knowledge, and the inability of any single overarching framework adequately to illumine social experience. Theoretical approaches that have claimed such adequacy have often proven too broad and abstract to explain particular ideological, material, and historical relationships, or too narrow to yield insights about larger cultural patterns.[14]

Yet to the extent that feminism seeks not just to challenge but to construct a social vision, its alliance with postmodernism becomes more difficult. Many theorists are left in the awkward position of claiming that oppression exists while challenging our capacity to be sure of it. This postmodernist paradox leaves feminists both denying our ability to know reality and demanding accounts that more adequately reflect it.

In response to these concerns, the essays that follow offer varying perspectives. However, their place in this collection implies a common premise: it is possible to remain skeptical about Theory while recognizing the need for theories, for multiple accounts from multiple disciplines at multiple levels that avoid privileging any single framework. In place of metanarratives that claim universal application, this volume argues for contextual, situated analysis.

A commitment to plural and provisional accounts does not, however, commit us to agnosticism toward the accounts offered. All understandings may be partial but some are more incomplete than others. Not all theories are equally self-critical, respectful of data, or attentive to women's experience.[15] We cannot cede the struggle for knowledge to those less respectful of its limitations. We can, however, be more self-critical about the partiality of our understanding and more explicit about the values underlying it.

We can also be more attentive to the logical implications of those values, and to their relevance for the contemporary women's movement. Although the definition of feminism has varied over time and culture, in modern American society it usually signifies commitments to gender as a category of analysis and to gender equality as a social goal. Yet what exactly these commitments entail has proven increasingly problematic. Here again, feminism finds itself intertwined with postmodernist tendencies that it can neither wholly embrace nor renounce. As Regenia Gagnier's essay notes, much recent feminist work, like other critical theories from which it draws, envisions human subjects with fractured identities—subjects who are culturally situated and divided by class, race, ethnicity, sexual orientation, and so forth. Yet how can feminists rally around the concept of Woman once they deny that any such universal category exists?

This paradox has implications for feminism as a political as well as a theoretical movement. There are obvious risks in deconstructing the identity on which practical struggle is grounded. Feminists traditionally have claimed authority by aspiring to speak from women's experience. Yet this experience warns against homogenizing women's lives and undervaluing their different cultural circumstances. As many of this volume's essays reflect, women by no means speak with one voice on matters of public policy. And such policies often require formulation from a stance of partial ignorance. We seldom have adequate information about the differential effects of legal or legislative mandates on discrete groups of women.

If "women" is in some respects too broad a category to be useful, it can also be too narrow. That is the dilemma that philosophers John Dupré and Alison Jaggar make clear. Any ethical and political framework adequate to challenge sexual inequality must similarly condemn the other forms of social injustice with which such inequality intersects. But broadening the focus also risks diffusion and division. These risks contribute to recurrent tensions between theory and practice in the women's movement. In principle, we need to fight "on all fronts at once." In practice, can we afford to?[16]

But can we afford not to? While the essays in this volume by no means resolve this tension, they do suggest ways to reformulate it. We cannot escape difference by what Frye labels an "additive method," attaching an endless string of qualifying adjectives to the label woman (white, middle-class, middle-aged, heterosexual . . .).[17] We can, however, seek a richer appreciation of the relationships between these characteristics and the shared experience that bridges them. The factors that divide women can serve also as a basis for enriching their perspectives and uniting them with other subordinate groups.

By building on these affinities, feminism can in some measure recast the dualisms that gave it birth. On a conceptual level we can work toward greater "critical consciousness."[18] Through cross-disciplinary work, we can deepen perceptions of our gendered nature of theory and our theories about gender. These perceptions can, in turn, inform a political agenda that seeks coalitions against injustice and the ideologies underlying it. In that sense, a focus on sex-related differences invites us to look both beneath and beyond them. A better understanding of our differences permits a better understanding of our commonalities—our common needs, aspirations, and humanity—and the social progress they demand.

PART ONE

Historical and Theoretical Overviews

Feminism and Sexual Difference in Historical Perspective

KAREN OFFEN

The challenge of postmodern thought has engaged the attention of scholars in many fields, not least in feminist theory. As debate has proceeded, however, the voices of historians have been missing or heard only discreetly in the background. It is high time that historians of women and of feminism enter this debate. Practitioners of the historical craft, especially those who work on comparative history, have much to contribute to this endeavor.

At the core of the feminist project lies the claim of solidarity or common cause among women as a group across lines of religion, class, race, and other historically significant divisions. This claim has generally rested on a common set of female values and aspirations, rooted more often than not in motherhood and nurturance and also in an effort to reclaim for women the right to define what "women" are and should be.[1] It bears emphasis that this was from the beginning a call for solidarity, not a description of reality. In earlier centuries perhaps even more than today many factors divided both women and men. Like the assertion in our own Declaration of Independence that all men are created equal, the claim for female solidarity was a brave and utopian assertion. The French journalist "Jeanne-Victoire" put it this way in 1832, in an all-women's newspaper, *La Femme libre* [The free woman]: "Liberty, equality—that is to say, a free and equal chance to develop our faculties: this is the victory we must win, and we can succeed only if we unite in a single group. Let us no longer form two camps—that of the women of the people and that of privileged women. Let our common interest unite us. To this end, let all jealousy among us disappear."[2] From the early nineteenth century to our own time, female solidarity has been an aspiration posited in recognition of the oppression of women as a group by men as a group; such solidarity was never and is not today a given. What is at stake in the debate between postmodernists and feminists is whether this aspiration to female solidarity should continue to provide a foundation for political action.

Contemporary American feminist theory and practice offers evidence of a growing breach between elite (or intellectual) and popular culture, in this instance represented by speculative academics who are more comfortable with complexities and movement activists and members of the general public who are not. The hierarchical preference given to theory may threaten communication—and effective cooperation—with grass-roots organizers. This collection reflects that schism. A sharp disjuncture exists between the recognizably feminist voice of Gloria Watkins (Bell Hooks), who seems to speak in the tradition of concrete action and the valuation of women qua women in extant communities, and the postmodern theoretical proposals of John Dupré and Jane Collier and Sylvia Yanagisako, who in effect are proposing to reduce the sociocultural effect of physiological differences between the sexes to one set of factors no more or no less important than many others and to posit, in a fashion now called postmodernist, a sociopsychological fragmentation of identities. But are these individuals ultimately committed to the same project?

Just as historians are attempting to bridge the gap to the public through women's history, to arouse interest in the historical project of women's emancipation in order to achieve advances in our own time, theorists with postmodern tendencies seem determined to broaden that gap. Is the emancipation of women as a group relative to men as a group no longer a central concern in our time? What should be the social significance of differences in what some call "biology" when they mean reproductive physiology? Should reproductive physiology make a sociocultural difference? Are the values associated with childbearing and nurture imposed only from outside, as some would argue, or do they arise from women's experience throughout history of their own bodily existence? Have reproduction and the requirements of maternity ceased to provide unifying ground? Is the availability of reliable birth control measures and the declining need in industrial societies for constant reproduction responsible for a changing perspective on women's potential for solidarity? Or does sheer bodily similarity and the social construction of its meaning continue to override efforts at deconsolidation? Has the historical conflict for women between the family and freedom been resolved? Can one have it "both ways," as Alison Jaggar and Regenia Gagnier hope? From the historical viewpoint, and despite clever arguments to the contrary, there is reason to doubt it.

Feminism is a political project, and political projects continue to entail choices from which there may be no retreat. Are you with us or against us? Are you ally, enemy, fellow traveler, fifth column? Intellectuals and theorists have historically resisted making hard political choices in the name of higher, seemingly more complete, more complex wisdom. In the process, they have often condemned themselves to political impotence. That is why, in revolutionary times, intellectuals and theorists—those whose thinking is in advance of the common horde's—have always been among the first to be brought before the firing squad. What I am asking here is for us to consider, from a historical perspective, whether the radical new postmodern politics (postmodern feminism, as some call it) suggested by many of the theorists in this volume and elsewhere is really visionary or simply evasive. Can this politics be qualified as "postmodern feminism" or is it rather "postfeminist postmodernism"? How useful to the emancipation and advancement of women is the postmodern critique, particularly its deconstruction of the category "women"? Will it help us to eradicate the subordination of women as a group by men as a group? Or is it a threat to the feminist project? What meaning should feminists attribute to the category women?

In fact, according to the three broad criteria I have sketched out elsewhere for recognizing feminists, postmodern thinking about women fails all the tests.[3] The fragmentation of identities it proposes, specifically the dissolution of the category women, threatens the historical feminist project; its effect is neatly encapsulated in the English limerick about the centipede and the toad:

> The Centipede was happy quite,
> Until the Toad in fun
> Said, "Pray which leg goes after which?"
> And worked her mind to such a pitch,
> She lay distracted in the ditch
> Considering how to run.[4]

Without the category women, the feminist project founders. The category women is essential in relation to the equally essential category men. This dualism persists in our sexed bodies and in our cultural constructions of their meaning.

Dualism is much criticized by postmodern theorists. Yet, a striking feature in the history of human thought is the persistence of dualism—of the male/female dichotomy, sameness/difference, subject/object, yin/yang, right/left, up/down, abstract/concrete, and so forth. Even those who seek to transcend dualism often fall back on dualistic terms, as when John Dupré juxtaposes "essentialism" and "antiessentialism." As others have pointed out, such dualism is deeply enmeshed in Western languages, and hence in our thinking. Nowhere is this more so than in the popular mind. The domestic/public dichotomy has come down to us from Roman law; nature/culture was a staple of eighteenth-century Enlightenment thought; the privileging of reason over feeling (and the identification of these terms with male and female) dates from seventeenth-century post-Reformation efforts to reconstruct the European mental universe.

Study of history, in particular the history of women and of feminism, has much to offer contemporary theoreticians. In many interdisciplinary collections, including this one, history has (as I have said) most often been honored in the breach, for historical data and interpretation have the untidy effect of muddying the crystalline waters of theory. One gets little sense when reading contemporary postmodern theory on difference of the place of such theory in the historical "long view"—that is, not over the last twenty to thirty years, but over centuries of human development.[5] To make only one point, neither the history of women nor the history of feminism, nor yet thought about sexual difference, began in 1859–60 with the contributions of Darwin and Marx. To suggest that they did ludicrously oversimplifies the past.

A historical perspective on such matters first entails cross-cultural comparisons. These would draw their data not primarily from the simpler, far less populous societies documented in the anthropological profession's Human Area Resources files, but from complex, populous, highly organized societies. Such comparisons would reveal both the distinctively Anglo-American tenor of the discussions of difference that characterize so much contemporary theory in the United States and the incipient imperialism of such models. What is revealed is an atomistic focus on the liberation of the human individual—a sort of Hobbesian or Leibnitzian monad devoid of distinguishing characteristics. While pointing to the complexity of human identity and inferring its fragmentation, such a perspective reveals itself as existing apart from any notion of community, state, or national sociopolitical goals. This approach to autonomy and the "reconstruction of individualism" could hardly occur in most other Western countries, much less in the rest of the world, where even today sociopolitical goals (such as struggles over territory, the creation of new nation-states, and the restructuring of old ones) continue to override the struggle for individual identity by women and by men. Our emphasis is not the "traditional" one some have suggested, but very exceptional. What some take to be our "cultural assumptions" are the result of once radical assertions that were deployed as weapons in a unique, successful attack on hierarchical religious and political authority in a society where men have systematically subordinated women since at least the thirteenth century.[6]

The history of feminist theory and practice can illuminate these claims. Briefly put, in the seventeenth and eighteenth centuries (in the wake of the Protestant Reformation and Catholic Counterreformation), European sociopolitical critics elaborated their criticism of theological explanations of the natural and social world by articulating what became known as the scientific approach. They invoked physiological, materialistic explanations of social phenomena to displace the claims of religious authority. The social construction of the human and animal body became a metaphor for the body politic as well. The materiality of the human body and sexual differences were called upon to explain and in particular to rejustify basic social arrangements.[7] Here, not with Darwin, we must look for, locate, and contextually examine the so-called biological arguments for sexual difference, as well as early anthropological studies, which emerged and continue to function in many instances as exercises in cultural criticism. The rise of biodeterministic thinking about the sexes is situated here, and it must be contested here. Darwin's use of such arguments merely confirms an earlier development.

What we can call a tradition of feminist contestation of male domination also launches itself in this early modern period, even before a word existed to epitomize it. The roots of this critique are distinctively Western European but by no means wholly English, as is often claimed.[8] The importance of the French contribution—informed by the radical skepticism of the philosopher René Descartes, with its mind/body dualism—requires underscoring. What is of particular interest is that throughout the nineteenth century and well into the twentieth, French feminists, like the surrounding French high culture in which these ideas were elaborated, not only accepted but insisted on physiological dualism between the sexes and on female experience as mothers as grounds for the project of emancipating women, even demanding a redistribution of political and social power on their behalf. In France notions of complementarity of the sexes and "equality in difference" were fully elaborated. These influenced feminist thinking throughout the rest of Europe and in European colonies and dependencies.[9]

As Carl Degler correctly suggests, notions of biological or physiological difference were widely used in the United States to argue for women's emancipation: what bears underscoring is that our experience was by no means unique. In twentieth-century Europe, such arguments led to extensive protective labor legislation for women, to state-funded maternity leaves with job security for employed women, and to nationally funded family allowance programs. These programs, though by no means always constructed to women's specifications, did benefit many women in the short run.[10] Such programs were explicitly rejected in the United States.

What requires explanation is American *resistance* to such projects on women's behalf amid the many European initiatives that underlay the development of the twentieth-century welfare state.[11]

Historically speaking, two intertwined strands can be identified in European (and also in American) feminist thinking.[12] The first of these, which I have called *relational feminism,* emphasizes the family, the couple, or the mother/child dyad as the basic social unit of the nation. Physiological differences between the sexes thus become the linchpins for a visionary construction of equitable social differences. The requirements of community, not the needs of the individual, dictated the sociopolitical program, and what some call *womanliness* and others *femininity* was asserted as an enduring and worthy social characteristic. The emphasis was placed on female-defined values. The second strand, individualist feminism, privileges the individual, virtually without reference to the community or group. Physiological differences and hence sociopolitical differences are muted, and equality of individuals and their claim to certain "rights" or entitlements, based on an eighteenth-century model devised for male heads of households (not single men), is uncompromisingly asserted. Within individualist feminism womanly qualities or attributes are necessarily downplayed.

Until very recent times, relational feminism has remained the historically dominant strand in the Western world. Individualist feminism, identified by Europeans (especially since the late nineteenth century) as distinctively Anglo-American, has been a minority phenomenon. Prior to the midnineteenth century it was restricted to notions of moral and intellectual development for women; only recently have material conditions of immense prosperity in North America and Great Britain allowed it to flourish and dominate public discourse. Even Mary Wollstonecraft, who is often thought of as championing an archindividualist concept of women's rights, insisted that "the being who discharges the duties of its station is independent; and speaking of women at large, their first duty is to themselves as rational creatures, and the next in point of importance, as citizens, is that which includes so many, of a mother." To read this statement in the context of her work is to discover that her notion of a rational creature did not override the sex-role related duties expected by society.[13]

As late twentieth-century feminist scholars, we take a great deal for granted. It is important to remind ourselves that the questions we ask today and the goals we now set for women could not be asked or set, had not many of the earlier goals of feminism been achieved. For one, educational goals—women's admission to literacy, to formal education from the primary level to the university, have largely been realized in the Western world (though by no means in other parts of the world). The religious and secular marriage laws that long oppressed married women as a legal class, relieving them of authority over their own persons and property without distinction of social class, race, or ethnicity have been radically reformed in most Western countries. Secular divorce laws have been enacted, most recently in Italy and Spain, over the bitter opposition of the Catholic church. Women now vote in many of the world's countries and enjoy civil, political, and even economic rights that only a hundred years ago were but dreams and aspirations. Such laws are not always as progressive as some feminists would like, but the institutionalizing of rights in law marks a giant step forward. Enforcement is another matter.

More excruciating problems, notably questions concerning professional and economic opportunities for women that free them from dependence on men and from poverty, questions of sexual violence and prostitution, and reproductive control, remain on the agenda. Political and educational emancipation for women is still an issue in many parts of the non-Western world. It would be foolish to claim that feminists even in the Western world have achieved all goals for women's emancipation. The problems that remain are difficult, deeply rooted, and without question woman-specific.

In response to those who suggest that "postmodern feminism" is a project for individual human emancipation that would neutralize or render irrelevant the question of gender predicated on sexual difference, or that questions of race, class, ethnicity (and perhaps also creed) should have equal weight, let me invoke the counterchallenge posed by the Swedish feminist activist Ellen Key. In 1904, during an era of European nationalism, rampant materialism, a major socialist challenge to capitalism, and state concern with the politics of motherhood, Key prophetically wrote: "We are here face to face with the profoundest movement of the time, woman's desire of freedom as a human being and as a personality, and in this we are confronted with the greatest tragic conflict the world's history has hitherto witnessed. . . . The struggle that woman is now carrying on is far more far-reaching than any other; and if no diversion occurs, it will finally surpass in fanaticism any war of religion or race."[14] I submit that Key's prophecy retains its relevance in our time, and that we are not yet at the point where the feminist project can cede terrain to a postfeminist postmodernism or decree its own dissolution. To think otherwise is badly to misread the past—the history of feminist struggle—and to compromise prospects for a feminist future in which the subordination of women will have become a thing of the past.

The challenge to feminist theory today is not to downplay, minimize, or counterbalance the importance of sexual difference relative to other and also significant and unhealthy cultural manifestations of difference (whether race, class, religion, or other), but to rethink the strategies for female solidarity, now that reproduction and motherhood no longer offer all women a common framework, and to envision ways of restoring and maintaining for the long term a balance of power in society between the sexes. This can be accomplished only by confronting and challenging the conditions that perpetuate and threaten constantly to reinvent male dominance and female subjection. My prediction is that physiological sexual difference will always dictate a differential cultural construction of gender until such time as the reproduction of the species within a given culture ceases to be an issue. We are not there yet. Even if my prediction is wrong, however, the useful question for our society is not "what if" gender didn't matter, but "how to" construct gender in such a way that the opportunities and choices available to individual women and men are maximized while the goals of the society's future, including reproduction and parenting, are satisfactorily met. Study of the historical record reveals that difference, especially sexual difference, has often led to hierarchy, dominance, and grave inequalities, but it does not show that such differences must necessarily have that result. Rethinking and reclaiming sexual difference—and the category women—in a way that avoids the construction of domination/subordination hierarchies remains a viable theoretical and political project for our time.

Feminist Postmodernism:
The End of Feminism or
the Ends of Theory?

REGENIA GAGNIER

Drawing upon a pragmatic distinction, one could include within feminist studies the descriptive or analytic study of sex (biology or zoology); gender (women's and men's, or girls' and boys', experience of gender, masculinity and femininity); and women's experience (motherhood, female sexuality, female bonding, etc.). Feminist studies asks the question, What are the aspects of reality that bear upon the construction of gender and the situation of women? Within such a pragmatic distinction, feminist theory could be defined as systemic synthesis of the data of feminist studies, including causality, methodology, and metaphysics as well as normative issues in ethics or politics.

I want to keep this pragmatic distinction between feminist studies and feminist theory because it is important to recognize that the papers in this collection are all within feminist theory. Whatever their discipline, the authors ask questions synthesizing what feminist scholars in history, literature, biology, or economics have labored to provide, and they present what each discipline can bring to bear on the general area of feminist theory, systemic approaches to gender inequality. Given the interdisciplinary, theoretical, and speculative breadth of the collection, I am impressed by an apparent tendency toward what in my own field of cultural criticism would be called a feminist postmodernism. In this essay I shall provide a preliminary critique—an examination of the conditions of possibility and the limits—of what appears to be an incipient feminist postmodernism, beginning with its relation to alternate feminist projects.

SEXUAL DIFFERENCE AND
DIFFERENCES AMONG WOMEN

One such alternative feminist project is clarification of the "sexual difference" alluded to in the volume's title, *Theoretical Perspectives on Sexual*

Difference. This includes, above all, the beliefs about differences between men and women that have rationalized gender inequality. They have been *the* overriding concern of modern feminism since its inception in the Enlightenment and continue to hold—if confusedly and incoherently, as Rhode reminds us—a major place in ethics and jurisprudence. As the biologist and activist Anne Fausto-Sterling writes in *Myths of Gender: Biological Theories about Women and Men,* a work that effectively challenges many purportedly scientific claims for biological differences between the sexes, "The claim of difference has been and continues to be used to avoid facing up to very real problems in our educational system and has provided a rationale for discrimination against women in the workplace."[1] This notion of difference, which sanctions less demanding education for girls, low wages for women in the labor force, no financial compensation for work at home, and prohibition of women's full engagement in public life, remains the principal target of feminism, and scholars and activists (like Ruth Hubbard in biology and Deborah Rhode and Catharine MacKinnon in law) will continue to address it.

Yet there is a further notion of difference, one that has emerged within feminism itself and whose articulation may even be claimed as a product of feminist methods of research and practice. This is the notion of differences among women. At least since the consciousness-raising of the 1960s, feminist scholars and activists have, despite all obstacles, made their work known to one another. Consequently, one of the major products of feminism is awareness of differences in experience and opinion where we once thought uniformity and solidarity prevailed. Feminist theory has long proven itself equal to the battle of difference between men and women. Its task today is to take into account differences among women.

Yet taking into account these differences in practice entails a rejection of feminism's metanarratives. Anthropologists reject the notion that there are presocial or universal domains of social relations such as the Marxist reproductive and productive and look for the symbolic and social processes that make these domains appear "natural." Philosophers replace sex difference pictures for numerous overlapping constructions, so that feminism is not a unified field or subject matter but a political project. Psychologists explore the possibility that identity is founded on multiple relationships, that no person (like the mother) or symbol (like the phallus) can hold a single, unvarying place in everyone's psyche, and they call for a more critical approach to gender in psychoanalytic theory and practice. Sociologists have amassed persuasive evidence that there is no easy way to analyze gender construction without accounting for multiple differences, including differences of race, ethnicity, and class.

It cannot be overemphasized that these critiques of earlier feminist theorizing are rejecting precisely the stories of oppression that gave earlier feminism its discursive unity, the stories that provided slogans that incited action: the distinction between public and private, the nurturing mother, the centrality of gender in psychoanalysis, even the notion of universal male dominance. Such stories have been culturally relativized—not politically neutralized, but examined in detail in culturally specific environments—and criticized as essentialist or reductionist. Where we used to see simple sex difference or a crude dualism we now see heterogeneity. This view reflects feminist postmodernism.

POSTMODERNISM AND FEMINISM

Outside feminism, the concept of postmodernism has drifted (despite considerable protest) from its origins in aesthetics to widespread usage in interdisciplinary cultural criticism.[2] With respect to individuals, postmodernism refers to the diffusion and dispersal of the centered, self-reflective subject among multiple signifying practices, namely, the practices involved in the construction of meaning and value. With respect to society, it refers to the heterogeneity and nontotalizable quality of the social; it presents the social bond as an effect of the multiplicity of historical meanings and values that intersect in individuals. In postmodernist theory, categories like race, class, or gender are too reductive to describe the complexity of social identities. Accordingly, postmodern group alliances look like affinities or coalitions rather than identities, and they are characterized by fluidity, the ability to mobilize and disperse. Some theorists call them microresistances.[3] Feminists may recognize the postmodern condition by juxtaposing it with the ideological and institutional apparatuses of Victorianism: commercialism/early industrialism, nationalism, realism, the patriarchal nuclear family, separate spheres, and liberal feminism versus multinationalism, self-reflexivity, home work economies, women-headed households, "hyphenated" feminisms (see the quotations from Sandra Harding and Audre Lorde below), and the erosion of gender itself. Postmodernism is often represented by the antiorganic figure of pastiche—random accumulation and mere contiguity. Thus a common geopolitical emblem of postmodernism is Los Angeles, the city of Angels and Dodgers, with its superluxury multinationally financed megahotels rising on the plain of Spanish-speaking ghettos, the sprawling city of sentimentality and spectacle without center. Clearly, in such an arena—if this is the world of the future—any universal, totalizing theory may miss most of reality. And postmodernism duly denies the legitimacy of any universalist theoretical ground for social critique, especially the "master narratives" of the Enlightenment—progress toward material well-being, truth, and justice (as we Victorianists say, bread, knowledge, and freedom).

Feminists can and cannot be postmodernist. They cannot easily reject an

authoritative theoretical or political ground, for the bottom line of feminism is that the oppression of women exists, and its normative project is to
make the world better for women. On this point feminists agree, although
many of us would extend the emancipatory project beyond women. Yet we
may well need a "postmodern" theory of ethics and politics to further that
project.

Many of the essays in this collection reflect *this* postmodern view. They
demand that we, as scholars and theorists, first, incorporate an appreciation of heterogeneity and historical contingency (Hubbard and Dupré);
second, render each manifestation of male dominance in its relative specificity and autonomy (Collier and Yanagisako); and third, incorporate an
appreciation of the complexity of social identities (Thorne, Chodorow,
Deaux and Major).

Thus we will not have a dualism of sex difference but pluralisms, differences. Since heterogeneous differences are inextricable in individuals and
the social arena, politics (or common objectives in Rhode's sense) rather
than identities or essences must provide unity. If feminist "theory" is
needed at all, it will theorize this new emancipatory politics for women and
others.

The emphasis on difference and plurality under political auspices parallels other current theoretical work. Indeed my formulation above of the
demands upon us is indebted to other theorists including Nancy Fraser
and Linda Nicholson. Here is Ruth Hubbard, biologist, in an earlier work,
on differences between women:

> The very notion that there exists a prototypical woman who can be
> described in ways that reflect and have meaning for the lives of the many
> different women living in very different geographical, economic, political,
> and social settings needs to be challenged.[4]

Alice Jardine, literary critic, presents the figure of "woman" as the sign of
difference, alterity, the previously excluded and marginalized:

> In considering this new semiosis of woman, one is drawn to what would
> seem to be a . . . concern among the theoreticians of [post]modernity: a
> search for that which has been "left out," de-emphasized, hidden, or
> denied articulation within Western systems of knowledge. Gynesis has
> taken its place in France within a movement away from a concern with
> identity to a concern with difference, from wholeness to that which is in-
> complete, from representation to modes of presentation, metadiscourse
> to fiction, production to operation, and from Universal Truth to a search
> for new forms of legitimation through para-scientific models.[5]

Sandra Harding, philosopher of science, challenges foundationalist assumptions of a "women's standpoint" epistemology:

Finally, we shall later examine the important role to be played in emancipatory epistemologies and politics by open recognition of gender differences within racial groups and racial and cultural differences within gender groups. "Difference" can be a slippery and dangerous rallying point
for inquiry projects and for politics, but each emancipatory struggle needs
to recognize the agendas of other struggles as integral parts of its own
in order to succeed. . . . For each struggle, epistemologies and politics
grounded in solidarities could replace the problematic ones that appeal to
essentialized identities, which are, perhaps, spurious.[6]

Audre Lorde, poet, and one of the major spokespersons for feminist
"hyphenization," describes how some differences are exploited as racism,
sexism, ageism, heterosexism, elitism, and classism:

> Much of western European history conditions us to see human differ-
> ences in simplistic opposition to each other: dominant/subordinate, good/
> bad, up/down, superior/inferior. In a society where the good is defined in
> terms of profit rather than in terms of human need, there must always be
> some group of people who, through systematized oppression, can be
> made to feel surplus, to occupy the place of the dehumanized inferior.
> Within this society, that group is made up of Black and Third World
> people, working-class people, older people, and women.
>
> As a forty-nine-year-old Black lesbian feminist socialist mother of two,
> including one boy, and a member of an interracial couple, I usually find
> myself a part of some group defined as other, deviant, inferior, or just
> plain wrong . . . Certainly there are very real differences between us of
> race, age, and sex. But it is not those differences between us that are
> separating us. It is rather our refusal to recognize those differences, and
> to examine the distortions which result from our misnaming them and
> their effects upon human behavior and expectation . . . It is a lifetime
> pursuit for each one of us to extract these distortions from our living at
> the same time as we recognize, reclaim, and define those differences upon
> which they are imposed.[7]

As these quotations, with the exception of Jardine (whose interest is
primarily in narrative) make clear, this is not the postmodernism that
rejects all authoritative theoretical or political ground. But the quotations,
like the papers in this collection, *are* postmodern in their rejection of any
foundationalist or simple sense of identity based upon gender distinction
alone, as well as in their suspicion of other dualistic and politically-charged
distinctions between subjectivity and objectivity, inner and outer, and fact
and value. That is, they are all postmodern in their awareness of the
fractured or unorganic quality of our identities, what current jargon (to my
mind conveniently) labels "postmodern hyphenization."

If one is a forty-nine-year-old Black lesbian feminist socialist mother of
two, including one boy, and a member of an interracial couple, one's

allegiance at moments of crisis can never simply be to "women" and one's identity cannot simply be "a woman." Moreover, if one is thoughtful, one's alliances will be overdetermined in particularly righteous ways: one will not be feminist, for example, at the cost of being racist. This applies to groups, caucuses, or parties as well as to individuals. Understanding the fractured quality of our experience, the many aspects of ourselves that have personal and historical claims, should be the basis of our political and theoretical agenda.

FEMINIST POSTMODERNISM AND POLITICS (INSIDE THE WHALE)

Respect for difference, the mark of postmodernism in feminism, is evident in the academy. Most feminist scholars have ceased to look for *the* deep structure of sexism and have produced more concrete scholarship. Feminist studies, that is, has reached maturity without subsiding into authoritarianism. At its best, I believe, it has resisted the *auteur* practice of theory, avoiding (*the*) grand theory and (*the*) great theorist; it has no Derridas, Lacans, Foucaults, or Bartheses, but rather the richness and complexity of history, literature, science, and scholars of goodwill and cooperative efforts. In the past ten years my own field of periodization, Victorian studies, previously dominated by a few great men who could have been called Victorians themselves (so deeply did they identify with their data), has been permanently altered by social history and gender studies. In literature as in law, "theorists" tried to persuade us that the boundaries of our "interpretive communities" were defined by, and limited to, literature departments and professional schools on the East or West Coasts. They forgot that some of us were feminists at least as much as we were literary critics and lawyers, and that we were as impressed by the new social movements of the 1960s at least as much as they were by their respective professions and institutional apparatuses. When these "theorists" spoke of "our interpretive communities" in literature or in law, we were wondering, like Tonto to the Lone Ranger, "What do you mean—'our,' white man?" And now both cultural studies and critical legal studies (CLS) with its "fem crit" wing demonstrate that the interpretive communities of law and literature are not nearly so uniform and monolithic as they thought. CLS and cultural studies merit brief comment since they reflect the recent institutional politicizing, or raising to political consciousness, of two main disciplines, law and literature.

CLS was fueled in 1977 not by philosophical hermeneutics but by the feeling that legal theory had come to justify the status quo.[8] CLS's first task was to critique the "Law and Economics" theorists and the "rights" theorists for their rationalization of inequality. Its principal method was "trashing," or "delegitimating," what we in cultural studies call deconstruction. Its second task was to propose something else, to transform the institution of the law.

First CLS challenged what it called "liberalism" in politicolegal theory (which is not to be confused with the New Right's evident sense of "liberalism" as pertaining to communists, perverts, drug abusers, and baby killers). The fundamental problematic of liberalism as CLS defined it is the relation of atomistic individuals in pursuit of self-interest to the state or society, created as a social contract. In its rejection of this liberalism, CLS forced a reexamination of liberalism's relation to the state in the service of radical social change. It first attacked the dualistic foundations of liberal thought, distinctions between state of nature and social order, subjective and objective, private and public, in order to propose that we deal with the problem of human association, or autonomy and relatedness, in other ways. For example, Robin West, both a sympathizer with and a feminist critic of CLS, has argued, probably correctly, that the autonomous individual of liberal legalism—the individual who creates value by satiating his desire with choices subject to consensual constraint—is an essentially *male* creation of political theory. Positing that women, for both biological and cultural reasons, have been at least as other-regarding as self-regarding, and that the constraints upon their so-called choices may not necessarily have been attributable to consent, West observes that the liberal theory of the human being with its apparatus of liberal (i.e., procedural as opposed to substantive) rights may definitionally exclude half of humankind. Liberal legalism, that is, posits one kind of subjectivity, that of human beings who maximize individual self-interests limited by rights arrived at consensually, to the exclusion of women, for whom connectedness to others is prior to individuation. Thus other-regarding, women provide for others' needs at least as much as their own.[9] CLS saw no distinctive mode of legal reasoning that could be contrasted with political dialogue, and it accordingly asserted that law *was* politics. It rejected liberalism for entailing limited possibilities for human association and social transformation, insisting rather that human possibility was a product of history, not nature, and could be changed. CLS's critique of liberal legalism was effectively postmodern in its deconstruction of dualist tradition and its emphasis on the realm of law as one of contest, including sex discrimination, rather than essence.

Like CLS, cultural studies is more like a coalition than an organic movement, but also like CLS, it includes some common practices and goals. Like CLS's assertion that law is politics, cultural studies stopped asking why there was no "Shakespeare's sister" (a female equivalent in poetic genius to Shakespeare) and considered that the production of the literary canon, the consumption or *meaning* of imaginative literature, and the status of the literary community's cultural capital were within the realm of politics. Like CLS's delegitimation, cultural studies has deconstructed such knots of ideology in literature as subjective/objective, self/other, public/private, and extraordinary/everyday, and like CLS, it has viewed deconstruction that merely works on the status quo as ultimately a conservative practice. Like CLS's positive program to transform the law by reintegrating it with everyday life, cultural studies wants to reintegrate the extraordinary (called Art or Literature) with the ordinary (called popular culture). Like CLS's critique of the liberal subject, cultural studies reevaluates subjectivity, situating the "literary subject" in relation to other past, present, and even future forms as a product of culture rather than nature. Like CLS's assault on hierarchy, cultural studies replaces Culture with a capital "C" as an elite cultural capital with a pluralistic, diverse conception of cultures. Just as CLS deconstructs an essentialist notion of the law as impartial justice for essentialist subjects, so cultural studies demystifies Culture as the bearer of timeless and transcendent truth and beauty. All these projects have profound implications for the study and practice of gender.[10]

Yet with these reflections upon feminist postmodernism in the academy, one wonders whether the emancipatory project described by commentators such as John Dupré is limited to academic work and communities. Within the academy one priority (a pleasure, really) is to admit *and* graduate women and minority students and to hire *and* promote women and minority faculty. We should seize the opportunity of large-scale faculty retirement in the next decade to make efforts in this direction, for we cannot forget how few of us as yet pursue our work in environments of commitment and security. But feminist postmodernism presses well beyond the academy.

If, as Dupré suggests, we substitute an essentialist picture of sex difference with a picture of numerous differences, we shall find that gender, like other differences that give us cause to worry, derives from politics. There are many differences, but only some are exploited as rationalizations of inequality. Recognizing that other exploitative differences, like race, class, sexual orientation, physical labor, and so on (to the extent that they are exploitative) derive from politics, that there is a structural analogy between race, class, gender, and the rest, keeps the nonessentialist picture expanding to what may be the most significant emancipatory project in human history. This project, that began with recognition of differences among women, in its most utopian reaches will cease to operate through political differences but rather, as Jaggar says so elegantly after Marx (and some mothers), will operate through the satisfaction of different needs: to each according to her needs, from each according to her abilities. Yet if exploitative differences derive from politics, value, at least for most feminists, does not. Value centrally includes the material conditions conducive for flourishing life. These can be achieved only by changing the material world, a world that uses people as means rather than ends. Feminists in the academy are adding immeasurably to our understanding of that world. The point, however, is to change it.

If feminist theory is the systemic synthesis of the data of feminist studies, and feminist studies now shows the structural similarity of gender inequality and other forms of discrimination, then feminist theory must now provide a theory of justice in a world of complex identities and contingent and temporary unities. Anything less will probably, at this point, be redundant.

Furthermore, our postmodern suspicions concerning "theory" should not hinder us from the practice of theorizing about what justice in a postmodern world would look like. Whether a theory of justice in a postmodern world is a concept insufficiently postmodern cannot be answered until we have done a great deal more critical work on the notion of "theory," which probably qualifies as the most appallingly underanalyzed trope in contemporary intellectual life. In philosophy of science, to take just one example from an appropriately dynamic field, there is a move toward replacing traditional conceptions of theories, like evolution, as systems of axioms, with more complex articulations of practice, heuristic paradigms, and so on.[11] It is not clear that a theory of justice in a postmodern world is insufficiently postmodern in conception. On the other hand, it is equally unclear that a "theory" is necessary to the politics that feminism has taught us to comprehend.

An issue of more immediate concern is why we should call such a politics feminism. As the feminist picture expands for many of us into a more inclusive emancipatory project, unified only by a political goal of quality of life, will we lose the solidarity we had, or thought we had, as women, for women? I see no reason why we cannot fight—in popular postmodernist fashion—on all fronts at once. Pacifica Radio does. (Even in a postmodern world, some things are constant.) I also see no reason why we should not call such politics "feminism" as well as any other name, since feminist method has been instrumental in comprehending this politics. I like to retain the term *feminism* in honor of the feminist practice that taught us what a few leftists or separatists may have seen but never so well expressed: where we thought we were unified and monolithic there was difference, and where there was difference we had to ensure that it not be silenced.

We may assume that in a postmodern world there are no uncontested grounds for belief. When I say that I want to change a world that uses people as means rather than ends someone else will say, "So what? What are 'people,' anyway, but a vestige of discredited humanism in a postmodern cyborg world?" "And what are ends but vestiges of the same teleological humanism?" and so on and on.[12] Therefore, those of us who agree that *people* includes some things that do better when they are fed and protected from climatic trauma than when they starve, burn, freeze, or drown, and agree that we would rather have them do better, cannot simply assert our preference for keeping this belief in view. When listing or funding local, national, or international priorities, we must persuade others to adopt our view. There is simply no higher authority.

At this point we do not need a theory so much as we need to persuade indifferent bystanders that a larger emancipatory project is in their interest. We need the postmodern equivalents of the feminist stories that provided slogans that incited action. This activity may not require anything so academic as a theory. We may recall that the enemy is pretty powerful, despite its lack of coherence, consistency, or precise usage:

> [The French theorist of the New Right] Alain de Benoist considers that in attributing a fundamental role to universal suffrage, democracy places all individuals on the same level and fails to recognize the important differences among them. Thence derives a uniformization and massification of the citizenry, upon whom is imposed a single norm which shows the necessarily totalitarian character of democracy. In the face of the chain of equivalences equality = identity = totalitarianism, the New Right proclaims the "right to difference," and affirms the sequence difference = inequality = liberty. De Benoist writes: "I call 'right-wing' the attitude that considers the *diversity* of the world, and hence inequalities, as a good, and the progressive homogenization of the world, favoured and brought about by the bimillenarian discourse of the totalitarian ideology, as an evil."[13]

At the very moment when we are acknowledging the differences among women, it is time for feminists to join others whose differences have been made to rationalize inequality in an elective affinity or coalition. To paraphrase Jesse Jackson at the 1988 Democratic National Convention, some of us came on immigrant ships, some on slave ships, and some of us on a long-deferred citizenship. But whatever ship we came on, we're in the same boat tonight.

I conclude with a final observation from one more manifesto of feminist postmodernism, Donna Haraway's "A Manifesto for Cyborgs." Haraway is talking about our victory over essentialist and reductionist theory and the urgency not to limit ourselves to what I should call an aesthetic appreciation of difference, to remember that, however diverse we are, we are engaged in a struggle: "In the consciousness of our failures, we risk lapsing into boundless difference and giving up on the confusing task of making partial, real connection. Some differences are playful; some are poles of world historical systems of domination. 'Epistemology' is about knowing the difference."[14]

PART TWO

Sociobiological Theories of Difference

Darwinians Confront Gender; or, There Is More to It than History

CARL N. DEGLER

To Charles Darwin sex was everything; he was largely oblivious to the social construction of the differences between the human sexes that today we denominate *gender*. What he observed in the behavior of the two sexes he assumed stemmed from the differences in their bodies. "Man is more courageous, pugnacious, and energetic than woman and has a more inventive genius," he wrote in *The Descent of Man*. And though he knew that contemporaries like John Stuart Mill did not believe there were differences in the mental powers of the two sexes, he thought that analogies with lower animals' sexual characteristics made those differences probable in human beings. No one doubts, he contended, that sows differ in disposition from boars, bulls from cows, or stallions from mares. "Woman seems to differ from man in mental disposition," he noticed, "chiefly in her greater tenderness and less selfishness." Women are kind to children and thus by extension to others as well; men are competitive and ambitious. Insofar as mental abilities were concerned, Darwin thought "the chief distinction in the intellectual powers of the two sexes is shown by man's attaining to a higher eminence, in whatever he takes up, than can woman." He challenged those who doubted him to compare lists of men and women who achieved eminence in the arts, history, science, and philosophy. They would find, he confidently maintained, that "the two lists would not bear comparison."[1]

Darwin may have been convinced that his conception of humankind placed women in a position inferior to men's, but contrary to what has often been contended, Darwinian evolution could be and was used to broaden opportunities for women, to change the status quo. Lester Frank Ward, for example, often referred to as the founder of American sociology, was not only a fervent and committed Darwinian but also the originator of what he called the "gynecocentric view" of human development. An avid student of biology, Ward concluded from his study of nature that females were the "primary" or fundamental sex and the male was "secondary in the organic scheme, that originally and normally all things center, as it were, about the female."[2] Males provided only the variation in heredity that was necessary for evolutionary change. It was the female, especially among mammals, who nurtured the young and thus made the continuation of life possible. According to his theory, in the remote past women were venerated because the role of males in reproduction was unknown. When men learned of their part, his theory argued, they began to assert themselves, ultimately overthrowing women's predominance in "a profound social revolution."[3] Men were able to accomplish their revolution because of the operation of the Darwinian principle of sexual selection, which Ward accepted fully. It was natural, he contended, that a female, wishing to advance the species, should seek to make the male strong, handsome, and vigorous, and hence "should always choose the largest and finest specimens" among the males contending to mate with her.[4] Once man had become bigger and more aggressive and, as Ward put it, "his egoistic reason, unfettered by any such sentiment as sympathy, and therefore wholly devoid of moral conceptions of any kind" began to come into play, he naturally drew upon that superior strength and exacted "from woman whatever satisfaction she could yield him. The first blow he struck in this direction," Ward theorized, "wrought the whole transformation," that is, her total subordination.[5]

Although Ward expounded his gynecocentric view of humanity at length only in 1903 in his book *Pure Sociology* he had suggested it as early as 1888 in a popular journal, whence it was picked up by others, notably by two women feminists, who made it the basis of their defense of women's aspirations. Eliza Gamble in her book *The Evolution of Woman* (1894) followed Ward when she wrote that "the female is the primary unit of creation, and that the male functions are simply supplemental or complementary." And though critical of Darwin where she had to be in order to defend women's rights in society, she believed that Darwin had "proved by seemingly well established facts that the female organization is freer from imperfections than the male, and therefore that it is less liable to derangements." She was especially interested, as was Ward, in showing woman's moral superiority, which she contended would make woman the equal of man in the qualities necessary for civilization once women had been vouchsafed equality of opportunity to develop them. According to her, motherhood was the root of human sympathy. Darwin may not have admitted it, she contended, but the logic of his argument showed "that the maternal instinct is the root whence sympathy has sprung, and that it is the source whence the cohesive quality in the tribe originated."[6]

A few years later, in 1898, Charlotte Perkins Stetson, later to be known as Charlotte Perkins Gilman, published *Women and Economics,* where she, too, drew upon Ward's explanation for women's suppression and argued for the release of women from the bondage Darwinian sexual selection had permitted men to fasten upon her sex. She clearly recognized biologically rooted differences between the sexes. Indeed, that was the point of her book: the world needed women's social and mental contribution if modern civilization was to be truly human.[7]

Lydia Commander, an early twentieth-century sociologist, was not dependent upon Ward's gynecocentric theory, but there can be no doubt that she, like Gilman and Gamble, found in biology a means for defending woman's right to equality of opportunity, in this case in regard to employment. "Woman is the working human creature," Commander wrote in 1909 in the *American Journal of Sociology.* "To work is an inherent tendency of woman's nature; with man it is an acquired characteristic. Woman works from instinct; man from habit," she insisted.[8] Like Gilman, Commander was convinced that women were more cooperative, more humane, and more concerned with life. In short, from the beginning of Darwin's influence on social theory, biological arguments were developed both to support and to confine the widening of women's social horizons. Contrary to what some recent opponents of biological explanations have contended, historically no necessary connection exists between the use of biological arguments and any particular social or political ideology.

The use of biology as a means of accounting for differences between men and women declined noticeably during the early twentieth century, largely as a result of new social science research and the activities of women themselves. Rosalind Rosenberg has shown how women social scientists at the turn of the century successfully prodded their male colleagues to abandon their belief in sexual differences.[9] And as early as 1922, Stanford University psychologist and designer of intelligence tests Lewis Terman was able to write that "mental tests have at last vindicated woman's claim to intellectual equality with man."[10]

This abandonment in academic and scientific circles of Darwin's emphasis on the biological limits of female capabilities went in tandem with such significant social changes as opening higher education, the professions, and eventually politics to women. The biological limits on women that some Darwinians had once discerned now carried little weight, even though everyone recognized that only women bore and nursed babies. That fact of physiology left a residue of biological restriction in the minds of many people, including some leaders of the women's movement. Florence Kelley and Jane Addams, to name but the most prominent, thought that maternity was so central to a woman's life that it needed to be taken into consideration when seeking to expand woman's economic and social activities. A whole body of social legislation on behalf of working women—the so-called protective legislation—stands as a monument to that belief.

New investigations into the relation between biology and women's behavior did not begin until at least the 1960s, when a new feminist movement emerged. Some members of the new movement explicitly rejected the view that anything inherent in woman limited her ability or aptitude for social roles. Obviously women were still the sole bearers of children, but no longer could it be said with any scientific or physiological justification that they were the only persons capable of rearing or nurturing children. In an age when cow's milk could be made almost equal in nutrient quality to mother's milk, women were no longer obliged to be the sole rearers of children if that office interfered with or limited their public roles. At about the same time, advances in contraceptive knowledge and technology empowered women to have complete control over their reproductive system so that pregnancy was no longer a physiological obstacle to virtually any public role. Socially the most striking measure of the transformation wrought by the new feminist movement in the United States was the admission of women not only into the once distinctively male domain of the military services, but also into the military academies themselves, something permitted in no other society enlisting women in the armed services except Canada.

The assumption behind such a radical redefinition of possible roles for women seemed to be that women were in all respects except childbearing interchangeable with men. Or more precisely, the category *woman* is so various and so overlapping with the category *man* that it is no longer possible to say what is a man or a woman except in regard to reproduction. The world that was expected to follow from such an assumption has been described by one recent feminist writer, Anne Fausto-Sterling, as one of "total equality." She portrayed it as a world in which "men and women would fully share political and financial power; no one would be unable—in the midst of great wealth—to feed and clothe their children adequately. Men and women would be represented equally, according to their equal abilities, in all walks of life."[11] Concealed or implied in this statement is the denial of any biological controls over or influences on behavior that social or cultural forces could not alter. Whatever history or socialization had created, human will could undo.

Proponents like Fausto-Sterling of a completely social origin of human behavior argue that no reliable evidence suggests that women and men differ in any significant way besides reproduction. Even differences in athletic achievement, according to Fausto-Sterling, are disappearing as the social opportunities for women's participation in competitive athletics have broadened and deepened. As she wrote in conclusion, "If the gap between highly trained male and female athletes were to continue to close at the current rate, in thirty to forty years men and women would compete in these sports on an equal basis."[12] Presumably the only explanation for human behavior is culture or history. Other deniers of sex differences opt for an agnostic position. "It is *not* possible to tease apart genetics and other biological factors from environmental and learning factors in human development," insists biologist Ruth Bleier. "From conception the relationship between the actions of genes and the environment of fetus are inextricable."[13]

As is evident from the books of Bleier and Fausto-Sterling, one of the reasons for such vehement denials of a biological basis for female behavior has been the emergence in the last two decades of a new interest on the part of natural and social scientists in biological explanations for human behavior. The arguments they make are worth looking into for two reasons. The first and less important reason is that, contrary to what is often said by opponents of biological explanations, the underlying motivation goes beyond simple social conservatism or defense of the status quo. For one thing, as we have seen already, there is no clear connection historically between the advocacy of biological explanations and the defense of the status quo. For another, modern proponents of a biological approach to human behavior are more often than not ideologically liberal and social reformist in outlook.[14] The more important reason for exploring this revival, especially as it appears in the writings of social scientists, is that the underlying rationale provides a theoretical framework within which to examine sex differences.

What is that theoretical framework? It is the application to human behavior of an old and now scientifically recognized theory, namely, Darwinian evolution, a fundamental principle of which is that human beings are an integral part of the continuum of life on earth. The operative word here is *integral*. Almost all modern students of human behavior give lip service to the Darwinian principle that human beings are included in the process of evolution through natural selection, but in practice many see a sharp disjunction between animals and human beings when they try to account for human behavior.

It is quite accurate, as Ruth Hubbard has stated, that because behavior leaves no fossil remains, we have no definitive proof of homologous as opposed to analogous behavior in animals, much less in human beings. And that issue has been a matter of concern among some students of sociobiology.[15] Yet in general terms there is little doubt that animals inherit their behavior as well as their morphology, or bodily shape. Female sea turtles lay eggs in holes on ocean beaches, from which offspring emerge and immediately head to sea. Salmon return to breed to the rivers in which they were hatched. And animal breeders, as Darwin himself pointed out, produce breeds of pigeons, dogs, and other domestic animals with diverse behavioral characteristics as well as strikingly different bodily shapes. It requires no great leap of faith to believe that over the millennia of evolutionary time certain patterns of behavior among animal species have been inherited as well as reordered by natural selection. For those reasons it is surprising to see a biologist like Ruth Bleier remark that because contemporary animals are not our direct precursors, "It is no more logical to look at chimpanzees or mice to gain insight into our behavior than it would be to look at our behavior to gain insight into theirs."[16] Such a conclusion denies the fundamental basis for a good deal of behavioral and experimental psychology, the scientific field of ethology, and a good deal of experimental medicine. All of those fields and others proceed on the assumption, by now widely accepted, that human beings are genetically descended from other species in varying degrees as a result of the operation of natural selection. From those origins our behavior as well as our morphology have evolved.

A fundamental assumption of Darwinian evolution to which most professional students of human behavior subscribe is that there is continuity between animals and human beings. The character of that continuity is what many social scientists are now seeking to identify. To ignore or to deny such continuity in attempting to account for human behavior, they argue, is to open a wide gulf between animals and human beings. Doing this asserts that somehow human beings have transcended the principle that all living things are part of the grand continuum of life. To follow that line means that when we study human beings we must abandon Darwin's powerful explanatory scheme, returning to the old homocentric conception of nature, the historic taproot of humanity's hubris. Perhaps we should abandon Darwinian evolution when dealing with human beings, for what remains biological or genetic in our behavioral makeup may be inconsequential and trivial. That, however, is not the view held by most biologists or by an increasing number of social scientists who have begun to reexamine the role of biology in human behavior.

A prime catalyst in reviving interest in biological explanations is Edward Wilson's treatise *Sociobiology* and its popularized companion, *On Human Nature*. Yet his work is no more than the culmination, in an admittedly provocative form, of a large body of new knowledge about animal behavior or the science of ethology. Most of the principles of sociobiology have been derived from the close observation of animals in the wild and from specially contrived experiments with wild animals.

Insofar as sex differences are concerned, the most relevant sociobiological principle is called *differential reproductive strategies*. Simply put, it states that males and females, especially among mammals, have different approaches to reproduction because of the nature of sexual reproduction. For females the cost of reproduction is high, entailing a high investment of energy in the form of large eggs and, most important, long periods of gestation and lactation. For males reproduction is quick, cheap, and easy. The distinction is the basis of Darwin's principle of sexual selection. Morphological differences between males and females (bright colors and extravagant plumages on males among certain species of birds) are often accounted for by the female's choice of mate, presumably on the basis of the male's potentialities for good paternal investment in offspring.

Some social scientists have used this ethological principle to identify the biological roots of the common observation that women are generally more reluctant to engage in sex than men. Women, like other female mammals, have a higher personal investment in (incur a higher cost from) offspring than men and hence are more circumspect. As sociobiologically inclined anthropologist Donald Symons has phrased the point: "Selection favored the basic male tendency to be aroused sexually by the sight of females. A human female, on the other hand, incurred an immense risk, in terms of time and energy, by becoming pregnant, hence selection favored the basic female tendency to discriminate with respect both to sexual partners and to the circumstances in which copulation occurred." Or to put it another way, in human females sexual arousal is not necessary for reproduction, though it is in human males, a difference that enhances male sexuality by tying it to nature's imperative of reproduction. A social as opposed to a bioevolutionary explanation for a less insistent urge for copulation in women is that they would suffer social punishment in certain societies if they emulated male sexual assertiveness. Symons' response is that even in societies in which female sexual activity is virtually without social constraints men generally have a greater sexual drive than women.[17]

Such a biological explanation for male and female sexual differences is useful in accounting for certain historically recognized differences in the behavior of men and women. The separation of reproduction from sexuality in women helps us to understand how it was possible in times past to deny women's sexuality: to do so did not affect reproduction, as a comparable denial or repression of male sexuality would have. The recognition of differential sexuality would also help to account for the presence through a good part of recorded history of pornography directed at men and of female prostitution. Since according to the theory of male reproductive strategy males must be ready at any time to copulate, their sexual arousal mechanism will be much more closely attuned to potential stimulation than females'. Given the high visual acuity of human beings, it is not surprising that pictorial pornography, almost all of which has been directed at males, is common in a variety of cultures. Similarly, given the male's propensity for more frequent and more indiscriminate copulation, recourse to prostitutes would be much more common among human males than among females. None of this implies or defines what ought to be normative sexual behavior for females today; nor as a general statement does it tell us anything about the normative sexual behavior or attitudes of individual women in the past. It suggests that there is a fit between the predictions of the interpretation and the general sexual behavior of women in history. (The counterargument that in a social order in which men were no longer dominant women's sexual behavior would *not* differ from men's begs the question. It assumes the conclusion that is at issue and for which historical evidence is presently lacking.)

Not all the social scientists who have been reexamining sexual differences have necessarily been inspired by Edward Wilson and sociobiology. One of them, Alice Rossi, the well-known sociologist and feminist leader, has specifically differentiated her views from those of Wilson. She emphasizes instead that the ease with which the sexes learn certain things varies according to differences in their biological or evolutionary history. Rossi's point of view is significant because of her important role as a feminist who once had no place for biology in discussing the roles of women. In 1977 and again in 1978, however, she concluded, after a good deal of investigation into sex differences, that "cultural determinism" had gone too far. The supporters of that view, she wrote, "had got themselves into an untenable position. Instead of replacing outdated biological theories with new, accurate knowledge, they were forced to deny that there are any physiological differences between men and women."[18] Yet she has by no means abandoned her commitment to the achievement of equality for women. Equality, she insists, should not be confused with sameness. "Difference is a biological fact" in men and women, "whereas equality is a political, ethical, and social concept. No rule of nature or of social organization says that the sexes have to be the same or do the same things in order to be social, political, and economic equals."[19]

Rossi's basic point is that because of the physiology determined by evolution, men and women differ, in her words, in their "predisposition to care for infants and in their ability to learn those caretaking skills." Human societies show great variations in child-rearing, she concedes, "but there is little or no variation in the cultural rule for the relationship of mothers and children: a close bond between them is the universal demand."[20] She discusses at some length the endocrinal and other evidence for seeing this relation as biologically based. She sees it as also evolutionary in that survival of the infant has depended upon mothering behavior, as has the survival of young among other mammals. She is careful to note that she is not describing a "maternal instinct" in women, merely a parental response triggered by pregnancy. Her argument comes close, at one point, to that of the sociobiologists when she explains why the female-child bond is universal: because of differences in sexual reproduction. "Biologically men have one sexual drive—to mate. But in female physiology there is a closely woven connection between sexuality and maternalism."[21] Because she thinks women are physiologically structured for reproduction, she believes the nature of that structure cries out for further study in place of a glib assumption of the absence of physiologically derived mental effects from childbearing. She specifically recommends, for example, the study of stress during pregnancy.

Rossi warns that until the biological roots of parental behavior are studied and understood alterations in the family on behalf of equality may well be counterproductive. Once they are understood, the differences impeding certain social goals can be compensated for if that is desired. (She means the training of fathers to be as competent parents as mothers.) She has no doubt that the "mother-infant relationship will continue to have greater emotional depth than the father-infant relationship because of the mother's physiological experience of pregnancy, birth, and nursing."[22] But if the social goal is for fathers to be active child-rearers, they will need social training to overcome the lack of evolutionary history. And if women are to be integrated into the military, they will need comparable training "for generations to come." The evolutionary aspect of her perspective comes through in her remark that "any slackening of such compensatory training . . . will quickly lead to a regression to the sex-role tradition of our long past."[23]

Interestingly enough, Rossi's delineation of differences in parenting roles for women and men comes close to that which Nancy Chodorow has sketched in her book *The Reproduction of Mothering*, though she specifically rejects Rossi's reasoning. She even agrees with Rossi in seeing maternity and sexuality linked. Chodorow concludes that "women's heterosexuality is triangular and requires a third person—a child—for its structural and emotional completion. For men, by contrast, the heterosexual relationship alone recreates the early bond to their mother; a child interrupts it."[24] The connection between child-rearing and women, Chodorow agrees, is deeply rooted, "despite the wish to share it with men." A century after human beings first learned that child care need not be confined to women, she observes with some sadness, "Women continue to be primary parents both within the family and in alternate child-care settings. Even when we look at contemporary societies where non-familial child care is widespread—Israel, China, the Soviet Union, Cuba—women still perform this care."[25] To Chodorow the differences stem from deep sociopsychological conditioning rather than from biology. The results, however, are the same as Rossi's, even to the need for compensatory education for males. Only the explanations differ, presumably because Chodorow is understandably but unnecessarily fearful of the implications that might be drawn from biological explanations. She is sufficiently fearful not only to doubt that biology has anything to do with mothering by human beings, but also to doubt that it affects the mothering behavior of animals.[26]

Despite Chodorow's apparent fears, a biologically rooted explanation for human mothering based on Darwinian evolutionary theory seems more intellectually satisfying than an explanation based on psychoanalysis. For one thing, evolutionary theory has the virtue of being more parsimonious (fewer assumptions have to be made) and more widely accepted than Freudian theory. For another, from a purely evolutionary point of view, the female is by definition the prime parent among mammal species, since lactation is the prime basis of offspring survival. Chodorow very nearly admits that point in her discussion of Rossi's biosocial interpretation when she says Rossi has no explanation for mothering after weaning.[27] But social scientists who are willing to consider biology as affecting human behavior often wonder why biology must be the sole explanation of a pattern of behavior in order to be acknowledged as part of an explanation. One of the weaknesses of the cultural-determinist case is the implicit assumption that if any learning or cultural influence can be identified as affecting a behavior pattern, then a biological or inherited influence has been eliminated. That seems to be the approach that Nancy Chodorow and Ruth Hubbard have implicitly followed, even if Hubbard gives lip service to the idea that both culture and biology are operative. Most students of human behavior—or mammalian behavior—would say as much. Few if any of them hold that genes or inheritance can alone account for behavior. The great majority of proponents of a biological component in human behavior would agree with Hubbard that culture and biology generally work together. Unlike Hubbard, however, they are interested in identifying as specifically as possible the contributions of both biology and culture. That cultural and biological evolution generally work together is the central assumption in the work of young evolutionary theorists in anthropology like William Durham, and Robert Boyd and Peter J. Richerson.[28]

Undoubtedly, as Chodorow's and Hubbard's anxiety attests, the greatest stumbling block to identifying any biological or evolutionary base for human behavior is the fear that to acknowledge such influence is to sanction it as right, that is, as necessary, or what is worse, as determining what ought to be. It needs to be said repeatedly that whatever human beings want to do socially or individually should be determined by their values, not by their biology. To claim otherwise would be to fall into the naturalistic fallacy, permitting nature to determine human choices. If a woman does not want to bear a child, biology ought not to be the justification for requiring or even expecting that she do so. If she does want to have a child, that fact does not determine that she ought to be the sole rearer of it. Certainly history, with its rich record of celibate organizations, suicides, and deliberately childless marriages, provides ample and convincing evidence of the power of human values to deny "obvious" biological or evolutionary influences.

Unfortunately, some supporters of human sociobiology, among whom must be included Edward Wilson, have sought to ground human ethics and values in biology, contending that in time we will discover that what we value in this world derives from our biological evolution, and that those values cannot be significantly altered. I say that it is unfortunate because it is so extreme, so intellectually imperialistic, as to bring into disrepute the whole idea of recognizing any biological bases for human behavior. One does not have to accept Wilson's or anyone else's subsuming of human ethics under biology in order to perceive continuity between our animal past and our human present. What social scientists who are interested in the biological roots of our actions are asserting is that our evolutionary past, like our cultural past, continues to influence us. Yet neither past is so controlling that we cannot seek ways to alter or modify its influences. If we are to do that, we must understand how our biological past does affect us, shape us, and perhaps restrict us. Then we can pursue other means to accomplish the ends that our biology seems to deny us. Whether we do or do not seek other ways depends on what kind of society or behavior we prefer. Our values are ultimately determined by us, not by evolution or natural selection, which has no goal or purpose. And because nature sets no goals or values for us we should not be fearful of explanations that include a biological or evolutionary component. At the same time, to identify how our biological inheritance may be shaping our behavior in the present may help us to arrive at sounder answers to old questions.[29]

In 1987 the philosopher Philip Kitcher published a severe critique of sociobiology, the substance of which was captured in its title, *Vaulting Ambition*. The aim of the book, as he explains on his opening page, is finally to finish off sociobiology as a serious approach to explaining human behavior. The book is a powerful and in some ways a devastating criticism, often on a point-by-point basis, of the pretensions and sometimes poorly defended propositions of leading proponents of sociobiology. But to imagine that such detailed, particularistic criticisms will end the appeal of biological or evolutionary explanations is to misunderstand the nature of that appeal. Even Stephen Jay Gould, a persistent and powerful opponent of sociobiology, acknowledged in the course of a laudatory review of Kitcher's book that "clearly, there must be a potential evolutionary science of behavior. If we wish to call this enterprise sociobiology (broad version) then no right-thinking person can oppose it."[30]

Contrary to what Kitcher and other opponents of Wilson's sociobiology contend, the primary appeal of sociobiology among social scientists is not its alleged usefulness in defending the status quo. Many of the supporters of a biosocial perspective do so for the reason expressed by the Dartmouth political scientist Roger Masters. "I am convinced," Masters wrote in 1979, "that the biological approach to social behavior . . . will ultimately unify the social sciences."[31] Others see such an approach as a way to understand better how we got to be what we are today. It needs to be emphasized that a biological perspective on human behavior is not hard science. It is closer to explanatory modes like Marxism or Freudian psychology. It offers suggestions how one might account for human behavior within a framework that is consonant with a powerful theory of nature, Darwinian evolution. Above all, a biosocial approach bridges that gulf between animals and human beings that cultural determinism insists upon and against which all our understanding of the animal world argues. After all, if Darwin was right, we should expect to find continuity between our biological past and our cultural present. The precise lineaments or character of that continuity constitute the research agenda for the nature of human nature.

Ruth Hubbard (in her essay in this volume) and others maintain that the very idea of human nature is a false and misleading concept. History is replete with uses of that concept that have been not only wrong but dangerous. Yet it is a biological fact that human beings are a species, and like all species we differ from as well as display similarities with other species. Since there has also been a long and well known historical discussion about the differences between animals and human beings, it seems evasive to deny the reality that lies behind that history, to conclude simply that human beings are what we do—to use Hubbard's words. As Bleier and Hubbard have pointed out, it is true that there is a great diversity among human societies today and yesterday. That diversity is the stuff of history as well as of anthropology. But few of the practitioners of those disciplines would deny that there are also characteristics—*universals* as they are sometimes called—shared by all or the great majority of human groupings. Among such universals is certainly language, another is bipedalism, a third is sociality, a fourth is the sexual division of labor, a fifth is the mother-child dyad, a sixth is the incest taboo, a seventh is social stratification, an eighth is patriarchy (absence of matriarchy), and a ninth is kinship, to name only the less controversial. A biosocial approach to human nature suggests that explanations for at least some of the universals in human social behavior are likely to be found in the biological history of human beings. It certainly may be difficult to establish those explanations, but since we believe that behavioral universals among other species contain at least some inherited component, would it not be reasonable to do the same when we are seeking to account for behavior in our own species?

Investigations of the biological roots of human society will put into proper context the social or cultural interpretation of human action. To exclude persistent biological influences from our explanations of human behavior, as cultural determinists do, is simply to reduce human beings to empty slates upon which history or experience writes what it will and out of which, presumably, emerges a human being. That denial of influences from our biological past has caused some modern students of human nature to probe beneath culture. John Maynard Smith is a biologist, to be sure, but one who is clearly skeptical of the validity of human sociobiology.

"The main generalization to have emerged from ethology," he has written, "is that animals, including higher animals, cannot be understood as blank sheets on which the environment writes what it will. Instead, animals must be seen as having a complex internal structure which ensures that they will learn to do some things very readily and others hardly at all. The same is likely to be true in man—as is becoming increasingly obvious from work in linguistics and psychology."[32]

Mary Midgley, an English philosopher, defines the same issue humanistically. For her culture alone is not sufficient to account for human behavior. Why are we social animals at all, she asks, except for our biological inheritance? And how can culture alone account for natural feelings like "our strong and special affection for our children," which are more than "just loose facts about us; they are the sort of things that constitutes our central good. Moral surgeons who want to cut them out because of their dangers . . . misconceive their function. We are simply not in a position to replace them with something else which will not be worse."[33] Not surprisingly, in her recent book *Women's Choices,* written in conjunction with Judith Hughes, Midgley applies her principle to sex differences, especially in regard to child care.[34] Once again, she scathingly rejects cultural determinism.

One of the reasons Midgley opposes cultural determinism is that it fails to account for human resistance to culture. The great philosophers of social existence, like Rousseau, Marx, and Freud, she observes, all saw human beings at odds with their social environment. The implication is that the human core is something beyond a cultural creation. Human beings are a product of their biological, as well as their cultural history.

Let me close this review of the revival of interest among social scientists in a biological basis for human behavior with some remarks from the eminent anthropologist Margaret Mead. Mead made her reputation emphasizing the cultural sources of sex differences. Her first book, *Coming of Age in Samoa,* was an early landmark in the pursuit of that approach. By the 1960s, however, Mead's approach had shifted, even before Alice Rossi's had, to recognizing a significant role for biology in differentiating the behavior of the two sexes. In 1968, at a symposium on war, she called attention to the close historical connection between warfare and human males, and as she put it, the exclusion of women, "with a very few brief exceptions," from "the habitual use of weapons." She went on to say that it is "important to take into consideration the possibility that the biological bases of aggression in the two sexes—in human beings as in other animals—may differ significantly. The female characteristically fights only for food or in defense of her young, and then fights to kill, and may be without the built-in checks on con-specific murder that are either socially or biologically present in males. Arming women," she warned, "as has been done in this century in Israel, the USSR, Indonesia and Vietnam, may be a suicidal course."[35] I do not quote Mead to imply that she may be right about the consequences of enrolling women in combat forces. But given Mead's intellectual history, her forthright statement reveals how widespread and persuasive the acceptance of a role for biology in the study of sexual differences has become among social scientists.

Global versus Local
Perspectives on
Sexual Difference

JOHN DUPRÉ

Most attempts to understand the nature and behavior of human beings have assumed, explicitly or implicitly, that an essentialist answer should be sought. It has been presumed that such understanding would require the discovery of some fundamental and universal property or properties, intrinsic to all normal humans, which could provide the key to the explanation of human behavior. It has also been supposed that essential properties distinguish men from women, so that the sexually dimorphic aspects of human behavior would be amenable to the same analytic approach. A starting point for this paper is that both of these essentialist theses are false.[1]

Without denying that there are (more or less variable) intrinsic properties common to humans or distinguishing men from women, I do deny that such properties can get us very far in understanding human behavior if they are not studied in relation to their historical and cultural contexts. If anything counts as "human nature," it must be the product of the interaction between biological, intrinsic features and cultural, extrinsic features. Since culture, at least, is highly variable, so must be human nature; and within the various forms of human nature will be equally diverse elaborations of male and female "natures."

A somewhat different line of thought leads to a similar conclusion. This is perhaps most familiar in the characterization of much recent feminism as "white middle-class feminism." Underlying this criticism is the observation that the problems faced by women will differ according to whether

This paper owes a great deal to discussion of the central issues with Regenia Gagnier, who also made valuable criticisms of earlier drafts. It has also benefited greatly from detailed comments on an earlier draft by Deborah L. Rhode.

47

and how gender discrimination interacts with race, class, and other forms of social discrimination. (This is an issue about which I shall say more toward the end of this paper. For now I present it only as the political analogue of theoretical antiessentialism.)

A background assumption of this paper is that the categories "man" and "woman" have no universal explanatory force that goes much beyond the strictly physiological. This conclusion would be widely, though not universally, accepted by contemporary feminists. Certainly essentialist biological theories, of which the most notable contemporary example is human sociobiology, have come under heavy fire from feminist critics.[2] But this criticism, while it has illuminated many important questions, has raised others perhaps equally pressing. I shall discuss two such questions.

My first question concerns the theoretical background to the antiessentialist assumption just outlined. When we reject the essentialism of sociobiology, are we rejecting the only theoretical perspective through which we can achieve coherence between our understanding of ourselves and our understanding of biology? Developments deriving in part from criticisms of sociobiology may help answer this question. Specifically, as I shall argue below, contemporary theories of cultural evolution, qualified by recent criticisms of evolutionary theory in general, can at least provide a historical perspective consistent with a fundamental emphasis on human diversity.

While my first question concerns the grounds of human diversity, my second question concerns the consequences: specifically, the consequences for feminist theory of taking diversity seriously. A primary focus of feminist theory is the relationship between, and the different behavior of, women and men. The emphasis on diversity within these categories, and their lack of essential defining characteristics, raises serious questions about how the very subject matter of feminism should be conceived.

To approach this latter question we must first distinguish between the different kinds of projects in which feminists are engaged. Historical, sociological, or anthropological studies of gender relations in specific times and places need be committed to no particular view as to the general applicability of their conclusions. Such studies may be seen as providing the data for more general feminist theories. But the possibility of any such general feminist theory is rendered problematic by the suggestion that there may be little homogeneity to the kinds "woman" and "man."[3]

As subsequent discussion suggests, the diversity of gender constructions does ultimately threaten the coherence of a purely *feminist* theory. If our understanding of different historical gender relations cannot be unified by an essentialist biological theory, then the only perspective that can unify them must be political. But a political theory that can both illuminate and unify the historically diverse constructions of gender difference will apply equally to the many other human divisions that cut across gender—such as race, class, and ethnicity—and that have been central in forcing recognition of gender role diversity. Thus I do not think one can make sense of a *purely* feminist theory. But I do take the logic that forces feminism to transcend the particular social inequity from which it arose to amplify, rather than diminish, the significance of the contemporary feminist movement.

ESSENTIALISM AND GENDER

Before expounding the biological arguments that ground what I am calling "essentialism," I must explain more fully what I mean by that term. The fundamental disagreement between essentialists and their adversaries concerns the scope of generalizations. Essentialism, in effect, offers a priori answers to questions about the range of applicability of generalizations. Or at least, once a "natural kind" has been (somehow) distinguished—a kind, that is, defined by the presence of the appropriate essence—it can be assumed that fundamental generalizations will be forthcoming that apply to all members of the kind. The identification of such a natural kind becomes a criterion of whether a generalization could be fundamental. It is characteristic of essentialist approaches to human behavior that apparent human diversity provides a challenge: the challenge to find the underlying regularities that explain away the apparent diversity.

The essentialist who assumes that humans constitute a natural kind and that within this kind a further essential distinction exists between men and women is committed to searching for gender-based generalizations with a broad extension across cultural and historical contexts. The antiessentialism that I am advocating denies any reason to expect such generalizations to be true. On this view, the extent of any gender-based generalization is a strictly empirical question. The defense of such a position will be the main objective of the following section of this paper.

One further preliminary, however, is essential. We must distinguish the view that gender identifies entities susceptible of essential definitions from the quite different idea that gender provides valuable analytic categories. The latter thesis I take to be established beyond question by the insights that gender-based analyses have provided into questions in history, anthropology, sociology, and many other areas. An indisputable achievement of feminist scholarship has been to show the inadequacy of social analyses that ignore this fundamental and omnipresent social division of power. The insights achieved by gendered analyses, however, in no way imply that homogeneous categories with some essential defining characteristic are being deployed. In common, I imagine, with the majority of feminists, I believe that this is not in fact the case.

It may be useful to illustrate the preceding distinction with one example.

For example, in theorizing animal evolution the concept of sex is a central analytic category. One could not, to take one familiar example, understand the evolution of peacocks without adverting to the subject of sex. More specifically, it has been supposed by biologists from Darwin down that the gaudy plumage of peacocks was to be explained by an evolutionary process in which peahens preferred mates with increasingly impressive costumes. However, it does not follow that sex is a uniform phenomenon throughout the animal kingdom; that sex in bees, for example, is essentially the same phenomenon as sex in birds. In fact, I am convinced that it is not. The idea that sex is an important force that has left its mark on numerous quite distinct evolutionary histories in no way entails that its effects should be recognizable as universal features of all sexually reproducing organisms.[4]

Returning now to gender, if gender categories were to be grounded in essences, it would have to be because of their ultimate traceability to biology. Essences are internal, intrinsic features of the objects that possess them. And the intrinsic features of organisms are paradigmatically (and by definition) biological.[5] Yet no biological basis for gender categories can be found or expected.

SOCIOBIOLOGY AND CULTURAL EVOLUTION

Since the nineteenth century, essentialist approaches to human behavior, and specifically to sexually differentiated behavior, have typically been grounded in the theory of evolution. The earliest versions of human sociobiology tended to treat human behavior as if it were directly genetically determined and could be explained simply by pointing to the reproductive advantages that would result from a particular pattern of behavior. For example, the tendency to aggressive competition for mates could be treated as an *adaptation* for maximizing sexual access in just the same technical sense as the opposable thumb is an adaptation for more efficient tool use. The assumption that any feature of an organism, including its behavioral dispositions, can be treated as an adaptation is often referred to (usually critically) as *adaptationism*. In the case of human behavior, the most obvious criticism of this approach is that human behavior is transmitted through culture rather than genes. Recent developments in human sociobiology have, therefore, paid particular attention to culture as a possible product of evolution. I shall focus particularly here on those developments. A major theme of this work has been to treat culture itself as fundamentally a biological adaptation, and hence as a way of reintroducing the universalistic adaptationism of earlier sociobiological theories in ways resistant to the more obvious criticisms of these earlier versions. I shall argue that such a treatment is untenable. It is crucial first to distinguish the evolution of culture, the general possibility of transmitting behavior through imitation and teaching, from the process of cultural evolution, the changes over time in the behavior that is transmitted. In light of this distinction, my major thesis is that, in contrast to the adaptationist approach, cultural evolution provides a framework within which real human diversity can be reconciled with an evolutionary understanding of human history. In this way I offer a plausible answer to the first question outlined in the introduction to this paper, the problem of reconciling a belief in human diversity with an evolutionary perspective on human origins. I believe that cultural evolution should be seen as a process with a major causal role in the *production* of human diversity.[6]

Sociobiology is a research program aimed at illuminating animal and human behavior, in part by a priori reflection—especially by applications of game theory—on what behavioral strategies would best favor the survival and reproduction of organisms that exhibited them. It is then assumed that the evolutionary process will somehow see to it that such behavior will be produced. In their earlier forms, these a priori speculations were carried out at the highest possible level of abstraction, and optimal behavioral strategies were postulated for males and females, for parents and offspring, and for parties to territorial disputes.[7] In the case of sexually differentiated behavior, it was inferred that males should be promiscuous, compete fiercely for females, and take little interest in their offspring; females should be monogamous and highly selective in their choice of sexual partner, and—faute de mieux—would have to look after the children. It was supposed that, other things being equal, these "optimal" behaviors would be exhibited by all species the members of which found themselves in these general roles.

Evidently, other things did not turn out to be equal. Although certain species could be found whose behavior realized the sociobiologists' wildest dreams—the aggressive behavior and disregard for their offspring of male elephant seals, for example, have figured largely in this discussion—it was not hard to find uncooperative species. Many species of birds, for example, turn out to be almost exclusively monogamous in both sexes. In a substantial number of species, especially fish and amphibians, the males do all the child-rearing. And most embarrassingly of all, at least to those who had hoped to include the human species in the grand synthesis, among chimpanzees, our closest relatives, the females turn out to be highly promiscuous. (Perhaps this would have lent considerable comfort to pre-Darwinian conceptions of apes as degenerate parodies of human beings.)

Partly in response to these empirical failures, and partly in response to deep theoretical criticisms, sociobiology has tended to move away from these all-encompassing claims. At its best, it combines detailed observation of particular species with cautious and highly qualified speculations about how particular forms of behavior might have evolved. Whether even this cautious and qualified approach will, in the long run, prove an illuminating way of studying animal behavior remains a matter of debate. In view of its detailed concentration on particular species, however, it is neither threatening nor of particular relevance to broad feminist interests.

Human sociobiology, on the other hand, has undergone some different developments. Most sociobiologists and their sympathizers have realized from the start that culture has some role in the determination of human nature. Culture, moreover, seems at first sight well suited to evolutionary analysis. Evolutionary theorists generally suppose that an evolutionary process will occur whenever a set of individuals exhibit what is referred to as "heritable variation in fitness." In a biological context "fitness" refers to the disposition to survive and reproduce, and "heritability" to a relation between parents and offspring, so that evidently we cannot move directly from the biological to the cultural context. But a fairly simple intuitive conception of cultural evolution is not hard to construct. A cultural item, say a particular belief or practice, may be considered heritable if there is some tendency for it to spread from one individual to another. Presumably this occurs by imitation, deliberate instruction, and related practices. Its "fitness" then is a measure of its tendency to be retained and transmitted. If cultural items vary in their tendency to be transmitted, it is easy to see that the "fitter" ones will tend to become more prevalent.

An important limiting case would occur for a cultural belief or practice that is transmitted solely from parents to offspring. In this case its evolutionary trajectory would be determined only by the effects it had on the general biological fitness of its carriers. Just as genes are automatically passed from parents to offspring, and the spread of genes is theorized to depend solely on the effect a gene has on the success of the organism at survival and reproduction, so could the same theoretical apparatus be applied to a cultural belief or practice. It could, more technically, be considered as simply an extragenetic mechanism of standard Darwinian inheritance.

One important component of cultural fitness, as this case brings out, is the effect, if any, on the viability of the carriers of the cultural practice. For example, a disposition to take poison will tend to die out even if its proponents are fairly successful proselytizers. If such behavior were (*per impossibile*) solely transmitted from parents to children, it would die out very rapidly. On the other hand, in so far as cultural variants may be transmitted much more widely, the significance of effects on viability are much less clear. As the tragedy at Jonestown illustrates, if the proselytizing skills of its adherents are great enough, even a trait as contrary to biological viability as poison-taking may become universal, or, in biological jargon, "spread to fixation."

Despite cases like Jonestown, a major theme of post-Wilsonian sociobiology has been to argue that cultural evolution will tend to converge on the same "optimal" state as that assumed for biological evolution generally. The central argument is that the capacity for culture must, after all, have evolved, and it could not have done so unless the forms of behavior to which it gave rise were, at least generally, biologically optimal. There might, for example, be biases in the structure of the mind that favor cultural choices—or at least procedures for making such choices—that promote biological fitness. According to this line of argument, therefore, the inclusion of culture in the analysis allows the original adaptationist conclusions to be salvaged.

I think that this last-ditch attempt to save the old sociobiological program is indefensible, and that the reasons for this may prove to be instructive. I see two main reasons for this indefensibility.[8]

The first difficulty parallels an influential critique that has recently been leveled against the general biological assumption that animals will evolve toward an optimal state. Steven Jay Gould and Richard Lewontin,[9] in particular, have argued that the whole adaptationist program, of which sociobiology is only the most notorious manifestation, is flawed by an unacceptable assumption of atomism. The attempt to identify the optimum state of a particular trait of an organism inevitably involves the assumption that that trait can be considered in isolation from the rest of the organism, an assumption that in fact can be seen to be false at every level of biological organization. Even at the genetic level, it is now acknowledged that it is seldom possible to identify a single piece of genetic material with a single trait of the organism, or vice versa.[10] At the macroscopic level, problems are more obvious, if no more serious. One now famous example of Gould's is the human chin. As a feature that distinguishes humans from our closest relatives one might imagine that the investigation of the adaptive function of the chin would be an interesting evolutionary problem. But Gould argues that the chin is merely a by-product of differing growth rates in two adjacent bone structures, and that such an investigation would therefore be wholly ill-conceived.

Returning to the analogous problem for culture, I imagine that some will already have been disturbed by my references to cultural items or variants. Reflection suggests that most significant aspects of culture are extremely resistant to atomization. Being born a Roman Catholic, or electing to become a born-again Christian, or deciding to pursue a career as a doctor or a politician will generally entail the adoption of a large cluster of beliefs and forms of behavior. I do not mean to imply that this cluster of practices will be entirely determinate, but I do suggest that adopting a large part of it will be a formal or informal condition of participation in these social forms. Presumably this structure is typical of a great deal of culturally determined behavior. A member of a society either buys the package or rejects it. And even this choice is not necessarily a real one, for in less pluralistic societies one may have little choice but to accept most of the cultural package. The upshot is that, as in general biological evolution, but more obviously in the cultural case, historical contingency enormously restricts the options available to an individual. Item-by-item optimization is not something that can be expected from the invisible hand of natural selection.

A second point is perhaps even more important in the present context. The supposition that culturally transmitted behavior will generally be biologically optimal, while grounded in the first place on general considerations about the very possibility of culture's having evolved, also requires some account of the detailed mechanisms by which cultural variants are to be optimized. By analogy with genetically based natural selection, the obvious account of these mechanisms will be in terms of a process in which individuals choose among cultural variants and receive some payoff for choosing the best. The payoff schedule will drive the overall pattern of choices toward the optimum. The argument that the capacity to make such choices must have evolved through natural selection then suggests that the selection process will favor choices that are biologically optimal.

One might attack this argument simply by pointing to the general difficulties with the assumption of optimality in evolution. But I think a more illuminating objection focuses on the implausible degree of individual autonomy implicit in the argument. For such an optimizing process to work at all it must be assumed that individuals choose among cultural possibilities unconstrained by anything but the actual (as opposed to merely perceived) benefits to themselves. To the extent that other individuals can influence those choices in their own interests, whether by some form of persuasion or by brute force, the process will fail. It is possible that the adaptationist will insist that such external imposition of choices must be the exception rather than the rule since culture did, after all, evolve. But this is a non sequitur. Even if such an argument establishes that the capacity for culture must *once* have been biologically adaptive, it does not show that it remains so. The evolution of the ability to transmit large amounts of information across generations was probably a highly beneficial adaptation. That ability may also have given rise to a process of cultural evolution largely decoupled from constraints of biological fitness. One of the most obvious and significant ways in which this decoupling could occur would be through different groups' acquiring the capacity to influence culture in directions that further their own interests rather than those of the society as a whole.

A natural feminist reaction to this issue is clear and direct. In the first place, arguments about what must have or should have evolved should be treated with great suspicion when they appear to conflict with what appears in fact to have evolved. Feminist research suggests overwhelmingly that for at least half of the human population for most of known history, cultural choices have been massively constrained by the interests of individuals other than those apparently making the choices. Socialist feminists would no doubt put this proportion much higher. Any feminist would at least insist that the nature and extent of external cultural imposition is a fundamental aspect of any adequate cultural analysis. At this point we touch on some of the most fundamental theoretical issues in feminist thought. In so far as apparent cultural choices—even apparently "free" cultural choices—seem to reflect the real interests of those in power rather than those doing the choosing, what are the mechanisms of cultural imposition? Or more important still, how can they be altered?

The foregoing discussion may now be summarized. We must distinguish the plausible assertion that human culture developed out of some sort of biocultural evolutionary process from the claim that this assertion allows us to reinstate the original adaptationist sociobiology. The latter claim raises at least two major difficulties. First, to the extent that cultures must be treated as integrated wholes (or at least as composed of large structured components rather than as mere assemblages of cultural traits) the amenability of such integrated wholes to adaptationist analysis is largely undermined. Only an implausibly atomistic conception of culture could provide anything approaching the range of possible choices for the postulated processes of selection to lead to "optimal" adaptations. The additional realization that the people who appear to make cultural choices are not always, and probably not even usually, the beneficiaries of those choices, undermines whatever remains of the project of treating those choices as constituting an optimizing process that conduces to the biological advantage of the "choosers."

The major conclusion I wish to draw from this discussion is that cultural evolution should be seen as a genuinely autonomous source of human diversity with no close connection to the imperatives (if such there be) of biological evolution. If cultural evolution is not constrained by biology to the perpetuation of reproductive "optima," then it provides a possible account, consistent with but distinct from a general evolutionary perspective, of the observed reality of cultural diversity.

Two points are relevant to feminism. First, since gender roles are embedded in specific cultural contexts, asserting the genuine diversity of those contexts implies the equally real cross-cultural diversity of gender roles. Second, and perhaps more important, once gender roles are acknowledged to be constructed by cultural forces, we can be optimistic about the possibility that they can also be changed by cultural forces, most notably political ones.

Perhaps ethnographic observations of cultural variation should be sufficient to establish all I have claimed. But it is a commonplace supposition
that science seeks to discover fundamental unity underlying apparent
diversity. Biologically oriented anthropologists, rather than being immediately discouraged by apparent cultural variation, seek to understand this
diversity in terms of basic biological forces, given particular shape by
specific initial conditions and ecological circumstances. (This exactly parallels the response of biologists to the diversity of animal behavior.) The
purpose of my preceding arguments has been to claim that we should
understand cultural variation predominantly in terms of strictly cultural
forces. If, as I have also argued, there is no reasonable expectation that
these forces will be significantly determined by underlying biological fact,
we must concentrate on social processes if we are to understand this
diversity.[11]

What I hope to have shown is that the contemporary feminist emphasis
on diversity, which implies that we cannot infer conclusions about women
or people in general from facts about one group of women or people, is
entirely compatible with a plausible and defensible perspective on human
evolution. In most of the remainder of this paper I want to explore some
theoretical and methodological implications of this conclusion.

DIGRESSION ON FEMINISM AND SCIENCE

In the preceding pages I have criticized certain scientific theses while
tacitly approving, if not endorsing, certain others. In the context of recent
feminist attention to what Sandra Harding[12] has called the "Science Question," my account may seem fairly conservative. If, as Harding and others
have argued, science is permeated by gender at every level, then it may not
seem worthwhile to describe a trend within science that merely appears to
be consistent with some common feminist positions.

I do not propose here to take a position on the general controversy about
feminism and science.[13] Certain broad theses are widely agreed upon by
feminist scholars working in this area. First among these is the assumption,
following a large body of work in post-Kuhnian history of science, that
science is never entirely value-free, but is always affected to some extent by
the extrascientific beliefs of its practitioners. Second, and more specifically
feminist, is the observation that science is, and always has been, one of the
most male-dominated of Western social institutions. From these together it
seems to follow that scientific theory is permeated by masculinist biases.[14]

The real controversy in feminism concerns how to conceive these biases,
and even more crucially, how feminists should respond to the scientific
enterprise. A range of possibilities is compatible with the preceding discus-

sion. For the more optimistic, the argument suggests that the concept of cultural evolution has possibilities for producing a nonsexist account of human evolution. At the very least, as I have argued, it does not treat human diversity as simply minor variations on a biologically determined theme, and, more important, it should suggest which factors might be the crucial determinants of social change.[15]

For those more pessimistic about the redemptive possibilities of science, my argument will be of less direct interest. But even the most extreme pessimists may acknowledge some rhetorical value to the demonstration that there are views of human evolution internal to the scientific hegemony that lend no support to patriarchal ideologies of biological determinism. To quote Sandra Harding, "Whatever the moral and political values and interests responsible for selecting problems, theories, methods, and interpretations of research, they reappear at the other end of inquiry as the moral and political universe that science projects as natural and thereby helps to legitimate."[16] For the most pessimistic, I offer the preceding discussion only as a modest example of this process being carried out with a particular feminist position as input to the scientific black box.

As Ruth Hubbard's remarks (in this volume) on the study of the evolution of behavior should make clear, speculations about the history and determining processes of human evolution remain at this time very much at the level of origin myths. The lack of evidence favoring one such story over another has allowed feminist critiques to reveal such myths as paradigmatic examples of the "scientific" elaboration of sexist ideology.[17] In cautiously recommending the concept of human cultural evolution, I should be seen as advocating a metamyth, a framework in terms of which other myths could be presented. This metamyth suggests the possibility of cultural change rather than the necessity of the status quo. Since some belief in progressive human possibility is a necessary feature of any feminist position, this is a significant advantage.

HUMAN DIVERSITY AND GENDERED ANALYSES

One way I have mentioned of stating the general thesis of this paper is to claim that the scope of gender-based generalizations must typically be assumed, lacking evidence to the contrary, to be very narrow. A central area to which this conclusion has relevance is the psychology of sexual difference. And I mean "psychology" here in the broadest possible sense, ranging from psychoanalytic theories of sexual difference to empirical studies of differences in behavior and capacity to accounts of developmental divergence between boys and girls. My point about such studies is not to question their potential legitimacy, but to highlight the unavoidable difficulty of determining the scope of the generalizations to which such research gives rise. Thus what I want to claim is that theoretical claims about human behavior, and in particular about sexually differentiated behavior, cannot be taken seriously without a simultaneous attempt to locate those claims within an appropriate cultural typology. Claims such as "women are more sensitive than men to emotional factors in decision making" or "men are more aggressive than women in sexual encounters" seem to me methodologically on a par with "animals eat meat" or "birds fly." It is not just that they are mostly false (cows don't; turkeys can't) but that, given our understanding of the determinants of human or animal variety, they do not provide plausible correlations of range and type of generalization. Unless they are based on very broad observational samples, in the first cases ethnographically and in the second taxonomically, they should not be taken seriously.

This point has great relevance to many areas of central concern to feminism. Rape, male violence, familialism, and pornography, for example, are not phenomena about which we should expect to formulate theories with much generality. Both their social significance and the typical circumstances of their occurrence may be expected to be specific functions of a particular cultural milieu. Generalizations beyond the specific cultural context will be fraught with danger.

Considering a theoretical perspective rather than particular issues, we may turn to psychoanalysis. Without proposing to offer an evaluation of psychoanalysis as a theoretical tool in its appropriate context, I do want to insist that its application requires an explicit claim about the cultural circumstances that give rise to the forces it describes. If we accept that Freudian psychoanalysis is highly illuminating of human behavior in Austria at the turn of the century, we may legitimately proceed first to isolate the cultural phenomena that make this true, and second, on the basis of such an analysis, extend its geographical relevance perhaps as widely as Western society in general, and its temporal relevance perhaps as far as the present. But a theoretical approach like psychoanalysis absolutely requires some such theory of cultural typology that explicitly addresses the question of its scope. There is nothing incoherent about very broad answers to this question. Some psychoanalytic theorists may believe that the mere fact of exclusively female child-rearing in any gendered society will produce characteristic gender-differentiated psychological consequences. But unless some universal biological mechanism is assumed to account for such a fact, it is wholly implausible to suppose that the effects in question would be insensitive to the great array of other cultural differences impinging on the child. I do not wish to accuse psychoanalytic theorists of such biologistic assumptions. As the survey article by Nancy Chodorow in this volume makes clear, some major trends in psychoanalytic theory are opposed to its original essentialist tendencies. What I do want to emphasize is how, in such an area of investigation, essentialist assumptions are always liable, perhaps implicitly, to occur.[18]

HUMAN DIVERSITY AND FEMINIST POLITICS

Feminist theory has tended to have a somewhat ambivalent attitude to the issue I am discussing. On the one hand feminists have increasingly recognized the importance of diversity and have been aware of interactions between gender and such distinct categories as race and class. They have certainly recognized the importance of combating the essentialist biologistic theories of sex and gender that have been the mainstay of patriarchal responses to feminism. But an obvious force is pushing feminists to different, but still fundamentally essentialist, positions of their own. If some essential notion of women and men cannot be retained, does feminism even make sense as a field of study?

I believe there is a sense in which feminist theory, as opposed to gender studies (see note 3), is *not* an ultimately coherent field of study. Perhaps there will always be distinctions of gender in human societies, and if so central areas of the social sciences, textual studies, and so on will continue to describe and theorize this aspect of social organization or its public representations; and of course gender distinctions could never be erased from history. But feminist theory involves a great deal more than that. Its primary source of coherence derives from politics rather than from the unified nature of its subject matter. The thesis that unites feminist scholars is not that some systematic understanding of gender differences is required, but that gender differences are an ethically indefensible, yet nearly universal, basis for systematic inequalities of power.

My general point may perhaps be best expressed by noting that most feminists, I take it, hope that at some time in the future feminism will no longer be needed. If we succeed in creating a society in which there are no politically significant gender categories, the most central aspects of feminist theory will become redundant. Whereas no amount of progress in geology, say, will make rocks go away, feminism, it is to be hoped, may eventually make distinctions of gender disappear.[19]

Although the subject matter of feminism—historically and geographically specific articulations of gender difference—is both highly varied and probably lacking in universal unifying principles, the political problem of feminism does, in the real world, present a quite coherent problem of sexual difference. And while cultural specifics of gender difference will obviously determine appropriate practical measures for addressing the political problem, I believe that there are ethical and political issues that entirely transcend these differences, and these, I believe, are the fundamental questions for feminism. The contrast between culturally specific articulations of gender difference on the one hand, and the attempt to formulate adequate ethical and political resistance to such differences, on the other, is what I have in mind in the title of this paper in contrasting the appropriateness of local and global approaches to sexual difference.

The last claim, that the political problem of feminism might be amenable to a quite general treatment, will no doubt require some explanation and defense. It is often assumed that if, as I have done, one accepts a strong thesis of cultural specificity and difference, one must be committed to an equally strong version of ethical relativism that will preclude any such culturally transcendent political position. I think this view is mistaken.

What I have in mind as a unifying conception of feminist politics must be understood at a fairly abstract level. The relativist argument I referred to above depends on considering ethical issues at too culturally specific a level. What most people think of as central ethical principles are quite detailed prescriptions concerning socially appropriate behavior: with whom it is appropriate to have sexual relations, or what are essential religious practices, for example. And such principles are highly culturally variable.

But such culturally local prescriptions must surely be analyzed—at least critically analyzed—as involving a mixture of, or interaction between, two very different things. On the one hand are the specific articulations of a social system; on the other, general principles governing appropriate ways of interacting with other human beings. The question of appropriate sexual partners provides an excellent illustrative case. We should surely regard strongly coercive practices, such as rape or sexual slavery, primarily in the light of general ethical principles; perhaps these should also prohibit sexual relations with small children. By contrast, if an issue like adultery is problematic it is not so simply as involving sexual relations with another adult person. To understand it as an ethical problem is to integrate that bare description of the act into the network of social values and meanings that constitute marriage in a particular social context. Assuming that, as barely described, the act involved is ethically unproblematic, I take it that adultery is an ethical issue only in the local, culturally specific sense.

This distinction is a difficult and sensitive one. It is no easy matter to analyze our own, still less another, culture in these terms. In the case of other cultures there is a constant danger of projecting our own categories inappropriately when we identify actions as "rape" or "slavery." We have no extracultural standpoint from which to make such judgments. Despite the difficulties, I want to insist that this distinction is essential. It is essential, at least for feminists, because we cannot be willing to accept the system of social values and meanings uncritically. And we can have a ground for criticism only if we adopt some more abstract ethical standpoint.

As feminists, we need to develop conceptions of justice, equality, and freedom as a basis from which to criticize and attack forms of gender differentiation that stand in the way of such ideals. The fundamental achievement of feminism must be the recognition of an entire dimension of injustice and oppression that has been largely ignored by traditional political theory, or, perhaps worse, consigned to the category of the natural and inevitable. But recognition is only the beginning of any solution. That will require first the development of our conceptions of ethics and politics in whatever ways are necessary to address adequately the injustices in question, and then the motivation of political action to remedy them.[20]

This leads me finally to a point mentioned in the introduction to this paper. While its conception as fundamentally political lends feminism coherence, it ultimately leads it to a kind of self-destruction. The extent of cultural difference suggests no single political problem of feminism exists. Instead there is a range of different social contexts, each with its own forms of oppression. Furthermore, all of these social contexts are partially constituted by distinct forms of inequality: economic, racial, religious, nationalist, imperialist, and so on. Everywhere gender differences interact with, and are perhaps partially constituted by, these other unequal distributions of power. But any ethical conception adequate to serve as a unifying basis for feminist analysis must certainly equally condemn these interacting forms of social inequity. Thus there appears a still deeper sense in which feminism is threatened by incoherence: the ethical conception required to hold it together inevitably expands to include many issues that are not specifically *feminist*. While I think there is no doubt that the same argument must apply to any specifically limited emancipatory movement, such as resistance to race, class, or ethnic oppression, it is perhaps the omnipresence of gender relations across this great array of social differences that has put feminism in the unique historical position to see that there can be no consistent stopping place for feminist politics short of comprehensive and systematic resistance to all these forms of oppression.

A common theme running through this essay, one that is the central point of antiessentialism,[21] has been the danger of assuming any preanalytic or a priori answer to the question of the scope of generalizations. Feminism starts by emphasizing the profound implications throughout society and our understanding of the world of the categories "man" and "woman." Yet it appears that as explanatory categories they are far too broad to be useful; they predict almost nothing about human behavior unless they are culturally and historically restricted. But this very fact, pointing as it does to the intersection of gender categories with many other categories that ground deep social inequities, leads inexorably to the observation that as ethical and political categories they are too narrow. It is these ambiguities of scope that I have tried to highlight with the suggestion that feminism is ultimately incoherent. Yet whether or not this is a genuine incoherence, it makes contemporary feminism potentially one of the most exciting emancipatory projects in human history.

The Political Nature
of "Human Nature"

RUTH HUBBARD

Biologists, social scientists, and philosophers have speculated about human nature. Is there such a thing, and if so, how does one describe it? Fortunately I do not need to review the history of such speculations, since Alison Jaggar has provided a lucid discussion of the main issues and has located the debates in their historical and political contexts.[1] What I can do is evaluate the biological suppositions that underlie the concept of a human nature.

The ambiguity of the term *biology* is at the heart of questions about what scientists do when they try to examine nature. We use the word to denote what scientists tell us about the nature of organisms and also the living experience. When I speak of "my biology," I am usually referring to how I experience my biological functions, not to what scientists tell me about them. I can also use the word as the name of the scientific discipline, as in "I am studying biology." These multiple meanings for *biology* reflect confusions and ambiguities about the connections between scientific descriptions and the phenomena in the real world that scientists try to describe. It is important that we be aware of this ambiguity when we think about "human nature." Are we describing the natures of real people—you and me—or an abstraction or reification that biologists construct? "Human nature" does not describe people. It is a normative concept that incarnates historically based beliefs about what human beings are and how they should behave.

Biologists' claims about human nature are embedded in the ways they learn about and describe living organisms. Most biologists, like other scientists, accept the notion that nature can best be described in terms of different levels of organization. These levels extend from ultimate particles, through atoms and molecules, to cells, tissues, and organs, to organ-

I want to thank Robin M. Gillespie for critical comments and discussion.

isms considered individually, and then to groups of organisms—societies. Biology nowadays is concerned with the range of levels from atoms and molecules through organisms, and also with groups of organisms and their relations with each other over time (evolution) and space (animal behavior and ecology). Some biologists learn about organisms by taking them apart; others observe whole organisms in the laboratory or the field. Yet these levels are not credited with equal authority. Most biologists (as well as chemists and physicists) believe that the "lower" atomic and molecular levels are more basic and have intrinsically greater explanatory potential. Thus we find scientists and science writers describing genes (which are molecules) as keys to "the secret of life" or as "blueprints" of the organism. Numerous biologists believe that we would understand a great deal more about ourselves and other animals if we knew the composition and sequence of all the genes on our chromosomes. This belief in the superior explanatory content of "lower" levels is usually referred to as *reductionism,* and at this time reductionism is the dominant mode of thinking among biologists.

Reductionists assert that the study of organs, tissues, and molecules can yield important information about how organisms, and hence societies, operate. For example, they attribute the existence of crime to the "criminal personality," and criminals are said to behave as they do because they have diseased brains, too much or too little of certain hormones or other critical substances, or defective genes. Reductionism is a hierarchical theory that proceeds from the bottom up.

The converse is sometimes called *holism.* It can be based on a similar analysis that accepts hierarchies of levels, but it assigns superior authority to the "higher" levels, the organism as a whole or the organism in its surroundings. It is a less popular system of explanation among scientists, but one that carries considerable weight among practitioners of "alternative" methods of healing such as acupuncture and massage, and among feminists and environmentalists. They see reductionist ways of conceptualizing nature as a threat to people and our environment because these focus on specific areas of interest as though they could be isolated from their context.

Biodeterminism is a form of reductionism that explains individual behavior and characteristics of societies in terms of biological functions. Feminists know it best in the form of Freud's notorious statement, "Biology is destiny." During the nineteenth and twentieth centuries, biologists have produced numerous biodeterminist explanations for the obvious differences in women's and men's access to social, economic, and political power. Among them are Darwin's descriptions of the greater "vigour" and more highly developed weapons of males, acquired over eons of evolution through competition among males for access to females. At the same time,

Darwin claimed, females sharpened their skills at discerning the most fit among their suitors and acquired coyness and the other wiles needed to captivate the best males. Biodeterminism has also prompted comparisons between the sizes of men's and women's brains and between brains of men of different races—which scientists used to "prove" the superiority of Caucasian men over men of other races and over all women.

A good deal of present-day research into presumed causes of social and behavioral differences between women and men relies upon reductionist explanations. These draw on hypothesized differences in hormone levels of female and male fetuses or on hypothetical genes for spatial skills, mathematical ability, and competitiveness and aggression in men and for domesticity and nurturance in women. The most pervasive and comprehensive of contemporary biodeterminist theories is sociobiology, which has as its project "the systematic study of the *biological basis* of all social behavior" (my italics).[2] Sociobiologists claim that the fundamental elements of human nature can be identified in traits that characterize all people (and selected animals as well) irrespective of their cultural or historical differences. Once these supposedly universal traits have been identified, for example, male aggression and female nurturance, sociobiologists argue that their universality is evidence that they are adaptive. The term *adaptive* in this context means that individuals who exhibit these traits leave more descendants than do other individuals and that they pass the traits on to their descendants. In this way the genes for more adaptive traits come to outnumber the genes for less adaptive ones until the more adaptive traits become universal.

Sociobiologists argue that animals, including humans, do things that help spread their genes about. Behaviors that let them do that most effectively become universal traits. Among males, these are behaviors that lead them to inseminate as many females as possible, hence male promiscuity; for females they are behaviors that optimize the ability to spot and attach themselves to genetically well endowed males and to take good care of the few precious offspring they can produce in their lifetime, hence female fidelity and nurturance.

This basic difference between male and female reproductive strategies is said to arise from the fact that males can produce large numbers of small sperm, whereas females can produce fewer but larger eggs.[3] From this seemingly trivial asymmetry, sociobiologists draw two conclusions that they assume are crucial for the evolution of important differences between females and males: (1) females are the scarce resource (few eggs) and (2) females invest more energy in each egg than males do in each sperm.

But there is no reason to believe that females expend more energy (whatever that means) in the biological components of reproduction than males do. Among mammals, females indeed produce fewer eggs than males do sperm, and females gestate the embryos, but it is not obvious how to translate these facts into energy expenditures. Is it reasonable to count only the energy males require to produce the few sperm that actually end up fertilizing eggs, or should one not count the total energy they expend in producing and ejaculating semen (that is, sperm plus spermatic fluid) throughout their lives (however one would do that)? What is more, a woman's eggs are laid down ("produced") while she is still in her mother's womb. So should they be credited to her mother's energy expenditures or to her own (however one might calculate them)?

There are other puzzles. Sociobiologists describe the growth of a fetus as an investment of energy on the part of the pregnant woman. But the metabolism of a mammalian embryo is part of a pregnant woman's metabolic functions. As she eats, breathes, and metabolizes, some of the food she takes in is used to build the embryo. Why does that represent an investment of *her* energies? I can see that an embryo that grows inside an undernourished woman may be a drain on her because it uses her body for its growth. But healthy, well nourished women have been known to live normal active lives, create art, compete in Olympic events, and feel "energized" rather than drained by their pregnancies.

In the nineteenth century, physicians argued that girls would not be able to grow up to bear children if they diverted the energy required by their developing reproductive organs to their brains by going to school and becoming educated, like boys.[4] And they spoke of menstruation and pregnancy as requiring energy as part of the self-serving ideology by which they portrayed all female reproductive functions as diseases that required medical (hence, of course, male) supervision. Sociobiological arguments that posit differences in the energy women and men invest in procreation to explain why men take less responsibility for the care of their children than women do may ring with scientific plausibility. But there is no way even to specify the variables, much less to do the necessary calculations to turn such hand-waving into scientific statements.

Sociobiologist Richard Dawkins takes sociobiological reductionism to its extreme by asserting that organisms are merely the gene's way of making more genes. He claims that everything organisms do is done out of self-interest, since organisms are only living manifestations of "selfish genes" engaged in the process of replicating themselves.[5] One of the obvious problems with this kind of formulation is that genes do not replicate *themselves*. Nor do eggs or sperm. Even many organisms do not reproduce themselves—at least not organisms that procreate sexually, like humans and most other animals discussed by sociobiologists. Sexual procreation involves a coming together of individuals with different genetic makeups, who produce individuals who are genetically different from their parents and from each other. This has made it difficult for biologists to know how to analyze the ways in which even simple Mendelian traits that involve differences in only one gene become established in a population, not to speak of the ill-defined behaviors that sociobiologists label selfishness, aggression, or nurturance.

Sociobiology can be criticized on many levels. Even within the reductionist, biodeterminist paradigm, human sociobiology allows far too much leeway for identifying and naming traits that are observed in different cultures and under different historical circumstances as the same and hence "universal," especially when these "same" traits are generalized to animals as well. In such an exercise everything—from sharp business practices and warfare to toddlers and young animals roughhousing to interactions scientists have observed among animals in the field, in zoos, or in crowded laboratory cages—becomes "aggression." The term *rape*, which refers ordinarily to the violent, sexualized assertion of power men impose on unconsenting women and occasionally on other men, has been used by sociobiologists as though it denoted nothing more sinister than males' efforts to spread their genes around. Hence sociobiologists have described what they choose to call rape among birds, fishes, insects, and even plants.[6] Contexts and cultural meanings are erased, and all that is left is reified traits, which are universalized when the same name is given to a multiplicity of behaviors. In this way sociobiological reductionism leads to absurd extremes of lumping diverse behaviors together and naming them to suit the scientist's purpose.

Obviously similarities exist between the ways animals and people behave. But the variety of animal behaviors on which to draw for models of human behavior is so great that one can prove any human behavior is "natural" if the criterion is merely that one can point to an animal that behaves that way. This brings me to a crucial problem with efforts to construct lines of evolutionary descent for behaviors among animals, as well as between animals and people. In attempting to establish continuities between different species that may be of historical—evolutionary—significance, biologists have learned to distinguish between two types of similarities: analogies and homologies. Analogies are similarities in appearance or function that have diverse biological origins. Examples are the wings of birds, bats, and insects, and the eyes of frogs, lobsters, and octopuses. Homologous structures may look less similar, but they exhibit important similarities of structure and function that point to a common ancestry. An example is the scales of reptiles and the feathers of birds. To establish lines of historical continuity, analogies are irrelevant. One must look for homologies, which usually requires culling the fossil record.

Behavior leaves no fossils. There are only observations of how contemporary animals (including people) act and interpretations of what their actions signify. This offers too much leeway for postulating connections and imagining possible lines of descent for similar behaviors in particular groups of people and kinds of animals. If we want to use biological observations to try to trace and describe our natural history (which is what sociobiologists want to do), we have to follow more rigorous rules. Resemblances in the ways different animals and people act should not alone lead us to conclude that a behavior has evolutionary significance and is genetically determined.

INTERACTIVE, DIALECTICAL, AND COMPLEMENTARY MODELS OF NATURE

To get away from reductionism *and* holism and from futile arguments about whether nature or nurture is more significant in shaping behavior, a number of scientists have stressed that both genetics and environment are important, and that their effects cannot be separated. The simplest model suggests that the effects are additive. On the basis of that kind of model Arthur Jensen and Richard Herrnstein have argued that 80 percent of intelligence is inherited, 20 percent due to environment.

Other scientists have pointed out that this interpretation is too simplistic and that nature and nurture interact in ways that cannot be numerically quantified because they are not additive but simultaneous, and always act together. For example, Lewontin has argued that we can assess the separate contributions of genetic and environmental factors that act jointly only under strictly controlled conditions that permit the experimenter to change just one variable at a time.[7] On the basis of such experiments one can construct graphs called norms of reaction that describe how specific changes in each variable affect the phenomenon under observation (such as the growth of a plant in various types of soil and under various conditions of moisture, temperature, and cultivation). But these graphs do not permit one to predict the reactions of different varieties of the same organism under the same experimental conditions, or the reactions of a single variety under conditions that one has not yet measured. Such experiments illustrate the complexity of the situation but do not yield information about the real world, in which changes do not occur one variable at a time or in controlled or controllable ways.

More recently, Lewontin, Rose, and Kamin, as well as Birke, have argued that this kind of interactive model, though less limited than simple additive ones, is still too static.[8] Lewontin, Rose, and Kamin propose a dialectical model that acknowledges levels of organization, such as the ones I have enumerated. They argue that no one level is more fundamental than any other. None "causes" or "determines" another, but all are related dialectically, mutually drawing upon and modifying the changes that may be produced at any particular level. Properties observed at a particular level cannot be inferred from properties at other levels because the levels are related dialectically. For example, one cannot predict the physics and chemistry of water from the properties of hydrogen and oxygen atoms. Nor can one predict the structures and functions of proteins from the properties of the amino acids of which they are composed, and even less from the properties of the atoms that make up the amino acids. This is not because we do not know enough about atoms or amino acids, but because new properties emerge when atoms or amino acids come together in different combinations. These properties must be discovered empirically. The same goes for the relationships between organisms and their genes or between societies and the individuals who live in them.

I like to call the dialectical model *transformationism*, an awkward term, but one that tries to signify that biological and environmental factors can utterly change an organism so that it responds differently to other concurrent or subsequent, biological or environmental changes than it might have done. At the same time, the organism transforms its environment, which includes other organisms.

We can visualize this kind of interaction or transformation by thinking about the interplay between biological and cultural factors that affects the ways boys and girls grow up in our society. If a society puts half its children into short skirts and warns them not to move in ways that reveal their panties, while putting the other half into jeans and overalls and encouraging them to climb trees, play ball, and participate in other vigorous outdoor games; if later, during adolescence, the children who have been wearing trousers are urged to "eat like growing boys," while the children in skirts are warned to watch their weight and not get fat; if the half in jeans runs around in sneakers or boots, while the half in skirts totters about on spike heels, then these two groups of people will be biologically as well as socially different. Their muscles will be different, as will their reflexes, posture, arms, legs and feet, hand-eye coordination, and so on. Similarly, people who spend eight hours a day in an office working at a typewriter or a visual display terminal will be biologically different from those who work on construction jobs. There is no way to sort the biological and social components that produce these differences. We cannot sort nature from nurture when we confront group differences in societies in which people from different races, classes, and sexes do not have equal access to resources and power, and therefore live in different environments. Sex-typed generalizations, such as that men are heavier, taller, or stronger than women, obscure the diversity among women and among men and the extensive overlaps between them for all traits except those directly involved with procreation. Most women and men fall within the same range of heights, weights, and strengths, three variables that depend a great deal on how we have grown up and live. We all know that first-generation Americans, on average, are taller than their immigrant parents and that men who do physical labor, on average, are stronger than male college professors. But we forget to look for the obvious reasons for differences when confronted with assertions like "Men are stronger than women." We should be asking: "Which men?" and "What do they do?" There may be biologically based average differences between women and men, but these are interwoven with a host of social differences from which we cannot disentangle them.

Recently some of us have begun to use yet another model to look at the different levels of organization, a model that draws on Niels Bohr's principle of complementarity. Bohr proposed complementarity as a way to think about the fact that light and other electromagnetic radiation can be described equally well as bursts of particles (quanta) or as waves spreading out from a point source. Classical physicists argued over which they really are; Bohr and other quantum theorists asserted that they are both. By complementarity Bohr meant that they are both at all times, not sometimes one, sometimes the other. Which description is appropriate depends on the instruments an observer uses to examine the radiation. When observed with a phototube or a photoelectric cell, light looks like a random succession of packets of energy; with a diffraction grating or a prism, it looks like waves.

Complementarity provides a fruitful model to integrate the different levels of organization and describe living organisms. The phenomena we observe at the subatomic, atomic, molecular, cellular, organismic, and societal levels are all taking place simultaneously and constitute a single reality. The distinctions between them are not part of nature. It is an outcome of Western cultural history and of the history of professionalization that we have developed separate academic specialties that describe these levels as though they were different phenomena. The only reason we think in terms of such levels is that we have developed specialties that draw distinctions between them. But physicists do not have access to more fundamental truths than molecular biologists have, and molecular biologists do not provide more basic descriptions than do the biologists who study cells or organisms. Biologists do not probe deeper realities than anthropologists or historians, only different ones. The fact that academic professionals value the explanatory power of these disciplines differently tells us something about the history and sociology of professionalization and about the alliances different disciplines have been able to forge with economic and political power, not about nature.

HUMAN NATURE

It is questionable whether the concept of human nature means anything. People's "nature" can be described only by looking at the things we do. To try to abstract or reify a human essence from the ways in which different groups of people have grappled with issues of survival in the range of geographical, ecological, and demographic settings that our species has populated is a dubious enterprise, because what one labels as "natural" depends on one's experience and viewpoint. People with different backgrounds are not likely to agree. Margaret Mead pointed out years ago that in societies with different, even opposite, sexual divisions of labor, people tend to believe that what women and men do follows from inherent differences in our natures.[9]

Sociobiologists presume that certain traits are inherent in our biological nature. Primary among them is selfishness, since it supposedly gets us to perpetuate our genes. A variant on selfishness is altruism of the kind that benefits the altruist (something like, "I'll scratch your back if you'll scratch my children's"). Then there are territoriality and a tendency toward establishing dominance hierarchies, which entered descriptions of animal behavior around the beginning of World War I, when a so-called pecking order was described among barnyard chickens,[10] a not very "natural" population. There are also the sex-differentiated characteristics of male aggressiveness and competitiveness and female coyness and nurturance, which supposedly follow from the asymmetry in our reproductive interests that I questioned earlier. Wilson includes in "human nature" various behaviors that make sexual relationships between women and men emotionally satisfying, such as fondling and kissing, religious and spiritual aspirations that generate the need to believe in something beyond oneself, and the incest taboo.[11] He acknowledges cultural influences but insists that biology contributes a "stubborn kernel" that "cannot be forced without cost."[12] Because sociobiologists posit that "kernel" of biological traits, honed over eons of evolutionary history, their human nature theories tend to be conservative and portray competitive, hierarchical, capitalist societies in which men dominate women and a small, privileged group of men dominates everyone else as the natural outcome of inborn biological propensities.[13] But competition and dominance hierarchies do not characterize all human societies,[14] and there is no reason to believe that our biology determines the ways we construct them.

Stimulated in part by insights gained in the women's liberation movement, a number of sociobiologists have recently published accounts that round out the traditional descriptions of female animals as reproducers.[15] They present females as active participants in the social life of the group, as aggressive, competitive, involved in dominance hierarchies of their own, and as initiators of sexual contact and promiscuous. It seems that the sexual revolution has overtaken the dominant, competitive male and the coy, submissive female.

In his chapter in this collection, Carl Degler points out that sociobiologists as individuals have a range of political views and commitments. This is true, but the sociobiological definition of human nature lends itself to conservative politics. It is not inconsistent for a sociobiologist to assert that Marxism is "based on an inaccurate description of human nature,"[16] or that women's liberation is doomed because "human societies have evolved toward sexual domination as though sliding down a ratchet,"[17] and that "even with identical education and equal access to all professions, men are likely to play a disproportionate role in political life, business, and science."[18]

Biology imposes limits on what people can do, but when we feel the need we usually try to overcome them—at times all too recklessly. Bareskinned, we live in the arctic; wingless we fly; we live under water without benefit of gills. In view of the ingenuity with which we have overcome our limitations, it might seem odd that scientists call on sometimes quite subtle hypothetical differences between women and men to explain gender inequalities and that research into sex differences arouses so much scientific and public interest. We must recognize that differences among people are of interest only if they are correlated with differences in power. Little, if any, research is done on biological or psychosocial correlates of differences in height, although folk wisdom suggests there may be some. But when it comes to dark-skinned and light-skinned people or women and men, every possibility of difference is explored—and always some scientists predict that it will be hard to overcome.

Yet people have undergone substantial physical as well as psychological changes during times of major political and economic transformation. For example, as a result of rationing and the social policies the British government enacted during World War II, a generation of children grew up in Britain that was healthier and looked significantly different from any that had gone before. People who participate in major political or personal changes that drastically alter the ways they live often experience simultaneous changes in the ways their bodies function—changes in their ability to work and concentrate, in sleep and eating patterns, muscle mass, shape and strength, body weight, skin color and texture, and many others. It is not that changes in our way of life *cause* our biology to change. All the changes are interconnected: *we* change. Women who have participated in the women's liberation movement are well aware of such changes— changes in our bodies as well as in our lives.

Another example: We tend to think of menstruation as purely biological, yet menstrual patterns and experiences are profoundly affected by the ways women live, and the menstrual and reproductive patterns of women whose ways of life differ can be very different. Research conducted with female college athletes has demonstrated menstrual changes induced by exercise and diet.[19] !Kung women who forage for food in the Kalahari desert in southern Africa have entirely different menstrual and reproductive histories from the ones we are accustomed to think of as normal or natural. These women walk a great deal as part of their foraging and eat food that, although nutritionally adequate, supplies very different proportions and kinds of carbohydrates, fats and proteins than do our Western diets. Also, they nurse their babies for longer times and much more frequently than we do.[20] As a result, the !Kung establish patterns of ovulation and menstruation that produce only four or five pregnancies and very few menstruations in a lifetime.[21] It seems quite possible that the regular monthly cycle that some Western ideologies have put at the core of female personality is an accompaniment of ways of life that have developed in the last few thousand years. During this time increasing numbers of people have ceased to live as nomadic foragers and have begun to cultivate land, form settlements, and build the kinds of cultural and political structures that have yielded historical records.[22] But even now, women (and no doubt men) in different parts of the world live diverse biological, as well as social and economic, lives. As I have tried to say, these aspects of our lives cannot be separated.

Biological differences between the sexes prevent us from achieving gender equality only in procreation, narrowly defined. To date, only men can produce sperm and only women can produce eggs and gestate. Women *and* men can now feed infants reasonably healthful imitations of mother's milk, at least in affluent societies. People's capacities to work at socially useful tasks and to nurture children and form nonexploitative and mutually satisfying relationships are not limited by biology, but by discriminatory economic and social practices.

Perspectives on Sociobiology, Feminism, and the Law

HERMA HILL KAY

EQUALITY AND DIFFERENCE IN FEMINIST LEGAL THEORY

For the past twenty-five years, American feminist legal scholars and practitioners have been trying to remove sex-based generalizations from the law.[1] Most of the scholarly analysis devoted to this end—and virtually all of the implementing litigation—has been carried on under the rubric of equality. The two major legal provisions used to attack classifications based on sex have been the constitutional concept of equality found in the Fifth and Fourteenth Amendments to the United States Constitution and the statutory antidiscrimination principle enacted in Title VII of the Civil Rights Act of 1964. Although neither of these provisions was originally designed to combat sex discrimination,[2] both have served that goal.[3] This effort has sought to remove legal barriers that hindered both sexes in making nontraditional choices affecting their public and private lives.[4] At its fundamental level, the legal campaign has attempted to eradicate patterns of sex segregation and related cycles of dominance and submission that have historically characterized male-female relationships in American society.

This feminist legal agenda was opposed by those who correctly viewed it as a challenge to established power structures, as well as by those who mistakenly, if understandably, viewed it as a repudiation of conventional values traditionally associated with the family. These opponents prevented the creation of a new legal tool especially designed to end classification by sex—the proposed Equal Rights Amendment (ERA) to the United States Constitution. The defeat of the ERA did not, however, mark the end of the

74

feminist legal attack on gender inequality. Rather, it may have stimulated new approaches to the problem of discrimination, including major efforts at reconceptualizing the meaning of equality between women and men.[5] The common ground these new theoretical approaches share is that they all address at varying levels the problem of difference.

To posit the existence of difference in the context of legal analysis, however, is to admit the possibility of rational classification between different groups. As Deborah L. Rhode has noted, historically, "arguments emphasizing sexual difference, even those designed to advance feminist causes, risked contributing to the stereotypes on which antifeminism rested."[6] Mindful of the hazards they confronted, the earliest feminist reconceptualizations of legal equality began cautiously. They focused on the undeniable biological reproductive sex differences between men and women, primarily stressing pregnancy.[7] They suggested that pregnancy might be taken into account under certain circumstances as an appropriate legal basis for the differential treatment of women and men in order to ensure substantive, rather than formal, equality.

Since the primary target of the earlier feminist battle for legal equality had been over-broad classifications inappropriately drawn on the basis of sex, including pregnancy,[8] the veterans of those battles did not greet the new approach with enthusiasm.[9] The immediate result was the "equal treatment-special treatment" debate that divided feminist legal practitioners and scholars over the issue of pregnancy in the workplace. The debate centered on two cases[10] challenging state statutes requiring the provision of reasonable leave for pregnant workers as a violation of federal law. Its implications, however, were much greater, ultimately pitting two opposing views of equality—formal versus substantive—against each other.[11] The resolution of the controversy in favor of the state statutes requiring pregnancy leave has not ended the theoretical debate. Instead, some participants have expanded its terms. Transcending the limitations of an analysis grounded in equality, they explore a celebration of difference.[12]

In its expanded form, however, the feminist legal discourse concerning difference may attract unwelcome support from an unexpected—and purportedly scientific—quarter. Proponents of sociobiology also celebrate differences between women and men. But unlike feminists, who invoke difference to liberate women from male domination, sociobiologists use sexual difference as a natural evolutionary justification for continued female exploitation. The juxtaposition of these diverse explorations of sexual difference may expose feminist theorists to the danger of having their work used to justify nonfeminist goals. This paper will contrast the content and purpose of feminist and sociobiological speculations concerning difference in the hope of lessening that danger.

SOCIOBIOLOGY AND SEX DIFFERENCES

THE DEVELOPMENT OF SOCIOBIOLOGY

Edward O. Wilson,[13] the father of sociobiology, explains that the most basic and universal sex difference common to the majority of organisms, including most animals, is the relative size of the sex cells, or *gametes,* of males and females. The egg is relatively large, while the sperm is small and motile. The egg contains the yolk that nourishes the embryo during its initial development. The female sequesters the embryo, and she may continue to care for the offspring during the postnatal period. Wilson concludes, "This is the reason why parental care is normally provided by the female, and why most animal societies are matrifocal."[14]

Richard Dawkins puts the point more pugnaciously in a chapter of his book *The Selfish Gene* entitled "Battle of the Sexes:"

> Sperms and eggs . . . contribute equal numbers of genes, but eggs contribute far more in the way of food reserves: indeed sperms make no contribution at all, and are simply concerned with transporting their genes as fast as possible to an egg. At the moment of conception, therefore, the father has invested less than his fair share (i.e. 50 percent) of resources in the offspring. Since each sperm is so tiny, a male can afford to make many millions of them every day. This means he is potentially able to beget a very large number of children in a very short period of time, using different females. This is only possible because each new embryo is endowed with adequate food by the mother in each case. This therefore places a limit on the number of children a female can have, but the number of children a male can have is virtually unlimited. Female exploitation begins here.[15]

From this difference in gamete size other differences follow, beginning with the division of labor within a two-sexed species. Dawkins claims that "it is possible to interpret all the other differences between the sexes as stemming from this one basic difference."[16] Charles Darwin[17] had earlier developed his theory of sexual selection to explain the existence of secondary sexual characteristics, which occur in many species, in addition to the purely functional differences in gonads and reproductive organs. Wilson and other sociobiologists derive from the concept of sexual selection characteristically different strategies followed by males and females to maximize their success in mating.[18] Once mating has occurred, however, the female's essential role becomes that of preserving the product of procreation, leaving the male free to mate successively.

Among mammals, the mother continues to provide the newborn infant with nourishment in the form of milk. Wilson emphasizes the universal importance of this fact to evolutionary trends:

> The key to the sociobiology of mammals is milk. Because young animals depend on their mothers during a substantial part of their early develop-

ment, the mother-offspring group is the universal nuclear unit of mammalian societies. . . . They are also distinguished by the absence of any species that shows reversal of sex roles, wherein females court the males and then leave them to care for the young.[19]

Wilson began the project of relating the body of evolutionary knowledge to human beings in the final chapter of his book *Sociobiology*. He there identifies the task of comparative sociobiology: to trace human qualities as closely as possible back through time. Eschewing more flamboyant efforts, he confines himself to an approach that establishes "the lowest taxonomic level at which each character shows significant intertaxon variation."[20] In this analysis, only the most conservative characters, defined as those that "remain constant at the level of the taxonomic family or throughout the order Primates," are chosen as the "ones most likely to have persisted in relatively unaltered form into the evolution of *Homo*."[21] When this has been done, Wilson tells us, "These conservative traits include aggressive dominance systems, with males generally dominant over females; scaling in the intensity of responses, especially during aggressive interactions; intensive and prolonged maternal care, with a pronounced degree of socialization in the young; and matrilineal social organization."[22]

In his subsequent book, *On Human Nature,* Wilson speculated more freely about the genetic basis of human behavior. He concluded that the accumulated evidence for a large hereditary component of human behavior is "decisive" and "unfavorable to the competing hypothesis which has dominated the social sciences for generations, that mankind has escaped its own genes to the extent of being entirely culture-bound."[23]

Applying his "general evolutionary theory" to contemporary human society, and deferring for the moment consideration of the "undeniably important plasticity controlled by culture," Wilson sketches out the following comparison between the biologically significant components of human and mammalian behavior:

> We are, first of all, moderately polygynous, with males initiating most of the changes in sexual partnerships. About three-fourths of all human societies permit the taking of multiple wives, and most of them encourage the practice by law and custom. In contrast, marriage to multiple husbands is sanctioned in less than one percent of societies. . . . Polygyny and hypergamy are essentially complementary strategies. In diverse cultures men pursue and acquire, while women are protected and bartered. Sons sow wild oats and daughters risk being ruined. When sex is sold, men are usually the buyers. It is to be expected that prostitutes are the despised members of society; they have abandoned their valuable reproductive investment to strangers.

> * * *

> The average temperamental differences between the human sexes are also consistent with the generalities of mammalian biology. Women as a

group are less assertive and physically aggressive. The magnitude of the distinction depends on the culture. It ranges from a tenuous, merely statistical difference in egalitarian settings to the virtual enslavement of women in some extreme polygynous societies. But the variation in degree is not nearly so important as the fact that women differ consistently in this qualitative manner regardless of the degree. The fundamental average difference in personality traits is seldom if ever transposed.

The physical and temperamental differences between men and women have been amplified by culture into universal male dominance. History records not a single society in which women have controlled the political and economic lives of men.[24]

Wilson thus summarizes his conclusions concerning the significance of these differences:

Here is what I believe the evidence shows: modest genetic differences exist between the sexes; the behavioral genes interact with virtually all existing environments to create a noticeable divergence in early psychological development; and the divergence is almost always widened in later psychological development by cultural sanctions and training. Societies can probably cancel the modest genetic differences entirely by careful planning and training, but the convergence will require a conscious decision based on fuller and more exact knowledge than is now available.[25]

The emergence of sociobiology as a scientific discipline did not go unchallenged.[26] In particular, the version of popular sociobiology advanced by Wilson and his followers has been subjected to searching criticism.[27] Wilson's ideas, however, form the theoretical basis for proposed changes in legal doctrine that would expressly recognize sex differences.

THE EMERGENCE OF LEGAL SOCIOBIOLOGY

Wilson's willingness to admit the possibility that the genetic code can be canceled through concerted societal effort appears not to be shared by some of his legal admirers who claim that biologically based behavioral sex differences can and should be used as the basis for legal distinctions supporting a conventional division of function by sex. Kingsley R. Browne argued in 1984 that, in view of the existence of sex differences in temperament, the feminist agenda of "attempting to achieve an androgynous society through anti-discrimination laws, affirmative action programs, and constitutional interpretation may be misguided."[28] Browne does not defend discrimination that "has nothing to do with genuine sex differences."[29] He does assert, however, that "certain forms of discrimination should be permissible because they are based on natural differences between the sexes."[30]

Drawing on the facts in litigated cases, Browne offers the following illustrations of sex-based legal classifications that he finds appropriate:

- An employer's pension plan under which female employees were required to pay in higher contributions than male employees in order to receive the same benefits upon retirement.[31]
- The exclusion of women from military combat.[32]
- A preference for mothers over fathers as the custodians of young children.[33]
- A state law prohibiting males, but not females, between the ages of 18 and 21 from purchasing a form of alcoholic beverage known as "near-beer."[34]
- The exclusion of males from jobs as airline cabin flight attendants.[35]
- The existence of single-sex schools, if their curricula and facilities are substantially equal.[36]

Browne grudgingly supports the invalidation on constitutional grounds of an Idaho state statute that preferred males to females as estate administrators. He does so not because the law was irrational but because "the incremental saving to the government was not sufficient to justify denying women as a class the opportunity to be administrators."[37]

Another advocate of implementing the teachings of sociobiology through legal rules is John H. Beckstrom, who has written two books and several articles on the subject.[38] Unlike Browne, Beckstrom does not limit his analysis to the biology of sex differences. Instead, he applies the "biology of altruism" to such diverse fields as probate and tort law.[39] Like Browne, however, Beckstrom advocates shaping child custody laws to conform with the fundamental concepts of sociobiology. He asserts that single mothers are more likely than single fathers to be solicitous parents because mothers are certain that their offspring carry one-half of their genetic material, while men can never be as sure of their parentage.[40] He also suggests that marriage laws should be drawn to encourage marriages between unrelated former in-laws, such as children and parents-in-law or brothers and sisters-in-law, because their common genetic bond with the children of the former marriage will make them excellent stepparents.[41]

I doubt whether the advocates of translating sociobiological learning into legal doctrine have adequately considered how that learning may be transformed by the law. After all, biology is not the first scientific discipline that has offered itself as the true guide to human behavior, nor is it the first to be proposed by its advocates as an appropriate source of legal theory. If legal institutions reflect their social and cultural settings—and that proposition, by now, is surely a widely accepted one—it is not surprising that the scientific assumptions of a society should also find a place in the law. The less obvious point, however, is that the law is not a mirror that gives a true reflection of the learning it takes from other disciplines. Rather, in applying that learning to concrete cases, law inevitably shapes what it views as

nonlegal material to suit legal ends. The not infrequent outcome is the
creation of a specialized legal understanding of the scientific data that is
unrecognizable or unacceptable to its source.

In what follows, I illustrate this point by examining a legal problem that
both Browne and Beckstrom have suggested should be solved through
application of sociobiological insights: the resolution of child custody disputes between separating parents. Since this problem has also emerged as
a focal point of feminist legal debate, the discussion provides an opportunity to contrast the differing contexts within which feminists explore the
legal relevance of sexual differences and sociobiologists justify selected
sexual differences as natural.

FEMINISTS AND SOCIOBIOLOGISTS EXAMINE CHILD CUSTODY

Both Browne and Beckstrom suggest that the sociobiological evidence
supports a legal doctrine that prefers mothers to fathers as custodians of
young children. Their reasoning differs slightly. Browne notes that "child-
rearing, virtually everywhere and in all times known, has been a female
occupation," adding in apparent explanation of this universal pattern that
"females are more nurturant than males from childhood."[42] Beckstrom
draws on the biology of human reproduction for the proposition that,
although "both males and females are predisposed to devote time and
attention to the nurture of children attributed to them to help assure that
those children reach maturity and are in a position to reproduce in turn,"[43]
the relatively greater certainty of mothers over fathers that the offspring
attributed to them in fact do carry their genetic material should tip the
balance in favor of single mothers as more solicitous parents. Both writers
conclude that maternal custody is, on average, best for young children.

Viewed from a sociobiological perspective, the Anglo-American law of
child custody is perverse indeed. At common law, in England, the father's
secure position as head of the household gave him the primary right to
custody and control of his children.[44] The English Lords had so little
concern for the biological link between milk and nurturance that we are
told the father had the right to demand possession of the infant even when
it was suckling at the mother's breast.[45] By the late nineteenth century,
however, the American courts had created a rebuttable presumption that
the custody of a young child should normally be given to the mother.[46]
This preference for the mother, sometimes called "the tender years doctrine," was not expressly based on a recognition of the mother's primary
biological nexus with the child. Rather, as Rhode notes,[47] it represented a
gradual reconceptualization of custodial premises away from emphasizing
fathers' rights toward a concern for the best interests of children, together

with an emerging view of mothers as more "fit" than fathers to serve as custodians.

Moving even further away from sociobiological explanations, Frances Olsen[48] offers an analysis of the rise of the tender years doctrine in ideological terms. Of the two dimensions she recognizes, one represents a shift from a hierarchical family headed by the father toward a supposedly egalitarian family of juridical equals, and the other represents a shift from conceptualizing the family as a corporate unit toward seeing it as a collection of individuals. Olsen argues that the legal recognition of the tender years doctrine represented both a victory and a defeat for women, since it simultaneously elevated women to a position of power within the previously hierarchical family and confined them within the home, thus limiting their options in the public world.

The tender years doctrine began to attract criticism during the latter half of the twentieth century as increasing numbers of women moved out of the home into the workplace and as feminists began their reexamination of the conventional role of women in the family. The quest for equality between women and men counseled both that women be treated equally in the public world long dominated by men and that women share their newly won power over children with men.[49] Today the tender years doctrine has been supplanted by the more general "best interests of the child" standard in most American states.[50] Frances Olsen argues that this development also represents both an ideological victory and a defeat for women by simultaneously vindicating the concept of sexual equality and isolating individual mothers losing custody from their political power base as women oppressed by a male hierarchy.[51] Her explanation of the rise and fall of the tender years doctrine is politically independent of sociobiological principles, and her analysis suggests that a return to the maternal presumption would have both advantages and disadvantages for women.

Legal doctrine governing child custody adjudication is not yet finally settled. The "best interests of the child" standard that replaced the tender years doctrine in most states has encountered severe criticism, as experience with adjudicated cases using that standard has demonstrated that it is essentially indeterminate.[52] Several alternative standards have been proposed, including joint custody with both parents;[53] sole custody with the child's psychological parent, who may or may not be a biological parent;[54] and sole custody with the primary caretaking parent.[55] In addition to these choices, legal sociobiologists like Browne and Beckstrom propose a return to the tender years doctrine.

The debate among feminists concerning difference has influenced their discussion of custody standards. Wendy Williams rejects the tender years doctrine as inconsistent with the goal of shared child-rearing by both parents; she prefers the primary caretaker rule.[56] Katharine Bartlett and

Carol Stack embrace joint custody as a strategy that will encourage fathers to participate in shared parenting during marriage as well as after divorce.[57] Other feminists, however, support a maternal preference, noting the unfairness of asking women to relinquish their authority in the home before they have fully attained equality with men elsewhere.[58] Martha Fineman has argued recently that feminists should advocate the perspective of custodial mothers not by proposing a return to the tender years doctrine but by supporting the primary caretaker rule as an easily administered, gender-neutral legal doctrine that rewards the day-to-day nurturing behavior characteristic of the experience of motherhood.[59]

These differing feminist perspectives are offered within a common context: their principal commitment is to the development of a female consciousness and a female identity drawn from the female experience. As Christine Littleton has pointed out,[60] the reality of living in a male-dominated culture necessarily conditions and distorts that female consciousness to the point that a clear feminist vision is difficult even to imagine, but the commitment itself is sufficient to identify and sustain the feminist project.

The sociobiological perspective is offered in the service of quite a different project. As Richard Dawkins puts it, "We are survival machines—robot vehicles blindly programmed to preserve the selfish molecules known as genes."[61] In that context, mother custody is preferred because the genetic bond between mother and infant ensures the child's survival more completely than the less certain bond between father and infant could guarantee. The sociobiological view of women is therefore an instrumentalist one in which women are valued primarily for their mothering capacity and their willingness to sacrifice themselves for their children. The use of this perspective as the foundation for a return to the tender years doctrine would impose a gloss on the legal rule that is entirely unacceptable.

WOMEN AS MOTHERS

If sociobiological perspectives support a return to the tender years doctrine in child custody cases, they may also be invoked more broadly to justify women's return to the home to fulfill their biological destiny as mothers. Such arguments were heard frequently in the 1930s, '40s, and '50s, when, as Rhode has noted,[62] public opinion and child welfare experts alike condemned those mothers who selfishly pursued careers at the supposed expense of their children. In recent years, such arguments have reappeared, this time drawing on sociobiological thinking to lend a scientific aura to the claim. Thus psychologist Selma Fraiberg relies both on the work of ethologist Konrad Lorenz concerning aggression in animal societies and on maternal deprivation studies of human infants conducted by Anna Freud and others to underscore the fundamental importance of mothering.[63] She concludes from an examination of these sources that unless a love bond is formed between the human infant and a nurturing adult that endures without rupture through early life, the "baby . . . is being robbed of his humanity."[64] The lesson is clear: women who put their own needs ahead of their infants' are irresponsible mothers, willing to imperil the future development of their children.

Less polemic than Fraiberg but no less confident of the central importance of sociobiological learning to human child-rearing practices is sociologist Alice Rossi. Rossi, who once saw clearly the obstacle to women's equality posed by the belief that motherhood is a full-time occupation for adult women,[65] now believes that the different parenting styles exhibited by men and women are rooted in sexual dimorphism, with females exhibiting an innate attachment to infants, while males must learn their social role as fathers.[66] She concludes that only by taking up the challenge of the biological component to human behavior can any ideology, including feminism, avoid becoming an exercise in wishful thinking.[67]

Such attitudes about the proper role of women have historically contained the potential for female repression disguised as a celebration of sexual difference. Christine Littleton compares the female "cult of motherhood" with the male warrior's "glory of battle" as opposite cultural symbols designed to cloak the unpleasant and even dangerous aspects of both functions behind a veil of glamor.[68] The cult of motherhood has attracted powerful contemporary religious support from Pope John Paul II. His recent apostolic letter on the dignity and vocation of women identifies virginity and motherhood as the unique dimensions and fulfillment of the female personality, and offers this meditation on motherhood and fatherhood:

> Human parenthood is something shared by both the man and the woman. . . . Although both of them together are parents of their child, *the woman's motherhood constitutes a special "part" in this shared parenthood,* and the most demanding part. Parenthood—even though it belongs to both— is realized much more fully in the woman, especially in the prenatal period. It is the woman who "pays" directly for this shared generation, which literally absorbs the energies of her body and soul. It is therefore necessary that *the man* be fully aware that in their shared parenthood he owes *a special debt to the woman.* No programme of "equal rights" between women and men is valid unless it takes this fact fully into account.
>
> Motherhood involves a special communion with the mystery of life, as it develops in the woman's womb. . . . This unique contact with the new human being developing within her gives rise to an attitude towards human beings—not only towards her own child, but every human be-

ing—which profoundly marks the woman's personality. It is commonly thought that *women* are more capable than men of paying attention *to another person,* and that motherhood develops this predisposition even more. The man—even with all his sharing in parenthood—always remains "outside" the process of pregnancy and the baby's birth; in many ways he has to *learn his own "fatherhood" from the mother.* One can say that this is part of the normal human dimension of parenthood, including the stages that follow the birth of the baby, especially the initial period. The child's upbringing, taken as a whole, should include the contribution of both parents: the maternal and paternal contribution. In any event, the mother's contribution is decisive in laying the foundation for a new human personality.[69]

Earlier in his missive, Pope John Paul II had made clear his opposition to the "masculinization" of women seeking relief from male "domination":

There is a well-founded fear that if they take this path, women will not "reach fulfillment," but instead will *deform and lose what constitutes their essential richness.* . . .

The personal resources of femininity are certainly no less than the resources of masculinity: they are merely different. Hence, a woman, as well as a man, must understand her "fulfillment" as a person, her dignity and vocation, on the basis of these resources, according to the richness of the femininity which she received on the day of creation and which she inherits as an expression of the "image and likeness of God" that is specifically hers.[70]

The culmination of this recent religious celebration of sexual difference is a reaffirmation of the conventional notion of separate spheres for men and women: women paramount in the home, men dominant in the external world. Science and religion, not for the first time, have formed a tacit alliance against feminism. In the face of that alliance, feminists must hold fast, also not for the first time, both to their capacity for nurturance and to their individuality as human beings. Kate Chopin's heroine, Edna Pontellier, provides an apt literary example of what is needed to survive such difficult times. As she explained to her friend Madame Ratignolle in 1899,

She would never sacrifice herself for her children, or for any one. Then had followed a rather heated argument; the two women did not appear to understand each other or to be talking the same language. Edna tried to appease her friend, to explain.

"I would give up the unessential; I would give my money, I would give my life for my children; but I wouldn't give myself. I can't make it more clear; it's only something which I am beginning to comprehend, which is revealing itself to me."[71]

The contemporary feminist fascination with difference coexists with the emergence of a conservative social movement committed to a return to traditional values and a celebration of women's primary role as mothers. One immediate result of this juxtaposition of two quite disparate projects might be the use of feminist theory to justify nonfeminist goals. This danger can perhaps be minimized by clarifying the content and direction of feminist theory. Even if such a danger materializes, however, feminists can ill afford to adopt a corrective strategy of silencing other female voices. An imposed unity of correct views can never be an appropriate goal for a movement devoted above all to the awakening of female consciousness. Instead, we should seek to broaden our interdisciplinary knowledge in order to understand and overcome obstacles to the feminist project newly reimposed in the name of science.

PART THREE

Psychological, Sociological, and Anthropological Perspectives on Difference

A Social-Psychological
Model of Gender

KAY DEAUX AND

BRENDA MAJOR

Psychology's record of considering gender has been, with too few exceptions, a tradition of sex differences.[1] Taking sexual dimorphism as a starting point, investigators have tried to establish, or in some cases refute, the existence of differences between women and men. Whichever conclusion is sought or reached, the debate has its origin in an implicit oppositional model.

This tendency to create oppositions between elements that can be dichotomized is a seductive feature of human thought. In a fascinating study by Barnes,[2] parents were asked to describe their children. Parents who had three or more children described each child in separate terms: for example, Jane is intellectual, Bill is sociable, and Pamela is athletic. Parents of two children, in contrast, succumbed to oppositional thinking: If Jane was a leader, Bill was a follower; if Bill was more sociable, Jane was less sociable. This tendency toward bipolar contrasts is probably exaggerated in the case of males and females, where there is consensus as to what the two categories are and where the categories serve as significant markers in most societies. Dualistic assumptions about gender may also preclude other relevant categories—race, class, age—from entering the analysis.

Those who conclude that there are differences between women and men often assume that these differences are stable. This stability is implicit, we

This essay was written while Kay Deaux was a Fellow at the Center for Advanced Study in the Behavioral Sciences, Stanford, where she was supported in part by the John D. and Catherine T. McArthur Foundation and received additional support from a grant by the National Science Foundation (BNS–8604993). Both authors would like to thank Jane Atkinson, Deborah Rhode, and Anne Firor Scott for their comments on earlier versions of this chapter.

would argue, whether nature or nurture is invoked as the cause. The "different voice" that Carol Gilligan[3] describes with reference to moral reasoning, for example, is attributed primarily to differences in socialization experiences. Yet as the historian Joan Scott[4] has suggested in analyzing the dualism expressed in this work, assumptions of differential experience often fall victim to a certain slippage, in which the original premise, namely, "Women are this way because of different experience" becomes "Women are this way because they are women." In Scott's words, "Implied in this line of reasoning is the ahistorical, if not essentialist, notion of women."[5]

As a group, psychologists have a pernicious tendency to develop a concept, devise a way to measure it, and then assume its reality. This reification creates a belief that people are, if their assessment scores so reveal, compulsive people, dependent people, aggressive people, and the like. These descriptions, in turn, connote both generality across situations and stability across time (despite numerous disputes within the discipline as to whether those assumptions are justified). In addition, the hypothesized dimensions often take on causal properties, as they are used to explain and justify actions that may seem consistent with the characterization.

This general tendency to infer causality from stability is particularly evident in analyses of sex differences, for which the explanatory concepts tend to be global. As the prototypical case, the conceptualization of "masculinity" and "femininity" was intended to represent the psychological essence of being male and female. It was not linked directly to biological sex but was capable of predicting those behaviors that tend to be associated with gender.[6] Slightly less broad at first glance, but equally pervasive in their implications, are such concepts as "instrumentality" and "expressiveness," or "justice" versus "caring." Like masculinity and femininity, these characteristics or behavioral styles are seen to reside primarily in one or the other sex and to dictate a wide range of outcomes and life choices.

Such diagnostic categories at most assess potentials and estimate probabilities. They do not dictate outcomes. As Hubbard suggests elsewhere in this volume, human nature as an abstract concept means very little.[7] To give this concept meaning, we need to look at the things people actually do. The viewpoint this represents may be too behaviorist for some. Yet while pure behaviorism is as out of fashion in psychology as in the wider intellectual community, Hubbard's injunction provides a useful antidote to the more global diagnoses some psychological and psychoanalytic models make. The analysis of gender is ill served by a reliance on inflexible and often ephemeral conceptions of the nature of woman and man. Attention to actual behavior, in contrast, demands a model that recognizes variability and similarity—as well as stability and difference.

A SOCIAL - PSYCHOLOGICAL
PERSPECTIVE ON GENDER

Our analysis is informed by a social-psychological perspective. In contrast to more traditional psychological analyses of gender that tend toward essentialism, a social-psychological perspective emphasizes the varying forces that influence women and men. Social psychology considers the situational influences on human behavior as a defining characteristic, assigning them a priority over individual traits and personality dispositions. From this perspective we ask quite different questions about sex differences in human behavior.[8]

Our model takes as its point of departure the behavior of women and men in dyadic interaction. Such social interactions can involve many forms of behavior—for example, leadership, social influence, moral choices, cooperation, and competition. Although the basis for our analysis is the empirical literature of psychology, we believe that the implications of the analysis go considerably beyond this domain. The emphasis is not on structural constants that program behavior but on conditions that foster variability and change. In contrast to developmental models of gender that deal with the acquisition of gender-linked behavior, our model is concerned with gender as experienced and enacted in a particular social context. The model is intended to supplement, not supplant, earlier theoretical models that stress the origins of specifiable tendencies and habits.

Fundamental to our perspective is the assumption that gender-related behavior is marked by flexibility, fluidity, and variability. Without denying that there may be some regularities in male and female behavior that are the result of biological propensity or socialization experience, we believe it is essential to recognize evidence of changes over time and circumstance. Acknowledging this variation makes the task of analysis more complex— but it is a complexity we need to confront.

A second assumption that underlies the current perspective is that women and men make choices in their actions. In contrast to the deterministic models offered by both psychoanalysis and behaviorism, our framework presumes a repertoire of possibilities from which individual men and women choose different responses on varying occasions with varying degrees of self-consciousness. In other words, gender-related behaviors are a process of individual and social construction. A number of commentators in other disciplines have argued a similar position. Scott, as one recent example, states that "there is room for a concept of human agency as the attempt (at least partially rational) to construct an identity, a life, a set of relationships, a society with certain sets of limits and with language."[9] The sociologists Gerson and Peiss describe gender as a set of "socially constructed relationships which are produced and reproduced through people's actions."[10] In both of these statements, as in our own model, an active dynamic replaces a passive determinism.

To assume flexibility and choice in an analysis of gender requires an appreciation of context. Choices are not made in a vacuum but are shaped by such transitory factors as the other people involved and the prevailing societal norms. In the present analysis, we reflect our disciplinary bias by emphasizing the immediate interpersonal context. Within such situations, individuals simultaneously react to others and present themselves. Social interaction can be viewed as a process of identity negotiation where individuals pursue particular goals for the interaction.[11]

Our view of gender-related behavior in terms of negotiated social interaction draws heavily on two theoretical perspectives in social psychology. Research on expectancy confirmation—sometimes called self-fulfilling prophecy—focuses on the active role of observers in maintaining or creating social reality through their cognitions or behaviors toward a particular individual. This process involves a sequence in which individuals take actions on the basis of their beliefs, and these actions then influence the behavior of the recipient, leading to a confirmation of the initial belief.[12] In applying this analysis here, we consider how the gender belief system of another can impact upon the individual woman, channeling her behavior in ways that support the stereotypic beliefs.

A second theoretical tradition concerns the factors that motivate an individual to vary how she presents herself to others. On the one hand, concerns with self-verification may lead the person to emphasize those underlying beliefs and characteristics that define a stable self-identity. On the other, external pressures may encourage the choice of self-presentation strategies that increase the likelihood of positive reactions from another. In either case the person shows a freedom of choice to select some facet of self from among a number of possible alternatives.

The model that we are developing attempts to deal both with the variation between people and with the variation in a given individual across situations and time. Clearly people confronted with the same situational pressures vary in their responses. Similarly, a single person may take a different course of action depending on the context in which the choice occurs. Dyadic interaction is our chosen testing ground, although our model has implications for other domains as well. In the model, two individuals bring specific beliefs and identities to an interaction, and their interaction occurs within a specifiable context. We do not assume that gender is always salient in these interactions. One of the objectives of our formulation is to specify and to predict just when gender substantially shapes the course of an interaction and when its influence is more muted. To make these predictions, we look at three influences: first, the individual woman or man; second, other individuals with whom the person interacts; and third, the context or setting in which the interaction takes place.

GENDER IDENTITY AND GENDER-BASED ACTION

Gender identity, as the term is typically used by psychologists, refers to a "fundamental, existential sense of one's maleness or femaleness, an acceptance of one's gender as a social-psychological construction that parallels acceptance of one's biological sex."[13] This sense of maleness or femaleness is acquired early in most people's lives. As Spence has stated, "It is inarguable . . . that gender is one of the earliest and most central components of the self concept and serves as an organizing principle through which many experiences and perceptions of self and other are filtered."[14]

Although the concept of gender identity is universal, substantial individual differences occur in the characteristics of these identities. First, people differ in the degree to which gender is a salient aspect of their identity. Chodorow, for example, has suggested that gender identity is differentially important to women and to men.[15] Data from a recent study of self-definition support this suggestion. When asked what identities were important to them, women were more likely than men either to mention gender spontaneously or to acknowledge gender as a central identity when questioned by the interviewer.[16] (Such findings are consistent with the argument that dominant groups have less need to be self-reflective than do groups who must define themselves vis-à-vis a more powerful other.)

A second way in which gender identities differ among individuals concerns the particular features associated with those identities. People may think of themselves as womanly, feminine, or feminist; within any of these general categories, the beliefs and behaviors associated with the label can differ dramatically. Two individuals who are equally conscious of their identities as women may, by virtue of experience or belief, have markedly different conceptions of what that identity means.

The influence of gender on social interaction depends heavily on the degree to which associations with gender are invoked, either consciously or unconsciously. In cognitive psychologists' terms, we can talk about the *accessibility* of gender identity—the degree to which concepts of gender are actively involved in a particular experience or are part of what has been called the "working self-concept."[17] Accessibility is affected by at least two sets of factors: the strength or centrality of that aspect of the self and features of the immediate situation that make gender salient.

For some people, gender will always be part of the working self-concept, an ever-present filter for experience. Individuals differ in how much gender is a chronically accessible aspect of self, and the prominence of gender identity can differ for the same individual across different situations and stages of life. Gender is more likely to shape a woman's experience, for example, when she has her first child or when she receives a diagnosis of breast cancer than it is on other less gender-linked occasions.

External cues can also evoke gender identity, moving it into the working self-concept. In a laboratory demonstration of gender awareness, for example, college students mentioned gender more often when their sex was a minority in a group situation than when it was a majority.[18] Kanter has vividly described how in other work environments gender becomes salient for the individual who is a token in an organizational setting.[19]

Not always recognized in feminist analyses is the fact that people have identities other than gender. A person may think of herself not only as a woman, but as a Black, a professor, an Easterner, or any of numerous other identities. These various senses of self may exist as independent units having little implication for each other. Or two identities may have different implications for action in the same setting and hence prove contradictory. Which identity is dominant in a situation in which both might be accessible depends both on the individual (the relative prominence of a particular identity in some hierarchy of identities) and on the situation (the degree to which circumstances make a particular identity salient). Gender is most likely to dominate interaction, by this account, when it is an identity of primary importance and when the situation contrives to make gender relevant.

Awareness of gender does not automatically dictate action. Instead people choose how to present themselves to others, with the choices reflecting a variety of motivations. Choices may be based on conscious intentions to present a particular stance or to convey a particular image; individuals may act for the sake of goals that are not clearly recognized in conscious thought. The motives of actions vary. One line of psychological investigation has stressed the degree to which individuals act to verify self-concepts, choosing actions that will be consistent with previous definitions of self.[20] An alternative perspective stresses the degree to which people are sensitive to the social significance of their conduct and strive to present themselves in ways that will ensure social rewards.[21] These two processes are not necessarily contradictory.[22] Rather, concerns with self-verification and self-presentation may be interwoven in any social interaction, as the individual uses both internal and external standards to monitor and shape behavioral choice.

Some empirical investigations have shown how gender concerns can alter the image one presents. In one study, for example, women presented descriptions of themselves to a man who was believed to hold either traditional or liberal views of the appropriate roles for women and men.[23] When the target of their presentation was a man possessing socially desirable characteristics (e.g., not in a steady dating relationship, attractive, wealthy), women modified their presentation to approximate the man's alleged views. In contrast, when the man was described as having traits that would presumably not motivate goals of continued interaction (e.g., currently engaged, unattractive, limited career goals), the women did not alter their presentation from what it had been at an earlier assessment. Such alterations are evident in men confronting women as well.[24] Another empirical study of self-presentational shifts found that women ate fewer available snacks when they were interacting with a desirable male partner as compared to a less desirable one. In extending their analysis, the investigators suggested that such eating disorders as anorexia and bulimia might be linked to self-presentational concerns, as women attempting to appear feminine choose behaviors that they believe are consistent with societal norms of femininity.[25]

THE INFLUENCE OF OTHERS

Social interaction occurs in a context in which certain expectations are conveyed by participants toward each other. Within a given setting, whether the dyadic case emphasized in our model or in a larger arena, the individual is generally aware of what is expected, prescribed, or typical in that setting. These expectations can shape the interaction so as to constitute a self-fulfilling prophecy. People interacting with each other may come to manifest the previously held beliefs of their companions.

We know, from both extensive research and common observation, that gender stereotypes are pervasive.[26] People typically believe that men and women differ in a wide range of personality traits, physical characteristics, role behaviors, and occupational positions.[27] Traits related to instrumentality, dominance, and assertiveness, for example, are believed more characteristic of men, while such traits as warmth, expressiveness, and concern for other people are thought more characteristic of women. These beliefs are not all-or-nothing ascriptions; rather, people make judgments about the relative likelihood that women and men will exhibit various characteristics.[28]

People not only have beliefs about women and men at the most general level. They also have clear images of certain types of women and men, such as businesswomen or blue-collar working men.[29] These types correspond to roles that men and women occupy in society and are often described in terms of physical features as well as personality traits. A macho man, for example, is most frequently characterized as being muscular, having a hairy chest and a moustache. Images of sexy women include references to the woman's hair, figure, clothes, facial appearance, and nail polish.[30] These beliefs, operating at various levels of specificity, serve as a framework or orientation for the individual approaching any particular interaction, and because information about physical appearance is both readily available and prominently coded, stereotypic thinking may be triggered quite early in initial encounters.

Of course individuals differ in the degree to which they endorse these beliefs and in the attributes they associate with gender categories. Some people may, as Bem has argued, be gender schematic, readily imposing stereotypical beliefs and making sharp distinctions between male and female. Aschematic people eschew such distinctions.[31] More generally, one can think of people as varying along a range of stereotypy, showing greater or lesser propensity to endorse the pervasive cultural beliefs.[32] It seems quite unlikely, however, that many people in contemporary society are unencumbered by some gender-linked expectations and beliefs.

As in the case of self, we do not believe that gender is always salient to the observer or that gender-related beliefs are necessarily activated in social interaction. Yet the obviousness of a person's sex in most instances makes it very likely to influence implicit assumptions. Kessler and McKenna argue that gender attribution is universal, taking precedence over many other forms of categorization.[33]

Both parties in an interaction can influence the likelihood of gender schemata's being activated. Specific features of a person's appearance can trigger a subset of gender beliefs in the mind of the observer, for example, shifting the expectancies from those associated with women and men in general to those linked to more particular subtypes. A woman with a briefcase elicits different associations for most people than does a woman in an apron and housedress. A woman with a low-cut blouse, slit skirt, and high-heeled shoes elicits more attributions of sexiness and seductiveness than does her more conservatively dressed counterpart.[34] Predispositions in the observer may lower the threshold for seeing gender relevance or influence the way in which a particular behavior is interpreted. Men, for example, are more likely than women to assume sexual intent in the friendly behavior of a woman.[35] An analysis of these beliefs is important because of their consequences. The expectancy confirmation sequence describes processes linking beliefs to actions. This link manifests itself in a number of ways, including active avoidance or termination of an interaction. A person can avoid individuals who are presumed undesirable, and such avoidance allows the retention of beliefs in the (untested) attributes of the undesirable one. More typically, perhaps, expectancies shape the form of interaction that occurs. To take an example from the employment realm, consider the case of a female manager whose supervisor believes her to be unfit for leadership positions. The supervisor might engage in such actions toward the woman as shunting her into a subordinate role that allows no room for the display of leadership qualities. The woman's subordinate behavior would then confirm the supervisor's initial belief independent of the woman's actual qualities.

SITUATION AND CONTEXT

The context in which an interaction takes place, like the characters of the actors, shapes the outcome. Context can be considered at many levels, from cultural norms and societal structures to the more immediate circumstances of an interaction. Although our analysis emphasizes immediate circumstances, we do not suggest that others are insignificant, for these more general forces shape, modify, and often limit the range of behaviors available to the individual actor.

Certain situations make gender more salient, increasing the likelihood that each of the participants will bring gender scripts to bear. Some environments, such as a nursery school or an automobile repair shop, are closely linked to gender. Other situations make gender salient because of the particular participants, as Kanter's analysis of tokenism illustrates.[36] Established norms can make gender more or less appropriate as an organizing principle.

To predict whether sex differences will be the rule or the exception, one must analyze the total set of influencing factors. The actual behavior of women and men in a situation depends on the relative weight of the three elements: the self-definitions and goals of each participant, the beliefs and expectations of the other, and the context in which the interaction takes place. By this analysis, sex differences, that is, observed differences in the actions of women and men, are one of several possible outcomes. In most cases this outcome could be altered relatively easily if one or more elements were changed.

The most straightforward predictions for observed behavior are possible when all forces press toward the same outcome. Using as an example a pair of entry-level managers in a corporation, we can describe conditions of maximal and minimal likelihood for the appearance of sex differences. Sex differences will be most likely, according to our analysis, when:

(1) The man and the woman have different conceptions of themselves as managers and different goals for their corporate experience.
(2) The supervisor holds strong stereotypic beliefs about women and men and is prone to act on those beliefs, creating different experiences for women and men.
(3) The situation is one in which men and women have traditionally assumed different roles and in which the organizational structure is based on a premise of different activities for women and men.

In contrast, sex differences should be rare when the opposite influences prevail. If women and men bring similar experiences and self-conceptions to a situation, if they aspire to the same outcomes, and if they are acting in a context within which sex discrimination is minimal, relatively few differences should be observed.

Both of these scenarios represent pure cases, in which the various influences converge toward a single outcome. In reality cases are rarely that simple. Women with identities and aspirations that match men's encounter situations that press for differentiation. Contexts that are seemingly neutral may still provide a venue for display of sharp differences between particular women and men. When two sources of influence produce contradictory pressures—one fostering difference and the other stressing similarity—what form does behavior take?

To deal with the complexity of frequently conflicting messages and pressures, we turn to a microlevel analysis of the social-psychological process involved in interaction. Rather than offering general statements of sex difference or similarity, we suggest that many dynamic factors must be considered. In each general domain—individual self-systems, expectancies of others, and contextual influences—the range of alternatives is great. With reference to the self-system, for example, people vary in the importance they attach to pleasing others versus verifying internal truths. If pleasing others is more important, situational factors should be much more influential. Characteristics of the other's expectancy that can be important include the desirability of the advocated behavior for the individual and the certainty with which that message is sent. *Who* is conveying the expectation also matters a great deal. A person is far more likely to confirm the expectations of those who are powerful, likable, and control rewards and outcomes than of those whose resources are more limited. Confirmation of another person's expectancies is more likely in public situations than in private, and more common in novel situations than in familiar ones.

The enactment of gender is a dynamic, not a static, phenomenon. People choose (although not necessarily at a conscious level) to act out gender-related behaviors and to vary their behavior with circumstances. Their choices reflect the joint contribution of cognitive factors like the accessibility of relevant beliefs and self-definitions, and motivational factors that relate to one's objectives for a particular interaction. Although we *use* observable behavior as a criterion, we *recognize* the determinants of these behaviors in mental acts. The actions of individual women and men cannot be understood without reference to social context. Changes in context mean changes in outcome, belying the stability of male-female differences so often posited.

The present analysis is more microlevel than some. We are concerned

less with human nature than with human actions; with where the repertoires of behavior come from than with how people make choices within
those repertoires. Our framework does not deny the usefulness of other
formulations, but we believe that the social-psychological perspective is a
valuable one. It offers little in the way of ultimatums. What it does, and
does in a way lacking in many previous accounts, is to affirm the range of
human behavior available to both women and men. By so doing, it moves
us away from the oppositional thought that has guided so much previous
work.

Children and Gender:
Constructions of Difference

BARRIE THORNE

When I first began observing in elementary schools as an ethnographer with gender on my mind, events like the following drew me and my notetaking like a magnet:

> On the playground, a cluster of children played "girls-chase-the-boys" or "boys-chase-the-girls" (they used both names). Boys and girls were by definition on different sides. In the back-and-forth of chasing and being chased, they used gender terms ("I'm gonna get that girl"; "Let's go after those boys") rather than individual names for members of the other side.

> In a combined fourth-and-fifth-grade classroom the teacher introduced a math game organized as girls against boys; she would write addition and subtraction problems on the board, and a member of each team would race to be the first to write the correct answer. As the teacher wrote two scorekeeping columns headed "Beastly Boys" and "Gossipy Girls," several boys yelled out, "Noisy girls! Gruesome girls!" while some of the girls laughed. As the game proceeded, the girls sat in a row on top of their desks; sometimes they moved collectively, pushing their hips or whispering, "Pass it on." The boys stood along the wall, several reclining against desks. When members of either group came back victorious from the front of the room, they would do the "giving five" hand-slapping ritual with their team members.

On such occasions—when gender divisions were highlighted and "the girls" and "the boys" were defined as separate, opposing groups—I felt I was at the heart of children's gender relations. But these moments are not the whole of social life in elementary schools; at other times boys and girls interacted in relaxed rather than bounded and antagonistic ways. An example from the same fourth-and-fifth-grade classroom:

This paper has benefited from helpful comments by Jane Collier, Cheris Kramarae, Deborah L. Rhode, Judith Stacey, Candace West, and especially Avril Thorne.

100

A student teacher had listed various activities on the board and asked students to choose one and sign up for it. Three boys and two girls had chosen to tape record a radio play. The teacher told them they could rehearse in the back of the room. They moved from their desks, settled in chairs at a round table (seated girl-boy-girl-boy-boy), and took turns leaning into the microphone and reading from the script. Now and then they stopped to talk and argue as a group.

I had to press myself to record the details of this situation; it seemed less juicy, less ripe for gendered analysis than the chasing sequence, the math game, or a same-gender group. This disparity in my perception of its relevance led me to ponder our frameworks for thinking about children and gender. These frameworks, which emphasize oppositional dichotomies, neatly fit situations in which boys and girls are organized as separate, bounded groups, and they obscure more relaxed, mixed-gender encounters. What kinds of frameworks can more fully account for the complexity of children's gender relations?

Is it "in the nature" of children that we should gear up different questions for them than we do for adults? Feminist scholarship has mostly centered upon the lives and experiences of adults; it has either ignored children, seen them as objects of adult (primarily women's) labor, or confined discussion of them to questions of "socialization" and "development."[1] In the last two decades our frameworks for thinking about adults and gender have moved beyond unexamined dualisms toward greater complexity. But when we focus on children, we tend to think in more simplistic ways—perhaps one reason for the lingering power of dualisms.[2]

THE DUALISTIC MODEL OF SEX DIFFERENCES

Most of the research on children and gender involves a search either for individual or for group sex differences. Both approaches conceptualize gender in terms of dualisms.

Studies in the "individual sex differences" tradition typically set out to explore possible statistical correlations between individual sex/gender (usually understood as an unproblematic male/female dichotomy) and a specific piece of behavior or measure of personality. The pieces that have been studied range widely, including such personality traits as self-esteem, intellectual aptitudes like verbal or spatial ability, such motivational structure as need for affiliation, and specific behavior, for example, the amount of time spent in rough-and-tumble play. Extensive research has studied whether parents and teachers interact (for example, touch or talk) differently with girls and boys. Sex difference studies specify and gauge behavior (for example, with tests of spatial ability or measures of time spent in rough-and-tumble play or talking with a teacher), aggregate across many individuals, and then look for statistically significant correlations by sex.[3]

The results of sex difference research are always a matter of statistical frequency, for sex/gender differences are never absolutely dichotomous. But where statistically significant differences are found, the language of frequency quickly slides into a portrayal of dualism ("boys engage in more rough-and-tumble play than girls"; "girls have greater verbal ability than boys"; "boys receive more teacher attention"). Many writers have cautioned against translating statistical complexity into a discourse of "the pinks and the blues," the tellingly dichotomous title of a popular television documentary on sex differences among children.[4] They have noted other related pitfalls in the sex difference approach, such as a bias toward reporting difference rather than similarity and a failure to distinguish statistical significance from the size of an effect.

But dichotomous portrayals may be unavoidable when one's basic strategy is to compare males and females. Individual sex categories[5]—female/male, woman/man, girl/boy—divide the population in half and are marked and sustained by daily social practices of gender display and attribution.[6] Sex difference research treats these categories as relatively unproblematic and continues binary framing with distinctions like similarity versus difference. Recent proposals to use phrases like "sex similarities and differences" or "sex-related differences," provide at best awkward and ambiguous tools for grasping the complexities of gender.

Although the situation is gradually beginning to change, sociologists and anthropologists have largely ceded the study of children to psychologists, who in turn have relegated the study of children to specialists in child development. The social science literature on children and gender reflects this division of labor. The focus has been more on individuals than on social relations, and the favored methods—laboratory experiments, observations organized around preset categories—strip human conduct from the contexts in which it is given meaning.

GROUP DIFFERENCES

When psychologists, sociologists, and anthropologists of gender have studied the social relations of children, they have primarily relied on a model of group differences that is founded on the prevalence of gender separation in children's friendships and daily encounters. Every observational study of children's interactions in preschools, elementary schools, and junior high schools in the United States has found a high degree of gender separation in seating choices and in the groups children form.[7] In a study of sixth- and seventh-graders in a middle school whose enrollment was half

Black and half white, Schofield found that while racial separation among the students was extensive, gender separation was even greater.[8]

After documenting widespread gender separation in children's social relations, most researchers have compared the separate worlds of boys and girls. The result is a by now familiar litany of generalized contrasts, usually framed as a series of dualisms: boys' groups are larger, and girls' groups are smaller ("buddies" versus "best friends"); boys play more often in public, and girls in more private places; boys engage in more rough-and-tumble play, physical fighting, and overt physical conflict than do girls; boys play more organized team sports, and girls engage in more turn-taking play; within same-gender groups, boys continually maintain and display hierarchies, while girls organize themselves into shifting alliances.[9]

There are problems with this separate worlds approach. Much of the literature, like that on individual sex differences, suffers from androcentrism: the "boys' world" is usually described first (as above) and more extensively; the less richly articulated "girls' world" seems explicitly (as in Lever's study)[10] or implicitly lacking.[11] Even where efforts are made to revalue the "girls' world" (as in Gilligan's reframing of Lever's work)[12] and to give both poles equal weighting, people still construe children's gender relations as polarities. The convention of separate worlds compresses enormous complexity into a series of contrasts: public/private, large/small, competitive/cooperative. It suggests a Victorian world of separate spheres writ small and contemporary.

Gender separation among children is not so total as the separate worlds rendering suggests, and the amount of separation varies by situation. For example, Luria and Herzog found that in a nursery school in Massachusetts two-thirds of playgroups were same-gender (one-third were mixed); 80 percent of playground groups of fifth- and sixth-graders in a public elementary school were same-gender (20 percent were mixed); in a private school, 63 percent of playground groups were same-gender (37 percent were mixed).[13] For many children in the United States, gender separation is more extensive on school playgrounds than in other daily settings. Girls and boys interact frequently in most elementary school classrooms, since adults organize much of the activity and usually rely on criteria other than gender. Children often report engaging in more cross-gender play in neighborhoods and in families than they do on school playgrounds; in these less populous situations they may have to cross gender and age categories to find playmates, and there are fewer witnesses to tease girls and boys who choose to be together.[14]

The occasions when girls and boys are together are as theoretically and socially significant as when they are apart, yet the literature on children's gender relations has largely ignored interaction between them. In much of the research on children's group life, "gender" has first been located in the separation of boys and girls and then in comparisons of same-gender groups.[15] Comparing groups of girls with groups of boys not only neglects the occasions when they are together but also ignores the complex choreography of separation and integration in children's daily interactions. Frequency counts provide snapshots of single moments, but they cannot teach us about the social processes by which gender is used—or overridden or ignored—as a basis for group formation.[16]

Finally, in relying on a series of contrasts to depict the whole, the separate worlds approach exaggerates the coherence of same-gender interaction and glosses extensive variation among boys and among girls. Characterizations of the "boys' world" suffer from a distortion akin to the "Big Man Bias" in anthropological ethnographies in which male elites are equated with men in general.[17] Larger, bonded groups of boys figure prominently in Joffe's ethnographic description of the "male subculture" of a preschool, Best's description of boys in an elementary school, Everhart's ethnography of a junior high and Cusick's of a high school, and Willis' study of working-class "lads" in a vocational secondary school in England.[18] Other less popular, disruptive, dominant, or socially visible boys—and girls (who remain invisible in the majority of school ethnographies)—appear at the edges of these portrayals, but their standpoints and experiences are voiced only indirectly. (Cusick reports that as a participant-observer he avoided "isolates"; "I was there to do a study not to be a friend to those who had no friends.")[19]

In the fourth-and-fifth-grade class in which I was a participant-observer,[20] a relatively stable group of four to six boys (often joined by a girl who successfully crossed gender boundaries) sat together in the classroom and the lunchroom and moved around the playground as a group, playing the team sports of every season. Because of the group's size, physicality, and social dominance, it *seemed* to be the core of the "boys' world" in that classroom—one more instance of the familiar generalization that boys are organized into "flocks" or "gangs." But other fourth-and-fifth-grade boys did not fit the model. Three of them were loners who avoided sports, preferred to stay indoors, and hung out at the edges of the playground. Three more were involved in an intense dyad-into-triad pattern similar to the social organization often generalized as typical of girls' friendships.[21] Two boys were recent immigrants from Mexico, spoke little English, were marginal in most classroom interaction, and on the playground often joined six to ten other Spanish-speaking, nonbilingual children in an ongoing game of dodgeball that was more mixed in gender and age than any other recurring playground group.

Depictions of girls' social relations have also masked considerable variation. While the fourth-and-fifth-grade girls I observed often used a language of "best friends" (dyads and triads did figure centrally in their social relationships), they also regularly organized into groups of five to seven doing "tricks" on the bars or playing jump rope. Hughes, who observed on an upper-middle-class school playground, and Goodwin, who observed Black children ages ten to thirteen in an urban neighborhood, also found that girls constructed larger groups and complex social networks.[22] Girls' social relations are usually depicted as more cooperative than those of boys, but ethnographers have documented patterns of dispute and competition in girls' interactions with one another, including ritual insults that are often said to be typical of boys.[23] Boys' social relations are usually claimed to be more hierarchical than girls', but type of activity affects mode of interaction. The group of neighborhood girls Goodwin studied constructed hierarchies when they played house (a form of pretend play that, tellingly for children's representations of families, involved continual marking of dominance).[24] But when the girls engaged in a task activity like making rings from the rims of glass bottles, their interactions were more collaborative and egalitarian.

FROM DUALISMS TO GENDER AS FLUID AND SITUATED

Instead of scrambling to describe girls (or girls' groups) in contrast to boys', we are beginning to develop more varied and complex ways of thinking about children and gender. This shift of interpretive conventions has been furthered by the work of anthropologists, folklorists, and sociologists, who are more prone than developmental psychologists to start with social relations and to emphasize social contexts and meanings.

Conceptualizing gender in terms of social relations breaks with the relatively static equation of gender with dichotomous difference. An emphasis on social relations is well developed in studies of social class and ethnicity. But what Connell calls "categoricalism" has hounded the study of gender: reliance on relatively unexamined, dichotomous sex (or gender) categories—male/female, woman/man, boy/girl—as tools of analysis.[25] I have already discussed this problem in sex difference research. It is also a problem in the use of gender as an untheorized binary variable,[26] and—coming from a quite different intellectual and political context—in feminist theories that take "women" and "men" as unproblematic categories.[27]

At the level of basic social categories, gender does operate more dualistically than class, race, or ethnicity. Our culture has only two sex categories, and every person is permanently assigned to one or the other with very few attempts to switch. In every situation each individual displays, and others attribute to her or him, characteristics associated with one or the other of the two categories.[28] The workings of social class and race and ethnic categories seem from the start to be far more complex and contingent than gender. Social class and ethnic categories are multiple, sometimes ambiguous, and may vary by situation. A person's social class or ethnicity may not be readily apparent, nor (as is the case with gender) do we always feel a need to know the class or ethnicity of those with whom we interact.

The distinctive features of sex categories lie behind what Wallman calls "the peculiar epistemology of sex"—the deep hold of dualisms on our ways of thinking about gender.[29] But dichotomous sex categories are only one part of the organizational and symbolic processes of gender. The two categories woman and man have multiple and changing meanings, as ethnographies of "femininities" and "masculinities" suggest.[30]

Shifting the level of analysis from the individual to social relations and from sex categories to the variable social organization and symbolic meanings of gender further unravels dichotomous constructions. When the topic is gender, there is no escaping the theme of difference. But the presence, significance, and meanings of differences are refocused when one asks about the social relations that construct differences—and diminish or undermine them.

How is gender made more or less salient in different situations? In specific social contexts, how do the organization and meanings of gender take shape in relation to other socially constructed divisions like age, race, and social class? How do children in varied positions (for example, popular, marginal, or more or less involved in teen culture) navigate and experience a given set of gender relations? By emphasizing variable social contexts and multiple standpoints and meanings, these questions open a more fluid and situated approach to gender.

SOCIAL CONTEXTS AND THE RELATIVE SALIENCE OF GENDER

Much of the research on children and gender has neglected the importance of social context. Children have been pulled from specificity and fixed by abstract stages of development. Studies of individual sex differences often generalize about girls versus boys without attending to variations in society and culture. A different perspective emerges when one shifts from individuals to group life, with close attention to social contexts.

Earlier I contrasted situations where gender is highly salient with those in which its importance is muted. When children play "boys-chase-the-girls," gender is basic to the organization and symbolism of the encounter. Group gender boundaries are charged with titillating ambiguity and danger,[31] and girls and boys become by definition separate teams or sides.

The idea of *borderwork*, used by Barth to analyze ethnic relations,[32] can also be used to conceptualize social relations maintained across yet based upon and strengthening gender boundaries. When girls and boys are organized as opposing sides in a math contest or in cross-gender chasing, members of both sides may express solidarity within their gender and playful and serious antagonism to the other. But borderwork is also asymmetric. Boys invade girls' games and scenes of play much more than girls invade boys'. Boys control far more playground space than girls. Girls are more often defined as polluting and boys as running the risk of contamination (for example, girls are more often defined as giving "cooties").[33] Difference is related to dominance in children's gender group arrangements, and the workings of power are complex. Girls do not always passively accept their devaluation, but sometimes challenge and derogate boys. They guard their play and respond angrily to invasions; they complain to adults.[34]

Moments of separation and of bounded interaction evoke perceptions of difference by participants and by the experts who observe them. In everyday life in schools, children and adults talk about the different "natures" of girls and boys primarily to justify exclusion or separation and in situations of gender conflict. Two examples from my field notes:

> A group of sixth-grade girls grabbed the football from the ongoing play of a group of boys [this was one of the few occasions when I saw a group of girls invade a group of boys on the playground]. The boys complained to the playground aide. She responded, "Why won't you let the girls play?" The boys replied, "They can't tackle; when we tackle 'em they cry."

> During lunchtime an aide who was frazzled by problems of discipline told the third-grade girls and boys they had to sit at separate tables. One girl turned to another and said, half in jest and half in earnest, "The boys are naughty and we're good."

Gender-marked moments seem to express core truths: that boys and girls are separate and fundamentally different as individuals and as groups. They help sustain a sense of dualism in the face of enormous variation and complex circumstances. But the complexities are also part of the story. In daily school life many situations are organized along lines other than gender, and girls and boys interact in relaxed and non-gender-marked ways. For example, children often play handball and dodgeball in mixed groups; girls and boys sometimes sit together and converse in relaxed ways in classrooms, the cafeteria, or the library. Collective projects, like the radio play described earlier, often draw girls and boys together and diminish the salience of gender.

Children's gender relations can be understood only if we map the full array of their interactions—occasions when boys and girls are together as well as those when they separate (Goffman coined the apt phrase "with-then-apart" to describe the periodic nature of gender segregation).[35] To grasp the fluctuating significance of gender in social life, we must examine encounters where gender seems largely irrelevant as well as those where it is symbolically and organizationally central.

Broadening the site of significance to include occasions where gender is both unmarked and marked is one of several analytic strategies that I believe can provide fuller understanding of children's gender relations. Our conceptual frameworks are whetted on the marked occasions. Extensive gender separation or organizing an event as boys against the girls sets off contrastive thinking and feeds an assumption of gender as dichotomous difference. By also seeing other contexts as relevant to gender, we can situate the equation of gender with dualism more accurately and understand something of the hold that conceptualization has on us in the thrall of our culture. By developing a sense of the whole and attending to the waning as well as the waxing of gender salience, we can specify not only the social relations that uphold but also those that undermine the construction of gender as binary opposition. We can also gain a more complex understanding of the dynamics of power.

MULTIPLE DIFFERENCES

In specific social contexts, complex interactions among gender and such other social divisions as age, race, ethnicity, social class, and religion are another source of multiplicity. General terms like *intersecting differences* obscure the complex, sometimes contradictory dynamics of concrete situations. The range of possibilities is better evoked by Connell and colleagues, who observe that different social divisions and forms of inequality may "abrade, inflame, amplify, twist, dampen, and complicate each other."[36]

In the world of elementary schools, age is a more formally institutionalized social division than gender. Being in the first, fourth, or sixth grades determines daily activities and the company one keeps. Different grades may be allocated separate turfs in the lunchroom and the playground, and those who venture out of their age-defined territory may be chastised. In some situations children unite on the basis of age, which then becomes more salient than gender. One day a much disliked teacher who was on yard duty punished a fourth-grader for something he didn't do. He was very upset, and others from his classroom who were playing in the vicinity and witnessed or heard about the incident perceived a great injustice. Girls and boys talked about the situation in mixed clusters and joined as a group to argue with the adult.

Adults (including sociological observers) who work in schools are accorded privileges denied to children. They are not confined to specific lines, seats, and tables; they can move more freely through space; and they have institutionalized authority. Teachers and aides sometimes use their authority to construct and enhance gender divisions among children, as in the cases of the teacher who organized girls and boys into separate teams for classroom contests and the noontime aide who ordered boys and girls to sit at different tables. But adult practices also undermine gender separation between children in schools. In the United States there is a long tradition of mixed-gender public elementary schools, with girls and boys sharing a curriculum and with an ideology of treating everyone the same and of attending to individual needs. Some structural pressures run against separating girls and boys in daily school life, especially in classrooms.[37] Adult practices work in both directions, sometimes separating and sometimes integrating boys and girls. Overall, however, school-based observers have found that less gender separation takes place among children when adults control a situation than when children have more autonomy.[38]

When children have constructed sharp gender boundaries, few of them attempt to cross. But adults claim the privilege of freelancing. In the schools I studied, when boys and girls sat at separate tables in school cafeterias, teachers and aides of both genders sat at either table, and the presence of an adult sometimes created a wedge for more general mixed seating. When the fourth-and-fifth-graders drew names for a winter holiday gift exchange, they decided (in a discussion punctuated by ritual gender antagonism) that girls would give to girls and boys to boys. The teacher decided that she would draw with the boys and suggested that the aide and I (both women) draw with the girls. Our adult status altered the organization of gender.

A mix of age, gender, and ethnicity contributed to the marginalization of two Latino boys in the fourth-and-fifth-grade classroom. The boys were recent immigrants from Mexico and spoke very little English. They sat in a back corner of the classroom and sometimes worked at a side table with a Spanish-speaking aide. The other children treated them as if they were younger, with several girls who sat near them repeatedly monitoring the boys' activities and telling them what to do. When the children were divided by gender, other boys repeatedly maneuvered the Latino boys and another low-status boy into sitting next to girls. These spatial arrangements drew upon a gender meaning—an assumption that being by girls is contaminating—to construct ethnic subordination and marginality.

Gender display may symbolically represent and amplify social class divisions. The students in the two schools I studied were largely working class, but within that loose categorization children's different economic circumstances affected how they looked, especially the girls. It was easier to spot girls from impoverished families than boys because the girls' more varied clothing was less adaptable (as in the case of a mismatched top and bottom) than the T-shirts and jeans the boys wore. Girls' hairstyles were also more varied and complex, providing material for differentiated display of style and grooming, and grooming standards were more exacting for girls than for boys. A fifth-grade girl whose unkempt hair and mismatched old clothing marked her impoverished background was treated like a pariah, while the most popular girl had many well-matched outfits and a well-groomed appearance. The top and bottom rungs of girls' popularity (positions partly shaped by social class) were defined by heterosexual meanings when children teased about a particular boy "liking" or "goin' with" a specific girl. The teasers most frequently named either the most popular girl or the pariah as targets of a boy's liking—the most and least probable and polluting targets of desire.

Attention to the dynamics of social contexts helps situate gender in relationship to other lines of difference and inequality. The meanings of gender are not unitary but multiple, and sometimes contradictory.

MULTIPLE STANDPOINTS

Exploring varied standpoints on a given set of gender relations is another strategy for deconstructing a too coherent, dichotomous portrayal of girls' groups versus boys' groups and for developing a more complex understanding of gender relations. Children who are popular or marginal, those defined as troublemakers or good students, and those who are more or less likely to cross gender boundaries have different experiences of the same situations. Their varied experiences—intricately constructed by and helping to construct gender, social class, ethnicity, age, and individual characteristics—provide multiple vantage points on the complexity of children's social worlds.

An array of social types, including the bully, the troublemaker, the sissy, the tomboy, and the isolate populates both fictional and social science literature on children in schools. If we shift from types to processes, we can get a better hold on the experiences these terms convey. For example, the terms *tomboy* and *sissy* take complicated social processes—changing gender boundaries and a continuum of crossing—and reify them into individual essences or conditions (for example, "tomboyism"). Crossing involves definition, activity, and the extent to which a child has a regular place in the other gender's social networks. Boys who frequently seek access to predominantly female groups and activities ("sissies") are more often harassed and teased by both boys and girls. But girls who frequently play with boys ("tomboys") are much less often stigmatized, and they continue to maintain ties with girls, a probable reason that, especially in the later years of elementary school, crossing by girls is far more frequent than crossing by boys.[39]

When girls are accepted in boys' groups and activities without changing the terms of the interactions (one girl called it being a "buddy"), gender becomes low. Heterosexual idioms, which mark and dramatize gender difference, pose a threat to such acceptance; one can't be a "buddy" and "goin' with" at the same time. The fifth-grade girl who was "buddies" with a group of boys navigated the field of gender relations and meanings very differently than did girls who frequently initiated heterosexual chasing rituals. Unitary notions like the girls' world and girls versus boys are inadequate for this sort of analysis. Instead, one must grapple with multiple standpoints, complex and even contradictory meanings, and the varying salience of gender.

ETHNOGRAPHIES OF SCHOOLING

In developing a contextual and deconstructive approach to understanding gender and children's worlds, I have been influenced by the work of other ethnographers, whose methods bring sensitivity to social contexts and to the construction of meanings. Ethnographers of education who work within "social reproduction theory" (asking how schools reproduce inequalities, mostly of social class and gender) have emphasized students' varying subcultures, some more conforming and some created in opposition to the official structure of schools. In an ethnographic study of working class "lads" in a vocational school in England, Willis gave attention to gender as well as to social class (the primary focus of this tradition anchored in Marxist theories).[40] Resisting the middle-class authority of the school, the lads created an oppositional culture of aggression and joking tied to the working class "masculine" subculture of factory workers. The lads' subculture, different from that of more conforming boys, helped reproduce their class position.

Recent research within this tradition has finally moved girls from the periphery more toward the center of attention. In a study of fifth-graders in U.S. schools, Anyon analyzed strategies related to social class that girls used both to resist and to accommodate institutionalized attempts to enforce femininity.[41] For example, some girls used exaggerated feminine behavior to resist work assignments; those who were "discipline problems" rebelled both against the school and against expectations of them as girls.

Connell and his colleagues, who have studied girls and boys of different social classes in high schools in Australia, use the plural notions *masculinities* and *femininities* to articulate an array of subcultures and individual styles or types of identity.[42] (I find it problematic that they mix, rather than carefully distinguishing, individual and group levels of analysis.) They conceptualize gender and class as "structuring processes" and argue that each school has a "gender regime," constructing, ordering, and arbitrating between different kinds of masculinity and femininity. "The gender regime is in a state of play rather than a permanent condition."[43]

These studies are important in part because they break with the pervasive determinism of conventional "sex-role socialization" literature on gender and schools. Instead of simply "being socialized" (the imagery of children in much feminist literature), girls and boys are granted agency in constructing culture and resisting it as well as in adapting to dominant ideologies. By positing a complex and plural approach to gender, these ethnographies also challenge simplistic dualisms like "the male role versus the female role" or "girls' groups versus boys' groups."

But for all their value, these conceptualizations leave unresolved some of the issues I raised earlier. They analyze gender primarily by emphasizing separation between boys and girls and comparing the dynamics and sub-cultures of same-gender groups. While the groups and subcultures are multiple, a sense of deep division (separate worlds) between girls and boys persists. How far such divisions may vary by situation or subculture is not made clear. Dualistic assumptions poke through the multiplicity.

A second problem with Connell's work is that while the plural mas-culinities and femininities seem useful, the patterns these ethnographers describe sometimes seem more classificatory (an ever-finer grid for fixing gender) than anchored in a close analysis of social processes. By what criteria should a given pattern of interaction be seen as constructing a femininity or a masculinity, that is, as being relevant to the organization and meanings of gender? Some "social reproduction" ethnographers like Everhart largely ignore gender in their analyses of students' everyday in-teractions.[44] Others, for example, Anyon and Connell and his colleagues, refer the entire field of interaction to notions of gender.[45] This variation points to a more general question. Is gender always relevant? Do some parts of social life transcend it? If our challenge is to trace the threading of gender (and gender inequalities) through the complexity of social life, how can we determine when and how to invoke gendered interpretations?

These difficult questions suggest the need for finer conceptual tuning. In every situation we display and attribute core sex categories: gender does have ubiquitous relevance. But there is wide variation in the organization and symbolism of gender. Looking at social context shifts analysis from fixing abstract and binary differences to examining the social relations and contexts in which multiple differences are constructed, undermined, and given meaning.

This contextual approach to gender—questioning the assumption that girls and boys (and men and women) have different "essential natures" best understood in terms of opposition—clearly resonates with deconstructive, postmodernist tendencies in feminist thought.[46] I reached a deconstruc-tive approach not by way of French theorists, however, but through the contextual and interpretive methods of ethnography.

Feminists have been more deconstructive and aware of multiplicities in thinking about adults than in thinking about children. We refer children's experiences to development and socialization, while granting adults a much broader scene of action. One way around that conceptual double standard is extending to children the frameworks (in this case, a fluid and contextual approach to gender) also used in analyzing the world of adults. In following that path, however, I have slid across a project that awaits close attention: grappling with differences of age, which, like gender, involve complex interactions of biology and culture. We should turn our critical attention to the dualism adult/child as well as to gender dualisms.

What Is the Relation between Psychoanalytic Feminism and the Psychoanalytic Psychology of Women?

NANCY J. CHODOROW

The relation of feminist theory to its disciplines, or discourses, of origin has always been problematic.[1] We have wanted to claim ourselves as Marxist feminists, phenomenological feminists, or feminist kinship theorists, always retaining (for purposes of analysis and identity) while transforming (for the same purposes) the core theoretical categories and methodological approaches of our chosen discourse. Psychoanalytic feminists face the same difficult challenge, but of all theoretical feminisms, psychoanalytic feminism has probably been most continually subject to dismissal or challenge. The relation of psychoanalytic feminism to psychoanalysis, as well as the feminist critique of psychoanalysis, forms a backdrop to any consideration of sexual difference in psychoanalytic perspective.

This essay does not take up the issue of the challenge to psychoanalytic feminism, which I and other psychoanalytic feminists have discussed extensively elsewhere.[2] Rather, it reflects on psychoanalysis and psychoanalytic feminism. It puts forth a case example of the dilemma posed for theory in general, and feminist theory in particular, when some claimants to theoretical persuasiveness demand scientific data as proof but debate what the "correct" data are, while others rely on interpretive strategies about data, on theoretical or narrative coherence or plausibility, on accord with life experience, on interpretive relevance to other texts, or on congruence with sociopolitical analysis and goals. As debates rage on these matters among the various discourses of psychoanalytic feminism, a problem emerges: psychoanalysts, unlike proponents of many of the other theories that feminists have drawn from, also claim to have much to say, clinically and theoretically, about gender and sexual difference, and they seem to be talking about areas of gender psychology that have little to do with any psychoanalytic feminist position.

Psychoanalytically derived theories about women, then, present themselves in several guises. On the one side, among psychoanalysts, debate that exhibits a range of positions and interests about women and femininity has become a topic of burgeoning concern in recent years. On the other side, psychoanalytic feminists—academic feminist literary critics, philosophers, social scientists, and epistemologists—engage in a distinctly different set of discourses about different questions.[3] Different discussions are going on, with rare mutual recognition, among different sets of people.

Briefly, psychoanalytic feminists begin, somewhat in the manner of the Freud of *Studies on Hysteria, Three Essays on Sexuality,* and "'Civilized' Sexual Morality and Modern Nervousness," from a critical, evaluative, liberatory position. We take gender and sexuality to be socially, culturally, and psychologically problematic and wish to understand how they develop and are reproduced in the individual and in society. Psychoanalysts begin, rather like the Freud who asks "how [a woman] comes into being,"[4] from a query about how the development and experience of gender and sexuality are played out in life: how, in individual cases, these do not follow the route prescribed or described as normal. Their evaluative stance tends to presume a bifurcation of masculinity and femininity in more or less traditional cultural terms and a heterosexuality with partners in complementary but different sexual roles. A small but growing number of feminist psychoanalysts—practicing psychoanalysts who identify themselves explicitly as feminists—borrow from and elaborate clinically upon the theoretical contributions of some psychoanalytic feminist theory, and a few psychoanalytic feminists make efforts to follow the changing psychoanalytic literature.

We are compellingly reminded of the professional and intellectual separation of worlds. For the most part, psychoanalysts do not seem to be aware of or to care much about the ferment in psychoanalytic feminist theory that is to the fore in a number of academic disciplines. They tend to identify themselves as scientists, practitioners of a scientific psychology or branch of psychiatry for whom empirical reality and direct clinical application have definite primacy if not exclusive claim to document truth. They are inclined to think that science can be value-free and have tended to see feminism as a political or politicized practice rather than as a theory that is relevant to their own theory or practice.[5]

So too, psychoanalytic feminists often seem to go about their work paying little attention to the claims of those who by profession would seem to have great authority to evaluate psychoanalytic claims. Psychoanalytic feminists are passionately interested in masculinity and femininity, but believe that traditional understandings of these are anything but value-free; they are imbued with an ideology of gender such that no claim about gender stands in itself. All claims, all "findings," are suspect and must be examined to discover those assumptions and practices that construct them in one way and not in another. Psychoanalytic feminist literary critics, philosophers, and epistemologists, who work more exclusively from text, "story," or theoretical argument, and who often adhere to a postmodernist skepticism about truth, in particular often feel that evidential claims need not affect their assessments about persuasive arguments.

For social scientists—who stand epistemologically between the empiricist scientism of psychoanalysts and the interpretive relativism of humanists, who privilege both empirical "reality" and theory but grant that value-free science does not exist, who draw upon a variety of interpretive and explanatory strategies—questions about the varieties of psychoanalytic theories of gender seem particularly problematic. It seems to me, however, that psychoanalytic feminists, who claim to draw upon psychoanalysis, must come to terms with what psychoanalysts *say* gender is about, even if and as we want to say something different. And since psychoanalysis is a deeply embedded cultural discourse and not just a therapeutic practice or value-free science, psychoanalysts would do well to consider seriously the debates and claims of psychoanalytical feminism.

PSYCHOANALYTIC THEORIES OF WOMEN AND GENDER

All modern developments, both psychoanalytic and feminist, are in dialogue with the traditional Freudian theory of the development of femininity. In this theory, first, sex difference does not matter until the phallic phase, around age four, at which stage "the little girl is a little man" with a masculine sexuality.[6] Second, for both sexes until puberty, sexual difference is defined in terms of presence or absence of the penis. The vagina (for classical psychoanalysis, *the* female sexual organ) is unknown, both consciously and unconsciously. Third, the development of heterosexuality and maternality in the girl are a secondary product of her sense of failed masculinity.

The classical view speaks not so much of gender as of sex and sexuality. Freud and his colleagues were concerned with the nature and meaning of bodily erotic experience and sexual orientation. Insofar as we can infer from this account, conceptions of gender identity (our sense of feminine or masculine self) and gender personality (males' and females' character, psychic structure, and psychological processes) are in the first instance tied to awareness of genital constitution: does a boy give up his mother (or his father) in exchange for his penis? Does a girl accept her "castration" or protest against it? Does she go through life seeking a penis? The creation of sexual orientation, the desire for parenthood, masculine and feminine identifications with the parent of the same sex, all result from what the child does with her or his sense of genital difference.

There was a major dissident position on female sexuality from almost as early as Freud discussed it, but active debate about the nature of femininity disappeared for some time. The topic was kept alive indirectly through clinical case discussion, but rarely in ways that constructed any fundamental challenge to the theory. In the last fifteen years or so, however, theoretical, clinical, and empirical discussion has emerged into active reformulation and debate. As I read the literature, contemporary psychoanalytic debate centers on two developmental issues.[7]

First, attention has focused especially on the question of genital awareness, when and how it develops, and what its impact is on gender identity, gender personality, and the sense of self. Against Freud's view that sex difference does not matter until the phallic phase, psychoanalysts now claim, on the basis of clinical and observational work with children as well as from their adult clinical practices, that genital awareness develops in the second year, in what would formerly have been called the pregenital period.

Two positions have been articulated within this view. One position understands early genital awareness as an awareness of sexual difference in the traditional sense: presence or absence of the penis is what matters.[8] In this view, the one-year-old girl's response to her discovered castration is the preeminent organizing influence throughout her life, not just on psychosexual development, sexuality, and the girl's turn to her father, but on ego and object relational development as well.

A second position agrees that genital schematization develops in the second year but provides different views of what this schematization is and its role in the formation of gender identity and gender personality. A variety of formulations challenge Freud's view that the little girl is a little man with a "phallic" (active, clitoral) sexuality who doesn't know her own feminine organs either consciously or unconsciously. Relying on a notion of primary femininity, this position argues that in both boys and girls a primary awareness and valuation (*cathexis*) of their own genital organs precedes the observation or schematization of genital difference. Such awareness proceeds directly out of body experience, though different writers consider it more or less affected by parental labeling and treatment.[9]

A second strand of recent psychoanalytic theories of feminine (and masculine) development focuses not so much on genital awareness as on gender identity, enlarging on arguments developed by Money and Ehrhardt, Stoller, and others that a cognitive labeling of gender or core gender identity—the sense of self as female or male—develops in the first few years of life (again before gender could be said to matter in the classical psychoanalytic view). As with the issue of genital awareness, writers take two positions on the question of gender identity. Like Freud's implicit view that gender identity is a matter of sexual orientation and genital constitution, the first and dominant position hinges gender identity—even if it is a cognitive self-label and not necessarily based on invidious comparison of the girl's with the boy's genitals—on genital awareness.[10] In this view, for example, the boy's first task in the establishment of his core gender *identity* is the discovery of his penis and its integration into his body image. His first step in gender *role* assumption is upright urination in identification with his father.

Against the psychoanalytic mainstream, an alternate account of the development of gender identity hinges this identity on cognitive and interpersonal factors and makes genital experience derivative.[11] Proponents of this view might agree that genital experience and self-stimulation occur in the young child, but they would take such behavior to be no more important than object relations, self-development, cognitive development, and other aspects of behavior. Against Freud's early claims, this alternate position asserts that the sense of femaleness is more easily attained than the sense of maleness and that male gender identity development runs a continual risk of being undermined by a primary feminine identification that emerges from a close tie to the mother. Core gender identity here is a composite result of biological forces, sex assignment and parental labeling at birth and in the early years, parental attitudes about that sex, family psychodynamics, and the infant's interpretation of these experiences.

No matter what the position endorsed, with little exception modern psychoanalytic developmental interest in female psychology has centered on a female sexuality defined as what girls make of their own genitals and genital difference. While in some ways an advance (in its confrontation of the empirically incorrect—as well as sexist—early Freudian theory of primary masculinity for both sexes), this modern approach reinforces and even extends psychoanalytic tendencies to put forth an essentialist view of gender identity and gender role. Whereas classical psychoanalytic theory begins from a more generically conceived sexuality and conception of fluid unconscious drives that in turn create genital experience (and character), for contemporary theories of gender, direct genital awareness and experience become primary determinants. Sexuality (as well as object relations and character) becomes more derivative.

PSYCHOANALYTIC FEMINISM

Any division of psychoanalytic feminism is partly arbitrary. Three self-identified approaches stand out, and I think the first two show large commonalities in comparison to the third. Here I distinguish an object-relations and an interpersonal psychoanalytic feminism from a Lacanian psychoanalytic feminism.

Following for the most part British object-relations theory, object-relations feminists put self-other relations and the development of a self (whether whole or fragmented, with its own agency or reactive) as that self is constituted through its consciously and unconsciously experienced relations in the center of development. The object-relations school has itself hardly dealt with gender difference or the development of gender, but their approach can be drawn upon in such a venture. I have argued that, as a result of being parented primarily by a woman, men and women develop differently constructed selves and different experiences of their gender and gender identity.[12] Through their early relationship with their mother, women develop a sense of self continuous with others and a richly constructed inner self-object world that continuously engages unconscious and conscious activity: "The basic feminine sense of self is connected to the world."[13] This psychic structure and self-other process in turn help to reproduce mothering: "Because women themselves are mothered by women, they grow up with the relational capacities and needs, and psychological definition of self-in-relationship, which commits them to mothering."[14]

By contrast, men develop a self based more on denial of relation and on a more fixed, firmly split, and repressed inner self-object world: "the basic masculine sense of self is separate."[15] The object-relations view argues that as a result of being parented primarily by a woman, masculinity develops a more reactive, defensive quality than femininity. Dinnerstein and I point to the mother blame, misogyny, and fear of the feminine that develops, especially in men, in reaction to the powerfully experienced mother (and internal mother image). We suggest that this fuels male dominance in culture and society and creates systematic tensions and conflicts in heterosexual relationships.[16]

Writers in the object-relations tradition, for example, Benjamin, Flax, and Fox Keller, have described how this arelational masculinity, based on a need to dominate women and deny femininity, has become institutionalized. Notions of scientific objectivity, the technical rationality of advanced capitalism, individualistic political and social theories that assume the inevitability of hierarchy and the need to create society out of asocial individuals, practices of erotic, scientific, and technical domination—all find their psychological roots as defensive institutionalizations of a rigid separateness needed by the masculine psyche and are built on a latent structure of anger and repudiation of women.[17] Feminist literary critics like Abel, Adelman, Hirsch, and Kahn draw from an object-relations perspective to investigate woman's voice, patterns of relationality, the mother image, and representations of inner worlds in women writers, as well as male writers' unconscious attitudes to mothers and feminine power.[18]

Thus the object-relations perspective takes the construction of masculinity and femininity to be interconnected and constitutes a critique of masculinity as well as a reformulation of our understanding of the female self. It stands the traditional Freudian understanding on its head, for it to some extent valorizes women's construction of self and makes normal masculinity problematic. Feminist object-relations theorists have also argued strongly for theoretical and developmental treatment of the mother as a subject—against psychoanalytic (including object-relational) tendencies to treat her as an object whose role is evaluated only in terms of the presumed needs and fantasies of the child.[19] This leads to a reformulation of the psychoanalytic self as well, emphasizing not only that separateness rather than connectedness needs explaining, but also that intersubjectivity and the mutual recognition of the self and the other are fundamental to psychological development.

The interpersonal, or cultural, or neo-Freudian group has created an account of female psychology similar for our purposes to the object-relations perspective. Baker Miller, a Sullivanian analyst, enunciated the main features of the interpersonal psychoanalytic perspective, and the group also draws on the theories of Gilligan.[20] Miller argues that women are repositories of qualities of affiliativeness, relatedness, empathy, and nurturance—qualities that object-relations feminism also describes—that are devalued and distorted in male-dominant culture and by men. She wants women to reclaim and value these traditionally feminine qualities. Much of the writing of the interpersonal group is based on clinical cases, and in these case descriptions women's problems are seen to inhere mainly in the denial and devaluation of affiliative qualities both by others and by themselves. Therapeutic cure consists in women's recognizing and accepting these qualities, in being caring and empathetic toward themselves. A second, less prominent strand in the cultural perspective focuses on problems women have in asserting anger and aggression, both of which have been repressed and denied by our male-dominant culture. Clinical work should also focus in this area.[21]

In a general way, Miller's original work attributed the developmental origins of the feminine qualities she described to cultural learning, and the Miller group continues to attribute women's qualities to cultural prescription and suppression. In its recent work, however, the implicit and occasionally articulated view seems to follow the object-relations perspective, emphasizing the influence of the mother-daughter relationship on the development of what they also now call the "self-in-relation."[22]

This general feminist perspective is bifurcated. As psychoanalytic theorists, object-relations feminists pay more attention to the complexities of the inner object world and to unconscious defenses, conflicts, and structuring of self. Interpersonal theorists emphasize unconscious dynamics less and pay more attention to cultural and personal evaluation of different qualities and capacities. Object-relations feminists, whose roots are in critical social theory as much as in psychoanalysis, tend to see the psychology of men and women as an intertwined conflictual whole, as part of a totality of social and psychological relations. Cultural school feminists do not discuss the psychology of masculinity except by comparative implication and seem to operate more in the context of an empirical psychology of sex differences and a separate-spheres feminism.

Object-relations theorists focus more on the problems that, along with strengths, inhere in women's psychology and are also more likely to focus on male development as a problem. Although they may valorize qualities traditionally associated with women, both social analysis and the greater attention to unconscious conflict lead object-relations theorists to hold a more tempered and critical view of these qualities. I argue, for example, that women's relational self can be a strength or a pitfall in feminine psychic life: it enables empathy, nurturance, and intimacy but threatens to undermine autonomy and to dissolve self into others. Women's mothering itself shares this ambivalent position, as it both generates pleasure and fulfillment and is fundamentally related to women's secondary position in society and to the fear of women in men. Flax stresses the difficulties women can have in recognizing differences with other women and argues that women's empathetic, different-voiced, relational self rests on the repression of selves bound up with autonomy, aggression, intellectual and interpersonal mastery, and active sexual desire. Benjamin describes women's tendency to seek separateness and recognition through a love for the father that becomes masochistically tinged.[23] In contrast, recent interpersonal writing seems to see women's relationality more exclusively in positive terms.

But these views have several features in common. Although both groups (especially the object-relations group) focus, like contemporary psychoanalysts, on the early infantile and preoedipal period as crucial to gender development and therefore on the crucial importance of the relation to the mother, they emphatically and by definition do *not* understand genital awareness and genital difference to be causal and central in gender identity and gender personality. We focus on the experience of *self with other* and how that comes to be organized and appropriated. Insofar as feminine development and sexuality are problematic, such problems are seen to inhere centrally and originally in issues of relation and of self—conflict in the mother, devaluation by the father, experiences of lack of fit, inadequately resolved development of self-esteem, agency, and wholeness—or in problems of cultural valuation. They are not built upon a primary, conflicted, genital schematization or problematic genital awareness (though they may be played out partly around such issues).

In a move controversial for any modern feminist theory that emphasizes the primacy of gender as a cultural meaning system or that stresses that gender is always situated in gender difference, the object-relations interpersonal perspective separates gender identity and gender personality. Qualities of self or self in relation (as well as denial of relation) and a generically constructed sense of self that is not necessarily tied to a sense of gender become more important than unconsciously or consciously experienced gender identity and cognition and assessment of gender difference. It is not because she knows she is female that a girl or woman experiences her self in relationship (though a boy's or a man's denial of relationality may very well be a product of his sense of appropriate masculinity). Her self-in-relation is a developmental product tied to her mother's sense of self, but not only to gender identity or gender role learning. The object-relations cultural perspective does not ignore conscious gender identity and the construction of gender or unconscious meanings of these, but it claims that this is not the whole of gender, and it embeds all three in object relations or a cultural sense of self. Because of this focus on qualities of self, the object-relations perspective in particular moves radically away from essentialist views of gender toward a view that constructs feminine and masculine personality and male dominance in a contingent, relationally constructed context.

Lacanian feminism, the second branch of psychoanalytic feminism, reacts, like the first, to the original psychoanalytic theory. But it also reacts to the object-relations position.[24] Lacanian feminists argue that Freud's account of how we become sexed shows how our very sexualization is asymmetrical and unequal. In this view, a linguistically constructed unconscious that *is* our sexuality (as opposed to the ego or internalized object relations) is the foundation of psychic life. Subjectivity emerges out of unconscious sexual drives. Sexualization and subjectivity are by definition constituted in terms of difference, an opposition between the sexes that is structured linguistically and not biologically. We are also born into this sexual/linguistic setting. It precedes us and makes inevitable the conditions within which we develop and the range of our possible sexual-subjective choices.

A person takes a place in the world as a subject only through entry into language and culture, and acquisition of subjectivity takes place through the intervention of a third person, the father (symbolized by his phallus), into the mother-child dyad, which is conceived to lie conceptually and emotionally outside language and culture. As the father and his phallus institute and constitute this symbolic intervention, the phallus stands for entrance into the symbolic realm of language and culture. In this view subjectivity is sexuality, and sexuality is defined exclusively in terms of sexual difference, the presence or absence of the phallus. Sexuality and subjectivity, rooted in the unconscious, are precarious for both sexes because they hinge on resolution of the castration complex.

In contrast to recent psychoanalytic views, the Lacanian position allows no primary genital awareness that is not tied to an awareness and cognizing of genital difference that, in turn, are located in language. Preoedipal knowledge of genital difference is an impossibility, since such knowledge is, as in classical psychoanalysis, tied to the oedipal transition and the castration complex. In contrast to object-relations feminism, Lacanian feminism recognizes no subjectivity apart from schematized sexual identity. Gender difference is all there is when it comes to our selfhood or subjectivity, and gender difference is experienced and cognized (through our placement in language) in terms of sexuality and genital schematization. Subjectivity and sexuality are interdependent; neither can develop without the other.[25]

Lacanian feminism makes radical psychoanalytic and feminist claims. It argues that no aspects to gender division, identity, or personality exist except for sexuality and symbolized genital difference and that subjectivity resides solely in sexuality. Every action is located in an unequal sexual world; we can never lose sight of our developmentally inevitable placement in a phallocentric culture. Lacanian feminism provides developmental underpinnings for a dominant theme in French and other feminisms concerning women's lack of self and sense of being the Other, her fundamental alienation from and objectification in culture.[26] On a more sociological plane, Lacanian-inspired theorists like Johnson and Rubin argue for the importance of the son's generational oedipal change of object and power position as he goes from involvement as a powerless subordinate with the powerful preoedipal mother to a position of dominance in relation to women. These theorists point to the girl's accession to oppression in a passive heterosexuality as men gain rights to her sexuality that she neither gains in theirs nor retains in her own. In this view, the oedipus complex and oedipal transition do not institute sex difference but male dominance.[27]

Lacanians claim that by focusing on the mother-daughter relationship or on a femininity defined apart from masculinity, object-relations feminists and primary femininity theorists fail to see these as systematically unequal social and psychological relations. Experience has meaning only in terms of sexual difference, and there cannot be a femininity defined in itself. Johnson argues that a focus on the mother obscures the father's critical role, which can be documented empirically as well as described through cultural analysis, in emphasizing and constituting gender-typed behavior and gender domination in the family. These writers criticize views that idealize women's qualities or ignore women's situation in a male-dominant culture and language, arguing that neither wholeness nor positive qualities are possible for men or women in such a culture.

We are presented in the contemporary period with three theories and three epistemological approaches to the question of psychoanalysis and gender. Psychoanalysts are interested in when genital awareness develops and whether boys and girls develop an awareness of their own genitals first or of the boy's only, whether they value their own genitals or only the boy's. They are interested in what gender identity means, and for the most part they tie this to questions of genital awareness. Object-relations and interpersonal feminists are concerned with gender-differentiated qualities of self that are separate from but related to gender identity and have developed theories that contrast the female's and male's self. They argue that qualities traditionally considered desirable and normal—firm ego boundaries, an emphasis on autonomy, an independent morality and impersonal superego, objectivity—are male defenses against connections to others and deeply inherent in a male-dominant society and culture. Whereas they may recognize that women need more access to autonomy, assertion, and an active sexuality, they see women's relational qualities as desirable and more fully mature than a defensive masculine autonomy. Lacanian feminists, by contrast, argue that such revaluation is wrong, that all people, but perhaps especially women, are stunted, perhaps inevitably, by a fractured subjectivity and sexuality imposed by placement in a phallocentric culture and language. Psychoanalysis cannot describe desirable qualities but is instead the best account we have of the iron cage of sexual inequality and male dominance.

What are the relations among these theories? Lacanians and French anti-Lacanians seem to have fundamental assumptions in common with the dominant psychoanalytic mainstream, locating gender difference in genital difference, but this is an accidental shared characteristic. It encompasses the scope neither of psychoanalysis, with its complex developmental account of the emotional meanings of the genitals, nor of Lacanian theory, with its specifically linguistic account of the relationship of sexuality and subjectivity. For most classical analysts (as for object-relations feminists) sexuality and subjectivity are distinguished, and it makes a difference whether we have primarily a speaking subject, in which location in language predominates, or a sexual subject, in which sexual difference and the phallus predominate. It is not clear that anything genital or sexual, as psychoanalysts think of this (or relational as object-relations theorists think of this), matters to Lacanians.

More important, the Lacanian argument is a logical argument about the structure of language and about us as its speakers. As developing beings, we *must* break out of the dyadic mother-child relationship, there *must* be a third term to institute this break, and the father, symbolized by his phallus, *is* this third term. Evidence cannot oppose this logic, since it is a logic, and Lacanians even have a language for dismissing evidence. Anything given, natural, or "real" is repudiated by definition on the symbolic level. Evidential claims based on psychoanalytic or developmental research—the research that most contemporary analysts and developmental psychologists rely on—that contradicts Lacanian theory about a genital phase in the second year, about a girl's primary positive awareness of her own genitals, about the nature of the early mother-child relationship, about language development or innate linguistic structures, cannot have impact on the account. Against queries about whether the actual presence or absence of the father makes a difference, Lacanians claim that the father is a symbol, definitionally present in language; his actual presence is irrelevant. We can linguistically describe or experience nothing outside the symbolic, which places us in that very phallic order against which we might want to find evidence.

Such views diametrically oppose those of most practicing analysts, especially in the United States, who see their work as scientific, as a product of the steady development of clinical and observational evidence. Psychoanalytic debates in the area of gender psychology concern the nature and interpretation of evidence; they are rarely cast in the language of theoretical logic. The psychoanalytic position, though apparently congruent with the Lacanian, fundamentally contrasts with it.

A different contrast obtains between object-relations and interpersonal psychoanalytic feminism and psychoanalytic gender theory. Whereas contemporary psychoanalysts take object relations and the self seriously, most have not applied these concerns to their approaches to gender. But object-relations feminists make the development, structure, and experience of self and self-other relations into a primary phenomenon in our consideration of gender, not a secondary reaction to drive development or genital experience. The object-relations developmental account concerning the role of fear of women, especially powerful women, in the development of masculinity may explain recent clinical findings about fears and avoidance of erotic transference in male patients of female analysts at least as well as and perhaps better than classic accounts about castration anxiety. But against "research" on genital awareness object-relations feminists can claim only that other things are psychologically more important.[28] Here the closing off of debate is substantively theoretical rather than epistemological.

Overlap and commonality between object-relations feminism and psychoanalysis are more often accidental than intentional. For example, both object-relations feminists and psychoanalysts have developed a version of a theory of primary femininity, but for object-relations feminists it is rooted in mother-daughter identification and shared selfhood, while psychoanalysts ground it in primary genital awareness.

Such a situation of substantive theoretical rather than epistemological conflict can lead to radically different interpretations of the same situation by people who both hold that clinical "evidence" matters. For instance, a classical analyst might say of a woman who has enormous performance anxiety and does much worse than she could in school and in testing situations that she unconsciously experiences success as gaining a penis. This reminds her of the early narcissistic injury when she learned that she could never have one, and she therefore develops inhibitions against success. Alternately, this fantasy of gaining (stealing) a penis induces oedipal guilt or fear of punishment. An interpersonal psychoanalytic feminist might understand this same woman to symbolize success unconsciously as a denial of connection to other students and friends, in which case her refusal to succeed becomes an affirmation of her self in relationship and her desires for affiliation and connection to other women.[29]

There are complex divisions between and within the two feminist positions. First, major disagreements exist concerning whether we should conceptualize psychological development in terms of object-relational and self experience or of linguistic placement in culture; whether we should conceptualize gender and male dominance in terms of consciously and unconsciously cognized sexual difference per se—in which case the genders can exist and have meaning only in relation one to the other—or in terms of qualities we can attribute to or feel as people of different genders; whether we should see sexuality as a product of relational development and its unconscious concomitants or as a linguistic location. Choices here hinge also on our developmental theories. In reaction to the nearly exclusive traditional psychoanalytic focus on the oedipus complex and the central role of the father in creating gender and sexuality, object-relations feminists center attention on the role of the mother in both preoedipal and oedipal periods. Lacanians retain and even extend the traditional position, arguing against the psychological centrality of the preoedipal and even oedipal mother and making the oedipal period and the relation to the father the exclusive generators of sexuality and subjectivity.

Second, equally fundamental epistemological and evidential differences pose a Lacanian feminist analysis of language and an argument that operate purely in the realm of theory, against the claims of some object-relations and interpersonal feminists for empirical and clinical reality. Here things are more complicated, because academic object-relations feminists arrange themselves on a spectrum in relation to textual versus empirical truth. In an internal division mirroring what begins to emerge as a deep schism within academic feminism, object-relations literary critics often share the Lacanian feminist commitment to textual analysis and a postmodernist skepticism concerning empirical reality. But object-relations social critics, while in no way part of the positivist mainstream of their fields, still wish to argue on empirical and clinical as well as theoretical grounds.[30]

Even as we argue among ourselves, all psychoanalytic feminists unite in opposition to what we perceive as overly biological psychoanalytic interpretations and to psychoanalytic claims to a value-free "scientific" study of gender and gender difference, a study that notices only by happenstance and in the occasional case that something is problematic in the construction and organization of gender. We also to varying extents and in different ways see masculine and feminine personality, development, and identity as interrelated, as part of a larger set of social, cultural, and psychological relations.

The various discourses have different truth criteria and different definitional realities. Clearly this calls for dialogue. On one side, psychoanalysis confronts a psychoanalytic feminism that has by and large considered only the psychoanalytic theory of femininity developed in the early years of psychoanalysis. Our problem as psychoanalytic feminists is the nature of our claim to appropriate psychoanalytic theory and findings and the grounds by which we choose what to accept and reject within this. Relying as we do on what we profess to be psychoanalysis, we cannot simply dismiss or ignore modern psychoanalytic work. In considering modern psychoanalytic claims, we must evaluate the extent to which female development is embedded in sexual difference or genital evaluation and experience. We need to ask how genital awareness affects gender identity and sexuality, how central it is compared to other areas of experience, to cognitive labeling, to cultural categories, to object relations, and to the development of sense of self more generally. Drawing on clinical evidence, we might also ask how important gender identity in the broadest sense is to women's sense of self.

Such a challenge has different meanings for different psychoanalytic feminists. Literary or philosophical critics, including most Lacanian feminists as well as some object-relations feminists, take psychoanalysis in whatever variety as a text or story. For them, evidence is less important and persuasiveness is measured in terms of consistency with a larger cultural story and resonance with other texts. Because we are more concerned, however interpretively, with an empirical world "out there," object-relations and interpersonal feminists who are social scientists or practicing clinicians must engage directly with psychoanalytic evidence. Contemporary psychoanalysis promises a substantial contribution to object-relations and interpersonal psychoanalytic feminism. Like the schools they draw upon, these theories are insightful about questions of self, other, and (hetero and homo) emotional orientation, but they have downplayed sexuality. Consideration of recent psychoanalytic views about primary femininity and genital awareness—if we can situate these socially and interactively rather than as essentialist, automatically generated dichotomies—might help to incorporate sexuality.

On the other side, psychoanalytic feminism makes important demands upon psychoanalysis and points to areas of potential expansion and revi-

sion. The gender of the analyst is a useful place to begin. As some psychoanalytic writers make clear, findings about male analysands' unconscious
fear of female analysts and inability to develop an erotic transference can
be understood only in a socially and culturally—as well as psychologically—gendered context. In a setting where they are passive and dependent upon a woman or mother figure in a position of power or authority,
reversing the dominant cultural and psychological definition of heterosexuality, men's sexuality freezes or is denied.

Object-relations and interpersonal psychoanalytic feminism also constitutes a basic challenge to and revision of classical psychoanalytic (and
Lacanian feminist) developmental theory and theories of gender identity,
as this feminism removes the centering of the gendered psyche from the
body and drives toward a recentering in the self and self with other,
questioning the extent to which female development, and by implication
women's lives, are embedded in and defined exclusively by sexual difference.

Lacanian feminism poses another kind of challenge, especially to psychoanalytic theories of gender, by offering a persuasive argument that
heterosexual desire is rooted in unequal relations and meanings of gender
and stressing the problematic and conflictual nature of all sexual identity
and desire. The interpretation is taken directly from Freud, but psychoanalysis has tended to call deviant and conflictual sexualities problematic
while seeming to assume that normal heterosexuality is relatively conflict-
and problem-free. Such a normative theory, supplemented by a theory of
perversion, cannot account for major features of heterosexuality, for instance, the pervasive intertwining of sexuality and aggression in men and
of radical gender asymmetries in violent sexual behavior.

I must stress here that the limitations I am discussing are relative, not
absolute. They do not warrant full-scale dismissal of psychoanalysis. Many
psychoanalysts think that women have been severely misunderstood by
their theory and want to claim value for women's traditional role and
physiology. Occasionally they criticize male bias and power in the creation
of theory, and some discuss the just role of anger in feminine emotional
life. But by and large one does not hear much challenge of the division of
gender and parental roles, of normative notions of sexuality, of "normal"
masculinity and femininity. Femininity may be resuscitated and valorized,
but there is little sense that masculinity is problematic. Psychoanalytic
feminism confronts psychoanalysis in all these arenas. (At the same time
psychoanalytic feminism has become so fashionable as to warrant treatment in a *New Yorker* article, and one begins to think that perhaps an
individual psychoanalyst working with troubled patients may be doing
more to change gendered lives than the psychoanalytic feminist and her
elegant interpretation of texts.)[31]

There is a final limitation in *all* the psychoanalytic theories of gender I have discussed: their inattention to, and in some cases inability to conceptualize, gender salience. Feminist theorists have begun to recognize the variable salience of gender in social and cultural life, to see gender as it relates to other identities and situated aspects of social and cultural organization.[32] This is probably true psychologically as well. We should be able to ask when, how, and why gender or sexuality is psychologically invoked, how each becomes relevant, and in relation to what other aspects of psychological and emotional life this happens. Psychoanalytic theories speak in universalist terms of "the girl," "the boy," "the man," "the woman." We need to know whether gender is a continuing, always dominant identity or feature of personality. We need to ask more about characteristics that tend to differentiate the genders but that are not necessarily conceptualized psychologically as a part of gender identity.

Neither psychoanalytic gender theorists nor psychoanalytic feminists discuss gender salience or have much way to conceptualize it. The concept of gender salience is redundant for Lacanian feminists, since sexuality is subjectivity. But interpersonal and object-relations feminists could build gender salience into their theories and haven't. Psychoanalysts across the theoretical spectrum assert that gender, usually as genital awareness, determines identity and psyche, but they do not locate this femininity in a more general or multifaceted sense of self. Gender is certainly part of what is often on people's minds, and it is part of what constructs (and constricts) their life consciously and unconsciously, but it is not all, and it is differentially salient at different times and places. A next step for all psychoanalytic feminists and psychoanalysts who reflect on women and gender will be to build gender salience into theories and practice.

Clinical psychoanalysis has something important to teach *both* psychoanalytic feminists and psychoanalytic theorists of sex and gender about gender salience and variability. Object-relations feminism has been interpreted to mean that the preoedipal mother-daughter relationship is almost all there is to the female psyche; Lacanian feminism seems to claim that the phallus is the phallus is the phallus; primary femininity psychoanalysts imply that the developmental meaning of the female genitals is self-evident. The clinical encounter reminds us forcefully that the symbolizations and transference meanings of relationships and body parts are manifold. It argues that any development and identity builds on multiple internal relationships and interpretations of experience and that no person, symbol, or organ can hold a single and unvarying place in anyone's psyche or symbolic system.

My own tentative view is that a melding of object-relations feminism and recent psychoanalysis might take us in the right direction. Against the essentialism of psychoanalytic gender theory, object-relations feminism enables an understanding of variability and fluidity in gender salience. It sees development as contingent on experience and what one makes of it, and it incorporates an understanding of gender characteristics like the self-in-relation that are not necessarily available as gender conceptions. At the same time, as a feminist theory it remains continuously cognizant of gender hierarchy and relations of inequality, even as it also sees these as multiple and situationally variable. Like clinical psychoanalysis, object-relations theory enables many developmental and psychological stories and leads to a recognition of variation, of ways that identities may or may not be invoked or experienced in different contexts and interpersonal or intrapsychic situations. This could, though it has not yet, enable recognition of historical and cultural specificity in gender psychology. By complement, a psychoanalytic feminist theory of gender must include understanding of sexuality and body experience, and the object-relations and interpersonal theorists have tended to downplay this area, which psychoanalysis has so intricately and intimately studied. Lacanian feminism also reintroduces sexual difference and sexuality, and it reminds us forcefully of another lacuna in the psychoanalytic approach: failure to recognize the intertwining of the psychodynamics of gender, sexuality, and male dominance as a constitutive cultural force. But Lacan puts us in an absolute sexual and subjective world with no room for salience or fluidity. One can only accept or refuse previously given sexual positions that are always and invariably present.

The answer to the question What is the relation between psychoanalytic feminism and the psychoanalytic psychology of women? is, Not much. Such a lack of relation should be of concern. Deeply problematic epistemological, theoretical, and substantive difficulties in professional communication must be dealt with as a preliminary step toward synthesizing or creating an adequate psychoanalytic and feminist understanding of women and men. I have tentatively outlined initial steps in this venture. Psychoanalytic feminism needs to develop an approach to gender that enables understandings of (1) the selves and object relational patterns of women and men; (2) the senses of maleness and femaleness; (3) sexual identities and interpretations of bodily experiences; (4) masculinities and femininities; (5) the fundamental interrelation of the unequal social and cultural organization of gender and its psychodynamics; and of (6) the fact that we are not always and in every instance determined by or calling upon these gendered and sexualized psychological experiences. Gender and sexuality should be seen to be situated in, as they help to create, life in general.

The Mode of
Reproduction
in Anthropology

SYLVIA   J.   YANAGISAKO

AND   JANE   F.   COLLIER

One of the first steps feminist scholars of the second wave took in the 1970s
was to distinguish gender from sex. By differentiating socially and culturally constituted gender differences from biologically given sex differences,
feminist social scientists[1] made explicit the conviction—evident as well in
the writings of feminist historians[2]—that our project consisted of analyzing gender rather than sex. This move held out the promise of enabling an
analysis of male privilege as the product of historically and culturally
constituted systems of gender inequality, not as the natural outcome of
biological differences between males and females.

In this essay we argue that the time has come to abandon the distinction
between sex and gender—at least as it is currently conceptualized. As
enabling as this distinction was in an earlier phase of feminist scholarship,
it has now become constraining. At a time when feminist scientists and
philosophers of science[3] are showing us that biologists, like the rest of us,
can apprehend the world only through cultural lenses, the distinction
between sex and gender is impeding our realization of the full implications

We would like to thank Jane Atkinson, Donald Donham, Sherry Ortner, Roger Rouse,
David Schneider, Judith Shapiro, Anna Tsing, and Harriet Whitehead for their helpful
comments and suggestions about earlier versions of our critique of analytical dichotomies. Deborah L. Rhode offered helpful advice for revising the present essay.

"The Mode of Reproduction in Anthropology" is a slightly modified and shortened
version of the authors' article "Toward a Unified Analysis of Gender and Kinship," in
Gender and Kinship, edited by Jane Fishburne Collier and Sylvia Yanagisako. Reprinted
with the permission of the publishers, Stanford University Press. © 1987 by the Board of
Trustees of the Leland Stanford Junior University.

of these apprehensions. Having conceded sex differences to biology in the interest of establishing our scholastic authority over socially and culturally constituted gender differences, we have limited our project and legitimized assumptions about sexual difference that return to haunt our theories of gender.

PROBLEMS WITH ANALYTICAL DICHOTOMIES IN THE STUDY OF GENDER

The core dichotomies used by anthropologists and other feminist scholars to analyze gender are nature/culture,[4] domestic/public,[5] and reproduction/production.[6] Each has been said to structure relations between women and men everywhere and, consequently, to offer a universal explanation of gender inequality. The opposition between the "symbolic" and the "practical"—a descendant of Emile Durkheim's distinction between the sacred and the profane—has also crept into attempts to understand the different interests of women and men through "practice theory."[7] Finally, essentialist dichotomies between women's and men's consciousnesses have been formulated by feminist anthropologists[8] who were seeking to correct the androcentric bias in ethnographic accounts.[9]

NATURE/CULTURE AND DOMESTIC/PUBLIC

In 1974 the nature/culture opposition and the domestic/public opposition were offered by the cultural anthropologists Sherry Ortner[10] and Michelle Rosaldo,[11] respectively, as explanations of a universal sexual asymmetry. Since then both oppositions have been widely utilized in the social sciences and humanities. At the same time, they have provoked sharp criticism.

Ortner's 1974 hypothesis that the symbolic association of a less valued "nature" with females and of a more highly valued, transcendent "culture" with males is the basis for the universal devaluation of females has been most persuasively challenged in Carol MacCormack and Marilyn Strathern's book *Nature, Culture, and Gender.*[12] In their introduction to this volume of edited papers, MacCormack and Strathern pose the critical question: when can we usefully translate a symbolic opposition found in another culture into one found in ours? Together the case studies in their volume demonstrate that our nature/culture opposition does not do justice to the range of configurations of gender meanings found in other societies. Strathern, for example, builds a convincing case that the Hagen opposition between "mbo" and "rømi" is not homologous to the nature/culture opposition in our culture but constitutes an opposition with both different symbolic meaning and social consequences.[13] The strength of Strathern's argument rests as much on her explication of *our* conception of the nature/culture dichotomy as on Hagen conceptions. Maurice and Jean Bloch also explore our conception of the nature/culture dichotomy in an essay analyzing historical changes in the usage of *nature* in eighteenth-century France.[14] They demonstrate that we cannot presume that the terms we use in discourse about our culture will provide a straightforward, unambiguous analytical focus for analyzing other cultures or historical periods.

While the nature/culture opposition draws on a Lévi-Straussian symbolic-structuralist perspective, the domestic/public opposition is more in line with a structural-functionalist perspective of the sort that has prevailed in anthropological studies of kinship. Rosaldo first construed the domestic/public opposition as the "basis of a structural framework" necessary to explain the general identification of women with domestic life and men with public life and the consequent universal cross-cultural asymmetry in the evaluation of the sexes. At the core of this identification of women with devalued domestic life lay their role as mothers. "Women become absorbed primarily in domestic activities because of their role as mothers. Their economic and political activities are constrained by the responsibilities of childcare and the focus of their emotions and attentions is particularistic and directed toward children and the home."[15]

Rosaldo later acknowledged the problematic theoretical implications of the domestic/public opposition and came to share Rayna Reiter's[16] view of the domestic/public opposition as an ideological product of our society and a legacy of our Victorian heritage, which "cast the sexes in dichotomous and contrastive terms."[17] As critics of this opposition have pointed out, attempts to salvage it cannot escape from the self-defeating circularity inherent in its initial formulation.[18] The claim that women become absorbed in constraining and devalued domestic activities because of their role as mothers is tautological given the definition of "domestic" as "those minimal institutions and modes of activity that are organized immediately around one or more mothers and their children."[19]

REPRODUCTION/PRODUCTION

In the last decade another analytical dichotomy has gained prominence in the social science literature on gender. Several writers attempting to develop a Marxist theory of gender while bringing a feminist perspective to Marxist theory have argued for the need to develop a theory of relations of reproduction.[20] Olivia Harris and Kate Young note that the proliferation of studies centered on the concept of reproduction in Marxist literature has emerged not only from a feminist concern with the status of women, but among other things from the concern of some Marxists to "break conclusively with economistic versions of a Marxism which places too great an emphasis on the forces of production."[21]

These writers take as their starting point Friedrich Engels' formulation of the distinction between reproduction and production. In contrast to

Karl Marx, who used these terms to describe a unitary social process,[22] Engels tended to treat production and reproduction as two distinct, although coordinated, aspects of the process of social production: "This, again, is of a twofold character: on the one side, the production of the means of existence, of food, clothing and shelter and the tools necessary for that reproduction; on the other side, the production of human beings themselves, the propagation of the species."[23]

It is not surprising that Engels' formulation would receive so much attention from Marxist-feminist social scientists, as it is one of the few early Marxist statements offering an explicit approach to gender. Much of the literature on the subject of women and capitalist development employs Engels' distinction. In their critique of Ester Boserup's neoclassical comparative study of the role of women in economic development,[24] the economists Lourdes Beneria and Gita Sen argue that scholars should attend to the role of reproduction in determining women's position in society.[25] They rightly fault Boserup for her distinction between "economic activity" and "domestic work," which leads her to exclude such activities as food processing—largely a female activity—from her description of economic activity in agricultural societies.

The concept of reproduction used by Beneria and Sen, however, proves more a liability than an asset. They define reproduction as including not only biological reproduction and daily maintenance of the labor force, but also social reproduction, the perpetuation of social systems.[26] Yet in their analysis of the ways in which the status of women has changed with economic transformations, reproduction is reduced to "domestic work." Accordingly, when they discuss industrial society, they equate "housework" with reproductive work[27] and assume the household is the focal point of all sorts of reproduction.[28]

The social historians Louise Tilly and Joan Scott employ a similar distinction in their history of women's work in industrializing England and France. For them reproduction is by definition a gendered category: "Reproduction activity is used here as a shorthand for the whole set of women's household activities: childbearing, child rearing, and day-to-day management of the consumption and production of services for household members."[29] This unfortunate equation of reproductive activity with *women*'s household activities excludes anything men do from the category of reproductive activity and is blind to men's contribution to "childbearing, child rearing, and day-to-day management of the consumption and production of services for household members." This makes it impossible for Tilly and Scott to attain their goal of writing a history of the changing relationship between the reproductive work of women and men, for there can be no such history of change when, by their definition, men do not engage in reproductive work.

The best attempt to clarify the confusion surrounding usages of the term *reproduction* and its relation to production is Harris and Young's comprehensive review of the concept. They propose to salvage it by isolating different meanings of the concept, which they see as located at "different levels of abstraction and generality" and which "entail different types of causality and different levels of determination."

Here we have isolated three senses of the concept of reproduction for discussion which seem to us to cover the major uses of the term and to illustrate the confusion that has resulted from their conflation. We feel it is necessary to distinguish social reproduction, that is, the overall reproduction of a particular social formation from the reproduction of labour itself; and further to distinguish the latter from the specific forms of biological reproduction.[30]

By teasing apart these different meanings of reproduction, Harris and Young do an excellent job of displaying the density and complexity of the concept. Yet their attempt to isolate these meanings into analytically useful levels generates new problems. For example, if we try to distinguish the reproduction of labor from social reproduction—that is, the overall reproduction of a particular social formation—we quickly run into problems. Harris and Young admit that "to talk of the reproduction of labour is in itself perhaps too limited; it would be more accurate to talk of the reproduction of adequate bearers of specific social relationships, since we also wish to include under this category classes of non-labourers."[31] Once the reproduction of labor slips into the reproduction of "adequate bearers of specific social relations"—which presumably includes such social categories as males and females as well as serfs and capitalists—it becomes indistinguishable from the process of social reproduction. If capitalists are being reproduced, then relations of capital must be simultaneously reproduced just as, if males and females are being reproduced, then gender relations must be reproduced.

Most important for our argument here is the fact that all the authors who draw upon Engels' distinction between production and reproduction locate the construction of gender relations and consequently women's subordination in the reproductive process. The productive process, regardless of the mode of production it comprises, is conceptualized as theoretically independent of gender considerations.

PRACTICAL/SYMBOLIC

Feminist scholars trying to understand how systems of gender inequality are reproduced and transformed have contributed to the development of a "practice approach" in anthropology.[32] Originally developed by Pierre Bourdieu in opposition to structuralism and structural-functionalism,[33] practice theory is neither a theory nor a method, but rather a key symbol "in the name of which a variety of theories and methods are being developed."[34] A practice approach focuses on the ways in which women and men, through their everyday practices, reproduce or transform the social systems of domination that constrain their lives.

The focus on agency, strategy, and the interests of individuals inherent in practice approaches can easily lead, however, to an implicit analytical opposition between the "practical" and the "symbolic" which brings with it an implicit opposition of gender. Bourdieu, for example, in discussing marriage strategies among the Kabyle of North Africa, implies that women seek "practical" advantage while men pursue "symbolic" goals. Because women are excluded from "representational kinship," they are "thrown back on to . . . practical uses of kinship, investing more economic realism (in the narrow sense) than the men in the search for a partner for their sons or daughters."[35] Like the poor,[36] women are "less sensitive to symbolic profits and freer to pursue material profits."[37] Bourdieu's comments about Kabyle women can too easily imply that women operate outside of and apart from symbolic systems.

The implication that women do so operate stems from the word *symbol,* whose use conjures up a misleading opposition with the nonsymbolic. One dictionary, for example, defines a *symbol* as "something that stands for or represents another thing,"[38] which makes nonsymbols things that do not stand for or represent something other than themselves. If symbols require interpretation, nonsymbols are—by this logic—transparent. They are simply what they are.

The conceptual opposition between symbols and nonsymbols leads to two analytic impasses. First, when social scientists define certain actions as symbolic, they risk setting themselves the task of ferreting out the "true meaning" of these actions—a task that too often results in reducing symbolic action to familiar motivations, such as self-interest or the oedipus complex. Second and more important for our argument, social scientists risk presuming that actions not labeled symbolic have obvious—that is, pragmatic and equally familiar—aims. Rosaldo has observed that by "separating the symbolic from the everyday, anthropologists quickly come upon such "universal" facts as correspond to their assumptions, and fail to see that common discourse as well as the more spectacular feats of poets and religious men requires an interpretive account."[39] So Kabyle women who pursue "practical" aims appear to operate outside symbolic systems of meaning. And many anthropologists continue to view the sexual division of labor in society rather as an extension of "biological facts" that set up functional prerequisites than as an aspect of a symbolically mediated system of social identities.

Attempts to differentiate actions into the "symbolic" and the "practical" have an unfortunate tendency to reproduce Durkheim's sacred/profane opposition,[40] an opposition that is inherently gendered. It is not merely that Durkheim overlooked women's participation in rituals and treated women's tasks as fulfilling biological rather than social needs. By defining as sacred those practices that represented and reproduced certain kinds of collectivities—such as moieties, tribes, and whole nations—Durkheim privileged male domains of action. A central dimension of male dominance in most, if not all, societies is men's authority to define their actions and the social relations they organize as constructing culturally valued collectivities. Durkheim's concern with "official" collective action led him to slight the practices of women and children and to relegate them to the domain of the nonsymbolic. It is an irony of intellectual history that practice theory, whose developers deliberately set out to analyze everyday practices and not the rituals that concerned Durkheim and his followers, should have led to labeling only some actions as symbolic, thus reproducing the sacred/profane opposition.

In the end, the practical/symbolic opposition is a variant of the nature/culture opposition. Just as "nature" is always culturally defined and therefore variable across time and space, so the "practical" is always symbolically constructed. The "practical" goals that women pursue when they seek to destroy the collectivities that men create and valorize, such as patrilineages or extended households, are as motivated by ideological representations of collectivities—such as harmonious families—as are the "symbolic" goals of men.

WOMEN'S CONSCIOUSNESS/ MEN'S CONSCIOUSNESS

One of the first changes called for by feminist scholars in the social sciences was the correction of androcentric views that had paid little attention not only to women's activities and roles but also to their views of social relationships and cultural practices. Within anthropology this feminist challenge was useful for calling into question seemingly natural social units like the "families" that anthropologists continued to discover everywhere as long as they confounded genealogically defined relationships with particular kinds of culturally meaningful social relationships.[41] By questioning the assumed unity of families, households, and other sorts of domestic groups, feminist anthropologists revealed the diversity and sometimes conflicts of views, interests, and strategies among members of supposedly solidary groups, opening the way to a richer understanding of the dynamics of these groups and of their interaction with other social units.[42]

At the same time, feminist anthropologists have come to realize that correcting the androcentrism of the past without reproducing its conceptual error in inverted form requires considerable rethinking of our notions of culture and ideology. Unlike scholars in some disciplines who have borrowed from Carol Gilligan[43] the idea of a "woman's voice," anthropologists appear to have left behind naive claims that female field-workers intuitively understand the subjective experience of their female informants because of their sex. Most anthropologists have also rejected claims for a universal "woman's point of view" or a universal "womanhood."[44] Anthropologists do not even assume a unitary woman's point of view *within* one society that cuts across significant differences in, for example, age, household position, or social class.

Despite this skepticism about the existence of a unitary woman's point of view in any society, anthropologists appear to have been less critical of the notion of a unitary "man's point of view."[45] Because they are socially dominant over women, it is tempting to treat the cultural system of a society as a product of men's values and beliefs and to assume that it is shared by most if not all of them. This assumption is implicit in the concept of a "male prestige system," which Sherry Ortner and Harriet Whitehead have proposed for understanding the organization of gender in any society: "The cultural construction of sex and gender tends everywhere to be stamped by the prestige considerations of socially dominant male actors."[46] And: "Women's perspectives are to a great extent constrained and conditioned by the dominant ideology. The analysis of the dominant ideology must thus precede, or at least encompass, the analysis of the perspective of women."[47]

In the quotations above, Ortner and Whitehead assume that men's perspectives are not also constrained and conditioned by the dominant ideology. Instead ideology and the perspectives of social actors are conflated. Even in those hypothetical cases where men as a whole are socially dominant over women as a whole and share the same values, beliefs, and goals, however, it seems a mistake to construe men's perspective as encompassing the larger cultural system more than women's perspective does. Like women's views, men's views are constrained and conditioned by the form of their relations with others. The men and women in a particular society may construe women's ideas and experience as more restricted than those of men,[48] and this may be reflected in the appearance that men have knowledge of events and things that women do not. But this appearance does not justify the analytical incorporation of women's views into a supposedly more inclusive male ideology. The task should be to make analytically apparent the social and cultural processes that create such appearances.

The concept of male prestige system rests on an implicit domestic/public analytic dichotomy. Because it posits an encompassing male sphere and an encompassed female one, it assumes that "domestic life" is "insulated from the wider social sphere" (although its degree of insulation may vary) and that "domestic life" is concerned with "gender relations" and "child socialization." In writing about social change, for example, Ortner observes, "To the degree that domestic life is insulated from the wider social sphere . . . , important practices—of gender relations and child socialization—remain relatively untouched."[49]

The reemergence of a form of the domestic/public dichotomy in the concept of male prestige systems brings us full circle and poses—in a particularly dramatic way—the question Why do feminist scholars keep reinventing this dichotomy or transformations of it like reproduction/production and practical/symbolic? If (as we have argued) these oppositions presume the difference we should be trying to explain, why do we find them so compelling? Why do they seem, as Rosaldo claimed even when she argued against using domestic/public as an analytic device, so telling?[50]

We suggest that the answer lies in our own cultural conception of natural sex differences. Although we claim to analyze socially and culturally constructed systems of *gender,* unexamined assumptions about biological sex differences pervade our analytical concepts. The analytical dichotomies discussed here are ultimately transformations of one another because they are all variations on the same theme.

GENDER AND THE "BIOLOGICAL FACTS" OF SEXUAL REPRODUCTION

The grounding of our understanding of gender in ideas about biological sex is reflected in Judith Shapiro's discussion of the distinction between sex and gender that has become a convention in feminist scholarship. She observes that the terms *sex* and *gender*

> serve a useful analytic purpose in contrasting a set of biological facts with a set of cultural facts. Were I to be scrupulous in my use of terms, I would use the term "sex" only when I was speaking of biological differences between males and females, and use "gender" whenever I was referring to the social, cultural, psychological constructs that are *imposed upon these biological differences.* . . . gender . . . designates a set of categories to which we can give the same label crosslinguistically, or crossculturally, because they have *some connection to sex differences.* These categories are, however, conventional or arbitrary insofar as they are not reducible to or directly derivative of natural, biological facts; they vary from one language to another, one culture to another, in the way in which they order experience and action.[51]

Because gender is defined as having "some connection to sex differences," assumptions about biological differences between males and females pervade the analytic concepts we use to study the cultural construction of gender relations. And to the degree that feminist scholars studying gender have left sex differences to the biologists, they have failed to notice that our understanding of "biological sex differences" is also socially constructed.

According to our culture, the biological difference between men and women is rooted in their different roles in sexual procreation. Anthropologists studying kinship in other societies do not ask what relationships are involved in the reproduction of humans in particular societies. They assume that humans are reproduced through sexual intercourse and its physiological consequences: pregnancy, parturition, and perhaps lactation. Nor have anthropologists studying gender asked what differentiates females from males. They have simply assumed that the sexes are differentiated by their biologically different roles in sexual reproduction.

Like anthropologists studying kinship who assume that such specific social consequences as the family flow from the biological processes of reproduction, feminist anthropologists studying gender have assumed that specific social consequences follow from the fact that women "bear" the children. For example, the assumption that women *bear* the greater burden and responsibility for human reproduction pervades gender studies, in particular those works employing a reproduction/production distinction. This notion is almost invariably a metaphorical extension of emphasizing the fact that women *bear* children. It is not a conclusion based on systematic comparison of the contributions of men and women to human reproduction in particular societies.

Notions about the social consequences of biological reproduction underlie all these analytic dichotomies and render them invalid for explaining the social construction of gender. Because cultural focus on biological procreation casts women as "bearing" the children, while men are "free" from further participation in reproduction after the moment of coitus, the dichotomies already encode notions of female constraint and male privilege. The devaluation of "nature" and women's association with it accompany the idea that men are "free" after coitus but that women must bear the "natural" consequences of pregnancy, parturition, and lactation. The higher value of the "public" sphere is subsumed beforehand in ideas about the socially constraining effects of childbearing.

The distressing tendency to equate reproduction with women's household activities derives from the symbolically meaningful and institutionally experienced opposition that our culture draws between the production of people and the production of things. When Harris and Young[52] consider the social reproduction of a particular social formation—which in Marxist terms entails the reproduction of a particular mode of production—they do not see gender as relevant because, although both women and men are involved in production, they do not appear to be involved as "males" and "females." Their sexual attributes do not appear to be crucial in structuring their relations. Yet Harris and Young see women as "females" and men as "males" when they are involved in the reproduction of labor, because in our cultural model the production of people is thought to occur through processes of sexual procreation. Since women "bear" the children while men are "free" after coitus, analyses of "reproduction" tend to degenerate into studies of women's activities.

The same ideas underlie the tendency to see women as engaged in practical activities while men pursue symbolic goals. Durkheim explicitly equated women with the profane because of their supposed involvement in the natural processes of breeding and feeding.[53] Men's supposed freedom from such natural processes allows them to focus on constructing symbolic orders—to develop "male prestige systems."

Attempts to separate the study of gender from the biological facts to which gender differences are seen to be universally connected seems doomed to fail, because such attempts start from a definition of their subject matter that is rooted in those biological facts. It is impossible to know what gender would mean if it were entirely disconnected from sex and biological reproduction. We have no choice but to begin our investigations of others with our own concepts. But we can unpack the cultural assumptions, embodied in our concepts, that limit our capacity to understand social systems informed by other cultural assumptions.[54]

BEYOND REPRODUCTION

We do not doubt that men and women are different any more than we doubt that individuals differ, generations differ, and societies differ. But we question whether the difference in reproductive function that our culture defines as the universal basis of the relations between males and females constitutes the structural basis of gender relations in other societies and even in our own. Like kinship studies, gender studies have foundered on the unquestioned assumption that the biological difference in the functions of females and males in human sexual reproduction lies at the core of the cultural organization of women's and men's relations. Only by calling this assumption into question can we discover how cultures construct the relations between women and men. And we can ask a central question: how has our culture come to focus on coitus and parturition as the moments that above all others constitute maleness, femaleness, and human reproduction?

Our realization that the model of sexual reproduction and sexual difference so widely used is a particular mode of thinking about relations between people enables us to question the "biological facts" of sex. In dismantling the notion that sex is to gender as biology is to culture, we enlarge our analytical project to encompass the symbolic and social processes by which sex as a system of difference is itself culturally constructed.

PART FOUR

Feminist Ethical and Political Theory

Thinking like
a Woman

SUSAN MOLLER OKIN

An influential claim in recent moral development literature is that women's moral thinking tends to differ significantly from men's. Such a claim is not new. For thousands of years—and long before the birth of liberal individualism—male political theorists have asserted that women are potentially subversive of the public interest and the common good. Several different, though related, explanations have been given for these allegations. One charge against women is that they are the source of sexual disorder unless strictly secluded, controlled, in some cases even segregated almost entirely from men.[1] In addition, as far back as classical Greece, women were perceived as subversive of the public good because of their orientation toward the sphere of private life and their feelings for those close to them—especially their families. Plato, though well known by now to feminists for his unusual insights about the malleability of female nature, clearly thought nonetheless that women as members of private families constituted a particular threat to the pursuit of the general welfare. In the ideal state he depicts in the *Republic,* where the family is abolished, women are included within the philosophic ruling elite. But once the ideal community begins to degenerate and women become private wives again, Plato regards them as a significant source of further corruption. He gives two reasons. First, women are depicted as a passive focus for the men's growing acquisitive impulses.[2] But as well as this, women are portrayed as an active influence in the turning away from the public good to private acquisitiveness. Plato alleges in a revealing passage that young men would be led astray by their mothers' complaints about their husbands' lack of concern for wealth and prestige. Such young men would come to prize

I wish to acknowledge the helpful critical comments of Carol Gilligan, Robert O. Keohane, Nona Plessner Lyons, Deborah L. Rhode, Nancy Rosenblum, and Iris Young on an earlier version of this paper. Thanks to Elaine Herrmann for typing the manuscript and to Elizabeth Wingrove for checking references.

personal honor and wealth over the publicly oriented values held by their more rational fathers.[3] In the *Laws,* too, where no attempt is made to abolish private property or the family, the female sex is described as "disordered" and as "generally predisposed by its weakness to undue secrecy and craft."[4] Clearly Plato perceives the influence of women's private orientation as something that must be constantly resisted.

Plato's questioning of the necessity for and sharpness of the public/private division of human life is rare among political philosophers. Turning to more recent thinkers, we find that the necessity for the two distinct spheres is either assumed or confirmed.[5] Hegel's is the modern archetype of the claim that women's private family orientation is both natural and socially necessary but at the same time renders them potentially subversive of the needs of the state.[6] The family, according to him, being characterized by feeling, altruism, and particularity, is ruled by divine law, with woman as its guardian not by accident or by choice but by nature.[7] The state, built on reason and universality, is ruled by human law, with man as its guardian. While the two types of law are connected, and neither the family nor the larger community is complete without the other, only the man inhabits both realms and "is sent out by the Spirit of the Family into the community in which he finds his self-conscious being."[8] Whereas men can live in both spheres and, in addition to their public, rational role, are able to live "a subjective ethical life on the plane of feeling" within their families, women have only the qualities required of the private sphere: "to be imbued with family piety is [their] ethical frame of mind."[9]

So women do not and cannot (according to Hegel) live the complete ethical life available to male citizens. And knowing his Greek tragedy very well, Hegel was well aware of the potential conflicts between the needs and interests of individual families and those of the whole community. Thus he perceived women's very feelings for and dedication to the particular world of their families as rendering them a threat to the community and its reason-based human law:

> Since the community only gets an existence through its interference with the happiness of the Family, . . . it creates for itself in what it suppresses and what is at the same time essential to it an internal enemy—womankind in general. Womankind—the everlasting irony [in the life] of the community—changes by intrigue the universal end of the government into a private end, transforms its universal activity into a work of some particular individual, and perverts the universal property of the State into a possession and ornament for the Family.[10]

As this revealing passage continues, Hegel speaks not only of woman's "ridiculing" the mature wisdom that is indifferent to private enjoyments and thinks only of the universal, but of her encouraging her children to do likewise. He speaks of her persistence in stressing the particular individuality of those close to her, an attitude that must be suppressed if the community is to be maintained.[11]

Not surprisingly, Hegel regards women and political power as incompatible. In plainer language than usual, he says: "When women hold the helm of government, the state is at once in jeopardy, because women regulate their actions not by the demands of universality but by arbitrary inclinations and opinions."[12] The very qualities that Hegel requires of woman if she is to be fit for her naturally predestined and immensely important role—her being guided by her feelings toward the preservation and good of the particular members of her family—are those that also make him see her as a threat to the larger community. Her particularistic altruism, her guidance by her feelings, her inability to reason in an abstract and universal way, all make her a good wife and mother but unfit her for participation as a citizen in the public realm of law and justice.

This way of thinking about women's moral proclivities recurs frequently in political theories. Bentham, for example, a contemporary of Hegel's who thought very differently from him about many things, expressed similar views about women. Though he at times argued for women's suffrage, he at other times argued against all political participation by women. His reasons were the same: men's judgment is based on reason, but women's is based on sympathy and feelings, especially for the members of their families; therefore they cannot be expected to uphold the principle of utility, the consideration for the happiness and suffering of all on which all good government and law must be built. While admirably suiting them for dedication to their families, their essential incapacity to universalize their moral judgments makes them a subversive force in the political arena.[13]

In the twentieth century, we find that Freud is clearly of this party. He proclaimed that "the first requisite of civilization is . . . that of justice—that is, the assurance that a law once made will not be broken in favour of an individual."[14] Justice demands that no one escape the restrictions on individual liberty that civilization requires. But love, except that of a few saintlike people who can universalize it, by its nature involves discrimination. Love and the institution that embodies it, the family, conflict with the interests of civilization. "The more closely the members of a family are attached to one another, the more often do they tend to cut themselves off from others, and the more difficult it is for them to enter into the wider circle of life." Predictably, just as for Plato, Hegel, Bentham, and others I have not mentioned, woman immediately becomes identified as the special guardian of love and the special enemy of justice. Women, "represent[ing] the interests of the family and of sexual life" and "little capable" of "instinctual sublimations," "soon come into opposition to civilization and display their retarding and restraining influence."[15] Because men become increasingly bound up with the demands of civilized life, women's resentment of and hostility towards it can only increase.

Unlike earlier theorists, Freud undertook to give a specific explanation of exactly how it is that women come to have the type of moral disposition that makes them so well suited to family life but so dangerous to "civilized" society, especially if they are to have any influence outside the private sphere. The difference in moral development of the sexes is explained, Freud argues, by their different passages through the oedipus complex. Whereas the male's fear of castration compels him to give up his oedipal attachment and to assimilate his father's superego, the female, discovering that she is already castrated, never overcomes her oedipus complex with the completeness that the male does. Thus Freud writes, though he says it is with hesitancy that he expresses it:

> I cannot evade the notion . . . that for women the level of what is ethically normal is different from what it is in man. Their super-ego is never so inexorable, so impersonal, so independent of its emotional origins as we require it to be in men. Character-traits which critics of every epoch have brought up against women—that they show less sense of justice than men, that they are less ready to submit to the great exigencies of life, that they are more often influenced in their judgments by feelings of affection and hostility—all these would be amply accounted for by the modification in the formation of their super-ego which we have inferred above.[16]

Apart from Freud, with his psychoanalytic case materials, the theorists discussed so far relied for evidence on their own informal observations and contemporary opinion. Only Plato in the *Republic,* with his complete abolition of the private realm, could envisage altering the conditions that led to what all regarded as women's deficient moral thought and functioning. For the others the attenuation of women's moral perspective was not really an issue. On the one hand they did not envisage the entry of women as serious participants in the political realm, and on the other hand they regarded women's moral peculiarities as functional for the private life of the patriarchal family, though not for political life. They were neither concerned with the deficiencies of their evidence nor interested in trying to separate out the specific and cultural—the *alterable* causes of women's allegedly different moral thinking—from the biological and seemingly inalterable ones.

Neither the virtual absence of evidence nor the lack of need to consider women as citizens applies today. The latest in the long heritage of discoverers and judges of women's moral thinking are some of the scholars of moral development of the Kohlberg school. In Kohlberg's fundamental schema he has distilled moral development into six hierarchically ordered stages, each of which is regarded as a Weberian ideal type.[17] At some risk of oversimplification, the stages can be characterized as follows, starting with the lowest. The first considers the avoidance of punishment. The second is characterized by the notion "I'll scratch your back if you'll scratch mine." Of the third, which is of particular significance here because Kohlberg and others have found that many more adult women than men remain at this stage, he says:

> Good behavior is that which pleases or helps others and is approved by them. There is much conformity to stereotypical images of what is majority or "natural" behavior. Behavior is frequently judged by intention—the judgment "he means well" becomes important for the first time. One earns approval by being "nice."[18]

The fourth stage—"law and order"—is oriented toward obeying the laws and other moral rules of one's given social order and respecting established authority. The fifth, while still valuing legalism, emphasizes the possibility of changing the law so as to make it conform better to social utility and individual rights, and is concerned with the formulation of procedural rules for reaching consensus on such matters. At the sixth and highest stage, "Right is defined by the decision of conscience in accord with self-chosen ethical principles appealing to logical comprehensiveness, universality, and consistency. At heart, these are universal principles of justice, of the reciprocity and equality of human rights, and of respect for the dignity of human beings as individuals."[19]

Stage 1 is characteristic of early childhood, and Stage 6 is very rare even among adults. A clear Stage 6 has been found by Kohlberg in only 4 percent of the college educated. A key concept necessary for progress, according to this developmental system, is what Kohlberg calls "reversibility" or sometimes "moral musical chairs." This means the ability to reason to a moral conclusion that holds no matter which person's position one assumes in the moral dilemma. At Stage 6, one is able to abstract totally in one's reasoning from any particular role in the dilemma. One of the reasons for Stage 3's low status on the Kohlberg scale is that the subject who remains at this level is perceived as empathizing only with others to whom he or she is personally attached.[20]

Kohlberg's moral development scale is, to say the least, not philosophically neutral, and it has been criticized on this account. He has recently undertaken to defend it on philosophical grounds.[21] But leaving this aside, there is another problem that has appeared in his system, though for a long time he paid little attention to it: women frequently failed to reach its higher stages. The original Kohlberg studies were all done, and the model developed, from an all-male population, as Gilligan and others have emphasized.[22] When women were included in subsequent Kohlbergian studies, some of the results were striking. At high school age about the same number of boys and girls were found to be at Stage 3, but a study of a college-age population found about twice as large a percentage of Stage 3 girls as boys, with the majority of girls at Stage 3. And a study of well-to-do parents of teenage children found about four times as many women as men at Stage 3. Kohlberg, assuming that this difference is due to the adult sex roles of the respondents, surmised on the basis of these findings that adult moral stabilization is a matter of "socialization," not "development." He concluded that "Stage 3 personal concordance morality is a functional morality for housewives and mothers; it is not for businessmen and professionals."[23]

But what of women as citizens? The most surprising thing about Kohlberg's reaction to women's supposed moral deficiency is that, finding it functional for family life, he pays no further attention to it. Unlike the earlier theorists who came to similar conclusions about women, however, he cannot just ignore the fact that women appear to lack what he regards as the essential characteristics of good citizenship. For in their time, women had little or no political influence. But in our society women, though noticeably sparse among the ranks of the most powerful, do compose, for example, approximately half of the eligible voting population and of those liable for jury duty. And since Kohlberg argues that our society is progressing toward the highest and most liberal stages of moral reasoning,[24] it seems strange that he does not concern himself with the half of the adult population that seems to constitute something of an obstacle in the way of such progress, being socialized for a sex role that requires a stage of moral thinking that men pass through or bypass in late childhood. In response to the challenge of Carol Gilligan, who argues that women's moral thinking— focused more on relationships and responsibilities than on individual rights—is not inferior to, but merely different from, Kohlberg's highest stages, he responds that, while perhaps an even higher level of ethics might be developed, encompassing both the ethic of justice and the ethic of love, "Such an ethic must still rely on Stage 6 fairness principles to resolve justice problems."[25] According to Kohlberg, whatever concessions he may make to the different style of moral thinking that is more typically female, it cannot substitute for justice, which is essential to the operation of an ethical society. Yet he does not seem concerned that, according to the findings of many of those applying his scale, women and justice do not mix.

What, then, are the common threads that run through all these pronouncements on women's moral and political thinking? Women are supposedly less capable than men—whether because of their "nature" or their social role—of putting reason above feelings and of abstracting from their own particular context, concerns, and loved ones to the greater good of the community. They are more liable to act in order to please those close to them and to gain their approval. They are supposedly either unsuited or less suited than men for the impartiality that is intrinsic to that first of political virtues—justice.

Turning to the question of how feminists have reacted to these characterizations of women, we find that we differ among ourselves on this matter as on many others. First, feminists differ both in the extent to which we concede any truth to the notion that men and women think differently about moral and political issues and about the nature of any such differences. To some of us it has been surprising that feminists have readily granted *any* validity to beliefs that have been employed so pervasively to deny women the rights of citizenship. Second, we differ profoundly in our agreement or disagreement with the hierarchical ordering of allegedly "male" and "female" types of thinking. Third, we differ in our views as to what any differences that exist might be due to. And fourth, depending at least in part on our answers to these three parts of the issue, we differ in our prescriptions for social changes. The several dimensions along which we differ yield many permutations, and therefore many positions that can be held. Many of these different positions have already been argued. There are so many permutations that one risks misclassification even in trying to identify a few of the major feminist positions. I will try to do so all the same, beginning with what I regard as some extreme feminist positions on the subject of men's and women's thinking and then turning to some more moderate ones.

Some feminists, not disputing that women as they are in patriarchal society think differently from men about important moral and social questions, have also shared with the theorists discussed above the judgment that the male model is the paradigm for human thought. Attributing what they regard as women's failings to the constraints of their private, narrow, and concrete existence, feminists of this kind have sought to free women— or at least some women—from those constraints. John Stuart Mill and Simone de Beauvoir present good examples of this vision of women's liberation.[26] While such feminists view women in their current state as intellectually limited, overemotional, and partial in their perspective, they attribute these characteristics to the subordination of women to the needs and interests of men. For most women as they actually were, at their respective times of writing, neither Mill nor de Beauvoir has much good to say. Though he insists on complete agnosticism as far as "women's nature" is concerned, Mill says about actual contemporary women: "I am afraid it must be said, that disinterestedness in the general conduct of life—the devotion of the energies to purposes which hold out no promise of private advantages to the family—is very seldom encouraged or supported by women's influence. . . . The consequence is that women's influence is often anything but favourable to public virtue."[27] De Beauvoir echoes this in her judgments—pervasive in *The Second Sex*—that women's passivity, inability to reason properly, and narrowness of vision render them a bad influence in the larger scheme of things.[28] She does not seem to find anything valuable in women's traditional life experiences. She has spoken much more recently of her luck in having "escaped" the "bondages" of matrimony and domesticity, and she makes it clear that she thinks a full and happy life can be lived without them, but not without the traditionally male experiences of the public sphere. She talks of "a certain number of women who can achieve full lives without submitting to women's limitations."[29] As this suggests, de Beauvoir is like Mill in that neither gives much thought to how most women might be enabled to enter the public realm. But both are certain that the only road to liberation for women is to join the world of men and to adopt their thought patterns. The foremost goal of their feminism, then, is for *some* women to be able to avoid the stunted and immanent realm of motherhood and the household. They should be able to live as men do, independent and individual, in the previously male— and presumably always predominantly male—world of reason and transcendence. For such feminists, especially de Beauvoir, the greatest intellectual compliment that could be given a woman would be "She thinks like a man."

For others the same assertion would be the greatest of insults. At this other extreme, partly in reaction to the above position, are some contemporary French feminists and such Anglo-American feminists as Mary Daly, Susan Griffin, and Mary O'Brien, who are close to them in some ways.[30] The French feminists I have in mind do not disagree with de Beauvoir or Mill about existing differences in the thinking of the two sexes—situating men at the abstract, rational, objective end of the scale and women at the concrete, emotional, subjective end—but they differ strongly about everything else involved. First, they regard women's thinking as decidedly superior and more human, and they blame the dominance of men's thinking for the present mess that the world is in, including the ecological crisis and the threat of nuclear extinction. Second, they assert that the reason the two sexes think differently is at least primarily because they are biologically distinct, because of the different construction of their bodies. Third, they see the replacement of male thinking by female thinking as the world's only hope for survival.

Although others concur in this position, the work of certain French feminists contains the clearest expression of it, perhaps because of their cultural context. They seem to be reacting against both French existentialist philosophy in general and de Beauvoir's existentialist feminism in particular. In the writings of Hélène Cixous, Xavière Gauthier, Claudine Herrmann, Luce Irigaray, Annie Leclerk and some others—in spite of differences among them—the message is that phallocentric, logocentric thinking has dominated Western philosophy and literature because of its patriarchal social context and that it is the enemy, to be rejected or over-turned in favor of female (preferably homosexual) thinking, which is different and liberating because of the different construction of women's bodies and, in particular, because of women's diffuse, multiple experience of sexual pleasure.[31] Women's language and thought are distinct and superior—more concrete, more focused on the contingencies of life, more emotional, less preoccupied with domination over others or over nature—because of women's different physical nature. Some versions of this theory contend that, with few exceptions, men cannot hope to comprehend wom-en's thinking. Some French feminists seem to have given up on the notion that reasoned discourse and logical argument lead to anything positive at all. The only feminist option is to reject totally male thinking and male language as well as male society. Rejecting men's logic, their rationality, their meaning, one must speak by means of "blank pages, gaps, borders, spaces and silences, holes in discourse."[32]

This rejection of rational discourse has aroused considerable reaction from other French feminists, including de Beauvoir and Catherine Clé-ment, who are not prepared so readily to concede the realm of argument to men.[33] While much is objectionable about de Beauvoir's devaluing of the entire traditionally female sphere of human life, her critique of the antira-tionalist strand of contemporary French radical feminism carries consider-able force. First, the illogic, meaninglessness, and dishonesty that abound in many of the prevailing male-dominated positions on important issues need to be attacked before we embark on a crusade against male logic and meaning. Second, given the uses to which biological determinism has been put, claiming that the two sexes' different ways of thinking are biological in origin involves a certain recklessness unless one also pays attention to the multitude of other plausible explanations.

One thing that de Beauvoir and most French antirationalist feminists seem to share, however, is the strong conviction that motherhood must be avoided at all cost. When the antirationalists speak of women's unique "vitality" as a determinative of female thinking, it is not the capacity to give birth that they have in mind, but sexual pleasure. English-speaking femi-nists have focused more on the mothering aspect of female biology. Mary O'Brien is the least impressionistic and most theoretical of the more ex-treme Anglo-American responses to such feminists as Mill and de Beau-voir, whose aim is for some women to emulate men if they can.

O'Brien is not as critical of what she calls "male-stream" thought, with its dualism and its excessive abstraction, as the most critical French or Anglo-American feminists. She is, nevertheless, still highly critical of it and defi-nitely reverses the male/female hierarchy established by male-stream thought on the subject. Although she acknowledges that the male-dominated tradition of political theory has important insights to offer, she believes that women hold the key to the way out of the morass that male-stream thought and action have created. Like some French feminists, O'Brien finds the roots of the difference between men's and women's modes of thinking in their biology, but what she considers determinative is women's power to reproduce and men's alienation from reproduction. Reproduction, however, like production, is subject to historical change. For O'Brien the decisive recent world historical moment has been the discovery of reliable contraception, which frees women from the necessity of continually reproducing while leaving them in their advantaged position as the owners of reproductive labor power. I think that O'Brien is clearly on the right track in looking to women's experience as reproducers for their special actual and potential contributions to human culture and thought. Unfortunately, she too tends toward biological determinism in her strong emphasis on pregnancy, birth, and the uncertainty of biological paternity, and in her almost total neglect of the long years of nurturing that follow. If O'Brien had taken child-*rearing* as seriously as she takes child*bearing,* she would have arrived at a more complete explanation of existing differences between the sexes and their modes of thought.

Others more moderate on the subject of women's and men's thinking have raised this and related issues. By calling them "moderate," I mean first that these theories neither reject male thought entirely nor seek to reverse totally the patriarchal valuing of men's thinking over women's. Second, they do not present biological explanations for the differences between the two sexes' modes of thinking, but find explanatory factors in the gendered social structure and in the two sexes' different experiences within it.

Jean Baker Miller explains women's psychology primarily in terms of women's powerlessness. As subordinates in a male-dominated society, they are required to develop psychological characteristics that please the dominant group and fulfill its needs. Such qualities as submissiveness, dependency, the desire to please and conform, lack of initiative, inability to act assertively or think independently, and the like have been regarded as signs of good adjustment and mental health in women, and as the opposite in men.[34] Sociological studies of sex-role stereotyping confirm these assertions.[35] The catch in all this stereotyping and in the socialization patterns that go along with it is that what has been regarded as a healthy *adult* turns out to be a healthy, well-adjusted *man.* The qualities fostered in women are seen as functional only for subordinate status. This fact has serious implications for those who both identify and wish to foster the development of a particular way of thinking about morality as more typically female.[36]

Second, though by no means inconsistent with Miller's, are the theories of such feminists as Chodorow, Dinnerstein, Flax, and Ruddick, who have focused on the influences on women both of being mothers and of being mothered.[37] These theorists have argued that the psychological (both personality and cognitive) differences between the sexes can best be explained by the facts that women mother and that children of both sexes are raised primarily by female parents, with consequent effects on their psychological development, particularly in its oedipal stage. Women's greater sense of connection with others, their empathy, their less decisive individuation and sense of autonomy, their nurturing capacities—and the opposite characteristics in men—are explained by these theorists as resulting from the gender imbalance of our parenting practices. As Chodorow puts it, it is neither biology nor sex-stereotyped socialization in general so much as being mothered that reproduces mothers.

Both the powerlessness theories and the mothering theories have made valuable contributions to our understanding of differences between the sexes. Taken together, and with the addition of some of O'Brien's insights into the influence of birth, they seem to provide a fairly full explanation of why we might find differences in female and male personality structure and modes of thinking. A thorough plumbing of the depths of men's and women's life experiences may yield so much explanatory material that biological origins need play a minimal role.

Here it will be useful to return to a point that the theorists discussed so far have assumed: that there *are* differences in men's and women's thinking about moral and political issues. There is little point in explaining something unless we know both that something needs to be explained and what it is. The Kohlberg data cited above seem to indicate that something does need explanation, but the extent and the nature of the differences require closer scrutiny. On these questions we can benefit from turning to the work of two feminist scholars of moral development, Constance Holstein and Carol Gilligan.

As I mentioned earlier, Kohlberg's moral development scale has been charged with not being gender-neutral. Both the definitions of the stages and the hierarchy in which they are arranged have been charged with gender bias. In a 1976 paper, Holstein finds that whereas young males tended to move from Stage 2 directly to Stage 4, the female pattern, for those who moved beyond Stage 3, was to move directly to Stage 5. She argues that, as defined by Kohlberg, "pure Stage 3 reasoning is not compatible with the traditionally instrumental American male role, nor is Stage 4 compatible with the traditionally expressive female role."[38] When Holstein tested respondents for liberalism versus conservatism on six issues, she found that while Stage 4 subjects of both sexes were relatively conservative, Stage 3 females were significantly more liberal than Stage 3 males, and were nearly as liberal as Stage 5 females. By contrast, Stage 3 males were more conservative than Stage 4 or 5 males. Since Kohlberg claims that his moral development scale is a ladder of progress toward liberalism, this finding about Stage 3 women is anomalous. It raises serious questions about the cohesiveness of the bundle of characteristics that are together regarded as defining Stage 3. It suggests in particular that males and females who are categorized as Stage 3 may be thinking very differently from each other. Holstein's conclusion is that Kohlberg's system is so highly cognitive in its orientation that it cannot account for or satisfactorily categorize "morally relevant emotions such as compassion, sympathy, and love," which seem to be consistently differentiated by sex.[39]

Gilligan's work has brought further into the open the question of whether it may be not women's problem but a problem in moral development theory that women's development does not easily conform to its pattern and that they fail to meet its highest standards. She is very much aware of the paradox that "the very traits that have defined the 'goodness' of women, their care for and sensitivity to the needs of others, are those that mark them as deficient in moral development" when the standards are derived from the study of men.[40] She does not claim superiority for the "different voice" she identifies as typically, though not solely, heard from women. But she justifiably insists that it must be given equal consideration in any satisfactory theory of moral development. She describes this voice as follows:

> In this conception, the moral problem arises from conflicting responsibilities rather than from competing rights, and requires for its resolution a mode of thinking that is contextual and narrative rather than formal and abstract. This conception of morality as concerned with the activity of care centers moral development around the understanding of responsibility and relationships, just as the conception of morality as fairness ties moral development to the understanding of rights and rules.[41]

A problem arises from the fact that it is not clear to what extent Gilligan is asserting generalizations about men's and women's moral thinking. Throughout most of the book, the language implies that strong general statements are being made about "men" and "women." By comparison, in the introduction Gilligan minimizes her intent to generalize about gender differences in moral thinking.[42] There have been numerous critiques, some of them based on extensive reviews of the literature, of the association Gilligan and her colleagues make of the two different voices with men and women.[43] For me three reasons stand out for thinking that the picture of differences in the moral development of men and women that is drawn in the bulk of Gilligan's book is exaggerated.

First, the numbers studied are small, and when the responses of just two individuals are compared at length the reader is given no indication of how typical or representative of the whole sample these particular responses are.[44] Second, several important chapters are based on the findings of a study of women making a decision about abortion. For some research purposes, this is clearly a perfect opportunity to study moral reasoning—at the high point of an important actual moral dilemma, and then again after its resolution. But it is a most inopportune example to choose if the purpose is to compare women's moral reasoning with men's.[45] Third, Gilligan seems predisposed to interpret talk of "rights" as referring to what are sometimes called "negative rights," that is to say, rights that require only restraint, and no *positive* responsibility, on the part of the corresponding obligation holder(s). She tends therefore to conflate talk about rights with individualism and even selfishness.[46] But as a number of moral philosophers have recently argued, many rights entail positive obligations and substantive responsibilities on the part of others,[47] and at least some of Gilligan's male respondents are ambiguous on this issue. In this light, the distinction between a "morality of rights" and "a morality of responsibilities" seems artificial and even obfuscating, unless it is meant simply to indicate where the greater emphasis is placed.

How far the picture of two different modes of moral thinking associated with women and men is overdrawn by Gilligan and her associates cannot be resolved here. But what is the *nature* of the difference? What is the "different voice" really saying? The virtue of Gilligan's work is that, because of the richness of its detailed quotations from respondents, it helps us to understand, far better than do more quantitative but less detailed findings, what the difference is. In particular, it confirms the idea that the core problem underlying Kohlberg's initial findings about women's moral inferiority is that his Stage 3 is a fundamentally confused and confusing amalgam of notions.

Stage 3 is characterized by two ways of thinking that seem both distinct from each other and indicative of very different levels of moral sophistication.[48] One characteristic of Stage 3 is the idea that moral behavior is what pleases or is approved by others. This is something that one would expect of children's moral thinking, although it would scarcely be surprising if it were more prevalent in adult women than men, given the emphasis placed on pleasing in female socialization. The other major characteristic of Stage 3 is that notion that moral behavior is what helps others. This characteristic is fundamentally ambiguous, and we can learn much from Gilligan's work about this ambiguity and therefore about the type of moral thinking that women seem to engage in more than men. The ambiguity consists in the fact that it is not clear *which* "others" are being referred to. Kohlberg seems to understand Stage 3 respondents to be concerned in their moral thinking with those others with whom they have personal relationships. "Customarily," he says, "Stage 3 decides by taking the roles of those with whom he has ties,"[49] and it is this limitation that makes him regard Stage 3 thinking as incomplete and unsatisfactory in its "reversibility." This limitation also makes him regard Stage 3 thinking as functional for housewives and mothers (who, he presumably thinks, should put their husbands and children first), but not as appropriate for participation in the public sphere, where one needs to be impartial.

Many of the passages quoted by Gilligan from women's responses, however, indicate the basic ambiguity of "what helps others." In some cases (and notably with the child Amy) it is clear that the respondent regards personal relationship and feelings for those who are close as important factors in moral decision making. In other cases it is not clear for which "other people" concern and responsibility are being expressed. But in many cases it is obvious that those "others" for whose suffering the female respondents express concern and feel responsibility are intended to include *far* more people than just their own circles of family and friends. As one says, "Acts that are self-sacrificing and that are done for other people or for the good of humanity are good acts." Another, mentioning "helping others," speaks of her "very strong sense of being responsible to the world." One woman defines morality as "a type of consciousness, a sensitivity to humanity, that you can affect someone else's life, you can affect your own life, and you have a responsibility not to endanger other people's lives or to hurt other people."[50] For some subjects, the responsibility they feel for others extends to those they do not know at all and to those whom they do not like. One woman, having talked of "that giant collection of everybody," says, "The stranger is still another person belonging to that group, people you are connected to by virtue of being another person." Another expresses the view that even though "you may not like them," other people are "part of you; that other person is part of that giant collection of people that you are connected to."[51] As Gilligan sums up such views, "The moral imperative that emerges repeatedly in interviews with women is an injunction to care, a responsibility to discern and alleviate the 'real and recognizable trouble' of this world."[52]

Although these responses quoted from Gilligan's data indicate that women's care and sense of responsibility for others are frequently universalized, she does not probe this issue fully. Many of the questions she poses investigate the conflict between self-interest and doing what helps others or prevents harm to them. But she gives little consideration to the issue that is so crucial in the light of the history of sex stereotyping about moral thinking—that of how women think when confronted with a moral dilemma involving a conflict between the needs or interests of family and close friends and the needs or interests of more distant "others." If we are to comprehend the significance of any tendency there might be in women to be concerned with caring, with responsibilities, and with relationships, and in men to be concerned with rights and justice, it is essential that we know how far women's caring and responsibility extend. We must find out whether and to what extent women and men weigh differently the moral significance of the needs of a distant stranger—a "far other"—and the needs of someone with whom they have a personal relationship—a "near other."[53]

What Gilligan's data clearly indicate, though she does not explicitly say so, is that the ambiguity of "others" in Kohlberg's definition of Stage 3 moral thinking is a serious flaw. Since the women quoted above do not talk in terms of laws, of rules, or of rights, they are unlikely to be classified as having attained Kohlberg's three highest stages of moral development. Because they talk in terms of helping and not hurting others, it seems likely that they would be classified in Stage 3. But insofar as Kohlberg understands Stage 3 respondents to be biased in their moral judgment in favor of those with whom they have personal ties, this classification would be erroneous, for these women express a fully universalizable concern for the welfare of humanity. Though apparently more utilitarian than rights-based, it is certainly not a moral stance that should be regarded as less advanced than Stage 4's "law and order" orientation, and among sophisticated moral philosophers some find utilitarianism more defensible than Kohlberg's rights-based Stages 5 and 6.

Women and men may well think about moral issues in different ways. The answer is not yet in; further research that overcomes some of the faults of previous methodology needs to be done. But Holstein's and Gilligan's findings suggest already that Kohlberg was not justified in interpreting more women's than men's remaining at his Stage 3 as meaning that their development is less advanced. Neither is he justified in his later characterization of the "different voice" that Gilligan identified as one that is "most vividly evident in relations of special obligation to family and friends."[54] As we have seen, many of those who speak in this voice use it to express as fully universalizable a morality of social concern as respondents who express themselves very differently, using the language of justice and rights. It is still not clear what "thinking like a woman" really means. But recent research in moral development certainly does not reaffirm the age-old judgment that women are more influenced than men by private attachment and less able to universalize in their moral reasoning.

Ethics from
the Standpoint
of Women

NEL NODDINGS

Until quite recently, the idea of ethics from the standpoint of women—or "female ethics" as some prefer to call it[1]—would have been called a contradiction in terms. Women had long been considered morally inferior to men and were thought to be ethically dangerous to them.[2] This inferiority was considered irremovable; it was a permanent privation inherent in a creature made explicitly for reproduction.[3] Women were credited with a certain goodness if they met the standards men established for them, but this goodness was not the ethical goodness that genuine moral agents can achieve. Such goodness requires a level of objective thinking and detachment considered beyond the capabilities of females. Female goodness, in the standard male version, consisted in obedience, industry, silence, and service. Woman's goodness, like that of animals and instruments, was measured in relation to her usefulness to males.[4]

It is not surprising, then, that there should be controversy—even among feminists—over the value of an ethics built on women's traditional role as nurturers. (An ethics of caring is not the only possible version of "female ethics," and I mention alternatives later.) Objections to this approach to ethics come from a variety of sources. One objection to an ethics of caring comes from those who believe that caring and nurturing are somehow natural or instinctive. Women are to be appreciated for their dedication and self-sacrifice in family life, but there is no reason to regard their nurturing as a manifestation of ethical agency. A second objection, coming largely from feminists, expresses the fear that an ethics built on such experience (if it were possible to build one) might be used to maintain women's servitude and aggravate the unfortunate tendency of women to blame themselves for everything that goes wrong in their relationships.[5] A third objection is that the very idea of a female ethic contradicts the supposed universality of ethics as the philosophical study of morality. A female ethic, from this perspective, would have to be classified with "business ethics," "personal ethics," and other specialized ethics that apply philosophical ethics to particular problems and domains. A genderized ethic could not, by definition, attain the status of ethics in philosophy.

But the construction of ethics from the standpoint of women is an important enterprise that may contribute significantly to both ethical thinking and general human welfare. Such an ethic has much in common with Christian agape; for example, it emphasizes needs over rights and love over duty, but it does not depend on divine commandment or seek divine favor. It contrasts sharply with the Kantian and utilitarian ethics that have dominated philosophical thinking. The first step in establishing the credibility of a project aimed at the construction of a female ethic is to defend the idea of a genderized ethic.

MALE ETHICS

Under what circumstances can we properly say that a philosophy—in particular, an ethic—is male? In a careful analysis of this question, Jean Grimshaw separates unimportant from important senses in which one might describe philosophy as "male."[6] First, Grimshaw contends that just because almost all philosophers have been male, it cannot be said that their philosophical theories are necessarily male. This way of branding philosophy male is not, however, quite so easy to brush off as Grimshaw suggests. Our judgment depends on how we assess philosophy's traditional claim to universality. If philosophical thought is by definition universally applicable, then the claim that philosophy has been male because men have been doing it would clearly be false. If we can show, however, that philosophy—or any other body of theorizing—is necessarily constructed from a perspective, then the fact that philosophers have been men becomes a more salient bit of evidence for the maleness of philosophy. But Grimshaw is right in pointing out that argumentation is required to support the complaint, and the argument might have to proceed branch by branch. It may or may not be easier to show the maleness of ethics than the maleness of, say, logic.

Second, the well-documented misogyny found in the writings of important philosophers cannot be used to label their entire body of thought as male. This seems clearly right. As Grimshaw points out, misogynist statements in one essay do not necessarily contaminate work in which women are not even mentioned.

If we suspect, however, that ethical thought does indeed proceed from a perspective, we may begin a search for ways in which a male perspective affects ethics implicitly. This procedure will at best show that *some* philosophy is male and cast some doubt on its claim for universality.

Consider Kant as the first example.[7] In an essay entitled "Of the Distinction between the Beautiful and Sublime in the Interrelations of the Two Sexes," Kant attributes a form of inherent, aesthetically motivated goodness to women; women are identified with the beautiful. In contrast, men are at their best associated with the noble and sublime. Women do not need to think deeply, Kant declared, because they have "a strong inborn feeling for all that is beautiful." If they are so foolish as to undertake and actually succeed at "laborious learning" or "painful pondering," they lose the very charm and goodness that would have developed naturally. Kant says, "A woman with a head full of Greek . . . or . . . mechanics . . . might as well even have a beard; for perhaps that would express more obviously the mien of profundity for which she strives."[8] Not only are most women incapable of thinking at the level required for moral reasoning: they *should not,* since such thinking tends to destroy the merits "proper to the sex."

When Kant develops his ethical theory, it is not surprising that he elevates duty and principle to positions far above love and inclination. For Kant, acts done out of love do not qualify as moral acts. Only those committed out of a conscious sense of obedience to principle are moral acts. Feelings and emotions are not to be trusted. One must detach himself from personal loves and longings to be truly moral, and Kant (along with Aristotle and Aquinas) clearly believes women are incapable of this sort of detachment. Confined to the morally supportive arena of home and family, guided by good husbands or fathers, women can contribute through their inherent gentleness and love of beauty to the joy and comfort of private life. But they are clearly unsuited for academic and political life.

The obvious congruence between Kant's view of the difference between men and women and his separation of moral acts from loving ones may lead us to infer that his moral philosophy is thoroughly contaminated by his views on gender. But as Grimshaw points out, "Kant could, without inconsistency, have retained his view about 'moral worth' but changed his view of women."[9] What we do not know, of course, is whether Kant would have changed his view of women or his view of ethics if he had been challenged with a thoughtful development of ethics based on some of the virtues he himself attributed to women. He might have been led to modify both, for the creation of a female ethics would have forced him to acknowledge that women can think philosophically, and an emphasis on caring and response to needs in that ethic might press him to admit that genuinely moral acts (acts reflectively committed) can be motivated and justified by fidelity to persons as well as fidelity to principles.

The important point is that Kant's moral philosophy, certainly one of the

most influential in all of Western ethics, is apparently unconsciously genderized. Recognizing this, we might respond in one of several ways when
we attempt to construct an ethical system. We might, for example, vow to
avoid genderizing our own ethical thinking; we might adopt a deliberately
genderized view that extols the virtues of our own sex; we might adopt a
genderized view critically on the grounds that no other is honestly available.

To construct an ethic free of gendered views may be impossible in a thoroughly gendered society. It is not even clear that such a construction is desirable, but if it is one might argue that it cannot be accomplished until we
have something like a balanced set of genderized ethics to analyze and then
to transcend. Joan Tronto has argued that "although an ethic of care could
be an important intellectual concern for feminists, the debate around this
concern should be centered not in discussion of gender difference but in
discourse about the ethic's adequacy as a moral theory."[10] Her reasons for
making this recommendation are cogent. She fears, for example, that any
assertion of gender difference in a society "that identifies the male as
normal" will relegate the distinctly female view to inferiority. This is an
important point, but there are a few others to keep in mind. First, it is not
clear that discussion of care would ever have arisen if women had not
initiated the discussion and responded to it with such recognition;[11] second, given that males have developed the criteria of adequacy for moral
theories, female discourse concentrated on these may find itself oddly
handicapped; and third, it may simply be necessary for women as moral
and intellectual agents to develop moral theories (and other theories as
well) through a careful articulation of their own female experience. Those
who do such work can remain mindful of Tronto's warning, and I believe
she is right that we should not get bogged down in disputes over empirical
claims concerning moral orientation. Even if many women do not display
signs of a caring orientation, and many men do, theories of care can clearly
be developed from analysis of the activities of care that have dominated
female experience for centuries. In this sense, the development of theories
of care may be genderized for a long time before the "transvaluation"
suggested by Tronto can even be approached.

The second possibility, building a frankly genderized ethic that favors
certain virtues thought to belong to one's own sex, is illustrated in the work
of Nietzsche. Here we encounter a consciously held and boldly articulated
masculine ethic. Nietzsche's ethic is not just male in the sense that Kant's is;
it does not simply reflect in its parallel structure a posited difference
between men and women. Rather, it is built on a deliberately chosen model
of masculinity that provides a foundation for the entire ethic. The morally
best man, the one to be emulated and obeyed, is the courageous warrior.
Slaves and women are to be despised. Any institution that embraces wom-

anly "virtues" or exhibits female-like traits is also to be despised. The church, with its gentle (if sometimes hypocritical) message of love and forbearance, falls into this category. Nietzsche said of churchmen that they "smash the strong, contaminate great hopes, cast suspicion on joy in beauty, break down everything autocratic, manly, conquering, tyrannical, all the instincts proper to the highest and most successful of the type 'man.'"[12]

Nietzsche uses his description of the warrior to build a prescription for human (masculine) life at its best, a new morality that goes beyond traditional conceptions of good and evil. Simultaneously, he uses his own description of women as a foil to illustrate much of what he takes to be wrong with Western culture. Both men and women can find admirable insights in Nietzsche's work despite his depraved misogyny,[13] but it is hard to imagine any significant change in his view of women that would not have necessitated a correspondingly profound change in his moral philosophy. His philosophy is overtly and proudly masculine, and much of it depends directly on the devaluation of women and all that is associated with the feminine.

Views very similar to Nietzsche's abounded into the twentieth century. Otto Weininger, whose work was apparently admired by Freud, published a book that was even more vitriolic than Nietzsche's in its condemnation of women. Like Kant, Weininger held that the truly feminine woman was incapable of genuine moral reasoning, but his assessment lacked a compensating admiration. Speaking of women he said, "In such a being as the absolute female there are no logical and ethical phenomena, and, therefore, the ground for the assumption of a soul is absent."[14] Weininger's "ethical" views were, like Nietzsche's, profoundly influenced by his misogyny. Unlike Nietzsche, however, who despised Kant's moral philosophy as unmanly in its emphasis on duty prescribed by universal principles, Weininger greatly admired Kant. As Bram Dijkstra points out, Weininger admired the individualism in Kant's position: "The birth of the Kantian ethics, the noblest event in the history of the world, was the moment when for the first time the dazzling conception came to him, 'I am responsible only to myself; I must follow none other; I must not forget myself even in my work; I am alone; I am free; I am lord of myself.'"[15] Where Nietzsche saw in Kant an emphasis on duty and therefore on weakness and subordination, Weininger detected the individualism that would characterize modern society and mark the admirable man.

All three men, Kant, Nietzsche, and Weininger, while differing dramatically on major points, carefully avoided anything in their ethical thinking that seemed to them to resemble the feminine. Traits that were admired had either to be denied of women (honesty and the capacity for rational thought are examples) or restricted to women (submissiveness and child-like innocence were often named in this category), and traits restricted to women had nothing to do with ethics. This way of approaching moral theory is both intellectually dishonest and morally wrong. When I speak of ethics from the standpoint of women, I do not mean that men should be excluded from either its descriptive or its prescriptive contents. Instead the ethic should frankly be developed from the experience of women. This leaves open the question whether it might also grow out of some forms of male experience.

The third possibility, that of adopting a genderized ethic for critical purposes, is hinted at in the work of William James, though he does not choose this strategy, letting the opportunity slip by. In his discussion of the warrior, James expresses the admiration traditionally directed toward this paradigm of masculinity, but he deplores the savagery and destruction of war. In an important sense he retains a masculine ethic while subjecting it to some criticism. Even though he wants to avoid the senseless violence of war, he wants also to avoid "effeminacy." "The fact remains," he says,

> that war is a school of strenuous life and heroism; and, being in the line of aboriginal instinct, is the only school that as yet is universally available. But when we ask ourselves whether this wholesale organization of irrationality and crime be our only bulwark against effeminacy, we stand aghast at the thought, and think more kindly of ascetic religion. . . . What we now need to discover in the social realm is the moral equivalent of war: something heroic that will speak to men as universally as war does, and yet will be compatible with their spiritual selves as war has proved itself to be incompatible.[16]

James suggests poverty as a life equally strenuous and heroic, a suggestion in part motivated by a fear of softness, of being like a woman. "Does not . . . the worship of material luxury and wealth, which constitute so large a portion of the 'spirit' of our age, make somewhat for effeminacy and unmanliness?"[17] he asks. He sees the violence, greed, and "prevalent fear of poverty," which he regards as the "worst moral disease from which our civilization suffers,"[18] but he does not seem to see that the traditional view of masculinity—one that defines itself in opposition to femininity—may be a substantial cause of this moral disease. James was on the right track when he began to call into question the kinds of commitments men should make in exercising their virtues. If he had realized that his analysis was embedded in a genderized perspective, he might have been able to explore the full range of human possibilities.

It is not necessary either to extol the virtues of one's sex blindly or to reject them wholesale in taking a genderized perspective, but if one is not aware that his or her perspective *is* genderized, one will miss a set of potential insights entirely. A female ethic built along Nietzschean lines might be instructive, but the notion is too outrageous for most of us even to consider, and at bottom it would be self-contradictory. What must be shown is that female experience, like male experience, can be reflected upon in a way that produces genuine moral insight and that failure to consider such experience and the virtues associated with it may condemn all of us to a state of moral dullness and incompleteness.

FEMALE ETHICS

The introduction of female ethics can hardly be construed as an attempt to genderize a field that has hitherto been gender-free; thus one objection to female ethics can be set aside. The other two objections remain. The first contends that the traditional activities and attitudes of women have nothing to do with ethics or even with a moral orientation from which ethics might be developed. The second expresses a concern that an ethics of caring might perpetuate the subordinate condition of women.

The first objection has two main parts: the common notion that traditional women's work does not require the kind of thought needed for moral agency and the more general claim that everyday experience is something to which ethics is applied, not something out of which ethics is developed.

Taking the first part of the objection, suppose that a phenomenology of work and interpersonal relations is necessary for the construction of ethics, is there reason to believe that a phenomenology of women's traditional work will uncover attitudes, ways of thinking, or modes of being that will contribute to ethical thought? This question has already been answered positively by a number of feminist thinkers and involves the analysis of such concepts and phenomena as caring,[19] virtues displayed in feminine life,[20] reproduction,[21] religious beliefs,[22] and maternal thinking.[23] The phenomena of caring are deeply embedded in ethical life, although theorists differ on the exact role of caring and its centrality to ethical theory.[24] Certain virtues have been attributed to women in their standard roles, but these virtues have not been considered important or even appropriate for men to develop, and both the philosophical account of birth and reproduction and the discussion of maternal thinking have induced lively debate on the relations between gender and ethical thought. A considerable revival of interest has taken place in restoring the role of ordinary life experience in ethics. Why, then, should there be resistance to the development of ethics from the traditional standpoint of women?

One reason for resistance is that, strictly speaking, there is no such thing as *the* standpoint of women.[25] Women's lives and voices differ. I, for example, speak not only as a woman but as middle-class, white, mother, and academic. Using such an expression as "the standpoint of women" risks an error similar to that in standard philosophy—a claim for universality that is patently false. This is an important objection, but it still may be important to articulate an ethical orientation that arises in the context of women's traditional work and gives attention to women's concerns. In doing this, we must choose topics that touch as many women's lives as possible, and we must also remember to invite a broad range of perspectives to join our own.

Another reason for resistance is the fear of being like a woman. Fear of being like a woman—of succumbing to effeminacy—has frequently influenced male philosophers, and now the same fear has infected many feminist thinkers. The feminist fear is not of being a woman but of being "like a woman"—of actualizing a hated stereotype. This fear is not entirely unfounded: as we have seen, the traditional view has not credited women with the capacity to think deeply about moral matters. It follows that the tasks traditionally charged to women cannot be either cognitively or morally demanding. Why, then, should we look at such activities as child-rearing, homemaking, and cooking and the "admirable" attitudes that have long accompanied them when we are interested in moral thinking? Some feminists have insisted that women must free themselves from these oppressive tasks if they are to attain full personhood and, by implication, moral agency.

An alternative view interprets female ethics as a field that attends philosophically to matters of moral significance to women: abortion, divorce, equal employment opportunity, pornography, rape, child care, surrogate motherhood, and the like. These are important topics for ethics to address, and one sense in which ethics can be approached from the standpoint of women is to begin with problems that are especially relevant to them. No feminist can object to the careful study of such problems, but some might object to analyzing them in the standard mode. They have an understandable fear of being "like a man," of treating problems as though they can be coldly abstracted from the situations in which they arise and from the people who experience them. A strength of the program to develop an ethics of caring is that it does not invoke already established theoretical frameworks through which to study the problems of women but assumes that taking the standpoint of women requires starting with the life experiences of women. And this does not imply that the traditional experience of women must be exalted or fully accepted. Such a start acknowledges that our foremothers often worked at worthwhile tasks, thought clearly and effectively, and developed virtues as valuable as those James wanted to preserve for men from the warrior model, while criticizing the way of life that confined women to a specific set of tasks. The process of working from experience toward ethics offers the possibility of locating new ethical issues and gaining critical insights into existing frameworks.

As an example of this last possibility, let us see what can be uncovered through a consideration of one task, cooking, that has figured prominently in female experience. Cooking has been so important in women's lives that it has come under scathing attack by some feminists. Charlotte Perkins Gilman led the way in this rebellion by warning women that trying to find the way to men's hearts through their stomachs would produce "fat, greasy husbands" along with vice and indigestion.[26] She wanted women to be freed from the task of home food preparation, and she hoped that cooking would become a professional enterprise. Gilman's vehement attack on home cooking is similar to Shulamith Firestone's polemic against child-bearing.[27] Both women felt that the activity under attack had to be abolished if women were to gain equality in public life, and both are subject to the same basic criticism: to attack activities that have been fundamental in women's lives is to elevate man's way of life above woman's prematurely and unreflectively. It risks losing the special contribution to thought that might be forthcoming from a careful analysis of women's experience in connection with these activities. One does not have to embrace the activities uncritically to take the standpoint of women, because female views arise from both participation in and resistance to these activities. But a woman's view cannot ignore them, as traditional views—those purporting to be man's (in the generic sense)—have done.

Gilman formulated her critique from a Marxist framework. Marx held that there are three components of labor: purposeful activity (the work itself), an object to be transformed, and an instrument to be used in accomplishing the work. When we read or listen to the stories women tell about food preparation, we see that something vital is missing in the Marxist view.[28] We need to ask not only what is being accomplished and how but *for whom,* in what setting, and with what attitude. To consider work as an economic concept seems right, but to consider it only an economic concept misses a large part of human experience. Much of women's work has been done, as Jane Roland Martin points out, with an emphasis on "caring, compassion, and connection,"[29] and one must ask how these attitudes can be maintained if the tasks under study lose their intimacy and become mere economic enterprises. As Marx worried over workers' alienation from their own labor under capitalism, women might be concerned with the loss of the tender personal interest that has often characterized "women's work." This concern need not culminate in a recommendation that all women rush back into the kitchen, but it might encourage us to think deeply about the sharing, cultural knowledge, and intimate responsibility for others that may be learned and practiced in the ordinary tasks of everyday life. The result of such thinking might be a recommendation in direct opposition to Gilman's: instead of converting cooking to a completely professional occupation, all family members should be involved in the preparation of meals.

Insights may also spring from considering the struggles of largely female occupations toward professionalization. Teaching, nursing, and early childhood education (or child care) are semiprofessions wrestling with important dilemmas. On the one hand, professionalization usually means a separation from intimate contact with clients. Why, for example, should a highly educated nurse be involved in spooning food into those who cannot feed themselves; washing, powdering, and gently rubbing sore bodies; assisting in the evacuation of bladder and bowels; soothing, cooling, warming; wrapping, dressing, combing; comforting? On the other hand, many nurses and nurse-theoreticians recognize these tasks as central to nursing. Jean Watson, for example, counsels that these tasks present "caring occasions," occasions in which both nurse and patient must decide how to relate to each other.[30] A professional nurse, in contrast to a kindhearted volunteer, can learn a good deal about a patient's condition and treatment through performing these tasks, and the loving attention of an authorized professional seems to raise the spirit of a patient. Just as a child or a tired spouse appreciates a special dish made just for him or her, a patient feels *regarded* when a professional nurse cares for his or her personal needs. The dilemma pits the natural desire of well-educated women to be "true professionals" against the hard-earned wisdom that values direct contact even when it requires what is called "menial labor." Resolution of the dilemma demands a careful redefinition of what it means to be professional, and taking the standpoint of women is a first step in this direction.

But is it appropriate to work this way in ethics? This question is not so controversial now as it would have been a few years ago. There is considerable philosophical interest today in ethical life as it appears in communities, occupations, and whole societies. The role of philosophy, in this view, is not to create ethics out of the heads of philosophers but to critique ethical life and bring some coherence to it. Some forms of foundational ethics, for example, clearly depend on background theories about the nature of experience, persons, and their relations to each other. A foundational ethics that does not posit self-evident basic premises, the intuition of basic moral knowledge, or an authoritatively established set of initial premises must build on a convincing description of human nature or experience.[31] Even if the ethical theory is neither foundational nor primarily concerned with moral knowledge and its justification, focusing instead on moral behavior and its correlate attitudes, such a grounding is necessary.

Recognition of the need to ground ethical theory in a psychology of human nature or experience is sometimes taken to mean that the moral orientation under development as an ethic requires empirical verification.

This is only partly true. Studies showing that women are more concerned than men with human relationships,[32] that professional women may have greater sensitivity for moral issues than their male counterparts,[33] and that women are more likely than men to be politically concerned with issues of war and poverty[34] are interesting and important. They contribute to the convincing description of human experience that will ground an ethics of caring. But from a philosophical perspective it is not essential to show that all women think this way or that the "different voice" to which Gilligan refers belongs only to women. The ethic is concerned with the logic and phenomenology of caring, not with the number of people who actually invoke it or live by it. Although a program of this sort does develop out of a certain opposition to the ways of the opposite sex (fear of being like a stereotypical man does influence some feminist thinkers—certainly those concerned with the ethics of caring), it does not necessitate a claim for the moral superiority of women. Most feminists rightly reject such a claim on the dual grounds that it is undemonstrable and that arguments from nature have not served women well in the past. The idea is to develop a phenomenology of women's experience that will provide an adequate grounding for the construction of ethics from the standpoint of women.

One must be cautious in assessing the present philosophical climate as receptive to the sort of program I have been discussing. The current revival of interest in practical ethics often centers on Aristotelian approaches.[35] Much of what I have said about studying ways of life and the tasks and attitudes characteristic of them is compatible with Aristotelian method, but an important difference must be noted and maintained. Aristotle's identification of virtues depended almost entirely on the establishment of exclusive classes and the activities appropriate to each. The virtues of women and of slaves were not those of educated citizens. He made no attempt to identify virtues in one class that might be cultivated in others by extending the range of privilege or sharing the array of common tasks. If he had made such an attempt, it would surely have moved in only one direction. One might try to inculcate the virtues of the highest class into lower classes, but one would never try to develop, say, feminine virtues in men.

Much of the same form of elitism can be found in current works that favor a return to Aristotle. Alasdair MacIntyre, for example, wants to begin the search for virtues in the sets of activities that he calls "practices," but he defines *practice* in an excruciatingly careful way to exclude all forms of therapy and management as well as many ordinary occupations from the class of practices.[36] Using such an approach we would surely end up with a hierarchy of jobs, persons, and virtues.

The feminist program outlined here has quite a different objective. It recognizes that, as Grimshaw says, "Theories . . . are not *only* ways of 'making sense' of the world. They may also be means by which one group of people may dominate or exercise control over another."[37] In our theorizing, we begin with ways of life in order to describe both strengths and weaknesses. The virtues we locate are not assigned permanently to a particular group or activity. Rather, we want to ask: If these virtues are worth maintaining, can they be developed if the ways of life in which they arose are abandoned? If not, can the ways of life be extended so that all human beings may develop them?

CARING AND SELF-SACRIFICE

The final objection to an ethic of caring as an example of a genderized ethic is expressed well by Barbara Houston:

> When I reflect on the history of women, I realize how much our caring has nurtured and empowered others. I see how good it has been, for others. However, I also see how terribly costly it has been for women. And so the first question that arises for me is one that arises for many of Gilligan's subjects. Can an ethics of care avoid self-sacrifice?[38]

This is an important question motivated by a realistic fear. Women who maintain a moral orientation of caring are often exploited, find themselves dependent on men or on welfare in order to care for their children, and are sometimes physically abused. In most such cases, philosophical questions could be raised about the interpretation these women put on caring. We could probably show that their interpretation is "not really caring" as it has been defined theoretically. Although there is some justification for such a theoretical approach—all of us, both men and women, need to learn more about appropriate forms of caring—it would be an arrogant and self-defeating response. An ethical theory constructed from the standpoint of women is not designed to control and dominate women (or men) but to make the world better and to make better sense of it. The reality described by Houston must be faced.

The most powerful response to Houston is that the ethics of caring is not intended as an ethic only for women. An ethical orientation that arises in female experience need not be confined to women. The possibility of confinement to women was a cogent reason for rejecting an Aristotelian approach to moral life. If only women adopt an ethic of caring, the present conditions of women's oppression are indeed likely to be maintained. This is exactly why an ethic of caring puts great emphasis on human interdependence and on moral education. An important task of moral education is teaching people how and why to care.

Kari Waerness has argued convincingly for "the rationality of caring."[39] She argues (as I did earlier) that any social theory resting its entire argument on an economic base is deficient. In her discussion of caring, she refers to "both labor and feelings":

> Caring is about relations between (at least two) people. One of them (the carer) shows concern, consideration, affection, devotion, towards the other (the cared for). The one needing care is invaluable to the one providing care, and when the former is suffering pain or discomfort, the latter identifies with her/him and attends to alleviating it. Adult, healthy people feel a need to be cared for by others. . . . Worn out, dejected, tired, depressed . . . we need or desire others "to care for us." In such situations we may feel that we have a *right* to our need for care being met. This means there must be others who feel that it is their duty or desire to honor this right.[40]

Waerness' concern to maintain or extend the attitude of love characteristic of private caring into public caring reflects the dilemma of the nursing profession. For present purposes, the important message in her argument is that caring is rational, that our universal desire to be cared for logically suggests the need for caring. Houston's worry is that the world can be too easily divided into two groups—the carers and the cared fors—and that women are all too likely to land in the first set. This problem is not one found only in ethics of caring. The so-called free-rider problem is a tough one whenever matters of charity (as contrasted with justice) are discussed.[41] People may acknowledge potential desires and needs, want remedies available for their own protection, yet not respond by making a personal contribution.

The solution probably has to involve both coercion and education. Corporations, professions, and educational institutions can be forced to provide better conditions for caring: child care, parental leaves, more time for interpersonal communication, cooperative evaluation. But coercion must not be pushed to the point where its users begin to model something that contradicts caring. Education must provide the attitudes that will make coercion acceptable. Sometimes adults, like children, welcome rules that give them legal reasons for doing what they really want to do or feel they should do. This is why educational programs of the sort suggested by Jane Roland Martin are so important: caring, compassion, and connection must become important values for all human beings, not just for many women.[42]

Although I have already said that I think it would be unproductive to respond to Houston solely in philosophical terms, a closer look at the philosophical underpinnings of caring is warranted. An ethics of caring is based on a relational ontology. It takes as a basic assumption that human beings are defined in relation. It is not just that "I" as a preformed, persistent individual enter into relations; the "I" of which we all speak so easily is itself a relational entity. I really am defined by the set of relations into which my physical self has been thrown. From this perspective, when I do something for someone else, I do it at least partly for me, too, since the other and I are members of a relation. A relational ontology is clearly at odds with the individualism that has dominated the last two centuries of Western thought and is still so powerful in the United States.[43]

Even though on an ontological level the self is already a relational entity, in practical, everyday life, people do enter relations, and Houston is concerned not only that women will too often occupy the position of carer (or "one-caring") in these relations but also that the moral worth of the carer seems to be conditional. She comments:

> Since an ethics of care takes as its ontology persons-in-relation and endows this fact of human relatedness with moral significance, the attribution of moral worth to persons appears to apply to them only as one-caring. . . . The unconditional worth of the *cared for* is unequivocally assumed. . . . But it is less obvious that unconditional value is assumed for the one-caring.[44]

Here I think Houston makes the error of supposing that a given person is either the one-caring or the cared for in some stable context. But this is not at all how the two are defined in my *Caring*.[45] Every human being capable of response is potentially both, and roles shift. As a possible cared for, each human being is worthy of moral regard. It is true that those who are capable of acting as carers occupy a special position in this moral scheme. Without people able and willing to care, there could be no cared fors, regardless of the need. But this is not a moral orientation in which only duty bearers can belong to the moral community. Even in the language of justice and rights, many theorists recognize that people may be rights bearers although they cannot for some reason assume moral duties (infancy would be an example).[46] In the language of caring and response, all beings capable of human response (and that has to be defined, of course) can call forth the obligation to respond. The one-caring, then, is unquestionably awarded what Houston calls "moral worth," for by definition she or he is capable of the most significant form of human response—caring.

The Possibility
of Feminist Theory

MARILYN FRYE

Imagine that a single individual had written up an exhaustive description of a sedated elephant as observed from one spot for one hour and then, with delighted self-satisfaction, had heralded that achievement as a complete, accurate, and profound account of The Elephant. The androcentrism of the accumulated philosophy and science of the Western world is like that. A few, a few men, have with a like satisfaction told the story of the world and human experience—have created what pretends to be progressively a more and more complete, accurate, and profound account of what they call "Man and His World." The Man whose (incomplete) story this is turns out to be a species of males to which there is awkwardly, problematically, and paradoxically appended a subspecies or alterspecies of individuals of which men are born but which are not men. It is a story that does not fit women and that women do not fit.

In the light of what is generally considered common knowledge (the official story of "Man and His World") a great deal of most women's experience appears anomalous, discrepant, idiosyncratic, chaotic, "crazy."[1] In that dim light our lives are to a great extent either unintelligible or intelligible only as pathological or degenerate. As long as each woman thinks that her experience alone is thus discrepant, she tends to trust the received wisdom and distrust her own senses and judgment. For instance, she will believe that her "inexplicable" pain is imaginary, a phantasm. In consciousness-raising conversations among themselves (however inten-

An earlier version of this work was delivered as an invited paper on the program of the Central Division of the American Philosophical Association, May 1, 1987, and the earliest work on it was supported by the Center for the Study of Women in Society at the University of Oregon. I am indebted at many points to conversations with Carolyn Shafer and to comments made by many women on the various occasions over the last five years when I have given talks in which I was working out various aspects of these thoughts.

tionally or unintentionally joined) women discover that similar "anomalies" occur in most of their lives and that those "anomalies" taken together form a pattern, or many patterns. The fragments that were each woman's singular oddities (often previously perceived as her own faults or defects) are collectively perceived to fit together into a coherent whole. The happy side of this is that we learn we are not sick or monstrous, and we learn to trust our perception. The unhappy side is that the coherent whole we discover is a pattern of oppression. Women's lives are full to overflowing with the evidence of the imbalanced distribution of woes and wealth between the women and the men of each class, race, and circumstance. In consciousness-raising the data coalesce into knowledge: knowledge of the oppression of women by men.

When women's experience is made intelligible in the communications of consciousness-raising we can recognize that it is in the structures of men's stories of the world that women do not make sense—that our own experience, collectively and jointly appreciated, can generate a picture of ourselves and the world within which we are intelligible. The consciousness-raising process reveals us to ourselves as authoritative perceivers which are neither men nor the fantastical, impossible feminine beings which populate the men's world story. Our existence is not inherently paradoxical or problematic. Our existence *is* an indigestible mass of discrepant data for the patriarchal world story. From the point of view of the discrepant data, that story appears appallingly partial and distorted—it seems a childish, and fantastic, albeit dangerous fiction. Assuming our perceptual authority, we have undertaken, as we must, to rewrite the world. The project of feminist theory is to write a new encyclopedia. Its title: *The World, According to Women.*[2]

The historically dominant Western man-made world story claims universality and objectivity but, from the point of view of feminists, conspicuously lacks both. Thinking to improve upon that story, we assumed ours should be both. By adding voices to the conversation, we expected to achieve a broader consensus in the intersubjective agreement that justifies the claim to objectivity and thus also a grounding for legitimate universalization.[3]

As many introductory philosophy textbooks will tell you, the Western tradition of philosophy presupposes the intelligibility of the universe—the doctrine that *it* and *we* (human beings) are such that it can be understood by us. The human knower, in principle any human knower, can, in principle, understand the universe.[4] This presupposes a fundamental uniformity of human knowers such that in principle any knower is interchangeable with any other knower. In practice it means that as you add to the group whose intersubjective agreement will count as objectivity, you are adding pieces of a single and coherent cosmic jigsaw puzzle. You may not know where the pieces fit, but you presume it is not possible that any of them do not fit. Noncongruence of observers' observations is either merely apparent or due to observers' mistakes or errors which are themselves ultimately explainable, ultimately congruent with the rest of the world picture. If one accepts this body of doctrine, one thinks all knowers are essentially alike, that is, are essentially like oneself; one thinks then that one can speak not just as oneself, but as a human being.

For feminist thinkers of the present era the first and most fundamental act of our own emancipation was granting ourselves authority as perceivers, and we accomplished that act by discovering agreement in the experiences and perceptions of women. It makes sense that when the feminist thinker assumes her authority as a knower, she claims her equal perceptual rights in the pseudodemocracy of the interchangeable knowers of the intelligible universe. It makes sense that she would carry over the assumption that all knowers are essentially alike into the supposition that all humans similarly positioned (in this case, as women in patriarchy) have in principle, as knowers, the same knowledge. She would think she could speak not just as herself but as a woman.

The new world writers had first to overcome the deceptions and distortions that made us unknown to ourselves. We have made remarkable progress: many, many of us have rewritten many chapters of our own lives and are living lives neither we nor our mothers would have imagined possible—or even imagined at all. We have deconstructed canons, reperiodized history, revised language, dissolved disciplines, added a huge cast of characters, and broken most of the rules of logic and good taste. But we have also discovered our own vast ignorance of other women of our own time. We have repeatedly discovered that we have overlooked or misunderstood the truths of the experience of some groups of women and that we have been overlooked or misunderstood by some other segment or school of feminist thought. We have had great difficulty coming to terms with the fact of differences among women—differences associated with race, class, ethnicity, religion, nationality, sexuality, age, physical ability, and even such variety among women as is associated just with peculiarities of individual history.

What we want to do is to speak of and to and from the circumstances, experience, and perception of those who are historically, materially, and culturally constructed by or through the concept *woman*. But the differences among women across cultures, locales, and generations make it clear that although all female humans may live lives shaped by concepts of Woman, they are not all shaped by the same concept of Woman. Even in any one narrowly circumscribed community and time, no female individual is a rubber-stamped replica of the prevailing concept of Woman. (The concept of Woman that prevails in my neighborhood is internally contradictory; nobody *could* fit it.) Furthermore, Woman is not the only concept or social category any of us lives under. Each of us is a woman of some class, some color, some occupation, some ethnic or religious group. One is or is not someone's sister, wife, mother, daughter, aunt, teacher, student, boss, or employee. One is or is not alcoholic, a survivor of cancer, a survivor of the Holocaust. One is or is not able-bodied. One is fat or thin. One is lesbian or heterosexual or bisexual or off-scale. A woman of color moves in the (Western) world as both "a woman" and "of color." A white woman also moves both as "a woman" and as "white," whether or not her experience forces upon her a clear consciousness of the latter. Lesbians must reject the question: Are you more fundamentally women, or lesbians? And we insist that heterosexual women recognize that everywhere they move as women they also move as heterosexual. No one encounters the world simply as *a woman*. Nobody observes and theorizes simply as *a woman*. If there are in every locale perspectives and meanings that can properly be called women's, there is nonetheless no such thing as *a* or *the* woman's story of what is going on.

Schematically and experientially the problem of difference in feminist theory is simple: a good deal of feminist thinking has issued in statements and descriptions that pertain to "women" unmodified for distinctions among them. These are the sorts of statements their authors want to be making. But when such statements and descriptions are delivered in public they meet with critics, who are women, who report that the statements are appallingly partial, untrue, or even unintelligible when judged by their own experience and by what is common knowledge among women of their kind, class, or group. This criticism seems to be (and I have felt it to be), devastating.

Feminism (the worldview, the philosophy) rests on a most empirical base: staking your life on the trustworthiness of your own body as a source of knowledge. It rests equally fundamentally on intersubjective agreement, since some kind of agreement in perceptions and experience among women is what gives our sense data, our body data, the compelling cogency which made it possible to trust them. It is an unforgettable, irreversible, and definitive fact of feminist experience that respect for women's experience/voice/perception/knowledge, our own and others', is the ground and foundation of our emancipation—of both the necessity and the possibility of rewriting, recreating, the world. Thus it is only by a violent dishonesty that we could, or can, fail to give credence to women's voices—even when they differ wildly and conflict. When we do give them credence it soon becomes clear that, taken as a whole, "women's experience" is not uniform and coherent in the ways required to ground a structure of knowledge as that has traditionally been understood.[5]

Thus has the feminist faith in and respect for the experience and voice of every woman seemed to lead us into the valley of the shadow of human-

ism—wishy-washy, laissez-faire, I'm O.K.–You're O.K., relativistic humanism (or more recently into the bottomless bog of relativistic apolitical
postmodernism)—where there are no Women and there is no Truth.
Which is not where we want to be.

The way out, or the way back in, I think, is to clarify how the practice of
feminist theory departed from the predominating modern Western epistemology even before some theorists began revising feminism into a form of
postmodernism.

The world story we have rejected is written in a code whose syntax respects
enumerative, statistical, and metaphysical generalization. Of these, enumerative generalization is probably kindest to particulars. But it is so weak
that to be true such a generalization must do a kind of violence by remark-
ing the unremarkable and unsaying everything that is worth saying about
the individuals in question. (For example, I hardly honor my colleagues in
the Michigan State University Philosophy Department by saying that they
all have offices on the MSU campus, which is the most substantial thing I
can think of that I know is unqualifiedly true of every one of them.)
Statistical generalization may be the next kindest to particulars since it is
cheerful about coexisting with (that is, ignoring) discrepant data. Metaphysical generalization, declaring this or that to be the what-it-is of a thing,
threatens the annihilation of that which does not fit its prescription. For
example, women are nurturant; if you are not nurturant you are not a real
woman, but a monster. All generalization seems unjust to particulars, as is
reflected in the aversion people so commonly have to "being labeled."
Generalization subsumes particulars, reduces them to a common denominator. Nomination is domination, or so it seems.

It might seem that in response to the embarrassment of these paradoxes,
we should retreat into autobiography or string suitable adjectives onto the
noun *woman,* and many of us have tried both. (Speaking as an able-bodied
college-educated Christian-raised middle-class middle-aged and middle-
sized white Anglo lesbian living in the Midwest, I can report that these
strategies both reduce one to silliness and raise serious questions about
adjective ranking in English.) More moderately, we might back up to
narrowing the subject of our claims to specific groups of women identified
by race, class, nationality, and so forth. In some cases we have done this—at
the risk, even so, of overgeneralizing or stereotyping—but what we have to
say, or what we thought we had to say, is not just a compendium of claims
about the circumstances and experiences of women of particular groups.
Our project is theoretical, philosophical, political. You have to have some
sort of genuinely general generality to have theory, philosophy, politics.

But feminism has been going at generality in another way from the
start. We need to pay more attention to what we have been doing. In

consciousness-raising there is a movement away from the isolation of the individual, the particular. But even in the most culturally homogeneous local consciousness-raising group, women's lives were not revealed to be as alike as two copies of the morning paper. We agreed neither in the details of our experience nor in opinions and judgments. We perceived similarities in our experiences, but we did not determine the relative statistical frequencies of the events and circumstances we found to be "common." And the question of what a woman is, far from being answered, was becoming unanswerable and perhaps unaskable. The generalizing movement of our "science" was not toward metaphysical, statistical, or universal generalization.

In consciousness-raising women engage in a communication that has aptly been called "hearing each other into speech."[6] It is speaking unspoken facts and feelings, unburying the data of our lives. But as the naming occurs, each woman's speech creating context for the other's, the data of our experience reveal patterns both within the experience of one woman and among the experiences of several women. The experiences of each woman and of the women collectively generate a new web of meaning. Our process has been one of discovering, recognizing, and creating patterns—patterns within which experience made a new kind of sense, or, in many instances, for the first time made any sense at all. Instead of bringing a phase of enquiry to closure by summing up what is known, as other ways of generalizing do, pattern recognition/construction opens fields of meaning and generates new interpretive possibilities. Instead of drawing conclusions from observations, it generates observations.

Naming patterns is not reductive or totalitarian. For instance, we realize that men interrupt women more than women interrupt men in conversation: we recognize a pattern of dominance in conversation—male dominance. We do not say that every man in every conversation with any woman always interrupts. (We do not hazard a guess, either, as to the exact statistical frequency of this phenomenon, though once someone did a study on it, and it turned out to be even higher than any of us suspected.) We do not close any questions about men's awareness of what they are doing, or women's experience of it. What we do is sketch a schema within which certain meanings are sustained. It makes sense of a woman's feeling stifled, frustrated, angry, or stupid when she is in the company of men. It makes sense of the women who lower the pitch of their voices and use the most elite vocabulary they can command when they want to be heard in a male realm. And when a man repeatedly interrupts me, I do not just dumbly suffer the battery; in knowledge of the pattern, I interpret this event, I know it as an *act*, as "dominating." Recognizing a pattern like this can also lead out along various associative axes to other discoveries. The pattern of conversational interruption readily suggests itself as a simile for the naming of other abridgements, interferences, and amputations we suffer but have not named.

Patterns sketched in broad strokes make sense of our experiences, but it is not a single or uniform sense. They make our different experiences intelligible in different ways. Naming patterns is like charting the prevailing winds over a continent, which does not imply that every individual and item in the landscape is identically affected.[7] For instance, male violence patterns experiences as different as that of overprotective paternalism and of incest, as different as the veil and the bikini. The differences of experience and history are in fact necessary to perceiving the patterns. It is precisely in the homogeneity of isolation that one *cannot* see patterns and one remains unintelligible to oneself. What we discover when we break into connection with other women cannot possibly be uniform women's experience and perception, or we would discover nothing. It is precisely the articulation and differentiation of the experiences formulated in consciousness-raising that give rise to meaning. Pattern discovery and invention require encounters with difference, with variety. The generality of pattern is not a generality that defeats or is defeated by variety.

Our game is pattern perception. Our epistemological issues have to do with the strategies of discovering patterns and articulating them effectively, judging the strength and scope of patterns, properly locating the particulars of experience with reference to patterns, understanding the variance of experience from what we take to be a pattern. As I see it, full reflective philosophical discussion of these issues has barely begun, and I cannot write the treatise that develops them either alone or yet. But I will survey some of the territory.

We have used a variety of strategies for discovering patterns, for making sense of what does not make sense. The main thing is to notice what does not make sense. Discovering patterns requires novel acts of attention. Consciousness-raising techniques typically promote just such unruliness by breaking the accustomed structures of conversation. Adopting practices designed to give every woman equal voice and equal audience, and to postpone judgment, defense, advocacy, and persuasion, the members of the group block the accustomed paths of thought and perception. In the consequent chaos, they slide, wander, or break into uncharted semantic space. In this wilderness one can see what does not make sense—incongruities, bizarreness, anomaly, unspeakable acts, unthinkable accusations, semantic "black holes."[8] These things are denied, veiled, disguised, or hidden by practices and language that embody and protect privileged perceptions and opinions. But they are often, perhaps characteristically, flagged by "outlaw emotions,"[9] and a powerful strategy of discovery therefore is to legitimize an outlaw emotion. You feel something—anger, pain, despair, joy, an erotic rush—that is not what you are supposed to be feeling. Everything invites you to stifle it, decide you are imagining it or are overreacting, or declare yourself crazy or bad. The strategy of discovery, enabled by the consciousness-raising structures, is to put that feeling at the center, let it be presumed normal, appropriate, true, real, and then see how everything else falls out around it. Over and over, for instance, women's pain, taken simply as pain—real and appropriate pain—uncovers and confirms the pattern and reiterated patterns of male violence. Similarly, giving any "minority" voice centrality in the force field of meanings reveals patterns to us.[10]

Other strategies of pattern perception are all the familiar strategies of creativity and of self-defense: cultivating the ability to be astounded by ordinary things, the capacity for loving attention, confidence in one's senses, a sensitivity to smokescreens and fishy stories, and so on.

Pattern perception and processes of checking such perception also require recognition that not everything that is intelligibly located by a pattern *fits* the pattern. A great deal of what I have said over the years about women is not true of me (as critics both hostile and friendly have often pointed out), and much of it is not true of most of the women to whom I have said it. One reason this is so is that many of the patterns we discover are not so much *descriptive* and *prescriptive*—patterns of expectation, bribe, and penalty from which many individual women manage to deviate to a greater or lesser extent by rejection, resistance, or avoidance. A very significant aspect of feminist theory is an *affirmation* of the disparity between the lived reality of women and the patterns of patriarchy. In the project of making oneself intelligible, it is as useful to recognize forces to which one is *not* yielding as it is to recognize forces by which one is being shaped or immobilized. For instance, there are kinds of prudishness, "modesty," and shame that shape women's experience of sexuality (not in all cultures, but certainly not only in Western ones). For the women who are not contaminated by these diseases it is nonetheless relevant to some of the meanings of their sexual experience that many women are thus shaped, that many men expect women to be so, and that the woman who is exceptional in this respect has acquired her own shape partly in resistance to the force of that mold and/or partly by some form of insulation or obliviousness that surely has other interesting manifestations. Recognizing the pattern and "placing" herself in the range of meanings it sets up will contribute to her understanding of herself and her world even if she is not a woman restrained and distorted by sexual shame.

But in addition to the fact that individual divergence from the pattern we perceive is not generally to be understood as a disconfirmation of the alleged existence or strength of the pattern, there are limits to how much any one pattern patterns. Patterns are like metaphors. (Perhaps patterns

are metaphors.) Just as an illuminating metaphor eventually breaks down
when persistently pressed, the patterns that make experience intelligible
only make so much of it intelligible at a time, and over time that range may
change. In pressing a good metaphor, one finds out a great deal by exploring its limits, understanding where and why it breaks down, and one
can do the same with patterns. An important part of pattern perception is
exploring the range of the pattern, and a way of going wrong is misjudging
scope.

An example of this sort of mistake that comes from the heart of some
important feminist theorizing is in perceptions of patterns of dependence
of women on men. Anyone who is oppressing another is very likely exploit-
ing social structures that coerce the other into some kind and degree of
dependence upon the oppressor (for otherwise the victim could and would
extricate herself from the situation). But the middle white American pattern of coerced one-on-one economic and psychological dependence of females on males with limited but real opportunities for individual women's
ad hoc escape from the trap is only a local working out of a higher order
pattern. In many cultural locales dependency is more collective, not primarily economic, more or less escapable, or more or less extreme. We can
err by taking one local expression of the pattern as a global pattern or by
thinking that there is no such global pattern because we see that not
everyone experiences the particular expression of it that has been brought
to our attention (for example, assuming that since single women are not
economically dependent on a husband, they are independent of men).

If the occupational hazard of pattern perceivers is misjudging scope, the
remedy is communication. The strategy by which one proceeds to test
pattern recognition involves many inquirers' articulating patterns they
perceive and running them by as great a variety of others as possible.
Others will respond by saying something like, "Yes, that makes sense, it
illuminates my experience," or, "That doesn't sound like my life, you're not
talking about me." Patterns emerge in the responses and signal the limits of
the meaning making powers of the patterns one has articulated. A pattern
is not bogus or fictitious either simply because things do not fit it (the nonfit
may be as powerfully significant as any fit) or simply because there are
limits to what it patterns.

One might consider requiring of the articulation of patterns that they
explicitly signal the limits of their powers and applications and then criticize those that do not or that signal it wrongly. But the similarity of
patterns and metaphors is salient again here. When one says that life is a
stage, one does not and cannot specify in precisely what dimensions and to
exactly what degree life is stagelike. One aspect of the power of metaphor
is the openness of its invitation to interpretation—it casts light of a certain
color, but does not determine how its object looks in that light to any

particular observer. The patterns articulated by the feminist theorist similarly have the power to make lives and experiences usefully intelligible in part because they do *not* fix their own applications but provide only a frame for the making of meaning. Neither patterns nor metaphors contain specifications of their limits. They work until they stop working. You find out where that is by working them until they dissolve. Like a metaphor, a pattern has to be appreciated, put to use. You may outrun its power without realizing you have if you are not paying attention to the voices and perception of many women.

The business of telling when one is just wrong about a pattern, when one is misperceiving, is very tricky for women in our current states of community, or lack of it. We work in a climate of inquiry where a mainstream knowledge industry works constantly to undermine our confidence in our perceptions, where political exigencies tempt us to forced unity, and where everything would keep women from forming epistemic community. In such conditions we operate without clear and dependable intuitions of plausibility and without adequate benefit of the monitoring function provided by a clear sense of audience. It is very hard to know when we are getting it right and when we are off the wall. Our first urgency, therefore, built into our situation and our method, is to be engaged with the greatest possible range of perceivers, of theorizers. What we are about is re-metaphoring the world. We need as many and various perceivers as possible to mix metaphors wildly enough so we will never be short of them, never have to push one beyond its limits, just for lack of another to take up where it left off.

The whole female population of the planet is neither a speaker nor an audience. It does not have a story. But communications among women—kin, friends, coworkers, writers and their readers, explorers and the audiences of their stories—have generated world stories in which the lives and fates of humans on this planet fall out along fault lines of female and male as prominently and consistently as on fault lines of wealth and of tribal, racial, or national identities. Those lines are characterized by women's doing more work and controlling less wealth than men, by men's doing far more violence to women than women do to men, and by men's world stories marginalizing, reducing, and erasing women. We have not assumed but discovered these patterns and their many ramifications. In this discovery we have also discovered the grounds of epistemic community. It is not a homogeneous community, and it does not have to be so in order to ground and validate feminist theory. In fact it *cannot* be so if it is to support the meaning making of feminist theory.

If a common (but not homogeneous) oppression is what constitutes us an epistemic community, what will happen when we free ourselves? First, I would suppose that a common history of oppression and liberation would hold us for a long time in a degree of community. Eventually, perhaps, we will fall into a happy and harmless theoretical disarray. What we are writing, *The World, According to Women,* has never been anything but an anthology, a collection of tales unified, like any yarn, only by successively overlapping threads held together by friction, not riveted by logic. There is no reason to predict or require that it must forever hold together at all. Perhaps eventually the category *woman* will be obsolete. But perhaps not.

Feminism: A
Transformational
Politic

BELL HOOKS

We live in a world in crisis—a world governed by politics of domination, one in which the belief in a notion of superior and inferior and its concomitant ideology—that the superior should rule over the inferior—affects the lives of all people everywhere, whether poor or privileged, literate or illiterate. Systematic dehumanization, worldwide famine, ecological devastation, industrial contamination, and the possibility of nuclear destruction are realities which remind us daily that we are in crisis. Contemporary feminist thinkers often cite sexual politics as the origin of this crisis. They point to the insistence on difference as the factor that becomes the occasion for separation and domination and suggest that differentiation of status between females and males globally is an indication that patriarchal domination of the planet is the root of the problem. This assumption has fostered the notion that elimination of sexist oppression would necessarily lead to the eradication of all forms of domination. It is an argument that has led influential Western white women to feel that feminist movement should be *the* central political agenda for females globally. Ideologically, thinking in this direction enables Western women, especially privileged white women, to suggest that racism and class exploitation are merely the offspring of the parent system: patriarchy. Within feminist movement in the West, this has led to the assumption that resisting patriarchal domination is a more legitimate feminist action than resisting racism and other forms of domination. Such thinking prevails despite radical critiques made by Black women and other women of color who question this proposition. To speculate that an oppositional division between men and women existed in early human communities is to impose on the past, on these nonwhite groups, a world view that fits all too neatly within contemporary feminist paradigms that name man as the enemy and woman as the victim.

185

Clearly, differentiation between strong and weak, powerful and power-less, has been a central defining aspect of gender globally, carrying with it the assumption that men should have greater authority than women and should rule over them. As significant and important as this fact is, it should not obscure the reality that women can and do participate in politics of domination as perpetrators as well as victims—that we dominate, that we are dominated. If focus on patriarchal domination masks this reality or becomes the means by which women deflect attention from the real condi-tions and circumstances of our lives, then women cooperate in suppressing and promoting false consciousness, inhibiting our capacity to assume re-sponsibility for transforming ourselves and society.

Thinking speculatively about early human social arrangement, about women and men struggling to survive in small communities, we see that the parent-child relationship with its very real imposed survival structure of dependency, of strong and weak, of powerful and powerless, was a site for the construction of a paradigm of domination. While this circumstance of dependency is not necessarily one that leads to domination, it lends itself to the enactment of a social drama wherein domination could easily occur as a means of exercising and maintaining control. This speculation does not place women outside the practice of domination, in the exclusive role of victim. It centrally names women as agents of domination, as potential theoreticians and creators of a paradigm for social relationships wherein those groups of individuals designated as "strong" exercise power both benevolently and coercively over those designated as "weak."

Emphasizing paradigms of domination that call attention to woman's capacity to dominate is one way to deconstruct and challenge the simplistic notion that man is the enemy, woman the victim; the notion that men have always been the oppressors. Such thinking enables us to examine our role as women in the perpetuation and maintenance of systems of domination. To understand domination, we must understand that our capacity as women and men to be either dominated or dominating is a point of connection, of commonality. Even though I speak from the particular experience of living as a Black woman in the United States, a white-supremacist, capitalist, patriarchal society, where small numbers of white men (and honorary "white men") constitute ruling groups, I understand that in many places in the world oppressed and oppressor share the same color. I understand that right here in this room, oppressed and oppressor share the same gender. Right now as I speak, a man who is himself victimized, wounded, hurt by racism and class exploitation is actively domi-nating a woman in his life—that even as I speak, women who are ourselves exploited, victimized, are dominating children. It is necessary for us to remember, as we think critically about domination, that we all have the capacity to act in ways that oppress, dominate, wound (whether or not that power is institutionalized). It is necessary to remember that it is first the potential oppressor within that we must resist—the potential victim within that we must rescue—otherwise we cannot hope for an end to domination, for liberation.

This knowledge seems especially important at this historical moment when Black women and other women of color have worked to create awareness of the ways in which racism empowers white women to act as exploiters and oppressors. Increasingly this fact is considered a reason we should not support feminist struggle even though sexism and sexist oppression is a real issue in our lives as Black women (see, for example, Vivian Gordon's *Black Women, Feminism, and Black Liberation: Which Way?*).[1] It becomes necessary for us to speak continually about the convictions that inform our continued advocacy of feminist struggle. By calling attention to interlocking systems of domination—sex, race, and class—Black women and many other groups of women acknowledge the diversity and complexity of female experience, of our relationship to power and domination. The intent is not to dissuade people of color from becoming engaged in feminist movement. Feminist struggle to end patriarchal domination should be of primary importance to women and men globally not because it is the foundation of all other oppressive structures but because it is that form of domination we are most likely to encounter in everyday life.

Unlike other forms of domination, sexism directly shapes and determines relations of power in our private lives, in familiar social spaces, in that most intimate context—home—and in that most intimate sphere of relations—family. Usually it is within the family that we witness coercive domination and learn to accept it, whether it be domination of parent over child or male over female. Even though family relations may be, and most often are, informed by acceptance of a politic of domination, they are simultaneously relations of care and connection. It is this convergence of two contradictory impulses—the urge to promote growth and the urge to inhibit growth—that provides a practical setting for feminist critique, resistance, and transformation.

Growing up in a Black, working-class, father-dominated household, I experienced coercive adult male authority as more immediately threatening, as more likely to cause immediate pain than racist oppression or class exploitation. It was equally clear that experiencing exploitation and oppression in the home made one feel all the more powerless when encountering dominating forces outside the home. This is true for many people. If we are unable to resist and end domination in relations where there is care, it seems totally unimaginable that we can resist and end it in other institutionalized relations of power. If we cannot convince the mothers or fathers who care not to humiliate and degrade us, how can we imagine convincing or resisting an employer, a lover, a stranger who systematically humiliates and degrades?

Feminist effort to end patriarchal domination should be of primary concern precisely because it insists on the eradication of exploitation and oppression in the family context and in all other intimate relationships. It is that political movement which most radically addresses the person—the personal—citing the need for transformation of self, of relationships, so that we might be better able to act in a revolutionary manner, challenging and resisting domination, transforming the world outside the self. Strategically, feminist movement should be a central component of all other liberation struggles because it challenges each of us to alter our person, our personal engagement (either as victims or perpetrators or both) in a system of domination.

Feminism as liberation struggle must exist apart from and as a part of the larger struggle to eradicate domination in all its forms. We must understand that patriarchal domination shares an ideological foundation with racism and other forms of group oppression, that there is no hope that it can be eradicated while these systems remain intact. This knowledge should consistently inform the direction of feminist theory and practice. Unfortunately, racism and class elitism among women have frequently led to the suppression and distortion of this connection so that it is now necessary for feminist thinkers to critique and revise much feminist theory and the direction of feminist movement. This effort at revision is perhaps most evident in the current widespread acknowledgment that sexism, racism, and class exploitation constitute interlocking systems of domination—that sex, race, and class, and not sex alone, determine the nature of any female's identity, status, and circumstance, the degree to which she will or will not be dominated, the extent to which she will have the power to dominate.

While acknowledgment of the complex nature of woman's status (which has been most impressed upon everyone's consciousness by radical women of color) is a significant corrective, it is only a starting point. It provides a frame of reference which must serve as the basis for thoroughly altering and revising feminist theory and practice. It challenges and calls us to rethink popular assumptions about the nature of feminism that have had the deepest impact on a large majority of women, on mass consciousness. It radically calls into question the notion of a fundamentally common female experience which has been seen as the prerequisite for our coming together, for political unity. Recognition of the interconnectedness of sex, race, and class highlights the diversity of experience, compelling redefinition of the terms for unity. If women do not share "common oppression," what then can serve as a basis for our coming together?

Unlike many feminist comrades, I believe women and men must share a common understanding—a basic knowledge of what feminism is—if it is ever to be a powerful mass-based political movement. In *Feminist Theory: From Margin to Center,* I suggest that defining feminism broadly as "a movement to end sexism and sexist oppression" would enable us to have a common political goal. We would then have a basis on which to build solidarity. Multiple and contradictory definitions of feminism create confusion and undermine the effort to construct a feminist movement so that it addresses everyone. Sharing a common goal does not imply that women and men will not have radically divergent perspectives on how that goal might be reached. Because each individual starts the process of engagement in feminist struggle at a unique level of awareness, very real differences in experience, perspective, and knowledge make developing varied strategies for participation and transformation a necessary agenda.

Feminist thinkers engaged in radically revisioning central tenets of feminist thought must continually emphasize the importance of sex, race, and class as factors which *together* determine the social construction of femaleness, as it has been so deeply ingrained in the consciousness of many women active in feminist movement that gender is the sole factor determining destiny. However, the work of education for critical consciousness (usually called consciousness-raising) cannot end there. Much feminist consciousness-raising has in the past focused on identifying the particular ways men oppress and exploit women. Using the paradigm of sex, race, and class means that the focus does not begin with men and what they do to women, but rather with women working to identify both individually and collectively the specific character of our social identity.

Imagine a group of women from diverse backgrounds coming together to talk about feminism. First they concentrate on working out their status in terms of sex, race, and class, using this as the standpoint from which they begin discussing patriarchy or their particular relations with individual men. Within the old frame of reference, a discussion might consist solely of talk about their experiences as victims in relationship to male oppressors. Two women—one poor, the other quite wealthy—might describe the process by which they have suffered physical abuse by male partners and find certain commonalities which might serve as a basis for bonding. Yet if these same two women engaged in a discussion of class, not only would the social construction and expression of femaleness differ, so too would their ideas about how to confront and change their circumstances. Broadening the discussion to include an analysis of race and class would expose many additional differences even as commonalities emerged.

Clearly the process of bonding would be more complex, yet this broader discussion might enable the sharing of perspectives and strategies for change that would enrich rather than diminish our understanding of gender. While feminists have increasingly given "lip service" to the idea of diversity, we have not developed strategies of communication and inclusion that allow for the successful enactment of this feminist vision.

Small groups are no longer the central place for feminist consciousness-raising. Much feminist education for critical consciousness takes place in women's studies classes or at conferences which focus on gender. Books are a primary source of education, which means that already masses of people who do not read have no access. The separation of grass-roots ways of sharing feminist thinking across kitchen tables from the spheres where much of that thinking is generated, the academy, undermines feminist movement. It would further feminist movement if new feminist thinking could be once again shared in small group contexts, integrating critical analysis with discussion of personal experience. It would be useful to promote anew the small group setting as an arena for education for critical consciousness, so that women and men might come together in neighborhoods and communities to discuss feminist concerns.

Small groups remain an important place for education for critical consciousness for several reasons. An especially important aspect of the small group setting is the emphasis on communicating feminist thinking, feminist theory, in a manner that can be easily understood. In small groups, individuals do not need to be equally literate or literate at all, because the information is primarily shared through conversation, in dialogue which is necessarily a liberatory expression. (Literacy should be a goal for feminists even as we ensure that it not become a requirement for participation in feminist education.) Reforming small groups would subvert the appropriation of feminist thinking by a select group of academic women and men, usually white, usually from privileged class backgrounds.

Small groups of people coming together to engage in feminist discussion, in dialectical struggle make a space where the "personal is political" as a starting point for education for critical consciousness, can be extended to include politicization of the self that focuses on creating understanding of the ways sex, race, and class together determine our individual lot and our collective experience. It would further feminist movement if many well known feminist thinkers would participate in small groups, critically reexamining ways their works might be changed by incorporating broader perspectives. All efforts at self-transformation challenge us to engage in ongoing critical self-examination and reflection about feminist practice, about how we live in the world. This individual commitment, when coupled with engagement in collective discussion, provides a space for critical feedback which strengthens our efforts to change and make ourselves new. It is in this commitment to feminist principles in our words and deeds that the hope of feminist revolution lies.

Working collectively to confront difference, to expand our awareness of sex, race, and class as interlocking systems of domination, of the ways we reinforce and perpetuate these structures, is the context in which we learn the true meaning of solidarity. It is this work that must be the foundation of feminist movement. Without it, we cannot effectively resist patriarchal domination; without it, we remain estranged and alienated from one another. Fear of painful confrontation often leads women and men active in feminist movement to avoid rigorous critical encounter, yet if we cannot engage dialectically in a committed, rigorous, humanizing manner, we cannot hope to change the world. True politicization—coming to critical consciousness—is a difficult, "trying" process, one that demands that we give up set ways of thinking and being, that we shift our paradigms, that we open ourselves to the unknown, the unfamiliar. Undergoing this process, we learn what it means to struggle, and in this effort we experience the dignity and integrity of being that comes with revolutionary change. If we do not change our consciousness, we cannot change our actions or demand change from others.

Our renewed commitment to a rigorous process of education for critical consciousness will determine the shape and direction of future feminist movement. Until new perspectives are created, we cannot be living symbols of the power of feminist thinking. Given the privileged lot of many leading feminist thinkers in terms of status, class, and race, it is harder these days to convince women of the primacy of this process of politicization. More and more, we seem to form select interest groups composed of individuals who share similar perspectives. This limits our capacity to engage in critical discussion. It is difficult to involve women in new processes of feminist politicization because so many of us think that identifying men as the enemy, resisting male domination, gaining equal access to power and privilege are the end of any feminist movement. Not only is it not the end, it is not even the place we want revitalized feminist movement to begin. We want to begin as women seriously addressing ourselves, not solely in relation to men, but in relation to an entire structure of domination of which patriarchy is one part. While the struggle to eradicate sexism and sexist oppression is and should be the primary thrust of feminist movement, to prepare ourselves politically for this effort we must first learn how to be in solidarity, how to struggle with one another.

Only when we confront the realities of sex, race, and class, the ways they divide us, make us different, stand us in opposition—and work to reconcile and resolve these issues—will we be able to participate in the making of feminist revolution, in the transformation of the world. Feminism, as Charlotte Bunch emphasizes again and again in *Passionate Politics*, is a transformational politics, a struggle against domination wherein the effort is to change ourselves as well as structures. Speaking about the struggle to confront difference, Bunch asserts:

A crucial point of the process is understanding that reality does not look the same from different people's perspective. It is not surprising that one way feminists have come to understand about differences has been through the love of a person from another culture or race. It takes persistence and motivation—which love often engenders—to get beyond one's ethnocentric assumptions and really learn about other perspectives. In this process and while seeking to eliminate oppression, we also discover new possibilities and insights that come from the experience and survival of other peoples.[2]

Embedded in the commitment to feminist revolution is the challenge to love. Love can be and is an important source of empowerment when we struggle to confront issues of sex, race, and class. Working together to identify and face our differences—to face the ways we dominate and are dominated—to change our actions, we need a mediating force that can sustain us so that we are not broken in this process, so that we do not despair.

Not enough feminist work has focused on documenting and sharing ways individuals confront differences constructively and successfully. Women and men need to know what is on the other side of the pain experienced in politicization. We need detailed accounts of the ways our lives are fuller and richer as we change and grow politically, as we learn to live each moment as committed feminists, as comrades working to end domination. In reconceptualizing and reformulating strategies for future feminist movement, we need to concentrate on the politicization of love, not just in the context of talking about victimization in intimate relationships, but in a critical discussion where love can be understood as a powerful force that challenges and resists domination. As we work to be loving, to create a culture that celebrates life, that makes love possible, we move against dehumanization, against domination. In *Pedagogy of the Oppressed,* Paulo Freire evokes this power of love, declaring:

> I am more and more convinced that true revolutionaries must perceive the revolution, because of its creative and liberating nature, as an act of love. For me, the revolution, which is not possible without a theory of revolution—and therefore science—is not irreconcilable with love. . . . The distortion imposed on the word "love" by the capitalist world cannot prevent the revolution from being essentially loving in character, nor can it prevent the revolutionaries from affirming their love of life.[3]

That aspect of feminist revolution that calls women to love womanness, that calls men to resist dehumanizing concepts of masculinity, is an essential part of our struggle. It is the process by which we move from seeing ourselves as objects to acting as subjects. When women and men understand that working to eradicate patriarchal domination is a struggle rooted in the longing to make a world where everyone can live fully and freely, then we know our work to be a gesture of love. Let us draw upon that love to heighten our awareness, deepen our compassion, intensify our courage, and strengthen our commitment.

PART FIVE

Policy
Perspectives

Definitions of Difference

DEBORAH L. RHODE

To those concerned with sexual equality, no issue has been more critical than sexual difference. Nor has any issue remained more divisive or elusive. For the last two centuries, most efforts to secure greater equality between women and men have proceeded in a legal framework preoccupied with the difference between them. Yet despite some major achievements, this framework has proven seriously inadequate in both theory and practice. Although the last quarter century has witnessed significant progress toward gender equality, substantial disparities between the sexes remain. Women are dramatically underrepresented in the highest positions of social, economic, and political power, and dramatically overrepresented in the lowest.[1]

The law's traditional response to such gender inequalities has focused on issues of gender difference. Analysis has proceeded in largely Aristotelian terms: the sexes should receive similar treatment to the extent they are similarly situated, and different treatment to the extent they are different in some ways relevant to important social goals. In theory, this approach has bordered on tautology. In practice, it has yielded results that are indeterminate and incoherent. Sexual differences have been both overlooked and overvalued. On some issues courts have transformed biological differences into cultural imperatives. On other questions women's special circumstances have remained unacknowledged and unaddressed. By taking difference as a given, traditional approaches deflect attention from broader issues surrounding its social construction and consequences. Part of the problem has been focus: legal analysis has been too much concerned with gender difference, too little with gender disadvantage. But part of the difficulty lies deeper, and reflects fundamental limitations of law as a strategy for social change.

The following analysis explores these limitations from a broader historical and cultural perspective. Of central concern is the way in which understandings of sexual difference shape law and law in turn shapes those understandings. The organizing premise is that legal ideology serves as an important social text, one that can illumine as well as influence cultural constructions of gender. What difference law makes in its response to difference is a crucial question for both social theory and public policy.

I.

Any coherent legal theory of sexual difference must begin by acknowledging the absence of such a theory in conventional legal decision making. That absence is in part attributable to the absence of women in governance structures. For more than two and a half centuries, understandings about gender have significantly affected American legal doctrine. Yet only in the past two and a half decades has gender discrimination given rise to significant legal remedies. Until recently, American constitutional traditions excluded concerns about women, just as women themselves were largely excluded from the processes of constitutional decision making. Although subject to the law's mandates, women were, until the last quarter century, largely unacknowledged in its text, uninvited in its formulation, and uninvolved in its official interpretation. An overview of the last two centuries of gender discrimination law reveals difficulties on three levels. One cluster of problems involves the circularity of traditional analysis. Courts and legislatures have often leapt from the fact of difference to the appropriateness of differential treatment without benefit of intermediate premises. A second set of difficulties involves the premises that legal decision-makers have invoked. Women's "essential" attributes have been exaggerated, denigrated, romanticized, and homogenized. Man has set the norm against which woman appears distinctive and often deficient. This preoccupation with "real" differences between men and women has obscured the differences among women and the way that other factors such as class, race, age, and ethnicity mediate these differences. A third group of problems relates to the law's consistently inconsistent reliance on difference. Some decision-makers have reached identical legal results from competing factual premises. In other cases the same notions about sexual distinctiveness have yielded opposite conclusions. Identical assumptions about women have served as arguments for both harsher and more lenient legal treatment, and for both including and excluding women from public life. These traditional approaches have all shared one final problem: the fixation on sexual difference has deflected attention from the disadvantages that have followed from it.

The simplest of conventional legal strategies has been to avoid difficulties by avoiding discussion. This approach has conflated description and prescription. The fact that men and women are different has provided sufficient justification for their different treatment. In the Supreme Court, a leading example of laconic analysis is an early twentieth-century opinion by Oliver Wendell Holmes. The case, *Quong Wing v. Kirkendall,* involved a licensing fee statute that offered exemptions for women but not men in laundry establishments with fewer than two employees. Writing for the majority, Justice Holmes declined even to hypothesize a plausible justification for the statute. Without further explanation, his opinion concluded that the "Fourteenth Amendment does not interfere [with state regulation] by creating a fictitious equality where there are real differences."[2] That the amendment had insisted on such equality in other contexts involving "real differences," such as race or alienage, was a matter that the Court discreetly overlooked.

On similar reasoning, courts throughout the nineteenth and early twentieth centuries found it "too plain for discussion" that a difference in sex justified a difference in law. In contexts ranging from criminal penalties to poll-tax exemptions, state judges were content to assume that since gender classifications "had always been made . . . from time immemorial" they were therefore "natural and proper to make."[3]

Other courts more intent on elaborating sexual differences generally ended up exaggerating them. In some instances, decision-makers ascribed these differences to nature, in others to nurture, but most often their analysis confused the two. One of the most graphic illustrations has involved criminal sentencing provisions. Until the last two decades, judges and legislators generally agreed that women's special attributes justified special treatment in penal contexts. One 1919 Kansas Supreme Court decision typified the "biology as destiny" approach:

> In structure and function human beings are still as they were in the beginning. "Male and female He created them." It is a patent and deep-lying fact that these fundamental anatomical and physiological differences affect the whole psychic organization. They create the differences in personality between men and women, and personality is the predominating factor in delinquent careers. . . . Women's individualities and peculiarities . . . [mark her as] radically different [and] . . . deman(d) special consideration in the study and treatment of nonconformity to law.[4]

As that opinion reflects, nineteenth- and early twentieth-century ideologies of difference generally proceeded from a male reference point. From that perspective, woman's "peculiar" attributes marked her not only as different, but also as deficient. Legal doctrine both reflected and reinforced prevailing cultural assumptions about females' limited physical, psychological, and cognitive capacities. These assumed inequalities in natural ability served to justify a wide variety of inequalities in social status. One of the most celebrated examples occurred in the post–Civil War

decades as an exclusively male legal profession contemplated the boundaries of its own exclusivity. Like most other licensed vocations during this
period, the law was closed to female applicants. In *Bradwell v. Illinois,*
Justice Bradley of the U.S. Supreme Court articulated prevailing understandings of domesticity as destiny and infused them with constitutional as
well as spiritual significance. According to the "Law of the Creator,"

> The natural and proper timidity and delicacy which belongs to the female
> sex evidently unfits it for many of the occupations of civil life. The
> constitution of the family organization, which is founded in the divine
> ordinance, as well as in the nature of things, indicates the domestic sphere
> as that which properly belongs to the domain and functions of woman-
> hood.[5]

Although the precise method of divine communication was never elaborated, it remained accessible to other courts as well. Judges in Wisconsin,
Pennsylvania, and the District of Columbia similarly concluded that wom-
en's nature was to nurture; any professional pursuits constituted a departure from the natural order and, "when voluntary, treason against it." The
"peculiar qualities of womanhood . . . its quick sensibility, [and] its tender
susceptibility," were "surely not qualifications for forensic strife."[6]

Such rhetoric was, of course, highly selective. The romanticization of
womanhood reflected biases of class, race, and ethnicity as well as sex. It
was, for example, never clear why women's "tender susceptibility" should
bar her from prestigious professions but not from more grueling and
indelicate occupations like factory and field labor.

With the gradual increase in women's education, employment, and political activism, legal enforcement of the sexes' separate spheres began to
loosen. Yet similar arguments about sexual difference recurred in other
contexts throughout the twentieth century. Woman's "natural" delicacy,
reproductive responsibilities, and physical "incapacities" rationalized her
exclusion from a wide array of activities ranging from shining shoes to mix-
ing drinks.[7] Until the mid-1970s, the reigning Supreme Court precedent
upheld females' categorical exemption from jury service on the ground
that their "enlightened emancipation" had not removed them from the
"center of home and family life."[8] Even when over half of all women were
in the paid labor force, the ideology of separate spheres lingered. That
ideology served to circumscribe male as well as female experience. For
example, as late as 1974 the Utah Supreme Court ruled that a father's
petition for custody of his four-year-old daughter was not entitled to equal
treatment since men and women were not "equally gifted in lactation."[9]

The area in which such sex-based stereotypes have had the most lasting
impact involved military service. Until the early 1970s, the armed forces
maintained quotas that restricted female participation to less than 2 per-

cent. Although that percentage rose substantially over the next decade, the increase occurred without judicial intervention. Challenges in the lower courts met with the same separate spheres ideology that had dominated legal discourse a century earlier in *Bradwell*. As one district judge in the late 1960s summarized the claim, "If a nation is to survive, men must provide the front line of defense while women keep the homefires burning." Since physical strength was "for the most part . . . a male characteristic," and combat could require physical strength, military service should remain a male responsibility.[10] Missing from that analysis was any acknowledgment of the changing technology of warfare and the growing evidence concerning females' ability to perform the vast majority of combat and non-combat-related tasks.[11]

Such acknowledgments were similarly lacking in the congressional deliberations that resulted in a male-only registration system during the late 1970s. These debates, like those surrounding the effect on an equal rights amendment on military service, reflected assumptions about difference in their most traditional and stereotypical form. Not all these assumptions proceeded from consistent factual premises. Some legislative narratives envisioned torrid scenes of foxhole seduction in which woman alternately figured as victim and vamp. Female warriors also variously appeared as Amazons with hand grenades or as debutantes in combat boots; neither image was acceptable. One Marine commander put the point directly:

> Biological convergence on the battlefield would not only be dissatisfying in terms of what women could do, but it would be an enormous psychological distraction for the male, who wants to think that he's fighting for that woman somewhere behind, not up there in the same foxhole with him. It tramples the male ego. When you get right down to it, you have to protect the manliness of war.[12]

In effect, that is what the Supreme Court did. In 1981, when upholding a male-only draft registration system, a majority of justices simply assumed that differences between the sexes justified differences in combat eligibility, and that such differences further justified females' exemption from registration requirements.[13]

The competing stereotypes that emerged in debates over military service are typical of those underlying other legal decision making throughout the last century. The persistence of such dichotomous images—woman as victim and victimizer—is emblematic of a final point about the ideologies of sexual difference: their inconsistent premises and indeterminate implications.

One form of inconsistency emerged most clearly in cases involving occupational exclusions, as decision-makers invoked quite different understandings of women's difference for identical ends. A leading example involved regulations concerning females and liquor. Although women had run taverns without apparent difficulties in colonial and frontier society, nineteenth- and twentieth-century lawmakers perceived dangers looming from all directions. Rationalizations for restricting female attendance or employment in bars rested on the same stereotypes that dominated debates over military service. Some decision-makers sought to shield unsullied womanhood from male aggression; others hoped to protect vulnerable men from female seduction.[14]

These competing caricatures of woman as both "Eve and little Eva" survived constitutional scrutiny in a celebrated Supreme Court decision during the late 1940s. At issue in *Goesaert v. Cleary* was a Michigan statute prohibiting women from service as bartenders (although not as waitresses in bars) unless they were relatives of male owners. The legislative history of the prohibition left little doubt that its proponents were more interested in protecting male bartenders from competition than in protecting female employees from assaultive behavior. It was, however, history that a majority of justices were prepared to overlook. As long as the legislature could imagine "moral and social problems" connected with female bartenders, it was not obligated to take account of "sociological insights" or actual experience.[15]

Antiquated as the *Goesaert* decision now appears, variations on the same theme reemerged in the 1970s in a similar context. The issue involved airlines' refusal to hire male flight attendants. In asserting that sex was a "bona fide occupational qualification" for the job, airline executives defended preferences for women on the same grounds that had earlier served to prevent women's employment. Pan American attempted to demonstrate that female attendants' maternal instinct made them better able than males to reassure passengers anxious in a "sealed enclave environment." Southwest Airlines, by contrast, emphasized woman's role as temptress; stewardesses in hot pants and high boots were allegedly essential to personalize Southwest's "sexy image" and take passengers "skyward with love."[16]

Although federal appellate courts ultimately rejected both the flying womb and flying bordello defenses, their history suggests a broader point about the indeterminacy of difference. Not only have conflicting assumptions about sex-based differences supported similar results; similar assumptions have supported conflicting results. Throughout the nineteenth and early twentieth centuries, theories about woman's "natural" roles served as rationales both for and against expanding her "natural" rights. These arguments about gender discrimination in legal contexts paralleled broader debates about the sexes' relative political and social status. To many antifeminists, it was abundantly clear that woman's special moral sensibilities would be compromised by involvement with civic or vocational pursuits. To many feminists, it was equally plain that these same womanly attributes were essential to "purify politics" and to supply missing dimensions in law and other professions.[17]

These double edges of difference have often been apparent in the legal contexts already noted. For example, in cases involving admission to the bar or service on juries, the same assertions about distinctive feminine attributes figured on both sides of the debate. Opponents of woman's entrance to the legal profession assumed that her "natural . . . delicacy" and "subordination of hard reason to sympathetic feeling" ill suited her for all the "nastiness of the world that finds its way into courts of justice." For similar reasons, exemptions from jury service appeared necessary to shield the tender sensibilities of womanhood from all the "indecent conduct" that legal proceedings exposed.[18] By contrast, advocates of female attorneys claimed that their "delicacy, refinement, and conscientiousness" would often accomplish more than the "severity and sternness" of a male.[19] Supporters of women on juries also invoked their distinctive feminine virtues—their ability to provide an "elevating or refining" influence or to respond with particular empathy to certain claims.[20]

Comparable arguments recurred in most other twentieth-century cases in which difference became decisive. Opponents of woman bartenders were concerned that feminine virtue would be compromised by exposure to intoxicated men; proponents were convinced that females would exert a "civilizing" influence on male customers. In debates over military service, some constituencies concluded that the values of care and compassion traditionally associated with women were incompatible with effective performance in war-related contexts. Other groups maintained that such values were essential to sound strategic decision making.[21]

In some cases where similar assumptions about difference pointed in different directions, the conflict was never acknowledged, let alone resolved. Although it was thought "too plain" for discussion that sex-based distinctions in criminal sentencing statutes were appropriate, it was less plain which way those distinctions cut. As late as 1970, courts were still invoking women's "special" attributes to reach opposing results. According to some legislative and judicial bodies, women's greater amenability to custodial regulation or lesser ability to withstand punishment justified shorter sentences. Other decision-makers concluded that unspecified differences in females' "physiological and psychological makeup . . . and their reaction as a class to imprisonment" dictated longer periods of penal supervision.[22]

For the past century, legal analysis of difference has been inescapably indeterminate. Conventional approaches have generated no coherent theory about what sorts of difference matter and why. The jurisprudence of gender has rested on circular reasoning and stereotypical assumptions. A more effective response to sexual inequality will require an alternative approach to sexual difference.

II.

Although discourses about difference sometimes have a place, they should begin—not end—analysis. By constantly presenting gender issues in terms of gender difference, conventional legal frameworks implicitly bias discussion. To pronounce women either the same or different leaves men as the standard of analysis. Further progress toward gender equality requires an alternative framework that focuses not on difference per se, but on the disadvantages that follow from it. Under this approach, the legitimacy of sex-based treatment does not depend on whether the sexes are differently situated. Rather, analysis turns on whether legal recognition of gender distinctions is more likely to reduce or to reinforce gender disparities in political power, social status, and economic security. This issue cannot be resolved in the abstract. It demands close attention to context and to the complexity of women's interests.

The rationale for this alternative framework may become more apparent in light of specific examples. Disputes involving preferential treatment offer a representative case in point. For the most part, courts have treated issues of benign discrimination, or special protection for women, in terms of difference. Attention traditionally has centered on the extent to which the sexes are differently situated. The alternative framework proposed here would focus on the consequences of specific legal responses to difference, and would remain sensitive to variations in those consequences for particular groups of women. Such an approach requires a level of contextual analysis that has been lacking in traditional legal approaches.

The most enduring example involves sex-based protective labor legislation. For almost a century, the law has vacillated between denying and exaggerating female employees' special needs. All too often women have ended up fighting each other over the value of protection rather than uniting to challenge the conditions that have made protection so valuable.

Sex-based protective statutes, such as regulation of hours, working conditions, and minimum wages, emerged in the late nineteenth and early twentieth centuries. Many of the initial statutes covered only women, a limitation encouraged by a celebrated 1905 Supreme Court decision, *Lochner v. New York*. There, a majority of Justices invalidated a sex-neutral maximum hours law as an unreasonable restraint on liberty to contract. The question that arose after *Lochner* was whether women's special circumstances justified special protection.[23]

To some judges, no such circumstances were apparent. In overturning sex-based night work restrictions, the 1907 New York Court of Appeals reasoned that "man and woman now stand alike in their constitutional rights. There is no warrant for making any discrimination between them with respect to the liberty of personal contract." Other courts similarly found no justification for regulating a woman's wages or work week and thereby restricting her "natural right to gain a livelihood."[24] Such egalitarian rhetoric was highly selective. When the issue was suffrage, jury service, management of marital property, or entry into certain occupations, women's natural rights became less evident. Moreover, in enshrining contractual liberty, these decisions ignored contractual realities. Few employees of either sex in fact were able adequately to protect themselves from exploitative working conditions, and women faced particular difficulties.

Some of those difficulties were related to asymmetries in domestic obligations. Whatever their employment status, women assumed the vast majority of household responsibilities. These duties, when coupled with the twelve-hour days common in female-dominated occupations, discouraged married women from working and imposed enormous hardship on those who had no choice. Since both workplace structures and social conventions kept most wives out of the paid labor force, female employees tended to be younger and less experienced than their male colleagues. These working women were unlikely to be union members or permanent employees with a large stake in advancement. Such characteristics helped confine women to low status, poorly paid, and tedious work, which further encouraged job turnover.[25]

This self-perpetuating cycle, coupled with overt discrimination, resulted in persistent wage disparities. Female workers in the early twentieth century averaged one-half to two-thirds the salaries of males. At the time when controversies arose over sex-based minimum wage laws, only about a quarter of women were earning even subsistence salaries.[26]

Yet the conventional sex-based response to these disparities helped in some ways to reinforce them. In both rationale and result, protective labor legislation often impeded equal opportunities for women in the workplace and equal obligations for men in domestic life. The difficulties in rationale emerged most clearly in a series of cases beginning with the Supreme Court's landmark 1908 decision, *Muller v. Oregon*. In *Muller* and its progeny, a majority of Justices sustained maximum hour and night work limitations for female employees on the basis of their maternal mission. In the Court's view, woman's reproductive functions, physical limitations, and special "disposition and habits of life" placed her at a disadvantage in the "struggle for subsistence." She had no alternative but to "look to [man] for protection." Since "healthy mothers [were] essential to vigorous offspring," it was appropriate to safeguard them from the "greed as well as passion of men" and from their own "indifference, error, recklessness or cupidity."[27]

In the aftermath of *Muller,* gender-based protective legislation became increasingly common and increasingly divisive. Within the feminist community, disputes intensified during the 1920s, after introduction of a constitutional Equal Rights Amendment in Congress. One camp of the woman's movement opposed the amendment because it would jeopardize sex-based preferences, particularly those in protective labor statutes; these opponents stressed women's different needs and circumstances. Proponents of the amendment were convinced that such special protections would "protect" women out of opportunities available to men. This debate not only divided the feminist movement for decades but also obscured the complexity of the concerns at issue. On both ideological and material levels, the consequences of preferential treatment were more mixed than the sameness/difference debate generally acknowledged.

For the majority of women, who worked in predominately female occupations, regulation of hours, wages, and working conditions produced some significant improvements. In those occupations, most employers adjusted to regulatory schemes without finding cheaper male replacements or reducing take-home pay. To the women who had once worked double days—twelve hours in the factory and another seven at home cooking, cleaning, laundering, and sewing—hourly restrictions were a substantial achievement. Although data on sex-based minimum wage guarantees are more spotty, the most exploited workers, particularly those in female-dominated industries, frequently obtained salary increases that made an appreciable difference in their quality of life.[28]

Yet the price of such protection was increased female unemployment and competitive disadvantage in contexts where male workers were available. By lobbying for restrictions on women's night work or overtime shifts, predominately male unions were often able to oust women from the most attractive positions. Some evidence suggests that restrictive maximum hours laws substantially increased unemployment among female immigrants and the minimum wage guarantees in certain states restricted opportunities for native women workers as well.[29] By foreclosing occupational mobility, such statutes locked women into crowded, sex-segregated employment and further depressed their bargaining leverage. Laws designed to preserve domestic roles frequently had the opposite result. Legislative bans on overtime forced some women to moonlight at jobs without overtime pay; prohibitions on night work compromised their ability to care for children or invalid relatives during the day. And since protective statutes generally exempted domestic service and farm labor, they offered little protection to women of color, who needed it most.[30]

Other consequences of sex-based protective legislation were similarly mixed and similarly difficult to assess. Some male workers obviously benefited from the exclusion of female competitors; others would have benefited more if regulations on hours, wages, and safety conditions had been available to all workers. By allocating overtime and evening work largely to men, protective labor laws encouraged domestic patterns that absolved husbands from many burdens, but also denied them many benefits of family life. The ideology of protection based on women's maternal mission also spilled over into other contexts where protection was far less desirable, such as exclusion from jury service or educational and military opportunities. Legal recognition of woman's separate and subordinate status thus in some measure reinforced it.[31]

Yet even with the advantages of hindsight, it is not self-evident whether sex-based protections were prudent interim strategies or inappropriate compromises. For feminists on both sides of this question, the ultimate goal was gender-neutral regulation and the last half century has witnessed a steady trend in that direction. In the late 1930s, Congress enacted, and the Supreme Court sustained, wage and hour provisions governing all workers. By the 1960s, restrictions covering only women were illegal except in certain limited contexts.[32] What remains unclear is whether more could have been accomplished sooner if legal reformers had not settled for less.

That question cannot be resolved at the abstract level where it is typically debated. In some circumstances, sex-specific statutes may have slowed momentum toward broader coverage, but in others they may have been a critical first step, given the political obstacles to reform and the practical exigencies facing most female employees. The common tendency has been either to applaud such regulation for responding to difference or to denounce it for contributing to difference. Both approaches ignore the complexity of the forces at work and the diversity of women's interests. Evaluation depends not only on historical evidence but also on historical interpretation: on which women, which industries, which period, and which social, economic, and ideological concerns receive emphasis. In this as in other contexts, the law's responses to difference have been double-edged and do not lend themselves to categorical pronouncements. This history should inform contemporary legal struggles.

III.

During the 1960s a variety of social, economic, demographic, and ideological factors converged to challenge traditional definitions of difference. Women's increasing work force participation, declining fertility rates, and growing political activism set the stage for new legislative initiatives on gender discrimination. Against this changing legal and cultural backdrop, courts began subjecting sex-based discrimination to heightened scrutiny. New constitutional standards permitted such discrimination only if it served important state interests that could not be achieved by alternative means. But while classifications based on gender roles met increasing resistance, classifications tied to biological attributes provoked greater ambivalence. At issue were the identical questions of sameness and difference that had given rise to the protective labor dispute a half-century earlier: to what extent should woman's special reproductive capacity entitle her to special legal status?

That issue took on particular significance in contemporary debates over maternity policies. Those debates provide a case study in the limitations of conventional responses to "real" difference. The modern dispute began with the Supreme Court's initial confusion about how to cope with pregnancy discrimination. In the mid-1970s, a majority of Justices upheld policies providing employee benefits for virtually all medical disabilities except those related to childbirth. What enshrines these decisions as landmark sex discrimination cases was the Court's unwillingness to treat them as such. The majority opinion in the initial case relegated the entire discussion of discrimination to a footnote. There, the Court announced its novel conclusion that pregnancy policies did not even involve "gender as such." Employers were simply drawing a distinction between—in the Court's memorable phrase—"pregnant women" and "non-pregnant persons." Preoccupied with difference rather than disadvantage, the majority perceived no issue of discrimination. Since pregnancy was a "unique" and "additional" disability, employers were entitled to exclude it from coverage.[33]

Never did the majority explain what made pregnancy more "unique" than the all-male disabilities, such as prostatectomies, that were fully covered. Rather, the Court's characterization assumed what should have been at issue and made the assumption from a male reference point. Men's physiology set the standard against which women's claims appeared merely "additional."

Following this series of cases, intense lobbying prompted passage of the federal Pregnancy Discrimination Act, which provided that pregnancy should be treated the same as other medical risks for employment-related purposes.[34] This remains, however, one of the many contexts in which equality in form has not resulted in equality in fact. The act requires only that employers treat pregnancy like other disabilities. It does not affirmatively require adequate disability policies. In the absence of statutory mandates, such policies have been slow to develop. A decade after the act's passage, about three-fifths of female workers were still not entitled to wage replacement for the normal duration of disability, and over a third could not count on returning to the same job after a normal period of leave. The United States stood alone among major industrialized countries in its failure to provide such benefits. Since about 85 percent of all women become pregnant at some point in their working lives, and over half return to the labor force within a year of childbirth, the absence of adequate maternity policies remains a significant problem.[35]

Efforts to improve that situation have given rise to new versions of old controversies over gender-specific protective statutes. The dispute came before the Supreme Court in the late 1980s in a case that again found feminists on opposing sides. At issue was a California statute which, like its analogues in other states, required reasonable leaves of absence for pregnant workers but not for other temporarily disabled employees. The defendant challenged the legislation as inconsistent with the federal Pregnancy Discrimination Act, which mandated that childbirth be treated the same as other disabilities. In rejecting that claim, a majority of Justices reasoned that policies like California's were consistent with the act's objective, which was to guarantee women's right to "participate fully and equally in the workforce."[36] While united in support of that objective, feminists have divided over whether "special" treatment for pregnancy is an effective means to the desired end.

Supporters of special legislative safeguards generally begin from the premise that women and men are differently situated with respect to reproduction. Although a no-leave policy creates hardships for both sexes concerning the disabilities they share, it places an additional burden on women. Pregnancy should not need to appear just like other medical risks in order to gain adequate protection. Why require females' assimilation to a male norm rather than fair recognition of their separate capacities? As long as legislatures are unprepared to mandate adequate protection for all workers, many feminists see partial coverage as an appropriate interim goal.[37]

The danger is that settling for intervention on behalf of the most politically sympathetic constituency could diminish pressure for more comprehensive approaches. Nor is that the only risk. Gender-based legislation has often worked to reinforce roles that are more separate than equal. While pregnancy is in some important sense unique, stressing that uniqueness has often exacerbated women's economic disadvantage and the stereotypes underlying it. Legislation that makes women more expensive reinforces incentives for covert discrimination. Feminists who oppose special protection are unwilling to see women once again protected out of any jobs desirable to men.[38]

Yet one lesson we learn from history is that there are limits to the other lessons we can draw from it. The adverse consequences of protective legislation earlier in this century occurred in a social context that lacked significant legal and social sanctions against gender discrimination. The current regulatory climate is somewhat different, although the problems of enforcing equal protection guarantees should not be underestimated.

Both the positive and negative consequences of maternity policies are likely to depend on various factors, including their scope, financing, and the particular climate surrounding enactment. Without further experience and research, it is difficult to predict how many women at what income levels would benefit and who would pay the price of gender-specific policies.

What complicates the issue still further are the mixed ideological messages that such policies may convey. In one sense, job-protected leaves may help break the stereotype of childbearing women as provisional employees with higher turnover and lower work commitment than their male colleagues. Yet to require that parental leaves be available only to mothers is to reinforce, both in fact and in appearance, unequal allocations of workplace opportunities and family responsibilities. "Mommy tracks" often become mommy traps. They limit women's career choices and reinforce assumptions that child-rearing is solely a mother's obligation. Few American companies have provided paternity or parental leave policies. Even where leaves are available, it has been rare for men to take one, and rarer still for them to do so for more than a brief one- or two-week interval.[39] Such asymmetries in parental roles circumscribe opportunities for both sexes. If, as much feminist psychoanalytic theory suggests, individuals can develop better capacities for nurturing by having significant attachments to a parent of the same sex during early childhood, then it is critical to develop policies that encourage paternal as well as maternal commitments.[40]

The complexity of this issue underscores the need to recast the framework in which it has generally emerged. As in other contexts, a focus on difference is ultimately unproductive. Women are both the same and different. They are different in their needs at childbirth, but the same in their needs for broader medical, child-rearing, and caretaking policies. To determine which side of the sameness/difference dichotomy to emphasize in legal contexts requires some other analytic tool, one that emphasizes not biological distinctions but the consequences of recognizing them in particular social, political, and economic circumstances.

This alternative framework, which focuses less on difference than on disadvantage, argues for the broadest possible caretaking policies for all workers. Sex-neutral strategies pose the least risk of entrenching stereotypes or encouraging covert discrimination, and offer the widest range of protections for disadvantaged groups. Although the consequences of women's special reproductive role should not be undervalued, neither should they be overstated. More women have access to maternity leaves than to broader disability and parenting policies. The absence of such policies presents recurring problems for the vast majority of employees, both male and female, throughout their working lives. Pregnancy leaves are only one aspect of an adequate parenting program, and provisions for working parents are only one aspect of an adequate strategy for dependent care. Disabled spouses, elderly relatives, and young children present needs that are difficult to meet under existing workplace structures.

An effective policy response would begin with federal legislation guaranteeing reasonable gender-neutral leaves for all temporary medical disabilities and short-term dependent care.[41] But to create a society truly committed to caretaking values will also require more fundamental changes in employment structures and welfare policies. It will demand a broad range of initiatives regarding child care, part-time work, flexible schedules, health insurance, and family support services.[42] Securing such changes will, in turn, require political coalitions that focus less on difference, and differences over difference, and more on crosscutting objectives and concerns. We cannot allow disagreements over interim strategies to obscure common long-term goals. The issue is not simply how well society accommodates women's particular biological capacities, but how highly it values intimate human relationships and the care-related obligations that such relationships impose. At stake are questions not only of gender equality but also of cultural priorities.

I V.

Comparable observations apply to other contexts that do not find women similarly situated to men, including poverty, divorce, sexual violence, reproductive autonomy, and occupational segregation. Although the last quarter century has witnessed progress in legal responses to gender discrimination, its legacy remains pronounced. All too often equality in formal mandates has not translated into equality in actual status. After two and a half decades' experience with equal pay legislation, we remained a fair distance from equal pay. Full-time female workers earned only about two-thirds of the annual salaries of full-time male workers (70 percent of weekly wages). Women were also more likely to be unemployed, or locked into low-paying, low-status occupations with few benefits or opportunities for promotion.[43] Despite judicial and statutory standards promising "equality" or "equity" for divorcing couples, most wives have secured neither equality nor equity. In the aftermath of dissolution, men's income generally has risen and women's has fallen; the vast majority of mothers find themselves with unequal family responsibilities and unequal resources to discharge them.[44] Although congressional reforms and constitutional challenges have eliminated most of the gender stereotyping that once dominated welfare regulation, such interventions have not addressed the growing feminization of poverty. In the late 1980s, two-thirds of all indigent adults were women and over half of female-headed families were below the poverty line. Restrictions on abortion and inadequacies in birth control programs have robbed many women of the ability to shape their own productive and reproductive lives.[45]

These gender differences vary across class, race, age, ethnicity, and sexual orientation. For example, women of color have suffered most from the inadequacy of societal responses to poverty, reproductive freedom, single-parent families, occupational segregation, and sexual violence.[46] Older women have borne a disproportionate share of the miseries that follow from unequal enforcement of divorce laws and limitations in assistance for displaced homemakers and dependent care.[47]

As these examples also suggest, many of the most significant legal challenges to gender-related differences have failed to reach the class of women for whom differences have carried the greatest disadvantages. To take an obvious illustration, Supreme Court decisions have to some extent recognized that women's control over the decision to bear a child is fundamental to their equality. However, neither courts nor legislatures have ensured the support structures necessary for all women to exercise that control. Without adequate public funding for abortion, child care, welfare assistance, contraceptive services, and medical insurance, individuals' reproductive choices will be highly constrained.[48]

The task remaining is to develop societal responses to sex-related differences that will neither perpetuate their adverse consequences nor obscure their differential effects. Such responses call for more than equal treatment in order to secure women's treatment as equals. And they require greater sensitivity to the difference difference makes for particular groups of women.

Although legal mandates can play an important part in the struggle for gender equality, their role should not be overvalued. The indeterminacies, inconsistencies, and inadequacies of the law's traditional responses to sex-related differences make clear its limitations as a vehicle for social change. Disputes over abstract legal principles can divert energy from concrete political struggles, and incremental reforms can deflect attention from the more basic economic and social problems that remain.

Yet recasting our legal understandings can also help reshape our social experience. Law can be a focal point for political mobilization and public education. Rethinking our legal approaches to sexual difference can force us to reconsider the consequences that have followed from it. The legal issues that have been most central to women's experiences are not only "women's issues." The "peculiar" concerns that lawmakers have traditionally ascribed to womanhood are concerns central to any struggle for a more just and humane society. The stakes in reimagining our legal alternatives are not simply equality between the sexes, but the quality of life for both of them.

Legal Perspectives on Sexual Difference

CATHARINE A. MACKINNON

> The measure of man is man.
> —Pythagoras

> [Men] think themselves superior to women, but
> they mingle that with the notion of equality between
> men and women. It's very odd.
> —Jean-Paul Sartre

Viewing gender as a matter of sameness and difference—as virtually all existing law and theory does in one way or another—is a way of covering up the reality of gender, which is a system of social hierarchy. Gender is an imposed inequality of power first, a social status based on who is permitted to do what to whom, and only derivatively a difference.

One of the more illuminating statements ever made about the so-called gender difference was by Jean Harris, former headmistress of the Madeira School, convicted for killing her former lover when, she testified, she had intended to kill herself instead. She said, "I wish I had been born a doormat or a man."[1] It is very different to be a doormat than it is to be a man. Differences between the sexes obviously do exist, descriptively speaking. But to focus on the fact that these are a woman's realistic options and that they are so limiting calls into question the explanatory value and the political agenda implicit in calling gender a difference. One is not socially permitted to be a woman and neither doormat nor man.

The differences attributed to sex are lines inequality draws, not the basis for those lines. Social and political equality are lived-out social systems that are basically indifferent to abstract conceptual categories like sameness and difference. Differences are inequality's post hoc excuse, its conclusory artifact. They are its outcome presented as its origin, the damage that is pointed to as the justification for doing the damage after the damage has been done. They are distinctions that social perception is organized to notice because inequality gives them consequences for social power, social

213

worth, social resources. Distinctions of body or mind or behavior are pointed to as cause rather than effect without realizing that they are so deeply effect rather than cause that pointing to them at all is a kind of effect. Inequality comes first. "Differences" come after. Inequality is a substantive system of disparity. "Differences" is an abstract system of false symmetry. To the extent this is true, a discourse of gender difference serves as ideology to neutralize, rationalize, and cover up disparities of power, including when it appears to be critical of them.

"Difference" in this view is the velvet glove on the iron fist of dominance. This is as true when differences are affirmed as when they are denied. It is as true when their substance is applauded as when it is disparaged. It is as true when women are punished for it as it is when they are protected in its name. A sex inequality in this view is not a difference gone awry. Deep antifeminism supports the persistent treatment of gender in scholarship, politics, and law as if it truly is a question of difference, when the gender difference is a construct of the difference gender makes.

Gender inequality pervades the way we think. If a concept like difference is a conceptual tool of gender and of inequality, it cannot deconstruct the master's house, because it has built it. Difference is what the gender system says gender is. Dominance, it denies. Only that might be a clue. Consider legal reasoning, in which analogy and distinction are methodological. In the peculiar way lawyers think, when you raise one issue, they have to talk about some other issue in order to act as though they are talking about the issue you raised. That is called reasoning by analogy, elevated with the social power of law and lawyers to a method. Like and unlike, similar and dissimilar, sameness and difference have become metametaphor through which the law puts its norm of equal treatment into effect.

Equality is a generic norm as well as a specific doctrine in the legal system. If you treat one situation one way, the question goes, do you have to treat another situation the same way? The answer is, See if the other situation is like or different from the first situation. Like and unlike are the test for equal and unequal. Like a lot of metaphors, the hold of this one is a lot more tenacious than it merits. Why should women have to be "like" men to be treated as equal citizens? Why should sex inequality have to be "like" racial inequality or any other inequality to be treated as invidious? Benjamin Cardozo once said of metaphors, "The word starts out to free thought and ends by enslaving it."

Equality, including sex equality, needs to be rethought. What is a gender question a question of? What is an inequality question a question of? Tacit answers to these questions underlie the law of sex discrimination, which is that area of the law in which the state applies the equality principle to issues of gender. Mainstream legal and moral theory tacitly give the same answer to both questions: these are questions of sameness and difference. The mainstream doctrine of the law of sex discrimination that results from the approach based on these answers has not provided sex equality for women in society. It has not guaranteed what is socially precluded to women in the United States, across class lines, on the basis of a condition of birth: a chance at productive lives of reasonable physical security, self-expression, individuation, minimal respect, and human dignity. Through conceiving and enforcing this condition as "the gender difference," the inner logic of sex discrimination doctrine can be seen to express the political logic of male dominance by effectively enforcing women's second-class status through state power.

According to the approach to sex equality that has dominated politics, law, and social perception, equality is an equivalence, not a distinction, and sex is a distinction. The legal mandate of equal treatment becomes a matter of treating likes alike and unlikes unlike, and the sexes are defined as such by their mutual unlikeness. Gender is socially constructed *as difference* epistemologically, and sex discrimination law bounds gender equality *by difference* doctrinally. Socially one tells a woman from a man by their difference from each other, but a woman is discriminated against on the basis of sex only when she can first be said to be the same as a man. A built-in tension exists between this concept of equality, which presupposes sameness, and this concept of sex, which presupposes difference. Sex equality becomes a contradiction in terms, something of an oxymoron. Difference, inscribed on society as the meaning of gender itself, and written into law as the limit on sex discrimination is thus the question on which the state's position on sex equality turns.

In sex discrimination law, the evil of sex discrimination becomes a "sex classification," legislators Linnaeus. A classification in law or in fact is or is not a sex-based discrimination depending upon the accuracy of its "fit"[2] with gender and upon the importance and validity of its purpose for government or business. A classification, in the classic formulation, "must be reasonable, not arbitrary, and must rest upon some ground of difference having a fair and substantial relation to the object of the legislation, so that all persons similarly circumstanced shall be treated alike."[3] Under the equal protection clause of the Fourteenth Amendment to the Constitution, if a rule or practice in question draws a gender line, it must correspond well to the reality of gender and must not be intended to discriminate. In addition, the relation between sex and the line's proper objectives must be better than rational but need not be perfect. In what has been termed "intermediate scrutiny"—a judicial standard of care for women only—sex lines are scrutinized more carefully than most, but not as strictly as some,[4] and are not prohibited absolutely, as they might have been under the dominant interpretation of the Equal Rights Amendment (ERA).[5]

Equality is comparative in sex discrimination law. Relevant empirical similarity is the basis for a claim to equal treatment. For differential treatment to be discriminatory, the sexes must first be "similarly situated" by legislation, qualifications, circumstance, or physical endowment.[6] This applies to sex the broader legal norm of neutrality, the law's version of objectivity. To test for gender neutrality, reverse the sexes and compare. To see if a woman was discriminated against on the basis of sex, ask whether a similarly situated man would be or was so treated. Relevant difference supports different treatment, no matter how categorical, disadvantageous, or cumulative. Accurate reflections of differences in situation are either noncomparable or rational, therefore not inequalities for legal purposes. Normative equality derives from and refers to empirical equivalence.

In this mainstream approach the sexes, by nature biologically different, are therefore socially properly differentiated for some purposes. Upon this natural, immutable, inherent, essential, just, and intrinsically wonderful differentiation, society is thought to have erected some arbitrary, irrational, confining, and distorting sex roles, or at least sex roles that do not work for everyone. These failures of socialization, nothing deeper, are the inequalities the law against sex discrimination primarily targets. As one scholar puts it, "any prohibition against sexual classifications must be flexible enough to accommodate two legitimate sources of distinctions on the basis of sex: biological differences between the sexes and the prevailing heterosexual ethic of American society."[7] Laws or practices that express or reflect sex "stereotypes," understood as inaccurate, overgeneralized attitudes often termed "archaic" or "outmoded," are at the core of this definition of discrimination.[8] Any real distinction, physical, or social, or that cannot be accurately traced to biology or heterosexuality, is not a discrimination but a difference.

Differentiation is thus the point of departure and return for sex discrimination law. Doctrinally speaking, two alternate paths to sex equality for women emerge within this mainstream approach to sex discrimination, paths that roughly follow the lines of the sameness/difference tension. The leading one is Be the same as men. This path is termed gender neutrality doctrinally and the single standard philosophically. It is testimony to how substance becomes form in law that this rule is considered formal equality. Because it mirrors the values of the social world, it is considered abstract, meaning transparent of substance; also for this reason it is considered not only to be *the* standard, but *a* standard at all. Legally articulated as the need to conform normative standards to existing reality, the strongest doctrinal expression of its sameness idea would prohibit taking gender into account (with limited exceptions). It is so far the leading rule that the words *equal to* are code for, equivalent to, the words *the same as*—referent for both unspecified.

For women who want equality yet find they are different, the doctrine provides an alternate route: be different from men. This equal recognition of difference is termed the special benefit rule or special protection rule legally, the double standard philosophically. It is in rather bad odor. Like pregnancy, which always brings it up, it is something of a doctrinal embarrassment. Considered an exception to true equality and not really a rule of law at all, it is the one place where the law of sex discrimination admits it is recognizing something substantive. Together with the Bona Fide Occupational Qualification (BFOQ) and the exception for unique physical characteristics under ERA policy, compensatory legislation, and sex-conscious relief in particular litigation, affirmative action is thought to live here.[9]

Underlying the differences approach is the philosophy of liberalism, applied to women. Here sex *is* a natural difference, a division, a distinction, beneath which lies a stratum of human commonality, sameness. The moral thrust of the sameness branch of the doctrine is to conform normative rules to this empirical reality by granting women access to what men have access to: to the extent women are no different from men, we deserve what they have. The differences branch, which is generally seen as patronizing but necessary to avoid absurdity, exists to value or compensate women for what we are or have become distinctively as women—by which is meant unlike men.

Most treatments of sex discrimination law, including those presented as feminist, revolve around these questions as if they are all there is, and concern themselves with which of these paths to sex equality is preferable in the long run or more appropriate to any particular issue.[10] My concern here is conceptually and politically prior. To treat issues of sex equality as issues of sameness and difference is to take a particular approach, here termed the differences approach because it is obsessed with sex difference. The main theme of its fugue is, "we're the same, we're the same, we're the same." The contrapuntal theme (in a higher register) is "but we're different, but we're different, but we're different." Its underlying story is: on the first day, difference was; on the second day, a division was created upon it; on the third day, occasional dominance arose. Division may be rational or irrational. Dominance either seems or is justified. Difference *is*.

There is a politics to this. Concealed is the substantive way in which man has become the measure of all things. Under the sameness standard, women are measured according to correspondence with man, our equality judged by our proximity to his measure. Under the difference standard, women are measured according to our lack of correspondence from man, our womanhood judged by our distance from his measure. Gender neutrality is the male standard, and the special protection rule is the female standard. Masculinity or maleness is the referent for both. Approaching sex discrimination in this way—as if sex questions are difference questions and equality questions are sameness questions—merely provides two ways for the law to hold women to a male standard and to call that sex equality.

This sameness/difference approach to sex equality questions has mediated what women have gotten as women from this state under the rubric of sex discrimination. It does take up a very important problem: how to get women access to everything women have been excluded from while also valuing everything that women are or have been allowed to become or have developed as a consequence of our struggle either not to be excluded from most of life's pursuits or to be taken seriously under the terms that have been permitted to be our terms. It negotiates what women have managed in relation to men. Its guiding impulse is We're as good as you; anything you can do, we can do. Just get out of the way. For women, it has accomplished some access to employment and education, to the public pursuits (including academic and professional and blue-collar work), to the military, and more than nominal access to athletics.[11] It has moved to alter the dead ends that were all women were seen as good for and to shift what passed for lack of physical training, which was really serious training in passivity and enforced weakness. The issue of the military draft[12] has presented the sameness answer to the sex equality question in all its simple dignity and complex equivocality: as a citizen, I should have to risk being killed just like you; the consequences of my resistance to this risk should count like yours count. The undercurrent is What's the matter, don't you want me to learn to kill . . . just like you? (The conflict might be expressed as a dialogue between women in the afterlife. The feminist says to the soldier: "We fought for your equality." The soldier says to the feminist: "Oh, no, *we* fought for *your* equality.")

Looking at outcomes, the sameness standard has mostly gotten men the benefit of those few things women have historically had—for all the good they did. Under gender neutrality, the law of custody and divorce has been transformed, giving men what is termed an equal chance at custody of children and at alimony.[13] Men often look like better parents under gender-neutral rules like level of income and presence of nuclear family, because men make more money and (as it is termed) initiate the building of family units. In effect men are granted a legal preference because society advantages them before they get into court, and the standards value men's social advantages above women's social disadvantages. Law is prohibited from taking that preference into account because that would mean taking gender into account, which would be sex discrimination. The group realities that make women more in need of alimony are not permitted to matter, because only individual factors, gender-neutrally considered, may matter. So the fact that women will live their lives as individuals, as members of the group women, with women's chances in a sex-discriminatory society, may not count or it is sex discrimination. The equality principle in this form mobilizes the idea that the way to get things for women is to get them for men. Admittedly, men have got them. Have women? Women still have not got equal pay *or* equal work, far less equal pay *for* equal work, and are close to losing separate enclaves like women's schools through this approach.[14]

Here is why. This approach is liberal idealism talking to itself. It presents how it wishes things were—women and men really equal, that is, the same—when, first, they are not; second, if they were, there would be little social inequality to address; and third, some of us have higher aspirations. So the sameness/difference approach is always being undermined by the problem it says it is trying to solve. In reality virtually every quality that distinguishes men from women is already affirmatively compensated in society's organization and values. Men's physiology defines most sports, their health needs largely define insurance coverage, their socially de-signed biographies define workplace expectations and successful career patterns, their perspectives and concerns define quality in scholarship, their experiences and obsessions define merit, their military service defines citizenship, their presence defines family, their inability to get along with each other—their wars and rulerships—define history, their image defines god, and their genitals define sex. For each of their so-called differences from women, what amounts to an affirmative action plan, otherwise known as the structure and values of American society, is in effect. But whenever women are different from men and insist on just not having it held against us, whenever a difference is used to keep us second-class and we refuse to smile about it, equality law has a paradigm trauma.

What this doctrine apparently means by sex inequality is not what hap-pens to us. The law of sex discrimination seems to be looking only for those ways women are kept down that have *not* wrapped themselves up as a difference, whether original, imposed, or imagined. Start with original: what to do about the fact that women actually have an ability men still lack, gestating children in utero. Pregnancy therefore is a difference. In main-stream doctrine it was sex discrimination to give women what they need because only women need it. It is not sex discrimination *not* to give women what they need because then only women will not get what they need.[15] This doctrine is transfixed by the bright vision of sameness like deer by hunters' headlights.

Move into imposed differences: what to do about the fact that most women are segregated into low-paying jobs where there are no men. Arguing that the structure of the marketplace will be subverted if compa-rable worth is put into effect (noting the radical potential of such a re-form)[16] the differences branch of the doctrine says that because there is no man to set a standard against which women's treatment is a deviation, there is no sex discrimination, only sex difference. Never mind that there is no man to compare with because no man would do that job if he had a choice (and because he is a man, he does, so he does not). Straightforward cases of sex discrimination run aground on the same rock. For example, in *Sears v. E.E.O.C.*, the plaintiff, E.E.O.C., argued that the massive statistical disparities between women and men in some categories of better-paying jobs showed sex discrimination. Alice Kessler Harris, assuming women's sameness with men in the name of feminism, supported them. The defendant, Sears, argued that women were different from men so did not necessarily want the same things men want—like better-paying jobs. Rosalind Rosenberg, arguing women's differences from men in the name of feminism, supported them. Given that the women in the empirical data overwhelmingly divided on gender lines, it is not difficult to understand why the lower courts found the differences approach compelling and exculpatory.[17]

Now move into the so-called subtle reaches of the imposed differences category: the de facto area. Most jobs require that the person, gender-neutral, who is qualified for them will not be the primary caretaker of a preschool child.[18] Pointing out that this raises a concern of sex in a society in which it is women who are expected to care for children is taken as day one of taking gender into account in the structuring of jobs. To do that would violate the rule against not noticing situated differences based on gender, so it never emerges that day one of gender in job structuring was the day the job was structured with the expectation that its occupant would not have primary child care responsibilities. Imaginary sex differences— such as between equally qualified male and female applicants to administer estates[19] or between males aging and dying and females aging and dying[20]—the doctrine can handle. But if women were not taught to read and write, as used to be the case (and women are still a majority of the world's illiterates), the gender difference between women and men in estate administration would not be imaginary. Yet such a society would be in even greater need of a law against sex inequality. Sex discrimination law can deal with illusions and mistakes. Disparate realities are something else entirely.

Clearly there are many differences between women and men. One could not systematically elevate one half of a population and denigrate the other half and produce a population in which everyone is the same. What goes unnoticed is that men's differences from women are equal to women's differences from men. There is an equality there. Yet the sexes are not socially equal. The sameness/difference approach misses the fact that hierarchy of power produces real as well as fantasied differences, differences that are also inequalities. What is missing is what Aristotle missed in his empiricist notion that equality means treating likes alike and unlikes unlike,[21] and no one has seriously questioned it since. Why should you have to be the same as a man to get what a man gets simply because he is one? Why is maleness an original entitlement, not questioned on the basis of *its* gender, so that it is women who want to make a case of unequal treatment in a world men have made in their image—this is really the part Aristotle missed[22]—who have to show in effect that they are a man in every relevant respect, unfortunately mistaken for a woman on the basis of an accident of birth?

The women benefited by gender neutrality, and there are some, show this method in highest relief. They are mostly women who have already been able to construct a biography that somewhat approximates the male norm, at least on paper. They are the qualified, the least of sex discrimination's victims. When *they* are denied a man's chance, it looks the most like sex bias. The more unequal society gets, the fewer such women are permitted to exist. The more unequal society gets, the *less* likely this doctrine is to be able to do anything about it, because unequal power creates both the appearance and the reality of sex differences along the same lines as it creates its sex inequalities.

The special benefits side, the difference side of the doctrine, has not compensated for the differential of being second-class. The double standard of its rulings does not give women the dignity of the single standard; neither does it suppress the gender of its referent—the female gender. The special benefits rule is the only place in mainstream doctrine where one can identify as a woman and not have that mean giving up all claim to equal treatment, but it comes close. Under its double standard, women who stand to inherit something when their husbands die have been allowed to exclude a small percentage of inheritance tax, to the tune of Justice Douglas' waxing eloquent about the difficulties of all women's economic situation.[23] If women are going to be stigmatized as different, it would be nice if the compensation would fit the disparity. Women have also gotten three more years than men get before we have to be advanced or kicked out of the military hierarchy as compensation for being precluded from combat, the usual way to advance.[24] Women have been excluded from contact jobs in male-only prisons because we might get raped, the Court taking the viewpoint of the reasonable rapist on women's employment opportunities.[25] We are also protected out of jobs because of our fertility. The reason given is that the job has health hazards, and somebody who might be a real person some day and therefore could sue—a fetus— might be hurt if women, who apparently are not real persons and therefore cannot sue either for the hazard to our health or for the lost employment opportunity—are given jobs that subject our bodies to possible harm.[26] Excluding women is always an option if equality feels in tension with the pursuit. Take combat. Somehow it takes the glory out of the foxhole, the buddiness out of the trenches, to imagine women out there.

You get the feeling that men might rather end the draft, might even rather not fight wars at all, than to have to do it with us.

These two routes to sex equality divide women according to their relations with men. Women who wish to step out of women's traditional relations with men and become abstract persons, to be exceptional to women's condition rather than receive the protections of it, are seen as seeking to be like men. They are served equality with a vengeance. If they win, they receive as relief the privilege of meeting the male standard, of paying the price of admission that men are trained for as men and are supposed to pay, even if regularly they do not. Women who assert claims in traditional role terms may, if they win, be said to be protected. Thus, women are excluded from guard jobs in contact positions in male prisons because of "their very womanhood" while the conditions that create women's rapability are not seen as susceptible to legal change. If courts learned that sexual harassment is as vicious and pervasive and damaging to women in workplaces everywhere as rape is to women guards in male prisons, could women be excluded from the workplace altogether?[27] At the same time that very few women are gaining access to the preconditions effectively to assert equality on male terms, women created in society's traditional mold are losing the guarantees of those roles to men asserting sex equality. Women asking courts to enforce the guarantees that have been an ideological part of the bargain of women's roles are getting less and less while also not receiving the benefits of the social changes that would qualify them for rights on the same terms as men. This is not a transitional problem. Abstract equality necessarily reinforces the inequalities of the status quo to the extent it evenly reflects an uneven social arrangement. The law of sex discrimination has largely refused to recognize that it is women who are unequal to men, and has called this refusal the equality principle.

If equality of rights rests upon a claim to similarity, and sex is actually a hierarchy, some men—failed as men—might rather readily qualify for women's special treatment, while few women would attain the prerequisites to claim equality with men. In fact, many of the doctrinally definitive sex discrimination cases that have reached the Supreme Court since 1971 have been brought by men.[28] Many have won. Women plaintiffs, by contrast, lose and lose and lose, often not even getting to the Supreme Court.[29] As a result of men's easier downward mobility combined with a man's comparatively greater access to resources and credibility, access men almost never lose, sex discrimination law's compensatory, preferential, or protective rationales on women's behalf have often been articulated in the context of challenges by men to sex-specific provisions that cushion or qualify but do not change women's status, and as often reinforce it in backhanded ways. One such case upheld a male-only statutory rape law against a sex equality challenge on the grounds that only women get pregnant, ignoring that young men also get raped, and raped women over the age of majority also get pregnant. Young males were incidentally preserved as sexual actors even when with adult women. The female population remained divided into categories of accessibility to sex by the drawing of an age line that kept little girls sexually taboo and thus sexually targeted, by definition unable to consent, while girls one day older were effectively considered consenting unless proven otherwise.[30] Another case preserved the male-only draft—and also men as society's primary combatants, its legitimate violence in their hands.[31]

Granted, some widowers are like most widows: poor because their spouse has died. Some husbands are like most wives: dependent on their spouse. A few fathers, like most mothers, are primary caretakers. But to occupy these positions is consistent with female gender norms; not surprisingly, most women share them. The gender-neutral approach to sex discrimination law obscures, and the protectionist rationale declines to change, the fact that women's poverty and consequent financial dependence on men (whether by marriage, welfare, workplace dependence, or prostitution), forced motherhood, and sexual vulnerability substantively comprise their social status *as women,* as members of their gender. That some men find themselves in similar situations at times does not mean that they occupy that status as men, as members of their gender. They do so as exceptions, both in norms and in numbers. Women, to claim being similarly situated with men, must also be exceptions. They must be able to claim all that sex inequality has in general systematically taken from them: financial independence, job qualifications, business experience, leadership qualities, assertiveness and confidence, a sense of self, peer esteem, physical stature, strength or prowess, combat skills, sexual impregnability—and, at all stages of legal proceedings, credibility. Sex discrimination law's rules are for society's exceptions. Taking the sexes "as individuals," meaning one at a time, as if they do not belong to genders, perfectly obscures the collective realities and substantive correlates of gender group status behind the mask of recognition of individual rights. It is only the woman who largely escapes gender inequality who is able to claim she has been injured by it. It seems one must already be equal before one can complain of inequality.

Under sex equality law, then, to be human still means, in substance, to be a man. To be a person, an abstract individual with abstract rights, may be a bourgeois concept, but its content is male. The only way to assert a claim *as* a member of the socially unequal group women, as opposed to seeking to assert a claim as *against* membership in the group women, is to seek treatment on a sexually denigrated basis. Human rights, including "women's rights," have implicitly meant only those men need to have legally recognized, those rights men have to lose. This may be in part why men persistently confuse procedural or abstract equality with substantive equality: for them, they are the same. Neither includes those rights women as women most need and never have had. All this appears rational and neutral in law because social reality is constructed from the same point of view.

Stereotyping—inaccurate or exaggerated misreflections—is the key injury in this view. It happens in the head or in symbolic social space. It freezes the process of objectification (of which it is a bona fide part) at its moment of inaccuracy, failing to grasp and being always potentially defeated by, images that become behaviorally and emotionally real. And most do. Taking, say, job applicants on an individual basis obscures rather than relieves this fact, although it surely helps some individuals. That women and girls may not *be* physically strong or appear physically intimidating compared with men and boys may be consequences as much as causes of the social image of proper womanhood as weak.

Sex discrimination law is entirely undercut by its concept of gender in a way that is prior to and largely determines litigation. The underlying strategy is to conceive of sex as a difference, to diagnose the evil of sex inequality as mistaken differences, to imagine that sex equality—the elimination of unreal differences—has been achieved, and to generate rules from this projected point as a strategy for reaching it. Feminism, by contrast, reveals that one cannot see the reality of sex unless one can imagine that it might be other than it is. To fail to do so is the misogyny of the right. But to suppose that legally assuming the situation really is otherwise in order to make it so is the sentimentality of liberalism. The sought-after inability to perceive sex differences also achieves an inability to perceive sex inequality. Nor can such an approach cannot distinguish separatism from segregation, nondiscrimination from forced integration, or diversity from assimilation.

Feminism radically questions whether the sexes are ever, under current conditions, similarly situated. Social circumstances, to which gender is central, produce distinctive interests, hence perceptions, hence meanings, hence definitions of principle. This observation neither reduces gender to thinking differently, rightness to relative subjectivity, nor principle to whose ox is gored. It challenges the view that neutrality, specifically gender neutrality as an expression of objectivity, is adequate to the nonneutral (objectified) social reality women experience. If differentiation were the problem, the similarly situated requirement and gender neutrality would make sense as an approach. Since hierarchy is the problem, they are not only inadequate, they are perverse. This analysis, in questioning the ultimate principledness of neutral principles,[32] suggests that the law to rectify sex inequality is premised upon, and promotes its continued existence.

The analytical point of departure and return of sex discrimination law is the liberal one of gender differences, which are thought rationally or irrationally to create gender inequalities. The feminist issue is gender hierarchy, which not only produces inequalities but shapes the social meaning, hence legal relevance, of the sex difference. To the extent that the biology of one sex is a social disadvantage while the biology of the other is not, or is a social advantage, the sexes are equally different but not equally powerful. The issue is the social meaning of biology, not any factual or object quality of biology. Similarly, both sexes possess a sexuality that occupies a place in "the heterosexual ethic." To the extent that the sexuality of one sex is a social stigma, target, and provocation to violation, while the sexuality of the other is socially a source of pleasure, adventure, power (indeed, the social definition of potency), and a focus for deification, entertainment, nurturance, and derepression, the sexuality of each is equally the same or different, equally heterosexual or not, but not equally socially powerful. The issue is the social meaning of the sexuality of women and men, the gender of women and men, not their sexuality or gender "itself"—if such a distinction can be made. To limit efforts to end gender inequality at the point biology or sexuality are encountered without realizing that these exist in law or society only in terms of their specifically sexist social meanings amounts to conceding that gender inequality may be challenged as long as the central pillars of gender as a system of power are permitted to remain standing.

So long as this is the way these issues are framed, women's demands for sex equality will always appear to be asking to have it both ways: the same when women are the same as men, different when we are different. But this is the way men have it: equal and different, too. The same as women when they are the same and want to be, and different from women when they are different or want to be, which usually they do. Equal and different, too, would only be parity. But under male supremacy, while being told we get it both ways, both the specialness of the pedestal and an even chance at the race, the ability to be a woman and a person, too, few women get much benefit of either. The sameness route ignores the fact that the indices or injuries of sex or sexism often ensure that simply being a woman may mean seldom being in a position sufficiently similar to a man to have unequal treatment be attributed to sex bias. The difference route incorporates and reflects rather than alters the substance of women's inferior status, presenting a protection racket as equal protection of the laws. In this way the legal forms available for arguing the injuries of sex inequality obscure the gender of this equality's reference point while effectively precluding complaint for women's sex-specific grievances.

When Deborah Rhode asked me to contribute to this volume on sexual difference, I responded "Difference? Who thinks *that's* the issue?" "Nearly everyone," she replied. She is right.

Gender Difference and Beyond: An Economic Perspective on Diversity and Commonality among Women

JULIANNE MALVEAUX

"Two out of three adults in poverty are women. What if they all were to go to the polls?" On a T-shirt or a poster the statement is a challenge—if poor women organized, things might be different. But would they? Do women in poverty share enough common ground that they could come together and change political realities? Would they come together despite differences in their path to poverty and the duration of their poverty? Would they come together despite racial differences?

"A woman is a husband away from poverty." This slogan, too, attempts to bind women together by gender. Implicit in the statement is the notion that men's earnings sustain families while women's do not. Men of color, who have lower earnings and labor force participation rates and higher unemployment rates than white men can work and still head families in poverty. The slogan about women, husbands, and poverty may make a strong case in an organizing attempt, but it is undergirded by racist and patriarchal assumptions. It implies that men are at the economic helm of families, while women do "secondary labor." It also ignores the fact that few men of color have had the opportunity to earn a family wage, few women of color the luxury of being "a husband away from poverty." Instead, in most minority groups, it generally takes two earners to move a family out of indigence.[1]

There is yet another slogan that rankles: "By the year 2000 all of the poor will be women or children." What does this suggest for men of color: genocide, full employment, or full incarceration? Again, a slogan designed to organize women and to illustrate their unequal position in society ignores or shrugs off the status of people and communities of color.

Why do the women who coin these slogans, who attempt to organize women along economic lines, fail to acknowledge issues of diversity? Are they so myopic as to perceive women's world as a white-only luxury? Do they understand that their slogans and their actions render Black women invisible in the very movements (around economic justice) that concern us vitally? Is invisible status conferred because there is power in numbers, because a mythical, broadly based "women's movement" needs to count all the bodies it can, whether they stand to be counted or not, because "women's studies" needs the broadest base possible (more than half of the population) whether this base is of one mind or not?

These paragraphs raise questions about the treatment and images of women of color in a set of overlapping institutions: the academy, the activist community, and the public policy arena. Slogans, organizing initiatives, legislative foci, and research efforts have attempted to portray "women" as some homogeneous community of people who come together through issues of gender difference. This has the effect of being a broad brush without bristles when differences among women are ignored, when the very different concerns of women of color are minimized because some initiative will "help all women." This is finger-pointing, but the desired response is an effort at examination of economic differences among women.

Slogans for organizing come from information about the status of women. Some of these slogans might be altered if the facts about economic differences among women were more closely examined. If women are to come together in strength instead of in frail coalitions bound only by the gossamer threads of gender, it becomes critical to examine this difference and to incorporate it into theory and policy development.

AIN'T I A WOMAN: MOTHERS, DAUGHTERS, SISTERS, AND MASTERS

Many of the issues that women come together around are economic and involve income, the distribution of jobs and promotions, college and graduate or professional school admission (and thus future income), child care, pension reform, and related issues. Though feminists have also been concerned about noneconomic issues, the focus on women's poverty, employment, and child care have been central questions in the women's movement. In fact, the phrase *the feminization of poverty* has been used as a rallying cry in the movement for economic justice for women. Yet while women generally experience more poverty than men do, the poverty level among whites (nearly 12 percent in 1985) is a fraction of the poverty level among Blacks (more than one-third). Early work on the feminization of poverty ignored that glaring fact.[2]

Ignoring differences distorts perceptions of Black women as severely as the perceptions of a mad Sylvia Plath peering through her bell jar. The use of the global term *women* without reference to differences among women renders Black women invisible. The genuflection to concerns of "race, class, and gender" without substantive examination of differences perpetuates the illusion of inclusion. Resisting the broad brush, Black women researchers, writers, and social theorists have had to fight for accuracy in the way we are portrayed. A goal is not only accuracy in the depiction and perception of Black women, but accuracy also in the depiction of Black communities. The link between Black women and Black communities is a critical one—to the extent that Black women are pivotal in Black communities, the appropriation of their images is a first step toward the destruction of positive images of Black communities. The process of cooptation has already begun, with discussions of teenage pregnancy and single motherhood giving way to discussions by social scientists (the term is used loosely) of "pathologies" to explain the economic status of Black families.

While it is true that most of the social scientists who have focused on "family pathologies" are men, it is amazing that so much of this work has gone unchallenged by the growing community of "feminist" social scientists. These feminists would do well to recognize that economic patterns among Black women have been duplicated, with a twenty-year lag, among white women. The female headship of white families has been rising in recent years just as the female headship of Black families rose rapidly in the 1970s. White female labor force participation rates, which once lagged nearly twenty percentage points below those of Black women, are now nearly as high as Black adult rates, and higher than Black female youth rates. By ignoring these patterns, some women's studies research ignores futures and glosses over significant racial differences among women. Consider studies of the "increased presence of women in the workplace" that ignore the fact that Black women historically have virtually been born broom in hand.[3] Terms like *juggling* seep into the scholarly literature to describe the multiple roles that Black women have held since they came to these shores: worker, mother, spouse. Feminists challenge the dominant approach to academia, to research, to policy, as they develop woman-centered approaches in these areas. But these women are usually connected—as mothers, daughters, sisters, wives—to those who have the greatest stake in the dominant approach. They may be oppressed by patriarchal economic systems, but through their familial connection to the architects and managers of those systems they are also beneficiaries of the oppression of men and women of color.

Perhaps Audre Lorde captured these contradictions best in her essay, "The Master's Tool Will Never Dismantle the Master's House."[4] The women who want to change the way the academy, research, and society work to include them are unwilling to make changes in the way the same society treats Black people. Yet the moral basis upon which they challenge definitions is rooted in the civil rights struggle, a struggle led by the Black community. The process of changing definitions and challenging society has enormous potential, but too many of the women who say they want change want partial change only, addressing issues of gender equity without looking at racial equity.

Ironies abound when women act on their desire to change realities for those in their race or class while ignoring the effects of such partial change on other women. Consider, for example, a group of women advisors (mostly white) to Lyndon Johnson, who felt the best way women could improve their status would be to make more maids (usually Black women or other women of color) available to them![5] Or consider registered nurses (mostly white) whose efforts to protect their jobs have motivated them to lobby to eliminate the jobs of licensed vocational nurses, mostly women of color.[6] These nurses say their effort is motivated by concern for "nursing quality," but organizations of licensed vocational nurses disagree. More recently, the National Organization of Women convened in 1987 around the theme "Feminization of Power," raising the question of whether powerful women want to bend the rules so that society will accommodate a few more of them, or whether they want to change society's rules so that far more women will have access to power. The focus on the feminization of power suggests the narrower of the two approaches.

In many ways feminism has, at its core, ignored and distorted the status of Black communities. Some of the distortion comes from the way some issues are claimed as "women's issues," presuming an alliance among women that excludes men. Black men have an equal stake in the racist treatment of the Black family and perhaps a greater stake in the way this treatment is manifested by direct oppression and exclusion of Black men. When education, family planning, pension reform, social service provision, and a host of related issues are seen as "women's issues," it undermines the interest that Black men (as well as other men) have in them.

But this is the heart of the matter. The white women who experience gender-based economic discrimination are the mothers, daughters, sisters, and wives of the patriarchs who have also institutionalized racial discrimination against Black people. Black women experience an economic oppression that has a basis in both race and gender. For white women to assume an alliance between themselves and Black women without taking matters of race and family (and thus, Black men) into consideration is a mistake. Too frequently this mistake characterizes feminist theory, scholarship, activism, and policy development.

DEFINING DIFFERENCE: THE LABOR MARKET STATUS OF BLACK WOMEN[7]

In the 1980s, the earnings of full-time Black women workers averaged about 93 percent of the earnings of full-time white women workers. Given this closeness, many researchers feel it makes no sense to talk about the labor market status of Black women as distinct from the status of other women. But income data only partially reveal this labor market status. Black women participate in the labor force slightly more than do white women, with the 1986 participation rate of adult Black women at 59 percent, compared to a white female labor force participation rate of 55 percent.[8]

Black women are more likely to work full time than are white women; when they work part time, it is more likely for economic reasons than is white women's part-time work.[9] At every educational level, Black women are not only more likely to work full time but also more likely to work full year than white women. The near parity in income levels that has been reported is an overstatement, since Black women have achieved this "parity" by working more.

Black women have consistently experienced higher unemployment (rates) than have white or Hispanic women, with their unemployment levels tending to be twice those for white women. In 1986, for example, the unemployment rate for adult white women was 5.4 percent, while the unemployment rate for adult Black women was 12.6 percent.[10] Black women lose their jobs more quickly than do white women during recession. They also find jobs more slowly than Black men, white men, and white women in periods of economic recovery. Their unemployment rates show less cyclical sensitivity than the rates of Black and white men, and unemployment rate improvement during economic recovery is more strongly correlated with the length of recovery than unemployment rate improvement for other race and sex groups.[11]

Perhaps the greatest difference in the status of Black and white women is the difference in occupational status. There is an important historical dimension to this occupational status. Before 1940, the majority (60 percent) of Black women worked as private household workers. A third of all Black women were so employed in 1960, but just 6 percent worked in private household jobs in 1980.[12] Partly because of this labor market legacy, Black women have experienced as much or more occupational segregation as white women, but in a different set of jobs. Even as Black women's occupational patterns shifted between 1960 and 1980, Black women have been both more heavily represented in "traditionally female" jobs than have white women and until recently more likely to be represented in service than in clerical jobs.[13]

Women have reduced their representation in "typically female" jobs since 1970. The reduction in the representation of Black women in traditionally female jobs ceased after 1977, while the reduction in the representation of white women in such jobs continued to decline after 1977. White women experienced less stratification from the outset and have left segregated jobs more rapidly than have Black women. While the quality of work among Black women changed, it changed because they moved from one set of stratified jobs to another, not because they left typically female jobs.[14]

The net result is a seeming similarity in the occupational status of Black and white women at present. One-third of all white women are clerical workers, as are 30 percent of all Black women workers. Twenty-three percent of all Black women work in service jobs, as do 16 percent of white women. Fifteen percent of Black women workers and seventeen percent of white women workers are employed in professional jobs. But Black women have moved out of service jobs and into clerical jobs while white women have moved out of clerical jobs into professional jobs. Black women tend to be employed in lower-paying, lower level, pink- and blue-collar occupations like manufacturing, service, and private household work (44 percent of Black women are so employed). They also experience an occupational segregation distinct from the occupational segregation white women experience. In addition to being employed in jobs that are "typically female," Black women are also employed in jobs that are typically, or disproportionately Black female. If Black women are either deliberately or traditionally crowded into a few low-paying jobs, they lower wages in those jobs where they cluster and reduce competition (or increase wages) in the jobs from which they are excluded. This concept of Black women's crowding explains, in part, why Black women receive lower pay than white women in similar occupations.[15]

Typically Black female occupations are defined as those where Black women's representation is more than twice their representation in the labor force. In service jobs, for example, they are overrepresented by a factor of three or four (three or four times their representation in the labor force) as chambermaids, welfare service aides, cleaners, and nurse's aides. Forty-one percent of the Black women who work in service occupations are employed in these four job classes.[16]

A similar analysis can be done for Black women in clerical occupations. Clerical work employs both the largest number and the largest proportion of Black and white women. The 1981 median clerical wage of $219 per week places the average clerical worker out of poverty but in the "near poor" category. Yet the range of clerical pay is broad: postal clerks in 1981 had median earnings of $382 per week, or almost $20,000 per year, while cashiers had median weekly pay of $133 per week, or less than $7000 per year. Interestingly, both of these occupations are typically Black female jobs.[17]

As with service work, an examination of detailed clerical occupations reveals those clerical enclaves that have become typically Black female. Nearly a quarter of all Black women are concentrated in just six of forty-eight clerical occupations. They are overrepresented by a factor of four as file clerks, typists, keypunch operators, teaching assistants, calculating machine operators, and social welfare clerical assistants. Except for the median wage of social welfare clerical assistants, all of these occupations have median wages associated with the near poor. Those occupations in which Black women are most heavily represented have pay levels at 125 percent or lower of the not very realistic poverty standard.[18]

Nearly 60 percent of clerical Black women work in typically Black female occupations, compared to 40 percent of clerical white women. Most of these Black women had wages at or below the near poor level in 1981. Nearly one in seven (13.7 percent) of Black clerical women work in typically Black female jobs and have earnings at the poverty line or lower. Another 31 percent of Black clerical women are both crowded into Black female occupational enclaves and among the working poor technically above poverty level. A lower but still sizable number of white women also work in typically Black female jobs with low earnings.

It is important to note that in 1981 nearly a third of Black clerical women were employed by government.[19] For many Black women, the fiscal health of federal, state, and local governments affects wage levels. Layoffs of government workers may have a greater impact on Black women clericals than on others both because of their heavy representation among government employees and because of their being recently hired municipal employees.

Occupational differences between Black and white women may mean that these women have different labor-market interests and choose different strategies for improving the status of women. Because of their high concentration in clerical jobs, white women may target these jobs for their organizing efforts. Though the highest concentration of Black women is in clerical jobs, the second largest number work in service jobs. Twenty-three percent of all Black women workers are concentrated in service there, compared to 16 percent of white women workers. Service jobs, then, are a probable target for Black women's organizing efforts. Trends in service work, such as the privatization of public services, will also have a different impact on Black and on white women.[20]

This discussion of Black women's economic status focuses at the lower end of the occupational spectrum, highlighting the persistence of some patterns: concentration in low-wage and part-time jobs with high unemployment rates. At the other end of the spectrum there has been some progress, with nearly 10 percent of all employed Black women (about half the percentage of employed white women) classified as "pioneers," or women who work in typically male professional, managerial, and crafts jobs. And though less than 1 percent of all Black women are entrepreneurs, the numbers have been growing and the businesses diversifying in the past decade.[21]

COMPARISONS, FAMILY WAGES, AND THE THIRD BURDEN OF BLACK WOMEN

The term *doubly disadvantaged* has been frequently used to describe the economic status and especially the labor-market status of Black women. The double disadvantage is described as membership both in a minority group and in the less economically powerful gender. But the term ignores another source of disadvantage for the Black woman—the labor-market disadvantage experienced by her spouse or members of her family unit. As Black male employment-to-population ratios declined to below 60 percent in 1984 (compared to white male employment-to-population ratios of more than 72 percent), and as the number of Black females heading households rose to more than 42 percent, the labor-market treatment of Black men may be perceived as a third for Black women.

Historically American employment practices have reflected patriarchal assumptions. Men have been the breadwinners in a family. Women historically participated in the labor market prior to marriage, sporadically during marriage, and occasionally after their children were adults, depending on social class. White men were paid a "family wage," a sum large enough (before 1970) to support a family. Black women, working-class white women, and a very small number of pre-1970 "career women" had continuous work histories but received lower pay.

Black men, because of racial occupational segregation, were denied the opportunity to earn a family wage, so Black women worked because they had to. Their earnings were necessary to Black family survival. Black women's wages continue to be critical to the economic status of Black families.

Still, some researchers persist in ahistorical attempts to turn this third disadvantage into an advantage for Black women in their comparisons of Black women to either Black men or white women. It is frequently noted, for example, that Black women's and men's incomes are closer together than are white men's and women's. For example, Andrew Brimmer reported that Black women were better represented among high-income women than Black men were among high-income men, failing to note the different types of discrimination that Black men, Black women, and white women experience.[22] Brimmer concluded that "the relative income deficit for higher-earning black women is 7.03 percentage points (in 1984) compared with a shortfall of 7.84 percentage points for black men." The comparison is a faulty one since he compared neither Black nor white women to white men. Comparisons like Brimmer's obscure real income deficits and tend to overstate Black women's progress, leading some to conclude that the relative closeness in Black male and female incomes means that Black women are "more liberated" than white women. Parity with a 15 percent unemployment rate is scarcely liberating, and low wages and single parenthood are no more so.

In an essay in the *New York Review of Books,* Andrew Hacker proffered the myth that "black women . . . have stronger representation than white women in professions and management."[23] Such assertions fail to allow for the fact that Black women have more relative participation in the labor force than white women. Black women experience no overall advantage vis-à-vis white women, since their "stronger representation" is in low-paying service jobs, not in the professions and management. Black women are also more strongly represented among the unemployed than white women are, a point to which Hacker failed to draw attention. Further, Black women employed in the professions and management are more likely than white women to work in such "typically female" professions as noncollege teaching and nursing. In 1985, there were 11.9 million workers in "executive, managerial, and administrative" jobs. Of these workers 301,000 (2.5 percent) were Black women, 348,000 (2.9 percent) were Black men, 3.9 million (32 percent) were white women, and 7.3 million (60 percent) were white men.[24]

If we take the same numbers and look at the occupational distribution of Black women compared to that of others, we find that 5.8 percent of all Black women work in "executive, administrative, and management" jobs, compared to 6.6 percent of all Black men, 9.7 percent of white women, and 13.8 percent of white men. A larger portion of the white population works in these jobs than the Black population. Again, the proportion of Black women in this occupation is lowest.

While it is sometimes useful to make comparisons between Black women and men, or between Black and white women, when these comparisons are taken out of historical context they distort the status of Black women. What purpose does it serve to note that Black women are better represented in the professions (vis-à-vis Black men, as compared to white women vis-à-vis white men), when neither Black men nor Black women are proportionally represented in professional jobs?

I have defined the third disadvantage, or third burden, as the burden beyond race and gender that Black women shoulder because of the labor-market treatment of Black men. From a quantitative standpoint, this burden can be measured by Black women's high labor force participation rates and proportional representation in the professions. There is a qualitative aspect of the third burden, as well, and it manifests itself in the dealings some Black women have with structural institutions in society as a result of their relationship to Black men.

In a public display of private fantasy, Bill Moyers predicted on national television that by the year 2000, 70 percent of all Black men would be on drugs, in jail, or unemployed.[25] Though it is possible to refute this prediction, that it was even advanced reinforces the notion of the third burden. If the numbers are just half as high as Moyers predicts, where does that leave Black women?

Consider the impact the criminal justice system has on both Black men and the women in their lives, women who are mothers, wives, sisters, and also workers. In California, Black men were five times as likely as their white "peers" to be arrested for felonies in 1980. Nearly 20 percent of the Black men who were convicted received prison sentences, compared to 15 percent of the convicted white men. The gap narrows from arrest to conviction, but this may indicate the frivolous nature of many of the arrests of Black men, who are stopped in their cars for "suspicion," arrested for loitering, and often incarcerated because of "mistaken identity."[26]

Although data have not been collected to substantiate this, few would dispute the assertion that these men's liaison to the "outside" world is a woman—mother, daughter, sister, wife. These women have the responsibility for raising money for lawyers, sandwiching trips to jail, and continuing to work and care for children. To the extent that Black men receive disparate treatment in the criminal justice system, Black women shoulder their triple burden, a burden beyond race and gender that is a function of the status of Black men in the workplace and in society.

Not every Black man will go to jail, nor will every working Black woman visit a jailed man. But the third burden placed on Black women when Black men are disproportionately affected by the prison system is mirrored in the burden they shoulder, whether corporate or clerical, when their men are negatively affected by race in the workplace. Black men's high unemployment adds to the burden Black women carry. Black men's limited opportunities for promotion adds to the burden Black women carry. The Black man who didn't get promoted will come home and share his bitterness and anger with the Black woman who may have her own reasons for bitterness. In her book "Angry Men, Successful Women," Bebe Moore Campbell talks about the negative effect that this burden can have on the relationships between Black professional men and women,[27] about how workplace frustration turns into anger in a relationship. When Black men do poorly and perceive their partners as doing "well," or when Black men attempt to impose traditional roles on women who do nontraditional work, anger is the likely result. Campbell has touched just the tip of the iceberg, since the third burden undoubtedly also affects working-class women and their spouses. The third burden may be added to by the fact that every member of a Black American household has been affected by racism, and every member of a Black American household depends in some way on the Black woman, who as spouse of household head usually holds primary responsibility for family management.

DIFFERENCE AND POLICY

While median income data suggest some similarity in the interests of Black and white women, the third burden implies key differences both in interests and in approaches to issues. The matter of approach is a perceptual one, yet these perceptions hamper the development of women's coalitions across racial lines. The frailty of Black and white women's alliances has been addressed by many writers, among them Paula Giddings in *When and Where I Enter: The Impact of Black Women on Race and Sex in America.*[28] From both a historical and a contemporary perspective, Giddings discusses the experiences of Black women as they have attempted to participate in white women's movements. Some of her discussions about NOW's history illustrate the racial myopia of white women. Giddings lists three disquieting aspects of the women's movement for Black women. First, she notes that the middle-class women who led the women's movement were the very women who had been the "bane of black women's existence." These were the women who had hired Black women as private household workers and failed to pay them fair wages. These were the white women who, in the words of Toni Morrison (quoted in Giddings), "sustained an eloquent silence in times of greatest stress," during Little Rock, Selma, and other civil rights crises.

Giddings' second concern with the white women's movement was the fact that this movement became popular just as the Black movement began to deteriorate. White women's characterization of themselves as "niggers" was seen as an affront to Black oppression. Third, Giddings writes that Black women were troubled by the "shrill tone (the women's movement) adopted against men." This concern reflects the fact that Black men have never been in a position economically to oppress Black women (although they may well be capable of other kinds of oppression).

Some of the concerns that Giddings raises about the early women's movement remain, and they are exacerbated by majority women's movements' tendency to be insensitive to the needs of Black women, their failure to address these needs, or their addressing them in a token manner. When feminist researchers sometimes genuflect before the altar of "race, class, and gender" before moving on with their majority women's agenda, it is no comfort to Black women. And majority women's movements' frequent failures to do outreach aimed for Black women is further proof that they perceive Black women as unnecessary or tangential to their movement.

White women's greater access to power and to the media is also troubling to Black women who find their long-standing concerns whitewashed and popularized (see, for example, my discussion of the politics around the feminization of poverty).[29] Though women's "agendas," with their focus on child care, job and pay equity, and other program thrusts, have some things to offer Black women, they are flawed for many Black women because the people who developed the agendas are often white women who have never had a dialogue with Black women. Lack of interaction may not invalidate policy proposals that improve the status of "all" women, but when a failure to talk suppresses information on differential impact, the possibilities for coalition are lessened. Black women's initial skepticism, for example, of comparable worth may have had its roots in the attitude, "If white women are pushing it, there must be something wrong with it." A careful examination of comparable worth as a policy suggests that it will be quite beneficial for Black women, although Black clerical women are more likely to be gainers than are Black women who hold service jobs.[30]

Some aspects of women's agendas are less important for Black women than they are for white women. The interest in pension and Social Security reform is a focus on capturing some of the economic gains that men have made. But a disproportionate number of Black men have little access to jobs, pensions, or Social Security. The matter of pension reform is more important for women who are married to men with long-term work histories, and these women are more likely to be white than Black. Similarly, the focus on "forcing" men to pay child support is one that must be placed in perspective. While all men should bear financial responsibility for the children that they father, Black men are less likely to be employed or to have earnings adequate to support two families than white men, which makes heightened child support enforcement an unrealistic approach to reducing Black poverty.

Feminist policy ignores Black women's concerns when it revolves around a definition of the oppressor as someone male and when it looks at economic discrimination in the same way as it does other forms of discrimination. Black men, Black women, and white women are disadvantaged by an economic structure that generates jobs and opportunities for white men first, but the bunching of men together regardless of race implies that Black men benefit from our economic system in the same way white men do. Such bunching also implies a similarity in the economic (as distinct from the labor-market) status of women regardless of race and ignores the fact that while occupational segregation limits work options for Black men, Black women, and white women, many white women still have access to assets beyond those that accrue from their work.

BEYOND GENDER DIFFERENCE

Issues of gender difference are compelling because the facts of gender-based inequity are glaring. Women are half of the population, but hold a small fraction of the elected offices in the United States and remain under-represented in other positions of influence in our society. Women earn less than men do, even in the same occupations and with similar qualifications and years of experience.

But "women" are not a homogeneous group of people. Women are white, Black, Hispanic, Asian, and Native American. We are mothers and single, disabled and well but at jeopardy because we may lack health insurance. Some of us are privileged and some not. We are joined by gender concerns, but these concerns bind us uneasily when issues of race and class are also considered. When relations among women mirror the inequitable relations of the broader society (with whites at the top and people of color at the bottom) the basis for bonding is further eroded.

Regardless of race and class, all women experience some measure of economic injustice. Women have less access than similarly situated men to money and credit, to employment, to pension funds, and to society's resources. Women's economic insecurity is compounded by the fact that we most often have the responsibility for the care of children and of aged or ill relatives. But there are important differences in the types of economic discrimination that women face, and great distances between the women forced to work below the minimum wage for their welfare checks in "workfare" programs and women who are denied promotions from associate to full professor.

An economic perspective on gender difference must of necessity focus on race and class and also on the family and community status of women. While there may be similarities in the way that individual women are situated, women are part of economic units like families and communities. The resources of these economic units have an impact on the status of individual women and may make major differences in women's economic status. Consider, for example, three clerical workers: one who heads a household, one who is married to a professional man, and one who is married to an unemployed man. A single set of workplace issues may join these women, but family circumstances make big differences in their perspectives on public policy.

When feminist theory and policy develop without sensitivity to differences in race, class, and family circumstances, the potential for broad-based cooperation among women is jeopardized. The third burden of Black women has been far too frequently ignored when economic issues of gender difference have been explored. For Black women and for many other women of color issues of gender difference can be explored only in conjunction with broader issues of racial difference and with particular attention to the socioeconomic status of families and communities.

Sexual Difference
and Sexual Equality

ALISON M. JAGGAR

The persistence and intensity of the perennial interest in sexual difference is not sustained by simple curiosity. Instead, it derives from an urgent concern with issues of sexual justice. For almost two and a half millennia, ever since Aristotle articulated the intuition central to the western concept of justice with his pithy but enigmatic dictum that justice consists in treating like cases alike and different cases differently, men and later women have debated the nature, extent, and even existence of the differences between the sexes and reflected on their relevance for the just organization of society.

These debates received both a fresh impetus and a new focus from the social and political revolutions that occurred in Europe and North America between the seventeenth and nineteenth centuries. The fresh impetus came from the economic and social upheavals that disrupted the seemingly natural order of feudal society, displacing women from their traditional work and raising urgently the question of what women's new place should be. The new focus derived from the enhanced prominence assigned by the accompanying political revolutions to the ideal of equality, an ideal that now became central to modern western ways of construing justice. Women of the emerging bourgeois classes seized on the increasingly popular rhetoric of equality, pointing out repeatedly that equality was not universal so long as it was restricted to males. In the three or four centuries that have elapsed since that time, the dominant theme in the modern western debate over the place of women in society has been the tension between the ideal of sexual equality and the apparent reality of sexual difference.

Equality is a contested ideal notoriously open to a variety of interpretations. In the first part of this paper, I outline two ways in which some contemporary feminists have construed equality in legal contexts, identifying some of the problems that accompany each construal. In the second, I argue that both these conceptions of sexual equality presuppose unacceptable interpretations of sexual difference, and I go on to sketch an approach to understanding sexual difference that is more adequate to recent feminist insights. I suggest that this alternative approach to sexual difference casts the initial construals of sexual equality in a new light, pointing to the need for rethinking and perhaps even moving beyond the traditional ideal of western feminism.

EQUALITY

SEXUAL EQUALITY AS BLINDNESS TO SEXUAL DIFFERENCE

Western feminists have not always been unanimous in demanding sexual equality. Even though this ideal inspired not only some of the earliest English feminists but also participants in the U.S. Seneca Falls Convention of 1848, most nineteenth-century feminists in the United States did not endorse such a radical demand, preferring instead to retain membership in women's separate sphere.[1] Despite the ideology of separate spheres, however, feminist challenges to such inequities in the legal system as women's inability to vote or to control their own property on marriage developed eventually into demands for identity of legal rights for men and women or, as it came to be called, equality before the law. By the end of the 1960s, mainstream feminists in the United States had come to believe that the legal system should be sex-blind, that it should not differentiate in any way between women and men. This belief was expressed in the struggle for an Equal Rights Amendment to the U.S. Constitution, an amendment that, had it passed, would have made any sex-specific law unconstitutional.

Nineteenth-century feminist demands for the suffrage and for property rights drew on a variety of arguments, sometimes claiming that women possessed distinctive ethical insight and nurturant capacities.[2] A persistent theme in the feminist argument, however, was insistence on women's capacity to reason, an insistence conditioned by the classical liberal assumption that the ability to reason was the only legitimate ground for the ascription of democratic rights. From the eighteenth century on, feminists have argued consistently that women's reasoning capacity is at least equal to men's (though not necessarily identical to it) and have attributed women's lesser intellectual attainments primarily to their inferior education.[3] Such arguments obviously tend to minimize the significance of the physiological differences between the sexes, since those differences are construed as irrelevant to the ascription of political rights. By the late 1960s and early 1970s, at the beginning of the most recent wave of western feminism, a conspicuously rationalist approach to women's equality was shared widely, though not universally, by English-speaking feminists, and arguments for so-called androgyny were common. The androgyny recommended typically was not physical, but mental and moral.[4]

Over the past two decades, western societies have seen a marked acceleration in the long process of dismantling legal discrimination against women. As the last of the formal barriers to women's entry into the so-called mainstream are being removed, however, it has become apparent that strict equality before the law may not always benefit women, at least not in the short term. Differences between the sexes have emerged as sufficiently significant to motivate some feminists as well as nonfeminists to recall the second part of the Aristotelian dictum: justice consists not only in treating like cases alike but also in treating different cases differently.

Contemporary feminists have identified a wide variety of differences between the sexes as relevant to sexual justice, though it should be noted that they are not always unanimous either about the list of differences or about the significance of its various items. What follow are only a few examples of differences between the sexes that many feminists claim it is unjust to ignore. Some of the differences seem almost inseparable from female biology, while others are linked more obviously with women's social circumstances.

The apparently biologically based differences between the sexes generally are connected with women's procreative capacity. The most evident and most frequently debated of such differences is women's ability to become pregnant and to give birth. In the now notorious case of *Gilbert v. General Electric* (1976), most feminists argued that a disability plan excluding disabilities related to pregnancy and childbirth discriminated against women, or treated women unequally, despite the indisputable fact that such a plan would fail "equally" to cover any man who became pregnant. A structurally similar example was a purportedly sex-blind ordinance forbidding firefighters to breast-feed between calls, an ordinance that of course applied "equally" to male and female firefighters.

Not all significant differences between women and men are related so directly to female biology. Many feminists have claimed that differences in the social situation of men and women may also make it unjust to apply identical standards of employment to both sexes. For example, they argue for the strategy of affirmative action in hiring on the grounds that it is necessary to make special efforts to counteract conscious and unconscious social bias against women and to ensure that women's opportunities are genuinely equal with men's. These feminists note, for instance, that the same piece of writing is rated lower when signed by a woman than when signed by a man and that job recommendations are both written and read with sexist prejudice. The circumstances of their lives, moreover, often have deprived women of the opportunity to become as well qualified as men. Apart from the damaging effects of sex-role conditioning on women's self-confidence and motivation, many women have been the victims of discrimination by being refused admission to the training programs that would enable them to acquire the most prestigious credentials. In addition, conventional family expectations concerning child care, housework, and the priority of a husband's career have limited many women's mobility and their time to acquire the best possible job credentials. Many feminists have argued that women's paper credentials may not always reflect accurately their real qualifications for the job and that different ("preferential") rather than identical treatment of the sexes may be necessary to select the candidate who has the most real ability or merit.

In the domestic sphere as well as in the market, some feminists recently have come to question whether justice is served best by treating men and women exactly alike. No-fault divorce settlements, for example, that divide family property equally between husband and wife, almost invariably leave wives in a far worse economic situation than they do husbands. In one study, for instance, ex-husbands' standard of living was found to have risen by 42 percent a year after divorce, whereas ex-wives' standard of living was reduced by 78 percent.[5] This huge discrepancy in the outcome of divorce results from a variety of factors, including the fact that women and men typically are differently situated in the job market, with women usually having much lower job qualifications and less work experience. Child custody is another aspect of family law in which feminists recently have questioned the justice of viewing men and women as indistinguishable. For example, some feminists have argued that the increasingly popular assignment of joint custody to mothers and fathers unfairly penalizes women because joint custody statutes increase the bargaining strength of men at divorce and thereby aggravate the dependence of women, threatening their economic rights, their ability to raise their children without interference, and their geographic mobility.[6]

It is possible to multiply indefinitely examples of situations in which identical treatment of the sexes appears to promote women's inequality rather than their equality, at least in the short term. We live in a society divided deeply by gender, in which differences between the sexes, whatever their cause, are pronounced and inescapable. When these differences are ignored in the name of formal equality between the sexes, continuing substantive inequalities between women and men may be either obscured or rationalized and legitimated. At least in the present social context, sexual equality in procedure often may ensure rather than obliterate sexual *in*equality in outcome.

SEXUAL EQUALITY AS RESPONSIVENESS TO SEXUAL DIFFERENCE

Within the last ten or fifteen years, increasing numbers of feminists have been challenging the assumption that sexual equality always requires sex-blindness. The growing public recognition that equality in areas other than gender relations is compatible with and may even require substantive differences in practical treatment adds plausibility to this challenge. For instance, equality in education ordinarily is taken to be compatible with, and even to require, the provision of different educational programs and bilingual or otherwise specially qualified teachers to serve the needs of children with varying abilities and disabilities. Similarly, there is increasing public willingness to provide special resources for people who are disabled or differently abled: readers for the blind, interpreters for the deaf, and adequate work space and access for those confined to wheelchairs.

Commitment to affirmative action in hiring probably constituted the first contemporary feminist challenge to the traditional sex-blind understanding of sexual equality. Affirmative action programs are generally uncontroversial among feminists because they are conceived as temporary expedients, as means rather than as ends. Typically such programs are defended as special protections for women (and other "suspect categories"), necessary in the short term in order to counter existing inequality of opportunity, but as something that should be abandoned once opportunities have been equalized. Rather than challenging the ideal of de-institutionalizing sexual difference, therefore, affirmative action ultimately presupposes that ideal.

Most of the other proposals for achieving sexual equality through the recognition of sexual difference are considerably more controversial than affirmative action, even among feminists. One such proposal is that employers should be forbidden to terminate or to refuse a reasonable leave of absence to workers disabled by pregnancy or childbirth even though such leaves may not be available to workers who are disabled for other reasons. The *Miller-Wohl* and *California Federal* cases, for instance, sharply divided the feminist legal community.[7]

Even more controversial than special pregnancy and maternity leaves are proposals to loosen the standard criteria of legal responsibility for women in some circumstances. For instance, there have been moves to recognize so-called premenstrual syndrome, which by definition afflicts only women, as a periodically disabling condition during which women enjoy diminished legal responsibility.[8] Other feminist lawyers have proposed that there should be special criteria for identifying self-defense, criteria that go beyond immediate life-threatening danger, in the cases of women who kill their abusive husbands.[9]

Sexuality is an issue that in recent years has generated particularly sharp disagreement among feminists over women's need for special protection. It is true that few contemporary feminists seem motivated to challenge the sexually differentiated way in which statutory rape laws are applied, in prosecuting adult men who have intercourse with consenting minor girls but failing to prosecute adult women who have intercourse with consenting minor boys. (The latter has even been judicially interpreted as an enriching educational experience for the boy!) Feminists have, however, been extremely divided over the merits of civil rights ordinances against pornography written by feminists in language that is pointedly not sex-blind. One model antipornography law drafted by Andrea Dworkin and Catharine MacKinnon claims that "Pornography is sex discrimination . . . a systematic practice of exploitation and subordination based on sex that differentially harms women." The model law admits that "The use of men, children, or transsexuals in the place of women . . . is pornography for the purposes of this law," but makes it clear that the use of women is paradigmatic, so that any person used as a pornographic object is being treated in a way that is characteristically feminine.[10]

It is easy to understand why most proposals for achieving sexual equality through the institutional recognition of sexual difference are controversial among feminists. The reason is that the supposed benefits of such recognition are bought only at a certain price to women. This price includes the danger that measures apparently designed for women's special protection may end up protecting them primarily from the benefits that men enjoy. This has happened frequently in the past. For instance, as one author remarks,

> The protective labor legislation that limited the hours that women could work, prohibited night work and barred them from certain dangerous occupations such as mining may have promoted their health and safety and guaranteed them more time with their families. But it also precluded them from certain occupations requiring overtime, barred them from others where the entry point was the night shift, and may have contributed to the downward pressure on women's wages by creating a surplus of women in the jobs they were permitted to hold.[11]

Similarly, American Cyanamid infamously "protected" the reproductive capacities of its women workers by forcing them to choose between being sterilized or losing their jobs.

A further problem with treating women differently from men is that it reinforces sexual stereotypes. Among the most familiar and pervasive of prevailing stereotypes are the correlative assumptions that men by nature are sexual aggressors and that women's very presence is sexually arousing and constitutes a temptation to aggression. In recent years these assumptions have been the basis of court decisions excluding women from the job of prison guard in Alabama maximum security prisons and even from the job of chaplain in a male juvenile institution.[12] Such decisions have not only the direct consequence of "protecting" women from jobs that may be the best paid available to them (in the case of the prison guard) or to which they may even feel a religious calling (in the case of the chaplain); they also have far-reaching indirect consequences insofar as they perpetuate the dangerous and damaging stereotype that women by nature are the sexual prey of men. This cultural myth serves as an implicit legitimation for the prostitution, sexual harassment, and rape of women, because it implies that such activities are in some sense natural. Other legislation designed to draw attention to the need to protect women's sexuality, such as legislation defining the subjects in pornography paradigmatically as female, may well have similar consequences.

Legal recognition of women as a specially protected category may also encourage homogenization or "essentialism," the view that women are all alike. In one form, this point is more than a century old: liberal feminists since John Stuart Mill have argued that treating women as a homogeneous group is unfair to exceptional individuals, whose interests and capacities may be different from those of the majority of their sex. Increasing feminist sensitivity to differences between groups of women as well as to differences between individual women now requires further elaboration of Mill's antiessentialist insight. As the present wave of feminism has rolled on, middle-class white feminists have been forced to recognize that their definitions of women's nature and women's political priorities too often have been biased by factors like race, class, age, and physical ability. Legislation that separates women into a single category inevitably will define that category in a way that makes a certain subgroup of women into the paradigm for the whole sex. One group of women may be penalized by being forced to accept protection that another genuinely may need. One example is insurance plans that require all female employees to pay premiums for coverage of disabilities arising out of pregnancy and childbirth but which do not require the same contributions from male employees. Such a requirement forces lesbians, infertile women, and women who are not sexually active to underwrite the costs of heterosexual activity by some women—and, of course, by some men.[13]

When the risks involved in the sex-responsive approach to sexual equality become apparent, feminist theory arrives at an impasse. Both the sex-blind and the sex-responsive interpretations of equality seem to bear unacceptable threats to women's already vulnerable economic and social status. In the next section I suggest that each interpretation of sexual equality rests on a construal of sexual difference that is inadequate for feminism.

DIFFERENCE

The sex-blind interpretation of sexual equality rests on an assumption that existing differences between women have relatively little social significance. The obvious defect of this denial is that it ignores the extent to which sex and gender affect every aspect of everyone's life. People's work and play, dress and diet, income level and even speech patterns are regulated by social expectations regarding the appropriate appearance and behavior of sexed individuals, so that on all these dimensions people vary systematically, though not solely, according to sex. Prevailing norms of gender may be and often are challenged by certain individuals in certain areas, but for most people most of the time these norms are simply the given framework of daily life. Feminists cannot deal with sexual difference simply by closing their eyes to its social institutionalization and refusing to recognize existing social and political realities.

The sex-responsive conception of sexual equality by definition is sensitive to these realities, but there are others to which it is blind. These are the realities of the differences *between* women, differences of race, class, sexual preference, religion, age, ethnicity, marital status, physical ability, and so on. Increasingly, contemporary feminists are recognizing that there is no typical woman, no essence of womanhood that underlies these other characteristics—which often constitute additional vectors of domination. Any conception of sexual difference that ignores these features is inadequate for a feminism seeking to represent the interests of all women.[14]

There is an additional problem with the conception of sexual difference that underlies the sex-responsive conception of sexual equality. This problem emerges when sex-responsiveness is justified, as it invariably is, in terms of "protection" or "compensation," terms suggesting that women are damaged or disabled in comparison with men. Sometimes women's disabilities are seen as resulting from social causes, war wounds sustained by women as a result of life in a male-dominated society; sometimes women's disabilities are seen as presocial in origin, akin to female birth defects. In either case, however, the sex-responsive interpretation of sexual equality usually rests on a conception of sexual difference according to which women are inferior to men at least in some ways.

In what follows, I outline an approach to understanding sexual difference that is more adequate to insights that feminists recently have emphasized. I focus especially on two characteristics of this approach.

A DYNAMIC APPROACH TO SEXUAL DIFFERENCE

In saying that a more deeply feminist understanding of sexual difference must be dynamic rather than static, I mean that it must reflect the continually expanding feminist awareness of the ways in which the history of women's subordination, especially as this intersects with the history of other subordinated groups, has shaped and continues to shape both existing differences between the sexes and the ways in which we perceive and evaluate those differences.

A more fully feminist understanding of sexual difference does not deny that deep differences may exist between the sexes, but it does not assume that these differences are presocial or biological givens, unambiguous causes of women's apparently universal inequality and subordination. Instead, feminists must be committed to exploring the ways in which not only women's cognitive and emotional capacities, but even our bodies and our physical abilities, have been marked by a history of inequality and domination: a mark imposed not just on the development of individual women but on the whole evolution of our species.[15] Thus the differences we perceive between men and women may be results as much as causes of sexual inequality.[16]

Such feminists argue that the ubiquitous context of sexual inequality has shaped not only our sex-differentiated genetic potential and the sex-differentiated ways in which we express that potential, but continues to influence our perception and interpretation of existing sexual differences, disposing us, for instance, to perceive a greater disparity between the sexes than exists. One example is the common perception that men are generally taller than women, a perception reinforced by the norms of heterosexual coupling, even though the mean difference in height between women and men is only a few inches, whereas the normal distribution of height within each sex is over two feet.

The context of social inequality is likely also to condition the values assigned to perceived sexual differences, so that male attributes are interpreted as assets and female attributes as defects. Social inequality of the sexes may even force revision of the standards by which sexual difference is measured, if men do not measure up well by those standards. The early development of I.Q. tests provides a clear example of this: when females performed better than males on the tests, their superior performance was taken as an indicator of the tests' invalidity and the tests were revised until the males performed up to the female standard. One doubts that the tests would have been revised if females had performed worse than males.

We noted above that an adequate understanding of sexual difference must be sensitive to the differences between women and women as well as to the differences between women and men. Like the differences between women and men, the differences between women of varying classes, ages, racial and ethnic backgrounds, and so on are not given prior to society, nor are they static and unchanging. Instead they too are influenced by social forces. In consequence, feminists must be committed to investigating how these differences, too, as well as our perceptions of them, are shaped by the changing circumstances of age, class, race, and ethnicity.

VALORIZING WOMEN'S DIFFERENCES

As a direct result of their awareness that social inequality has shaped not only perceptions of sexual difference and even difference itself but also the ways in which sexual difference has been valued, a number of feminists now are consciously reevaluating sexual difference. In addition to challenging biologically reductionist accounts of sexual difference, they have begun to look at difference in a more woman-centered way, not just as evidence of women's weakness but as a possible source of women's strength.

The most evident difference between the sexes is women's capacity to become pregnant and give birth. Existing sex-responsive conceptions of sexual equality typically have viewed this capacity as a disability for which women deserve social compensation. But more feminists now are emphasizing that the ability to give birth is a uniquely valuable potential. Some claim it is a potential that is valuable not only in itself but in its giving rise to characteristically feminine ways of approaching and dealing with the world, ways that may provide a basis for feminist reconstruction.

A wide variety of feminist arguments now purports to demonstrate that familiar western modes of conceptualizing reality in fact are distinctively masculine. Nancy Hartsock, for instance, argues that women's daily experience of transforming natural substances through activities like cooking, in addition to women's experiences in procreation (menstruation, coitus, pregnancy, childbirth, lactation), engender:

> opposition to dualisms of any sort, valuation of concrete, everyday life, sense of a variety of connectednesses and continuities both with other persons and with the natural world. If material life structures consciousness, women's relationally defined existence, bodily experience of boundary challenges, and activity of transforming both physical objects and human beings must be expected to result in a world view to which dichotomies are foreign.[17]

Feminine experience in Hartsock's view generates an ontology of relations and of continual process, an ontology she believes superior to an atomist metaphysics.

Sara Ruddick does not address the question of difference in the bodily experience of women and men, but she suggests that women's social experience of mothering may have political implications.[18] Ruddick claims that women's training and experience as mothers predisposes them to look for other than military means of conflict resolution. She believes that the work of preserving children's lives, as well as of nurturing and training children, gives women distinctive motives for rejecting war and distinctive practice both in peacekeeping and in nonviolent forms of resistance to oppression. Ruddick's work may provide part of the explanation for women's historic involvement in antiwar activity, and it may also help to justify the contemporary organization of such women-only groups to oppose militarism as the Greenham Common encampment in the United Kingdom and the Women's Pentagon Action, together with the Seneca Falls Encampment, in the United States.

Carol Gilligan's work on moral development recently has received wide-spread popular attention.[19] Gilligan is widely interpreted as claiming to have established that the moral development of women is significantly different from the moral development of men. On this interpretation, Gilligan claims to have discovered that women tend to construe moral dilemmas as breaches in relationships and seek to resolve those dilemmas in ways that will mend the holes in the relationship network. Supposedly, women are less likely than men to make or justify moral decisions by the application of abstract moral rules; instead they are more likely to act on their feelings of love and compassion for particular individuals.

Gilligan's work has aroused a storm of controversy. Her original sample was small, and others have been unable to replicate her findings of systematic differences in the moral development of women and men, especially when the studies have been controlled for occupation and class. Moreover, there are problems in Gilligan's interpretation of her data. Gilligan herself now sees the main significance of her work as consisting in hearing a different voice, a voice that is often but not exclusively female.[20] This voice reasons in a way that gives primacy to considerations of what Gilligan calls care rather than to considerations of justice, and she takes its existence to demonstrate that existing standards of moral rationality measure at best only one aspect of moral development. Gilligan has been clear that the so-called ethics of care is a supplement to rather than a replacement of what she perceives as a characteristically masculine ethics of justice. Some feminists, however, have taken Gilligan's identification of this supposedly feminine approach to morality to offer a basis for the development of an ethics that would be distinctively feminist and preferable or superior to the traditional western preoccupation with justice.[21]

When sexual difference comes to be understood in ways that are dynamic and woman-affirming rather than static and woman-devaluing, a new light is thrown on the ideal of sexual equality.

A DIFFERENT FEMINISM

A dynamic approach to understanding sexual difference helps to explain the inadequacy of both the sex-blind and the sex-responsive ways of construing sexual equality. Because it recognizes the reality of sexual difference, such an approach shows why a sex-blind procedure may be unjust if it makes sexual inequality in outcome more likely. Simultaneously, through its recognition both of differences between women and of the social genesis of many inter- and intrasex differences, it shows the dangers of self-fulfilling prophecy that lurk in the sex-responsive approach to sexual equality. A dynamic understanding of sexual difference demonstrates why feminism must rethink traditional interpretations of sexual equality. Contemporary feminist revalorizations of sexual difference indicate some directions in which this rethinking may proceed.

Equality has always been open to the charge (usually made by anti-egalitarians) that it involves a leveling down, a degradation of the exceptional to the ordinary, a reduction to the lowest common denominator. In the historical context of male dominance, the call for women to be equal with men may have appeared as a threat to some men, but certainly it was perceived by most feminists as a promise, the promise to grant them male privileges, to raise them to the level of men. The valorization of women's differences, however, makes the ideal of sexual equality suddenly far less attractive to feminists. Rather than appearing as the extension to women of the full human status enjoyed by men, sexual equality starts to look like an attempt to masculinize women and negate their special capacities.

From this alternative feminist standpoint, the two conceptions of sexual equality that we began by considering now appear as more similar than opposed. The debate whether feminists should ignore or respond to sex differences now is revealed as merely a debate over strategy: it is not a disagreement about the ultimate goal of feminism. In either conception of sexual equality, the goal of feminism is for women to be in some way the same as men, whether this sameness be interpreted as identical treatment or as access to the same opportunities.

While this goal may appear radical from the standpoint of male dominance, it can look conservative or even antifeminist to those who are concerned to rediscover the insights and values embedded in what they construe as women's traditional practice. For, at least in its current interpretations, the goal starts from the assumption that the male is the norm of humanity and so endorses the most fundamental tenet of male-dominant ideology. In this way the goal of sexual equality, as it is ordinarily conceived, may be thought to contribute covertly to the maintenance rather than the transformation of the status quo. Far from expressing the quintessence of feminism, the demand for equality with men may be perceived as negating feminism's most radical and distinctive vision.

This vision is blurred and indistinct, glimpsed by only a few feminists and invisible to many who dedicate themselves to the struggle for sexual equality. It begins to emerge, however, in feminist attempts like those mentioned above to delineate ways of conceptualizing and dealing with the world that are characteristically feminine. Some aspects of this supposedly feminine vision are shared at least in part by certain utopian communities of the past. In our time a form of the vision particularly inspires intentional feminist communities, such as women's music festivals or peace camps. It is a vision at once of community and of individuality, a vision of people who are connected primarily neither by rational self-interest nor by shared oppression but who instead are united simultaneously by a sense of common humanity and caring for specific individuals.

Equality as it is ordinarily construed seems largely irrelevant to this vision. As we have seen already, the idea of sameness is at the core of equality, the idea that people should be treated similarly because they are in some relevant respect alike. But at the same time that it emphasizes human similarity, the call for equality may be thought to obscure human difference. Equality deliberately turns away from the particularity and uniqueness of individuals and groups in their history and in their daily experience. Rather than responding directly to needs that are perceived immediately, equality abstracts from concrete people in their specific situations. It seeks to resolve conflicting interests by the application of an abstract rule.

The ideal of equality gained its popularity in a period when caste and class divisions were extremely rigid and regulated every aspect of people's lives in a highly conspicuous way. In a situation where some groups have privileges that others lack, where certain groups are systematically restricted and repressed, the call for equality is voiced spontaneously. It provides a rallying cry to abolish privilege, to end oppression, to unite people against injustice and domination. This cry in the past has served women well, inspiring heroic and often victorious struggles against women's legal disabilities and forcing the opening up of economic, social, and educational opportunities for women. In a world where women (or certain groups of women) are still at the bottom of the pile, where women in full-time jobs earn on average less than two-thirds of the male wage and still do 70 percent of the housework (with husband and children averaging 15 percent each), where one girl in four is subjected to male incest, almost one woman in three to rape and half of all married women to domestic violence, in a world such as this, which is our world, feminists cannot afford to abandon the rhetoric of equality.

Equality, then, is a weapon that feminists seem forced to use, but some fear that it may turn against feminism. For some feminists, the language of equality is not women's "mother tongue"; instead, it is a language that some men developed at a particular point in European history, a language that western women have borrowed and sometimes put to good use. In its prevailing interpretations it is a language of impartiality and abstraction, a language of rational distance rather than of close connection. It presupposes scarcity and a preoccupation with getting one's fair share. It conjures up a rationalized and bureaucratic society of procedurally regulated competition, not an abundant, sensuous, and emotional world rich with human uniqueness and diversity.

Ruddick has written that "to mothers, the ideal of equality is a phantom."[22] Certainly it is true that mothers typically are less concerned with

abstract procedures or with merit than with individual need. They respond
to the members of their families as concrete rather than as generalized
individuals.[23] Their actions are guided by intimate knowledge informed by
feeling, not by abstract principle and emotional distance. This is why some
see mothers as practicing an ethics of care rather than an ethics of justice.[24]

There are unmistakable parallels between this (admittedly idealized)
practice of mothers and the ideal of the classes society sketched by Marx in
his *Critique of the Gotha Programme*. In such a society, according to Marx, an
emphasis on equality of rights is likely to lead to inequality precisely
because people differ from each other. In such a society, equal right
becomes "*a right of inequality, in its content, like every right*" (italics original). It
creates inequalities by ignoring differences between individuals. "To avoid
all these defects, right instead of being equal would have to be unequal."[25]
Marx believed that these defects are unavoidable in the first phase of
communist society but that in a higher phase the principle of communist
distribution would be: "From each according to his [*sic*] ability, to each
according to his [*sic*] needs." To apply this Marxist principle certainly
would require a knowledge of individual circumstances at least as intimate
as that which mothers have of their families, and in advocating this principle Marx, like mothers, often has been seen as abandoning the ideal of
equality. Since equality, as we have seen, is a central feature in the western
conception of justice, one who interpreted Marx in this way might even say,
obviously anachronistically that Marx, like mothers, rejects an ethic of
justice in favor of an ethic of care.

Alternatively, one might deny that either mothers or Marxists are uncon-
cerned with equality. One might interpret them instead as reaching for a
more determinate and substantive conception of equality, equality of outcome or condition rather than equality of procedure or opportunity.[26] One
might say that neither mothers nor Marxists are rejecting equality, but
instead are groping toward a finer-grained and more adequate conception
of equality, one that does not presuppose a framework where justice is
wholly or even partially blind. One might even suggest that it is only by
removing her blindfold completely, permitting her to see the full particularity of human individuals, that we enable justice to achieve full equality
by making the discriminations necessary to treat genuinely like cases alike
and genuinely different cases differently.

CONCLUSION: HAVING IT BOTH WAYS

No matter whether one construes mothers and Marxists as reinterpreting
or transcending equality, there remains an enormous contrast between
their radical vision, now being appropriated and developed by some contemporary feminists, and the currently limited conceptions of sexual

equality employed in the daily struggle for sexual justice. Feminists seem caught in the dilemma of simultaneously demanding and scorning equality with men.

My own view is that feminists should embrace both horns of this dilemma, abandoning neither our short-term determination to reform existing society nor our long-term desire to transform it. We should develop both the pragmatic and the utopian strands in our thinking, in the hope that each may strengthen the other.

On the one hand, feminists should continue to struggle for women to receive a fair share of the pie, carcinogenic though it ultimately may be.[27] They should use the rhetoric of equality in situations where women's interests clearly are being damaged by their being treated either differently from or identically with men. It seems likely that neither of the two prevailing interpretations of equality is best in all circumstances. Sometimes equality in outcome may be served best by sex-blindness, sometimes by sex-responsiveness—and sometimes by attention to factors additional to or other than sex. Because perceived sexual differences so often are the result of differences in treatment, it seems prudent to advocate only short-term rather than permanent protections for women. For example, affirmative action and special legal defenses for chronically abused women seem less dangerous to women's status than premenstrual exemptions from legal responsibility. Some questions that have been presented as issues of sexual equality, such as antipornography ordinances and moves to draft women, may be decided better by reference to considerations other than those of equality.

Throughout the battle for sexual equality, it is necessary to remain critical of the standards by which that equality is measured. In particular, feminists should be ready constantly to challenge norms that may be stated in gender-neutral language but that are established on the basis of male experience, and so likely to be biased in favor of men. One example of such a norm is the ordinance forbidding firefighters to breast-feed between calls; another is the minimum height requirement for airline pilots, a requirement based on the seemingly sex-blind concern that pilots be able to reach the instrument panel. Feminist challenges to such norms should mitigate at least to some extent the concern that sexual equality simply will "masculinize" women by assimilating them to male standards. The need to redesign the organization of both paid work and of domestic responsibility in order to avoid this kind of male bias must surely modify the extremes of gender polarization.

Simultaneously with insisting on sexual equality in a world presently racked by scarcity and injustice, feminists should develop their long-term visions of a world in which equality is less a goal than a background condition, a world in which justice is not "the first virtue of social institutions,"[28] but in which justice and equality are overshadowed by the goods of mutual care. But this must be care in a new sense, not the feminized, sentimentalized, privatized care with which we are familiar; not care as a nonrational or even irrational feeling; not care as self-sacrifice (Noddings' "motivational displacement"), nor care as contrasted with justice. Feminists need to develop a distinctive conception of care, one that draws on but transcends women's traditional practice. Feminist care must be responsive both to our common humanity and our inevitable particularity. Neither narrowly personal nor blandly impersonal, it can consist neither in the mechanical application of abstract rules nor in an uncritical surge of feeling, but must transcend both rationalism and romanticism.[29]

The development of such a conception of care is a practical and political as much as an intellectual project. It cannot take place in a world that is structured by domination, where the public sphere is separated sharply from the private, and where inequality is justified in terms of such familiar, gender-linked, western oppositions as culture/nature, mind/body, reason/emotion—dichotomies in which each of the first terms is associated with the masculine and considered superior to each of the second. Instead, experimentation with ways of transcending equality requires an enriched and in some ways protected environment, a consciously feminist community dedicated to discovering less rigid and less hierarchical ways of living and thinking. We need not fear that such an environment will be so sheltered as to produce a weakened, hothouse plant. Far from being sheltered from the cold winds of the larger world, alternative communities may be particularly vulnerable to them. It is stimulating but hardly comfortable to live daily with contradictions.

PART SIX

Epilogue

Theoretical Perspectives
on Sexual Difference:
An Overview

ESTELLE B. FREEDMAN

The essays gathered in this collection reflect an important tension over gender difference that recurs across disciplines in contemporary feminist scholarship. In contrast to earlier discussions, which assumed the salience of gender differences, feminist theorists have increasingly rejected a unitary focus on gender, exposing the ways we have assumed gender salience rather than proven it. A close look at these essays, however, suggests that even among those scholars who attempt to deconstruct gender, gender difference is alive, well, and still critical both for scholarship and for politics—that is, for the design of our research and for our thinking about strategies of achieving equality. The "critique of difference," a critique of dualism or of dichotomous thinking, is one of several theoretical frameworks that coexist in the present volume and in feminist scholarship generally.

Like other contemporary works by feminist scholars, the essays here tend to fall within three major theoretical frameworks. The first view accepts gender difference, the second criticizes the notion of difference, and the third attempts to go beyond difference. Yet what we lack at present is a framework that neither uncritically embraces nor overcritically rejects ideas about male/female differences, a theory that recognizes gender variations without enforcing them. To some extent we can view the theoretical frameworks articulated in this collection as developmental stages of theory, for at times they seem to be sequential. But we should not imagine that one framework clearly improves upon or replaces an earlier one. Rather, they may be simultaneous and continually useful ways of thinking about gender that need not compete for intellectual dominance.

Ideas about male/female difference provided the earliest frame of reference informing feminist scholarship. These ideas drew upon two kinds of arguments. The first was essentially a biological explanation (more recently sociobiological), the second a social constructionist view. The biological explanation roots gender difference in genes or in reproductive strategies. In general, biological difference theories are most useful in explaining male dominance. They offer fairly pessimistic political implications for those committed to gender equality. They do not, for example, answer the question of how, politically, we can respond to gender differences that are rooted in genetic or species-survival strategies. Biological and evolutionist arguments about gender difference have been employed in the past by conservative antifeminists, such as the nineteenth-century American doctors who opposed women's higher education on the grounds that intellectual stimulation diminished women's reproductive capacity and thus contributed to "race suicide."[1] In our own time, feminists themselves have adopted sociobiological arguments, most notably in Alice Rossi's controversial 1977 essay, "A Biosocial Perspective on Parenting."[2] In this collection, Carl Degler's essay follows in this tradition, while Ruth Hubbard's critique exemplifies the dominant feminist response to sociobiological thinking. The argument for a biological basis of gender difference has been the one most easily dismissed by feminists, yet it is clearly important for us to confront this model, since it remains compelling for the larger audience beyond our ranks.

The second major early argument for understanding sexual difference rests on a range of social, psychological, and political explanations and can be summarized as the social constructionist view of gender. As Nancy Chodorow explains, psychoanalytic theories, including the object-relations and Lacanian schools, posit deep psychic origins of gender difference, rooted either in perceptions of genital difference or in parent-child relations. Although these theories leave more room for social change than do biological arguments, they perpetuate a male/female dualism, and their political implications can be almost as challenging for feminists as those of biological and sociobiological models. If gender differences are so deeply and early embedded within children, as some theorists propose, and if they are so pervasively reproduced by fundamental institutions that remain highly resistant to change—the family, the school, and the workplace— what kind of feminist politics can we envision short of revolutionary overthrow of these institutions?

Another theory of socially constructed difference, based on ethical and political considerations and usually associated with the work of Carol Gilligan, emphasizes women's unique moral development.[3] This "feminist valorization of women's differences," to use Alison Jaggar's phrase, is reminiscent of nineteenth-century concepts of female moral superiority, which elevated women to the position of guardians of the morality of society. Rather than assuming a biological basis for women's morality, as did the Victorian middle class, contemporary scholars like Nel Noddings offer concrete social facts to support the view that there is a "common feminine experience that logically leads to a distinct moral orientation."

Several authors represented in this collection struggle to understand the political implications of theories of woman's socially constructed difference. Jaggar seems reluctant to accept any theory of difference for strategic reasons. She argues that the feminist goal of equality, and particularly the politics of equality-based law, are confounded by arguments based on a unique female social or ethical stance. Both Deborah Rhode and Catharine MacKinnon criticize the ethical foundations of gender difference even as they explore the practical, legal, and epistemological problems of using a male standard to measure equality. In the end their legal scholarship remains in the socially constructed difference camp, because their analyses are grounded in concerns about both equality and difference. MacKinnon substitutes "dominance" and Rhode substitutes "disadvantage" when speaking of difference. These terms call attention to the critical element of power, which is often missing in the literature that emphasizes the valorization of women's differences. However, both "dominance" and "disadvantage" approaches are still essentially concerned about a difference between men and women. Although Jaggar and MacKinnon adopt opposite strategies in confronting the dilemma of difference and equality—Jaggar says take both; MacKinnon says take neither—each still works within a structure that views gender difference as central.

These papers thus fall, sometimes against their will, into the category of theories that ask What difference does gender make? However, another set of essays, represented in this collection primarily by social scientists, asks What difference does gender not make? I tend to think of this shift as one from "Rosaldo 1" to "Rosaldo 2": from Michelle Zimbalist Rosaldo's influential 1974 theoretical overview in *Woman, Culture and Society,* which encouraged the search for universal sexual asymmetry, to her 1980 *SIGNS* article, "The Use and Abuse of Anthropology," which directed us to look at the ways that gender intersects with a range of other social categories.[4]

Before illustrating such a shift within the papers collected here, it is important to point out that the scholarly project of questioning gender salience follows the lead of activist feminist politics. A variety of writers engaged in grass-roots politics since the early 1970s have insisted that race, class, sexuality, age, and physical ability require a redefinition of the category "woman" in every context in which a woman acts. Black writers in particular and women of color in general first raised this critique, from the Combahee River Collective Statement to the exposés of invisibility and exclusion in the women's movement included in the collection *This Bridge Called My Back.* The proliferation of multiple feminist identities—in such anthologies as *Home Girls, Nice Jewish Girls,* or *With Wings*[5]—presented us with a more diversified notion of sisterhood than we previously had been willing to acknowledge. As Bernice Johnson Reagon explained in a 1981 speech: "The women's movement has perpetuated a myth that there is some common experience that comes just cause you're women. . . . It does not matter at all that biologically we have being women in common. We have been organized to have our primary cultural signals come from some other factors than that we are women."[6]

What activists first acknowledged, scholars soon translated into theories that invoked postmodern and deconstructionist concepts in an attempt to "go beyond" gender.[7] Whether steeped in the language of postmodernism or not, many feminist scholars across disciplines came to share Rosaldo's concern for phenomena that a simple focus on gender dualism can miss. They responded to a call to understand the interaction of gender with other forms of inequality and with social forces that can give gender very different meanings, depending on its context. In this collection, Collier and Yanagisako's critique of dichotomous categories in anthropological accounts of kinship and gender provide a good example of the theoretical implications of Rosaldo's 1980 essay. Collier and Yanagisako propose that we study the "interaction of social and symbolic systems" in order to deconstruct gender and explore sets of categories more true to human experience than those channeled primarily through our Western, socially constructed, and gendered preconceptions. The essays by Barrie Thorne and by Kay Deaux and Brenda Major similarly reveal how preoccupations with gender can mask the ways gender intersects with race, class, and age, as well as how these categories change over time. Recurrent terms in these studies are *context, fluidity,* and *variation,* all of which contrast with the polarities associated with earlier theoretical frameworks that emphasized gender duality and asymmetry. These recent social scientific accounts echo John Dupré's philosophical criticism of the political limitations of over-generalizing about gender.

All of the authors in this last social constructionist camp share an impulse to go beyond gender, or, in the psychologist's language, to speak of "differential gender salience." The emphasis is on understanding the complexity that really exists when we speak about gender. I do not disagree with either the political or the theoretical project of expanding our definitions of gender to be both more precise and more variable. But I do not think such an effort requires us to claim that theories about gender must transcend the concept itself, no matter how fashionable such decentering practices may now seem. The challenge for feminist theory today is to expand, not restrict, our critique of gender inequality. We must seek both to question received wisdom about gender and to affirm gender as a category of reality that matters tremendously in our lives.

Like contemporary feminist scholarship in general, the essays collected here attempt to meet this challenge by refining rather than rejecting theories of gender difference. They expose the weaknesses of difference theories based on simple dualism and universal assumptions. They push our thinking in ever more sophisticated and complex directions. Yet what we are groping toward, I think, is not so much a new theory as a new strategy for our old one. The essays here suggest that where we go next is not so much a question of what we get to as it is a question of how we proceed.

If I seem to suggest here that the goal of transcending gender remains elusive, I do so for good reason. In a historical moment when the category "woman" continues to predict limited access to material resources, greater vulnerability to physical and psychological abuse, and underrepresentation in politics, the search for a theoretical transcendence of gender difference is difficult at best and frivolous at worst. An earlier generation of American women rejected theories of gender difference in the decades after the suffrage victory. By assuming a false universality of male and female experience, our predecessors undermined feminist politics.[8] Today, for both theoretical and political purposes, we must avoid the tendency to assume both a false unity across genders and a greater disunity within our gender than in fact exists. This is not to say that we cannot indulge in the privileges of theorizing, but let us not lose sight of the world within which our theories operate. The constraints that our social world imposes on building new theories can be healthy ones, reminding us that gender difference is still with us, and that understanding this difference still requires our best intellectual efforts.

Notes

DEBORAH L. RHODE: THEORETICAL PERSPECTIVES ON SEXUAL DIFFERENCE

1. Evelyn Fox Keller, "Is Sex to Gender As Nature Is to Science?" *Hypatia* 1 (1987); Jane Flax, "Post-Modernism and Gender Relations in Feminist Theory," *SIGNS* 12 (1987): 621; Catharine MacKinnon, "Toward Feminist Jurisprudence," *Stanford Law Review* 34 (1982): 703.

2. Louise Michele Newman, "The Problem of Biological Determinism," in Louise Michele Newman, ed., *Men's Ideas, Women's Realities: Popular Science, 1870–1915* (Newark: Pergamon, 1985). See also Edward Clark, *Sex in Education or A Fair Chance for the Girls* (New York, 1873).

3. Barbara Ehrenreich and Deirdre English, *For Her Own Good: 150 Years of the Experts' Advice to Women* (Garden City, N.Y.: Anchor, 1978); see Susan Moller Okin, "Thinking like a Woman," infra; Clark, *Sex in Education;* Carroll Smith Rosenberg, *Disorderly Conduct: Visions of Gender in Victorian America* (New York: Knopf, 1985), 259–60; Herbert Spencer, "Psychology of the Sexes," in Newman, *Men's Ideas,* 17, 23; Deborah L. Rhode, "Perspectives on Professional Women," *Stanford Law Review* 40 (1988): 1164.

4. See, e.g., Bernard, "Sex Difference: An Overview," in Alexandra G. Kaplan and Joan P. Bean, eds., *Beyond Sex-Role Stereotypes* (Boston: Little, Brown, 1976); Anne Fausto-Sterling, *Myths of Gender* (New York: Basic, 1985); Ruth Hubbard, Mary Sue Henifin, and Barbara Fried, eds., *Women Look at Biology Looking at Women: A Collection of Feminist Critiques* (Boston: G.K. Hall, 1979); Eleanor Burke Leacock, *Myths of Male Dominance: Collected Articles on Women Cross-Culturally* (New York: Monthly Review, 1981); Eleanor Maccoby and Carol Jacklin, *The Psychology of Sex Differences* (Stanford: Stanford University Press, 1974); *Child Development* 51 (1980) (symposium).

5. See Ruth Hubbard, "The Political Nature of Human Nature," infra; Ruth Hubbard and Marian Lowe, eds., *Genes and Gender: Pitfalls in Research on Sex and Gender* (New York: Gordian, 1978–79), vol. 2; Donna Haraway, "In the Beginning Was the Word: The Genesis of Biological Theory," *SIGNS* 6 (1981): 469; Merle Thornton, "Sex Equality Is Not Enough for Feminism," in Carole Pateman and Elizabeth Gross, eds., *Feminist Challenges: Social and Political Theory* (Boston: Northeastern University Press, 1987), 95.

6. In addition to the essays cited from this collection, see Carol Gilligan, *In a Different Voice* (Cambridge: Harvard University Press, 1982); Nel Noddings, *Caring: A Feminine Approach to Ethics and Moral Education*, (Berkeley: University of California Press, 1984); Mary O'Brien, *The Politics of Reproduction* (Boston: Routledge and Kegan Paul, 1981); and Sara Ruddick, "Maternal Thinking," *Feminist Studies* 6 (1980): 342. See generally Joan C. Tronto, "Beyond Gender Difference to a Theory of Care," *SIGNS* 12 (1987): 644.

7. For critical perspectives on Gilligan, see Catherine Greeno and Eleanor Maccoby, "How Different Is the Different Voice?" *SIGNS* 11 (1986): 310; Lawrence Walker, "Differences in the Development of Moral Reason: A Critical Review," *Child Development* 55 (1984): 677; Cynthia Fuchs Epstein, *Deceptive Distinctions: Sex, Gender, and the Social Order* (New Haven: Yale University Press, 1988), 76–94; Seyla Benhabib, "The Generalized and the Concrete Other: The Kohlberg-Gilligan Controversy and Feminist Theory," in Drucilla Cornell and Seyla Benhabib, *Feminism as Critique: Essays on the Politics of Gender in Late Capitalist Society* (London: Polity, 1987), 77–79; Ann Colby and William Damon, "Listening to a Different Voice: A Review of Gilligan's *In a Different Voice*," in Mary Roth Walsh, ed., *The Psychology of Women: Ongoing Debates* (New Haven: Yale University Press, 1987), and the bibliography in Walsh, *Psychology*, 275–77.

8. See sources cited in n. 7. For related work suggesting more similarities than differences in men's and women's leadership styles and political preferences, see, e.g., sources cited in Barbara Forisha, "The Inside and the Outsider: Women in Organizations," in Barbara Forisha and Barbara H. Goldman, eds., *Outsider on the Inside: Women and Organizations* (New Jersey: Prentice-Hall, 1981), 22; Rosabeth Moss Kanter, "The Impact of Hierarchical Structures on the Work Behavior of Women and Men," in Rachel Kahn-Hut, Arlene Kaplan Daniels, and Colvard Richard, eds., *Women and Work: Problems and Perspectives* (New York: Oxford University Press, 1982), 234, 236–45; Robert S. Erickson, Norman K. Luttberg, and Kent L. Tedin, *American Public Opinion: Its Origins, Content and Impact* (New York: John Wiley, 1980), 186–87; Jane S. Jacquette, "Introduction," in Jane S. Jacquette, ed., *Women in Politics* (New York: John Wiley, 1974), xiii–xxii.

9. See Susan B. Anthony and Ida Halsted Harper, eds., *History of Woman Suffrage* (Indianapolis: Hallenback, 1902) 4:178.

10. See, in addition to works in this collection, Joan Scott, *Gender and the Politics of History* (New York: Columbia University Press, 1988), 176–77.

11. Barrie Thorne, "Children and Gender: Constructions of Difference," infra.

12. Catharine MacKinnon, "Legal Perspectives on Sexual Difference," infra.

13. See Sandra Harding, *The Science Question in Feminism* (Ithaca: Cornell University Press, 1986); idem, "The Instability of the Analytic Categories of Feminist Theory," *SIGNS* 11 (1986): 645; Flax, "Post-Modernism"; Deborah L. Rhode, "Gender and Jurisprudence: An Agenda for Research," *University of Cincinnati Law Review* 56 (1987): 521; Catharine R. Stimpson, *Women's Studies in the United States* (New York: Ford Foundation); Pateman and Gross, *Feminist Challenges*.

14. Nancy Fraser and Linda Nicholsen, "Feminism and Post-Modernism" (unpublished manuscript, 1987); and Sandra Harding and Merrill Hintikka, "Introduction," in Sandra Harding and Merrill Hintikka, eds., *Discovering Reality: Feminist Perspectives on Epistemology, Metaphysics, Methodology, and Philosophy of Science* (Boston: D. Reidel, 1984), x; Linda Akoff, "Cultural Feminism versus Post-Structuralism: The Identity Crisis in Feminism," *SIGNS* 13 (1988): 405. See generally Jean-François Lyotard, *The Post-Modern Condition: A Report on Knowledge*, trans. Geoff Bennington and Brian Massumi (Minneapolis: University of Minnesota Press, 1984).

15. See Mary E. Hawkesworth, "Knowers, Knowing, Known: Feminist Theory and Claims of Truth," *SIGNS* 14 (1989): 553, 555, arguing that feminists must not privilege any single model of inquiry but should rather be reflective about levels of analysis, forms of explanation, standards of evidence, criteria of evaluation, and strategies of argumentation. See also Elizabeth Gross, "What Is Feminist Theory?" in Pateman and Gross, ed., *Feminist Challenges*, 192, 194–204.

16. Regenia Gagnier, "Feminist Postmodernism: The End of Feminism or the Ends of Theory?" infra.

17. See Frye, "The Possibility of Feminist Theory." See also Elizabeth Spelman, *Inessential Woman: Problems of Exclusion in Feminist Thought* (Boston: Beacon, 1988), 114, 167, for a critique of the "ampersand problem in feminist thought," the tendency to add race and class to gender analysis as if there existed some "generic woman."

18. Bell Hooks, "Feminism: A Transformational Politic," infra.

KAREN OFFEN: FEMINISM AND SEXUAL DIFFERENCE IN HISTORICAL PERSPECTIVE

1. For further discussion of these points, see my essays, "Liberty, Equality, and Justice for Women: The Theory and Practice of Feminism in Nineteenth-Century Europe," in Renate Bridenthal, Claudia Koonz, and Susan Stuard, eds., *Becoming Visible: Women in European History*, 2d ed. (Boston: Houghton Mifflin, 1987), 335–73; and "Defining Feminism: A Comparative Historical Approach," *SIGNS* 14 (Autumn 1988): 119–57.

2. "Appel aux femmes," *La Femme libre*, no. 1 (1832); English translation in Susan Groag Bell and Karen Offen, eds., *Women, the Family, and Freedom: The Debate in Documents, 1750–1950*, 2 vols. (Stanford: Stanford University Press, 1983), 1:146.

3. Briefly put, these criteria (which are delineated in the context of a historically sensitive definition of feminism) are three: (1) recognizing the validity of women's own interpretations of their experience and needs and acknowledging the values they claim; (2) exhibiting consciousness of, discomfort at, or even anger over institutionalized injustice toward women as a group by men as a group; and (3) advocating the elimination of that injustice by challenging the coercive power, force, or authority that upholds male prerogatives in a particular culture. For additional discussion, see Offen, "Defining Feminism," esp. 150–53.

4. Limerick by Mrs. Edmund Craster (d. 1874), in *The Oxford Dictionary of Quotations*, 2d ed. (London: Oxford University Press, 1955), 166.

5. For the long view of European women's history, complemented by substantial bibliographies, see the essays in Bridenthal, Koonz, and Stuard, eds., *Becoming Visible*, and Bonnie S. Anderson and Judith P. Zinsser, *A History of Their Own: Women in Europe from Prehistory to the Present*, 2 vols. (New York: Harper & Row, 1988).

6. In English society, the doctrine of *coverture* of women in marriage dates from the thirteenth century and eroded only slowly over the centuries. Married women's property acts in Anglo-American society are a nineteenth-century reform. The French case evolved in the opposite direction, culminating in the virtual dispossession of married women in the Civil Code of 1804. The evolution of gender distinctions in property law was critical to determinations of women's subordinate status, insofar as landed property was long deemed an essential precondition for the exercise of political privileges in European societies.

7. For a particularly interesting manifestation of this general development, see Londa S. Schiebinger, "Skeletons in the Closet: The First Illustrations of the Female Skeleton in Nineteenth-Century Anatomy," *Representations* 14 (1986): 42–82. See also Paul Hoffmann, *La Femme dans la pensée des lumières* (Paris: Editions Orphys, 1978), and Yvonne Knibiehler and Catherine Fouquet, *La Femme et les médecins* (Paris:

Hachette, 1983). For an account of the British case that does begin with Darwin, see Janet Sayers, *Biological Politics: Feminist and Antifeminist Perspectives* (London: Tavistock, 1982).

8. See, for example, Carolyn Merchant, *The Death of Nature: Women, Ecology, and the Scientific Revolution* (San Francisco: Harper & Row, 1979); Hilda L. Smith, *Reason's Disciples: Seventeenth-Century English Feminists* (Urbana: University of Illinois Press, 1982); and Christine Fauré, *La Démocratie sans les femmes* (Paris: Presses Universitaires de France, 1985).

9. See Offen, "Theory and Practice of Feminism."

10. See Jane Lewis, *The Politics of Motherhood: Child and Maternal Welfare in England, 1900–1939* (London: Croom Helm, 1980); the various essays in Renate Bridenthal, Atina Grossmann, and Marion Kaplan, eds., *When Biology Became Destiny: Women in Weimar and Nazi Germany* (New York: Monthly Review, 1984); and Karen Offen, "Women and the Politics of Motherhood in France, 1920–1940," Working Paper no. 87/293 (Florence: European University Institute, 1987).

The historical reexamination of the welfare state from a feminist perspective is in progress at the European University Institute, Florence, Italy, and at the Center for European Studies/Women's History Program at Harvard University. For the latter, see the photocopied proceedings, "Gender and the Origins of the Welfare State: Conferences at the Center for European Studies, 1987–88." For an illuminating comparison of the British and French cases, see Jane Jenson, "Both Friend and Foe: Women and State Welfare," in Bridenthal, Koonz, and Stuard, eds., *Becoming Visible,* 535–56.

11. On this subject, see the forthcoming proceedings from the March 1988 conference Women and the Progressive Era, National Museum of American History, Washington, D.C.

12. Further analysis of these two modes of argument and their consequences can be found in Offen, "Defining Feminism."

13. Mary Wollstonecraft, *A Vindication of the Rights of Woman* (1792); quoted in Bell and Offen, eds., *Women, the Family, and Freedom* 1:61.

14. From Ellen Key, *Love and Marriage* (1911; originally published in Swedish, 1904), quoted in Bell and Offen, eds., *Women, the Family, and Freedom* 2:25.

REGENIA GAGNIER: FEMINIST POSTMODERNISM: THE END OF FEMINISM OR THE ENDS OF THEORY?

1. Anne Fausto-Sterling, *Myths of Gender: Biological Theories about Women and Men* (New York: Basic, 1985), 14.

2. For major discussions of postmodernism in social theory, see Jean-François Lyotard, *The Postmodern Condition: A Report on Knowledge,* trans. Geoff Bennington and Brian Massumi (Minneapolis: University of Minnesota Press, 1984); Jürgen Habermas, "Modernity versus Postmodernity," *New German Critique* 22 (Winter 1981): 3–14; Fredric Jameson, "Postmodernism, or the Cultural Logic of Late Capitalism," *New Left Review* 146 (July/August 1984): 53–92; Mike Davis, "Urban Renaissance and the Spirit of Postmodernism," *New Left Review* 151 (May/June 1985): 106–12; Terry Eagleton, "Capitalism, Modernism, and Postmodernism," *New Left Review* 152 (July/August, 1985): 60–73.

3. See, for example, Donna Haraway, "A Manifesto for Cyborgs: Science, Technology, and Socialist Feminism in the 1980s," *Socialist Review* 80 (March/April 1985): 65–107.

4. Marian Lowe and Ruth Hubbard, eds., *Woman's Nature: Rationalizations of Inequality* (New York: Pergamon, 1983), 2.

5. Alice Jardine, *Gynesis: Configurations of Woman and Modernity* (Ithaca: Cornell University Press, 1985), 36.

6. Sandra Harding, *The Science Question in Feminism* (Ithaca: Cornell University Press, 1986), 18.

7. Audre Lorde, *Sister Outsider: Essays and Speeches* (New York: Crossing, 1984), 114.

8. The response to CLS has been voluminous. For the great collections see *Stanford Law Review*, vol. 36, nos. 1 and 2 (January 1984), *Harvard Law Review*, Special Volume on CLS (Harvard Law Review Association, 1986); and David Kairys, *The Politics of Law: A Progressive Critique* (New York: Pantheon, 1982). See also Mark Kelman, *A Guide to CLS* (Cambridge: Harvard University Press, 1987) and Roberto Mangabeira Unger's books *Knowledge and Politics* (New York: Free Press, 1976), *Passion: An Essay on Personality* (New York: Free Press, 1984), *The Critical Legal Studies Movement* (Cambridge: Harvard University Press, 1986), and *Politics: A Work in Constitutive Social Theory*, 3 vols. (Cambridge: Cambridge University Press, 1987).

For thoughtful critiques of CLS not in the collections, see especially Ward Harper, "Review Essay: The Critical Legal Studies Movement," *American Philosophical Association Newsletter on Philosophy and Law* (November 1987): 3–12; Drucilla Cornell, "Toward a Modern/Postmodern Reconstruction of Ethics," *University of Pennsylvania Law Review* 133/2 (January 1985): 291–380, and "The Poststructuralist Challenge to the Ideal of Community," *Cardozo Law Review* 8/5 (April 1987): 989–1022; and James Boyle, "Modernist Social Theory: Roberto Unger's *Passion*," *Harvard Law Review* 96/4 (February 1983): 1066–83.

9. Robin West, "Jurisprudence and Gender," *University of Chicago Law Review*, 55/1 (Winter 1988): 1–72, and "The Difference in Women's Hedonic Lives: A Phenomenological Critique of Feminist Legal Theory," *Wisconsin Women's Law Journal* 3 (1987): 81–145.

10. For a full exposition of a cultural-studies approach to subjectivity and value, see Regenia Gagnier, *Subjectivities: A History of Self Representation in Britain, 1832–1920* (New York: Oxford University Press, 1991).

11. For an emphasis on experiment over theory, see Ian Hacking, *Representing and Intervening* (Cambridge: Cambridge University Press, 1983). For a brief discussion of evolution and theory, see John Dupré, "Materialism, Physicalism, and Scientism," *Philosophical Topics* 15/1 (Spring 1988): 39–41.

12. For the figure of the cyborg, see Haraway, "Manifesto." Roughly, Haraway intends *cyborg* to represent the collapse of the distinction between the organic and the mechanical.

13. Ernesto Laclau and Chantal Mouffe, *Hegemony and Socialist Strategy: Towards a Radical Democratic Politics* (London: Verso, 1985), 174.

14. Haraway, "Manifesto," 79.

CARL N. DEGLER: DARWINIANS CONFRONT GENDER; OR, THERE IS MORE TO IT THAN HISTORY

1. Charles Darwin, *The Descent of Man and Selection in Relation to Sex* (New York: Modern Library, n.d.), 867, 873.

2. Lester F. Ward, *Pure Sociology* (New York, Macmillan, 1903), 296.

3. Ibid., 376.

4. Ibid., 326. Ward makes clear his indebtedness to Darwin, saying that the naturalist "makes an unanswerable case in favor of his principle of sexual selection" (327).

5. Ibid., 336.

6. Eliza Burt Gamble, *The Evolution of Woman: An Inquiry into the Dogma of Her Inferiority to Man* (New York: G.P. Putnam's Sons, 1894), 31, 44, and 61.

7. Charlotte Perkins Gilman, *Women and Economics* (New York: Harper Torchbooks, 1966). For a summary of her ideas see Carl N. Degler, "Charlotte Perkins Gilman on the Theory and Practice of Feminism," *American Quarterly* 8 (1956): 21–39.

8. Lydia Kingsmill Commander, "The Self-Supporting Woman and the Family," *American Journal of Sociology* 14 (1909): 752.

9. Rosalind Rosenberg, *Beyond Separate Spheres: The Intellectual Roots of Modern Feminism* (New Haven: Yale University Press, 1982).

10. Lewis Madison Terman, "Were We Born That Way?" *World's Work* 44 (1922): 660.

11. Anne Fausto-Sterling, *Myths of Gender: Biological Theories about Women and Men* (New York: Basic, 1985), 207.

12. Ibid., 219.

13. Ruth Bleier, *Science and Gender* (New York: Pergamon, 1984), 6. See also the essay by Ruth Hubbard in this volume for a similar denial that any separation of biological and cultural influences on human behavior is possible.

14. A sample of such politically liberal social scientists who draw upon biology in accounting for human behavior would include anthropologist Melvin Konner (Emory University), sociologist Alice Rossi (Boston University), psychologist Daniel Freedman (University of Chicago), sociologists Pierre Van den Berghe (University of Washington) and Joseph Lopresto (University of Texas, Austin), anthropologist William Durham (Stanford), and political scientist Roger Masters (Dartmouth).

15. See, for example, James W. Atz, "The Application of the Idea of Homology to Behavior," in Lester Aronson et al., eds., *Development and Evolution of Behavior* (San Francisco: W.H. Freeman, 1970), and Arthur L. Caplan, "A Critical Examination of Sociobiological Theory," in George W. Barlow and James Silverberg, eds., *Sociobiology: Beyond Nature/Nurture* (Boulder: Westview, 1980).

16. Bleier, *Science and Gender*, 37–38.

17. Donald Symons, "Darwinism and Contemporary Marriage," in Kingsley Davis, ed., *Contemporary Marriage: Comparative Perspectives on a Changing Institution* (New York: Russell Sage Foundation, 1985), 145–46, and Donald Symons, *The Evolution of Human Sexuality* (New York: Oxford University Press, 1979), 86–95, 111–12. Symons also points out that a sociobiological interpretation of sexuality would provide an explanation for the differences in female and male orgasms, about which students of women's sexuality like Shere Hite, Margaret Mead and others have commented.

18. Alice S. Rossi, "The Biosocial Side of Parenthood," *Human Nature* 1 (1978): 79. See her earlier and documented article: "A Biosocial Perspective on Parenting," *Daedalus* 106 (1977): 1–31. See also Melvin Konner, *The Tangled Wing: The Biological Constraints on the Human Spirit* (New York: Holt, Rinehart and Winston, 1982), chapter 6 for a discussion of Rossi's views and those of other recent studies of sex differences. Konner is an anthropologist and a feminist.

19. Rossi, "Biosocial Side," 72.

20. Ibid., 75.

21. Ibid.

22. Ibid., 79.

23. Ibid.

24. Nancy Chodorow, *The Reproduction of Mothering* (New York: Schocken, 1978), 207.

25. Ibid., 216.

26. Ibid., 29. Chodorow, of course, is not alone among social scientists in fearing to accept biology in accounting for behavior that seems inexplicable by culture alone. The cultural explanation is deeply ingrained in all fields of human behavior, and for good reason: biological explanations have been horribly misused. Without that historically derived fear, a biological explanation would probably not be absent, as it

presently is, from psychologist Carol Gilligan's depiction of male and female differences in her book *In a Different Voice* (Cambridge: Harvard University Press, 1982); sociologist Melford E. Spiro would not have fallen back on what he terms "precultural" explanations in *Gender and Culture: Kibbutz Women Revisited* (New York: Schocken, 1980). In his book he makes clear that his findings about the differential behavior of male and female kibbutzniks caused him to lose confidence in socialization or culture as a complete explanation of human behavior.

27. Chodorow, *Reproduction*, 28.
28. See William H. Durham, "Toward a Coevolutionary Theory of Human Biology and Culture," in Arthur L. Caplan, ed., *The Sociobiology Debate: Readings on Ethical and Scientific Issues* (New York: Harper & Row, 1978), 428–48; Robert Boyd and Peter J. Richerson, *Culture and the Evolutionary Process* (Chicago: University of Chicago Press, 1985).
29. One promising possibility is a sociobiological explanation for the incest taboo. See, e.g., Joseph Shepher, *Incest: A Biosocial View* (New York: Academic, 1983), and W. Arens, *The Original Sin: Incest and Its Meaning* (New York: Oxford University Press, 1986).
30. Stephen Jay Gould, *New York Review of Books* (September 25, 1986), 48.
31. Roger D. Masters, "Sociobiology: Science or Myth?" *Journal of Social and Biological Structures* 2 (1979): 245. For examples of other political scientists interested in a biosocial perspective see: Stephen H. Balch, "The Neutered Civil Servant: Eunuchs, Celibates, Abductees and the Maintenance of Organizational Loyalty," *Journal of Social and Biological Structures* 8 (1985): 313–28; Lynton K. Caldwell, "Will Biology Change Politics? A Commentary," *Politics and the Life Sciences* 1 (1982): 44–45; Steven A. Peterson and Alfred Somit, "Methodological Problems Associated with a Biologically-Oriented Social Science," *Journal of Social and Biological Structures* 1 (1978): 11–25.
32. J. Maynard Smith, "The Conceptions of Sociobiology," in Gunther S. Stent, ed., *Morality as a Biological Phenomenon: The Presuppositions of Sociobiological Research*, rev. ed. (Berkeley: University of California Press, 1980), 29.
33. Mary Midgley, *Beast and Man: The Roots of Human Nature* (Ithaca: Cornell University Press, 1978), 65, 76.
34. Mary Midgley and Judith Hughes, *Women's Choices: Philosophical Problems Facing Feminism* (London: Weidenfeld and Nicolson, 1983). On page 211, she provides a good example of how one applies the Darwinian insight to human behavior. She begins by pointing out the evolutionary nature of care of offspring by birds, noting that parents who fail to care for their offspring simply have fewer or no surviving young. "All surviving birds must be descended from ancestors whose parental motivation was quite strong. This evolutionary consideration, of course, applies equally to all other species where the young need prolonged care. . . . Our young have the longest period of dependence in the animal kingdom. On any view, at least up to the stage where social conditioning may be supposed to take over, the survival of our ancestors depended, as much as or more than that of other animals and birds, on strong, natural parental motivation."
35. Margaret Mead, "Alternatives to War," in Morton Fried, Marvin Harris, and Robert Murphy, eds., *War: The Anthropology of Armed Conflict and Aggression* (Garden City, N.Y.: Natural History Press, 1968), 228.

JOHN DUPRÉ: GLOBAL VERSUS LOCAL PERSPECTIVES ON SEXUAL DIFFERENCE

1. I argue against these essentialist positions in, respectively, John Dupré, "Human Kinds," in *The Latest on the Best: Essays on Evolution and Optimality* (Cambridge:

Bradford Books/MIT Press, 1987), 327–48; and John Dupré, "Sex, Gender, and Essence," *Midwest Studies in Philosophy* 11 (1986): 441–57.

2. See, e.g., Ruth Bleier, *Science and Gender: A Critique of Biology and Its Theories on Women* (Oxford: Pergamon, 1984); Anne Fausto-Sterling, *Myths of Gender: Biological Theories about Men and Women* (New York: Basic, 1985), chap. 6; and Ruth Hubbard's essay in this volume. The most comprehensive general critique of human sociobiology is Philip Kitcher, *Vaulting Ambition: Sociobiology and the Quest for Human Nature* (Cambridge: MIT Press, 1985).

3. Semantically, this distinction is sometimes expressed by a distinction between "gender studies" and "feminist theory," though it would be a mistake to suppose that these categories neatly divide the kinds of projects of feminists who have used these descriptions of their work. For further discussion see Regenia Gagnier's essay in this volume.

4. The parallel between sex and gender is discussed further in my "Sex, Gender, and Essence." There I also defend antiessentialist perspectives on both categories.

5. As will appear later in the paper, there is a sense in which I consider power disparity, or political inequality, potentially universal features of gender systems. However, I think it is clear that these are not the kinds of features that could be candidates for essential properties in the sense I am now considering.

6. I do not discuss here in any detail the criticisms of sociobiology. This task is very capably addressed by Ruth Hubbard (this volume). For further references see note 2. Familiarly enough, Darwin's theory was originally constructed as an explanation of biological diversity. I am suggesting that we should take seriously this analogy between biological and cultural evolution. I discuss this parallel further in "Human Kinds."

7. See, e.g., Richard Dawkins, *The Selfish Gene* (Oxford: Oxford University Press, 1976).

8. There are also serious technical reasons for rejecting the thesis of convergence of biological and cultural evolution. Recent work, sympathetic and internal to the study of cultural evolution, has shown in some detail how decision-making rules might have evolved which, under quite plausible circumstances, might well lead to biologically maladaptive behavior. For details see Robert Boyd and Peter J. Richerson, *Culture and the Evolutionary Process* (Chicago: University of Chicago Press, 1985). Discussion of these rather technical issues is not necessary for my present purposes.

9. Steven Jay Gould and Richard Lewontin, "The Spandrels of San Marco and the Panglossian Paradigm: A Critique of the Adaptationist Program," *Proceedings of the Royal Society of London,* B, 205 (1979): 581–98. As should be clear from this discussion I am, like Gould and Lewontin, very far from assuming that *biological* evolution is a process leading inexorably to optimal adaptation. For further criticism, see Richard Lewontin, "The Shape of Optimality," in John Dupré, ed., *The Latest on the Best.*

10. See especially Richard Lewontin, *The Genetic Basis of Evolutionary Change* (New York: Columbia University Press, 1974).

11. The particular project of explaining social organization in terms of (individual) biological factors is only one instance of a more general strategy of scientific reductionism. It is arguable that reductionism itself reflects deep ideological commitments. See Lynda Birke, *Women, Feminism, and Biology: The Feminist Challenge* (Brighton: Harvester, 1986), chap. 4; for more general discussion of reductionism see John Dupré, "The Disunity of Science," *Mind* 92 (1983): 321–46; and idem, "Materialism, Physicalism, and Scientism," *Philosophical Topics* 16 (1988): 31–56.

12. Sandra Harding, *The Science Question in Feminism* (Ithaca: Cornell University Press, 1986).

13. For discussion of this issue see Harding, *The Science Question;* Birke, *Women, Feminism, and Biology,* chap. 8; Fausto-Sterling, *Myths of Gender,* chap. 7; Helen Longino, "Can There Be a Feminist Science?" *Hypatia* 2 (1988): 51–64; Evelyn Fox Keller, *Reflections on Gender and Science* (New Haven: Yale University Press, 1985); Evelyn Fox Keller, "The Gender/Science System: Or, Is Sex to Gender As Nature Is to Science?" (*Hypatia* 2 (1988): 37–49.

14. Keller, "The Gender/Science System," contains an interesting discussion of the parallel between critiques of science (as mirroring nature) and critiques of gender (as mirroring sex).

15. This remark is oversimplified. Prima facie, there is nothing less determining about a cultural cause than about a biological cause. What is needed is a three-level system in which biological, cultural, and autonomous processes are distinguished. The last I conceive paradigmatically as involving action guided by systems of values. Such a system of values can be conceived as deriving from, but also transcending, cultural forces in a way analogous to that in which culture arises from within biology. (I discuss this more fully in Dupré, "Human Kinds," 345–47.)

16. Harding, *The Science Question,* 251.

17. See, e.g., Fausto-Sterling, *Myths of Gender;* Helen Longino and Ruth Doell, "Body, Bias, and Behavior: A Comparative Analysis of Reasoning in Two Areas of Biological Science," *SIGNS* 5 (1983): 206–27.

18. A valuable additional source, complementary to the present argument, is the attack on a number of the major dichotomies in terms of which feminist scholars have attempted to draw ultimately essentialist gender distinctions. See Sylvia Yanagisako and Jane Collier, "Toward a Unified Analysis of Kinship and Gender," in Jane Collier and Sylvia Yanagisako, eds., *Gender and Kinship: Toward a Unified Analysis* (Stanford: Stanford University Press, 1987).

19. This may suggest a simplistic view of feminist theory. In particular, many feminists want to make ethical and political claims that go far beyond the mere elimination of difference, for example the promotion of values now associated with the feminine. Alison Jaggar's essay in this volume proposes a position of this kind. Such an argument, however, could surely not be *feminist* as opposed to simply *ethical,* in a society not divided by gender.

20. A landmark attempt at such a project is Alison Jaggar, *Feminist Politics and Human Nature* (Totowa, N.J.: Rowman and Allanheld, 1983).

21. See Dupré, "Sex, Gender, and Essence."

RUTH HUBBARD: THE POLITICAL NATURE OF "HUMAN NATURE"

1. Alison Jaggar, *Feminist Politics and Human Nature* (Totowa, N.J.: Rowman and Allanheld, 1983).

2. Edward O. Wilson, *Sociobiology: The New Synthesis* (Cambridge: Harvard University Press, 1975), 4.

3. George C. Williams, *Sex and Evolution* (Princeton: Princeton University Press, 1975).

4. Edward H. Clarke, *Sex in Education* (Boston: James R. Osgood, 1874).

5. Richard Dawkins, *The Selfish Gene* (Oxford: Oxford University Press, 1976).

6. David Barash, *The Whispering Within* (New York: Harper & Row, 1979).

7. R. C. Lewontin, "The Analysis of Variance and the Analysis of Causes," *American Journal of Human Genetics* 26 (1974): 400–11.

8. R. C. Lewontin, Steven Rose, and Leon J. Kamin, *Not in Our Genes* (New York: Pantheon, 1984); Lynda Birke, *Women, Feminism and Biology* (New York: Methuen, 1986).

9. Margaret Mead, *Male and Female* (New York: Dell, 1949).

10. Donna Haraway, "Signs of Dominance," *Studies in History of Biology* 6 (1983): 129–219.

11. Edward O. Wilson, *On Human Nature* (Cambridge: Harvard University Press, 1978).

12. Wilson, *On Human Nature*, 147.

13. Idem, *Sociobiology*, chap. 27; "Human Decency Is Animal," *New York Times Magazine* (October 12, 1975).

14. Eleanor Burke Leacock, *Myths of Male Dominance* (New York: Monthly Review Press, 1981).

15. Samuel K. Wasser, ed., *Social Behavior of Female Vertebrates* (New York: Academic, 1983); Sarah Blaffer Hrdy, "Empathy, Polyandry, and the Myth of the Coy Female," in Ruth Bleier, ed., *Feminist Approaches to Science* (New York: Pergamon, 1986), 119–46.

16. Wilson, *On Human Nature*, 190.

17. Ibid., 134.

18. Wilson, "Human Decency Is Animal."

19. Rose Frisch et al., "Delayed Menarche and Amenorrhea of College Athletes in Relation to Age of Onset of Training," *Journal of the American Medical Association* 246 (1981): 1559–63.

20. Melvin Konner and Carol Worthman, "Nursing Frequency, Gonadal Function, and Birth Spacing among !Kung Hunter-Gatherers," *Science* 207 (1980): 788–90.

21. Nancy Howell, *Demography of the Dobe !Kung* (New York: Academic, 1979).

22. Barbara B. Harrell, "Lactation and Menstruation in Cultural Perspective," *American Anthropologist* 83 (1982): 796–823.

HERMA HILL KAY: PERSPECTIVES ON SOCIOBIOLOGY, FEMINISM, AND THE LAW

1. These generalizations are found in state statutes (e.g., former §15–314 of the Idaho Code provided that "of several persons claiming and equally entitled to administer [the estate of a decedent], males must be preferred to females, and relatives of the whole to those of the half blood"); acts of Congress (e.g., former 37 U.S.C. §401 provided that "in this chapter, 'dependent,' with respect to a member of a uniformed service means—(1) his spouse; * * * However, a person is not a dependent of a female member unless he is in fact dependent on her for over one-half of his support * * *"); and the practices of administrative agencies (e.g., an unwritten regulation of the Alabama Department of Public Safety requiring a married woman to use her husband's surname when applying for a driver's license). The U.S. Supreme Court held the first two sex-based generalizations unconstitutional; it affirmed without opinion a lower court judgment that sustained the third. See *Reed v. Reed,* 404 U.S. 71 (1971) (invalidating Idaho provision); *Frontiero v. Richardson,* 411 U.S. 677 (1973) (invalidating dependency requirement for spouses of female service members); *Forbush v. Wallace,* 341 F. Supp. 217 (M.D. Ala. 1971), aff'd mem. 405 U.S. 970 (1972) (sustaining Alabama regulation).

2. Carolyn Bird, *Born Female* (New York: Pocket Books, 1968), 1–15 (recounting how the word "sex" was added to Title VII); Ruth Bader Ginsburg, "Sexual Equality under the Fourteenth and Equal Rights Amendments," *Washington University Law Quarterly* (Winter 1979), 172 (pointing out the difficulty of elaborating "bold doctrine regarding sex discrimination when even a starting point is impossible to anchor in the constitutional fathers' design").

3. Wendy Webster Williams, "Equality's Riddle: Pregnancy and the Equal Treatment/ Special Treatment Debate," *New York University Review of Law and Social Change* 13 (1984–85): 329–31 (setting out the doctrinal framework established with the aid of the two legal provisions cited in the text).

4. Ibid., 331.

5. Jane Mansbridge, *Why We Lost the ERA* (Chicago: University of Chicago Press, 1986), 197 (noting that "the political death of the ERA has in fact corresponded to a flowering in feminist thought"). Some recent examples of the flowering include Christine A. Littleton, "Reconstructing Sexual Equality," *California Law Review* 75 (July 1987): 1279–1337; Martha Minow, "The Supreme Court 1986 Term: Justice Engendered," *Harvard Law Review* 101 (November 1987): 10–95; Deborah L. Rhode, "Association and Assimilation," *Northwestern University Law Review* 81 (Fall 1986): 106–45.

6. Deborah L. Rhode, "Perspectives on Professional Women," *Stanford Law Review* 40 (May 1988): 1168.

7. See, e.g., Ann Scales, "Towards a Feminist Jurisprudence," *Indiana Law Review* 56 (Spring 1981): 375–444; Sylvia Law, "Rethinking Sex and the Constitution," *University of Pennsylvania Law Review* 132 (June 1984): 955–1040; Herma Hill Kay, "Models of Equality," *University of Illinois Law Review* (1985): 39–88.

8. See, e.g., Katharine T. Bartlett, "Pregnancy and the Constitution: The Uniqueness Trap," *California Law Review* 62 (December 1974): 1532–66.

9. See Wendy Webster Williams, "The Equality Crisis: Some Reflections on Culture, Courts, and Feminism," *Women's Rights Law Reporter* 7 (Spring 1982): 175–200.

10. *California Federal Savings & Loan Association v. Guerra*, 479 U.S. 272 (1987); *Miller-Wohl Company, Inc. v. Commissioner of Labor and Industry*, 692 P.2d 1243 (Mont. 1984), vacated and remanded 479 U.S. 1050 (1987), opinion reinstated on remand 744 P.2d 871 (Mont. 1987). Both cases involved challenges by employers under Title VII of the Civil Rights Act to state statutes requiring pregnancy leave on the ground that the state statutes impermissibly discriminated on the basis of sex. The United States Supreme Court resolved the immediate controversy by upholding the California statute.

11. See, e.g., Linda J. Krieger and Patricia N. Cooney, "The Miller-Wohl Controversy: Equal Treatment, Positive Action and the Meaning of Women's Equality," *Golden Gate University Law Review* 13 (Summer 1983): 513–92; Williams, "Equality's Riddle," supra n. 3; Herma Hill Kay, "Equality and Difference: The Case of Pregnancy," *Berkeley Women's Law Journal* 1 (Fall 1985): 1–38; Lucinda Finley, "Transcending Equality Theory: A Way out of the Maternity and the Workplace Debate," *Columbia Law Review* 86 (October 1986): 1118–82.

12. See, e.g., Ann Scales, "The Emergence of Feminist Jurisprudence: An Essay," *Yale Law Journal* 95 (June 1986): 1373–1403; Littleton, "Reconstructing Sexual Equality," supra n. 5.

13. Edward O. Wilson, *Sociobiology*, abridged ed. (Cambridge: Harvard University Press, Belknap Press, 1980), 156.

14. Ibid.

15. Richard Dawkins, *The Selfish Gene* (Oxford: Oxford University Press, 1976), 152–53.

16. Ibid., 152.

17. Charles Darwin, *The Descent of Man, and Selection in Relation to Sex*, 2 vols. (New York: Appleton, 1871).

18. Wilson, *Sociobiology*, 158–64; Dawkins, *Selfish Gene*, 157–76.

19. Wilson, *Sociobiology*, 220.

20. Ibid., 275.

21. Ibid.

22. Ibid.

23. Edward O. Wilson, *On Human Nature* (Toronto: Bantam, 1979), 33.

24. Ibid., 130–33.

25. Ibid., 133–34.
26. See, e.g., Richard C. Lewontin, Steven Rose, and Leon J. Kamin, *Not in Our Genes* (New York: Pantheon, 1984); Ruth Hubbard, Mary Sue Henifin, and Barbara Fried, *Women Look at Biology Looking at Women* (Cambridge, Mass.: Schenkman, 1979).
27. See Philip Kitcher, *Vaulting Ambition* (Cambridge: MIT Press, 1985).
28. Kingsley R. Browne, "Biology, Equality, and the Law: The Legal Significance of Biological Sex Differences," *Southwestern Law Journal* 38 (June 1984): 617–702, at 619.
29. Ibid.
30. Ibid.
31. Browne, "Biology," 664–68. The U.S. Supreme Court invalidated this practice in *City of Los Angeles Department of Water & Power v. Manhart*, 435 U.S. 702 (1978).
32. Ibid., 668–73. The U.S. Supreme Court upheld the validity of male-only registration for compulsory military service in *Rostker v. Goldberg*, 453 U.S. 57 (1981). Plaintiffs did not challenge the combat restriction.
33. Ibid., 674–76. This illustration is discussed later.
34. Ibid., 676–78. The U.S. Supreme Court invalidated this law in *Craig v. Boren*, 429 U.S. 190 (1976).
35. Ibid., 678–82. This practice was invalidated in *Diaz v. Pan American World Airways, Inc.*, 442 F.2d 385 (5th Cir.), cert. denied, 404 U.S. 950 (1971).
36. Ibid., 682–84. The U.S. Supreme Court held that a state-supported single-sex nursing school could not refuse to admit an otherwise qualified male student in *Mississippi University for Women v. Hogan*, 458 U.S. 718 (1982).
37. Ibid., 697. One hopes that even Browne would concede that this example of sex-based discrimination was not based on a "genuine" sex difference.
38. John H. Beckstrom, *Evolutionary Jurisprudence* (Urbana, 1989); *Sociobiology and the Law: The Biology of Altruism in the Courtroom of the Future* (Urbana, 1985); "The Potential Dangers and Benefits of Introducing Sociobiology to Lawyers," *Northwestern University Law Review* 79 (December 1984 and February 1985): 1279–92; "Sociobiology and Intestate Wealth Transfer," *Northwestern University Law Review* 76 (April 1981): 216–70.
39. These applications are spelled out in the two articles cited in n. 38 supra.
40. Beckstrom, "Potential Dangers," 1288–89.
41. Ibid., 1290–92.
42. Browne, "Biology," 676.
43. Beckstrom, "Potential Dangers," 1289.
44. Joseph W. Madden, *Handbook of the Law of Persons and Domestic Relations* (St. Paul: West Publishing, 1931), 369–70.
45. Peter M. Bromley, *Family Law*, 5th ed. (London: Butterworth, 1976), 306.
46. Homer H. Clark, Jr., *The Law of Domestic Relations in the United States*, student ed. (St. Paul: West Publishing, Hornbook Series, 1988), 789.
47. Deborah L. Rhode, *Justice and Gender* (Cambridge, 1989): 154–60.
48. Frances Olsen, "The Politics of Family Law," *Law & Inequality* 2 (Feb. 1984): 6–16.
49. I have elaborated on this point elsewhere. See my "Models of Equality," *University of Illinois Law Review* (1985): 39–88. There I conclude, after analysis of U.S. Supreme Court cases dealing with race and sex discrimination, that the two groups of cases display different models of equality. The race cases show a one-way model of access, with black litigants asking to be treated like whites in specified circumstances, while the sex cases show a two-way model of access, with women asking to be treated like men in the public sphere, and men asking to be treated like women primarily in the private sphere.

50. Clark, *Domestic Relations,* 799–800.
51. Olsen, "Politics," 16–18.
52. Robert H. Mnookin, "Child-Custody Adjudication: Judicial Functions in the Face of Indeterminancy," *Law and Contemporary Problems* 39 (Summer 1975): 226–93.
53. See generally Jay Folberg, ed., *Joint Custody and Shared Parenting* (Washington: B.N.A. Books, 1984).
54. See generally Jay Goldstein, Anna Freud, and Albert Solnit, *Beyond the Best Interests of the Child* (New York: Free Press, 1973).
55. Richard Neely, "The Primary Caretaker Rule: Child Custody and the Dynamics of Greed," *Yale Law and Policy Review* 3 (Fall 1984): 168–86.
56. Williams, "Equality Crisis," 190 n. 80.
57. Katharine T. Bartlett and Carol Stack, "Joint Custody, Feminism, and the Dependency Dilemma," *Berkeley Women's Law Journal* 2 (1986): 9–41.
58. See, e.g., Rene Uviller, "Fathers' Rights and Feminism: The Maternal Presumption Revisited," *Harvard Women's Law Journal* 1 (1978): 107–30.
59. Martha Fineman, "Dominant Discourse, Professional Language, and Legal Change in Child Custody Decisionmaking," *Harvard Law Review* 101 (February 1988): 768–74.
60. Littleton, "Sexual Equality," 1333.
61. Dawkins, *Selfish Gene,* ix.
62. Rhode, "Professional Women," 1170–71.
63. Selma Fraiberg, *Every Child's Birthright: In Defense of Mothering* (New York: Basic, 1977).
64. Ibid., 62.
65. Alice Rossi, "Equality between the Sexes: An Immodest Proposal," *Daedalus* 93 (Spring 1964): 615, 624–25.
66. Idem, "A Biosocial Perspective on Parenting," *Daedalus* 106 (Spring 1977): 4–5.
67. Idem, "Gender and Parenthood," *American Sociological Review* 49 (February 1984): 15.
68. Littleton, "Sexual Equality," 1329. See also Williams, "Equality Crisis," 183, 190.
69. John Paul II, "Mulieris Dignitatem," *L'Osservatore Romano* n. 40 [1058] (weekly edition in English, October 3, 1988): 8.
70. Ibid., 5.
71. Kate Chopin, *The Awakening* (New York: Capricorn, 1964), 121–22.

KAY DEAUX AND BRENDA MAJOR: A SOCIAL-PSYCHOLOGICAL MODEL OF GENDER

1. The meanings associated with the terms *gender* and *sex* vary as a function of both academic discipline and political stance. In this article, we adopt the position defined by Deaux in "Sex and Gender" (*Annual Review of Psychology* 36 [1985]: 49–81.) *Sex* refers to the biologically based categories male and female. *Gender* refers to the psychological characteristics associated with those biological states, assigned either by observers or by the individual. In this usage, the term *sex differences* does not make any assumptions about causality (i.e., whether assumed or observed differences are biologically or experientially based) but refers to a categorization of individuals on the basis of biological features.
2. This study is reported in an unpublished doctoral dissertation from the Harvard Graduate School of Education (W. S. Barnes, "Sibling Influences within Family and School Contexts," 1984) and is described in Deborah Belle, "Ironies in the Contemporary Study of Gender," *Journal of Personality* 53 (June 1985): 400–05.
3. Carol Gilligan, *In a Different Voice* (Cambridge: Harvard University Press, 1982).

4. Joan W. Scott, "Gender: A Useful Category of Historical Analysis," *American Historical Review* 91 (1986): 1053–75.

5. Scott, "Gender," 1065.

6. For an excellent historical analysis of the assumptions underlying research on masculinity and femininity, see J. G. Morawski, "The Measurement of Masculinity and Femininity: Engendering Categorical Realities," in Abigail J. Stewart and M. Brinton Lykes, eds., *Gender and Personality: Current Perspectives on Theory and Research* (Durham: Duke University Press, 1985), 108–35.

7. See Ruth Hubbard's essay in this volume.

8. A full treatment of this model is presented in Kay Deaux and Brenda Major, "Putting Gender into Context: An Interactive Model of Gender-Related Behavior," *Psychological Review* 94 (July 1987): 369–89.

9. Scott, "Gender," 1067.

10. Judith M. Gerson and Kathy Peiss, "Boundaries, Negotiation, Consciousness: Reconceptualizing Gender Relations," *Social Problems* 32 (April 1985): 327.

11. For more discussion of negotiation of self in social interaction, see Michael Athay and John M. Darley, "Toward an Interaction-Centered Theory of Personality," in Nancy Cantor and John F. Kihlstrom, eds., *Personality, Cognition, and Social Interaction* (Hillsdale, N.J.: Lawrence Erlbaum, 1981), 281–308; also William B. Swann, Jr., "Quest for Accuracy in Person Perception: A Matter of Pragmatics," *Psychological Review* 91 (October 1984): 457–77.

12. For more extensive reviews of the empirical literature on expectancy confirmation, see John M. Darley and Russell H. Fazio, "Expectancy Confirmation Processes Arising in the Social Interaction Sequence," *American Psychologist* 35 (October 1980): 867–81; and Dale T. Miller and William Turnbull, "Expectancies and Interpersonal Processes," *Annual Review of Psychology* 37 (1986): 233–56.

13. Janet T. Spence, "Masculinity, Femininity, and Gender-Related Traits: A Conceptual Analysis and Critique of Current Research," *Progress in Experimental Personality Research* 13 (1984): 84. For more traditional discussions of gender identity, see Richard Green, *Sexual Identity Conflict in Children and Adults* (New York: Basic, 1974); John Money and Anke A. Ehrhardt, *Man and Woman, Boy and Girl* (Baltimore: Johns Hopkins University Press, 1972); Robert J. Stoller, *Sex and Gender: On the Development of Masculinity and Femininity* (New York: Science House, 1968).

14. Janet T. Spence, "Gender Identity and Its Implications for Concepts of Masculinity and Femininity," in T. Sondregger, ed., *Nebraska Symposium on Motivation* (Lincoln: University of Nebraska Press, 1985).

15. See Nancy Chodorow's essay in this volume.

16. For a preliminary report of these data, see Kay Deaux, "Incipient Identity" (paper presented as the Carolyn Wood Sherif Award Lecture at the meeting of the American Psychological Association, Atlanta, August 1988).

17. For more discussion, see E. Tory Higgins and Gillian King, "Accessibility of Social Constructs: Information-Processing Consequences of Individual and Contextual Variability," in Nancy Cantor and John F. Kihlstrom, eds., *Personality, Cognition, and Social Behavior* (Hillsdale, N.J.: Lawrence Erlbaum, 1981), 69–121; also Hazel Markus and Ziva Kunda, "Stability and Malleability of the Self-Concept," *Journal of Personality and Social Psychology* 51 (October 1986): 858–66.

18. Albert A. Cota and Kenneth L. Dion, "Salience of Gender and Sex Composition of Ad Hoc Groups: An Experimental Test of Distinctiveness Theory," *Journal of Personality and Social Psychology* 50 (April 1986): 770–76.

19. Rosabeth Moss Kanter, *Men and Women of the Corporation* (New York: Basic, 1977).

20. See William B. Swann, Jr., "Self-Verification: Bringing Social Reality into Harmony

with the Self," in Jerry Suls and Anthony Greenwald, eds., *Psychological Perspectives on the Self* (Hillsdale, N.J.: Lawrence Erlbaum, 1983) 2:33–66.

21. Erwin Goffman made the classic statement of this position in *The Presentation of Self in Everyday Life* (New York: Anchor, 1959).

22. For a thorough discussion of this point, see Philip E. Tetlock and A. S. R. Manstead, "Impression Management versus Intrapsychic Explanations in Social Psychology: A Useful Dichotomy?" *Psychological Review* 92 (January 1985): 59–77.

23. Mark Zanna and Susan J. Pack, "On the Self-Fulfilling Nature of Apparent Sex Differences in Behavior," *Journal of Experimental Social Psychology* 11 (November 1975): 583–91.

24. Rona Fried and Brenda Major, "Self-Presentation of Sex-Role Attributes to Attractive Others" (paper presented at the meeting of the Eastern Psychological Association, Hartford, 1980).

25. DeAnna Mori, Shelly Chaiken, and Patricia Pliner, "'Eating Lightly' and the Self-Presentation of Femininity," *Journal of Personality and Social Psychology* 53 (October 1987): 693–702.

26. For a review of the psychological literature on the gender belief system, see Kay Deaux and Mary E. Kite, "Thinking about Gender," in Beth B. Hess and Myra Marx Ferree, eds., *Analyzing Gender: A Handbook of Social Science Research* (Beverly Hills, Calif.: Sage, 1987), 92–117.

27. For the classic study of gender stereotypes, see Paul Rosenkrantz, Susan Vogel, Helen Bee, Inge Broverman, and Donald M. Broverman, "Sex-Role Stereotypes and Self-Concepts in College Students," *Journal of Consulting and Clinical Psychology* 32 (1968): 286–95. For more recent analyses of gender stereotypes among U.S. college students, see Kay Deaux and Laurie L. Lewis, "The Structure of Gender Stereotypes: Interrelationships among Components and Gender Label," *Journal of Personality and Social Psychology* 46 (April 1984): 991–1004; and in an international sample, John E. Williams and Deborah L. Best, *Measuring Sex Stereotypes: A Thirty Nation Study* (Beverly Hills, Calif.: Sage, 1982).

28. In recognizing that people have certain beliefs about gender, we do not assume that there is no basis in reality for these beliefs. Research indicates that *on the average* men score higher on measures of instrumentality and women score higher on measures of expressiveness. But these observed differences tend to be relatively small, generally smaller than assessed beliefs about the differences.

29. For discussions of gender subtypes, see: Richard D. Ashmore, Frances K. Del Boca, and David Titus, "Types of Women and Men: Yours, Mine, and Ours" (paper presented at meeting of American Psychological Association, Toronto, 1984); A. Kay Clifton, Diane McGrath, and Bonnie Wick, "Stereotypes of Women: A Single Category?" *Sex Roles* 2 (June 1976): 135–48; Kay Deaux, Ward Winton, Maureen Crowley, and Laurie L. Lewis, "Level of Categorization and Content of Gender Stereotypes," *Social Cognition* 3 (1985): 145–67; Dorothy Holland and Debra Davidson, "Labeling the Opposite Sex: Metaphors and Themes in American Folk Models of Gender" (paper presented at the Institute for Advanced Study, Princeton, 1983); Cathryn Noseworthy and Albert J. Lott, "The Cognitive Organization of Gender-Stereotypic Categories," *Personality and Social Psychology Bulletin* 10 (September 1984): 474–81.

30. Deaux et al., "Gender Stereotypes."

31. Sandra L. Bem, "Gender Schema Theory: A Cognitive Account of Sex Typing," *Psychological Review* 88 (July 1981): 354–64.

32. Carol Lynn Martin, "A Ratio Measure of Sex Stereotypes," *Journal of Personality and Social Psychology* 52 (March 1987): 489–99.

33. Suzanne J. Kessler and Wendy McKenna, *Gender: An Ethnomethodological Approach* (New York: John Wiley, 1978).
34. See Antonia Abbey, Catherine Cozzarelli, Kimberly McLaughlin, and Richard J. Harnish, "The Effects of Clothing and Dyad Sex Composition on Perceptions of Sexual Intent: Do Women and Men Evaluate These Cues Differently?" *Journal of Applied Social Psychology* 17 (February 1987): 108–26.
35. See Antonia Abbey, "Sex Differences in Attributions for Friendly Behavior: Do Males Perceive Females' Friendliness?" *Journal of Personality and Social Psychology* 42 (May 1982): 830–38.
36. Kanter, *Men and Women of the Corporation.*

BARRIE THORNE: CHILDREN AND GENDER: CONSTRUCTIONS OF DIFFERENCE

1. See Barrie Thorne, "Re-Visioning Women and Social Change: Where Are the Children?" *Gender & Society* 1 (1987): 85–109. The invisibility of children in feminist and sociological thought can be documented by reviewing scholarly journals. Ambert analyzed issues of eight widely-read sociology journals published between 1972 and 1983. At the top of the journals in the proportion of space devoted to children, *Journal of Marriage and Family* had only 3.6 percent and *Sociology of Education* only 6.6 percent of articles on children. The index for the first ten years of the feminist journal *SIGNS* has one entry under "child development," one under "child care," and four under "childbirth." See Anne-Marie Ambert, "Sociology of Sociology: The Place of Children in North American Sociology," in Peter Adler and Patricia A. Adler, eds., *Sociological Studies of Child Development* (Greenwich, Conn.: JAI, 1986) 1:11–31.
2. See M. Z. Rosaldo, "The Use and Abuse of Anthropology: Reflections on Feminism and Cross-Cultural Understanding," *SIGNS* 5 (1980): 389–417.
3. For reviews of some of the research on sex differences see Eleanor Maccoby and Carol Jacklin, *The Psychology of Sex Differences* (Stanford: Stanford University Press, 1974), and Jere E. Brophy and Thomas L. Good, *Teacher-Student Relations* (New York: Holt, Rinehart, 1974).
4. For example, see Carol Jacklin, "Methodological Issues in the Study of Sex-Related Differences," *Developmental Review* 1 (1981): 266–73; Maccoby and Jacklin, *Psychology of Sex Differences;* and Maureen C. McHugh, Randi Daimon Keoske, and Irene Hanson Frieze, "Issues to Consider in Conducting Nonsexist Psychological Research," *American Psychologist* 41 (1986): 879–90.
5. Here is the inevitable footnote on terminology, one more example of the definitional fiddling so prevalent in the social science literature on sex and gender. This perpetual fiddling reflects our ongoing efforts to locate subject matter, to construct appropriate levels of analysis, and to grapple with difficult problems such as how to weigh and simultaneously grasp the biological and the cultural. I am currently persuaded that: (1) we should conceptually distinguish biological sex, cultural gender, and sexuality (desire), but (2) we should not assume that they are easily separable. One of our central tasks is to clarify their complex, often ambiguous relationships—kept alive in the term "sex/gender system" (a term first put forward in Gayle Rubin, "The Traffic in Women: Notes on the 'Political Economy' of Sex," in Rayna R. Reiter, ed., *Toward an Anthropology of Women* [New York: Monthly Review Press, 1975], 157–210). We should muse about why, after all our careful distinctions, we so easily slip into interchangeable use of *sex, gender,* and *sexual.*

The phrase *sex category* refers to the core, dichotomous categories of individual sex and gender (female/male; girl/boy; woman/man)—dualisms riddled with the complexities of biology/culture and age/gender. While these categories appear to be rockbottom and founded in biology—hence "sex" category—they are deeply constructed by cultural beliefs and by social practices of gender display and attribution. *Gender* still seems serviceable as an all-purpose term linked with other words for finer conceptual tuning, e.g., "gender identity," "gender ideology," "the social organization of gender." In my discussion of "sex difference" research I use "sex" rather than "gender" because that has been the (perhaps telling) verbal practice of that tradition.

6. See Suzanne J. Kessler and Wendy McKenna, *Gender: An Ethnomethodological Approach* (New York: John Wiley, 1978); Erving Goffman, "The Arrangement between the Sexes," *Theory and Society* 4 (1977): 301–36; Spencer E. Cahill, "Language Practices and Self-Definition: The Case of Gender Identity Acquisition," *Sociological Quarterly* 287 (1987): 295–311; and Candace West and Don H. Zimmerman, "Doing Gender," *Gender & Society* 1 (1987): 125–51.

7. See reviews in Marlaine E. Lockheed, "Sex Equity in Classroom Organization and Climate," in Susan B. Klein, ed., *Handbook for Achieving Sex Equity through Education* (Baltimore: Johns Hopkins University Press, 1985), 189–217; and Eleanor Maccoby, "Social Groupings in Childhood: Their Relationship to Prosocial and Antisocial Behavior in Boys and Girls," in Dan Olweus, Jack Block, and Marian Radke-Yarrow, eds., *Development of Antisocial and Prosocial Behavior* (San Diego: Academic, 1985), 263–84.

8. Janet Schofield, *Black and White in School* (New York: Praeger, 1982).

9. See reviews in Daniel N. Maltz and Ruth A. Borker, "A Cultural Approach to Male-Female Miscommunication," in John J. Gumperz, ed., *Language and Social Identity* (New York: Cambridge University Press, 1983), 195–216; Barrie Thorne, "Girls and Boys Together . . . But Mostly Apart: Gender Arrangements in Elementary Schools," in Willard W. Hartup and Zick Rubin, eds., *Relationships and Development* (Hillsdale, N.J.: Lawrence Erlbaum, 1986), 167–84; and Maccoby, "Social Groupings."

10. Janet Lever, "Sex Differences in the Games Children Play," *Social Problems* 23 (1976): 478–87.

11. The invisibility and marginalization of girls in the extensive British literature on "youth subcultures" was first noted in Angela McRobbie and Jenny Garber, "Girls and Subcultures," in S. Hall and T. Jefferson, eds., *Resistance through Rituals* (London: Hutchinson, 1976).

12. Lever, "Sex Differences"; Carol Gilligan, *In a Different Voice* (Cambridge: Harvard University Press, 1982): 9–11.

13. Zella Luria and Eleanor Herzog, "Gender Segregation across and within Settings" (unpublished paper presented at 1985 annual meeting of the Society for Research in Child Development, Toronto).

14. Most observational research on the gender relations of preadolescent children in the United States has been done in schools. Goodwin's research on children in an urban neighborhood is a notable exception. See Marjorie Harness Goodwin, *Conversational Practices in a Peer Group of Urban Black Children* (Bloomington: Indiana University Press, in press).

15. Two decades ago there was a reverse pattern in research on adult interaction, at least in the literature on sociolinguistics and small groups. "Gender" was assumed to "happen" when men and women were together, not when they were separated. It took feminist effort to bring same-gender relations, especially among women (a virtually invisible topic in traditional research on communication), into that subject matter (see Barrie Thorne, Cheris Kramarae, and Nancy Henley, eds., *Language, Gender and Society* [Rowley, Mass.: Newbury House, 1983]). These inverse ways of locating gender—defined by the genders separating for children and by their being

together for adults—may reflect age-based assumptions. In our culture, adult gender is defined by heterosexuality, but children are (ambivalently) defined as asexual. We load the interaction of adult men and women with heterosexual meaning, but we resist defining children's mixed-gender interaction in those terms. Traditional constructions of children and gender exemplify the ideal of latency.

16. See Barrie Thorne, "An Analysis of Gender and Social Groupings," in Laurel Richardson and Verta Taylor, eds., *Feminist Frontiers* (Reading, Mass.: Addison-Wesley, 1983), 61–63; and idem, "Girls and Boys Together," 170–71.

17. Sherry B. Ortner, "The Founding of the First Sherpa Nunnery, and the Problem of 'Women' as an Analytic Category," in Vivian Patraka and Louise Tilly, eds., *Feminist Re-Visions* (Ann Arbor: University of Michigan Women's Studies Program, 1984).

18. Carole Joffe, "As the Twig Is Bent," in Judith Stacey, Susan Bereaud, and Joan Daniels, eds., *And Jill Came Tumbling After* (New York: Dell, 1974), 79–90; Raphaela Best, *We've All Got Scars* (Bloomington: Indiana University Press, 1983); Robert B. Everhart, *Reading, Writing and Resistance* (Boston: Routledge & Kegan Paul, 1983); Philip A. Cusick, *Inside High School* (New York: Holt, Rinehart and Winston, 1973).

19. Cusick, *Inside High School*, 168.

20. I was a participant-observer in two different elementary schools—for eight months in a largely working class school in California (there were about 500 students, 5 percent Black, 20 percent Hispanic, and 75 percent white), and for three months in a school of similar size, class, and racial/ethnic composition in Michigan. Most of the examples in this paper come from the California school, where I focused primarily on fourth- and fifth-graders. For further reports from this work, see my "Gender and Social Groupings"; "Girls and Boys Together"; and "Crossing the Gender Divide: What 'Tomboys' Can Teach Us about Processes of Gender Separation among Children" (unpublished paper presented at 1985 meeting of the Society for Research on Child Development, Toronto). See also Barrie Thorne and Zella Luria, "Sexuality and Gender in Children's Daily World," *Social Problems* 33 (1986): 176–90.

21. See Thorne and Luria, "Sexuality and Gender," 182–84.

22. Linda A. Hughes, "Beyond the Rules of the Game: Girls' Gaming at a Friends' School (unpublished Ph.D. diss., University of Pennsylvania Graduate School of Education, 1983); Goodwin, *Conversational Practices*.

23. Marjorie Harness Goodwin and Charles Goodwin, "Children's Arguing," in Susan Philips, Susan Steele, and Christina Tanz, eds., *Language, Gender, and Sex in Comparative Perspective* (Cambridge: Cambridge University Press, 1988).

24. Goodwin, *Conversational Practices*.

25. R. W. Connell, "Theorising Gender," *Sociology* 12 (1985): 260–72. Also see R. W. Connell, *Gender and Power* (Stanford: Stanford University Press, 1987).

26. See Judith Stacey and Barrie Thorne, "The Missing Feminist Revolution in Sociology," *Social Problems* 32 (1985): 301–16.

27. This problem is analyzed in Connell, "Theorising Gender" and *Gender and Power;* Hester Eisenstein, *Contemporary Feminist Thought* (Boston: G.K. Hall, 1984); Jane Flax, "Postmodernism and Gender Relations in Feminist Theory," *SIGNS* 12 (1987): 621–43; Bell Hooks, *Feminist Theory: From Margin to Center* (Boston: South End, 1984); and Sylvia J. Yanagisako and Jane F. Collier, eds., *Gender and Kinship: Essays toward a Unified Analysis* (Stanford: Stanford University Press, 1987).

28. West and Zimmerman, "Doing Gender."

29. Sandra Wallman, "Epistemologies of Sex," in Lionel Tiger and Heather T. Fowler, eds., *Female Hierarchies* (Chicago: Aldine, 1978). Also see Nancy Chodorow, "Feminism and Difference: Gender, Relation, and Difference in Psychoanalytic Perspective," *Socialist Review* 46 (1979): 51–70; Rosaldo, "Use and Abuse of Anthropology"; and Yanagisako and Collier, "Feminism, Gender, and Kinship."

30. See Paul Willis, *Learning to Labor* (New York: Columbia University Press, 1977); and R. W. Connell, D. J. Ashenden, S. Kessler, and G. W. Dowsett, *Making the Difference: Schools, Families, and Social Division* (Boston: Allen & Unwin).

31. On the charged nature of socially constructed boundaries, see Mary Douglas, *Purity and Danger* (New York: Praeger, 1966).

32. Frederik Barth, *Ethnic Groups and Boundaries* (Boston: Little, Brown, 1969).

33. See Thorne, "Girls and Boys Together," 174–75.

34. In an ethnographic study of a multiracial school in England, Fuller found that girls of varied social classes and ethnicities had somewhat different ways of responding to boys' efforts to control and devalue them. See Mary Fuller, "Black Girls in a London Comprehensive," in Rosemary Deem, eds., *Schooling for Women's Work* (London: Routledge & Kegan Paul, 1980), 52–65.

35. Goffman, "The Arrangement between the Sexes," 316. The phrase "sex (or gender) segregation among children" has been in widespread use, but as William Hartup suggested in comments at the 1985 meeting of the Society for Research in Child Development, the term *segregation* implies separation far more total and sanctioned than in most social relations among children in the United States.

36. R. W. Connell et al., *Making the Difference*, 182.

37. See David Tyack and Elisabeth Hansot, "Gender in American Public Schools: Thinking Institutionally," *SIGNS* 13 (1988): 741–60. British schools have institutionalized extensive gender separation, described in Sara Delamont, "The Conservative School? Sex Roles at Home, at Work and at School," in Stephen Walker and Len Barton, eds., *Gender, Class and Education* (Sussex: Falmer, 1983): 93–105.

38. See Luria and Herzog, "Gender Segregation," and Thorne, "Girls and Boys Together."

39. For a fuller analysis, see Thorne, "Crossing the Gender Divide."

40. Willis, *Learning to Labor*.

41. Joan Anyon, "Intersections of Gender and Class: Accommodation and Resistance by Working-Class and Affluent Females to Contradictory Sex-Role Ideologies," in Walker and Len Barton, eds., *Gender, Class and Education*, 1–19.

42. Connell et al., *Making the Difference;* S. Kessler, D. J. Ashenden, R. W. Connell, and G. W. Dowsett, "Gender Relations in Secondary Schooling," *Sociology of Education* 58 (1985): 34–48.

43. Kessler et al., "Gender Relations," 42.

44. Everhart, *Reading, Writing and Resistance*.

45. Anyon, "Intersections of Gender and Class"; Connell et al., *Making the Difference*.

46. On feminist postmodernism, see Flax, "Postmodernism and Gender Relations"; Sandra Harding, *The Science Question in Feminism* (Ithaca: Cornell University Press, 1986); and Toril Moi, *Sexual/Textual Politics* (London: Methuen, 1985).

NANCY J. CHODOROW: WHAT IS THE RELATION BETWEEN PSYCHOANALYTIC FEMINISM AND THE PSYCHOANALYTIC PSYCHOLOGY OF WOMEN?

1. Longer versions of this essay appear in my *Feminism and Psychoanalytic Theory* (Cambridge: Polity Press; New Haven: Yale University Press, 1989) and in the *Annual Review of Psychoanalysis* 17 (1989). Elizabeth Abel, Daniel Greenson, Lisby Mayer, Barrie Thorne, and Abby Wolfson made helpful comments on the essay. Deborah L. Rhode's reading helped shape its present form.

2. I discuss these issues especially in my introduction to *Feminism and Psychoanalytic Theory* and in "Feminism, Femininity and Freud," in the same volume; and in Jerome Rabow, Gerald M. Platt, and Marion Goldman, eds., *Advances in Psychoanalytic Sociology* (Malabar, Fla.: Krieger, 1986).

3. My labels here do not do justice to the complexities of these protagonists' identities. Some who have contributed prominently to the mainstream psychoanalytic literature about women would label themselves as feminist—critical of the sexual status quo as well as of the situation of women in the psychoanalytic profession. Some whom I consider to have contributed primarily to psychoanalytic feminism—Jessica Benjamin, Jane Flax, and I among object-relations feminists, Jean Baker Miller and her colleagues among interpersonal feminists, Juliet Mitchell among Lacanians— are practicing analysts or therapists.

4. Sigmund Freud, *New Introductory Lectures*, vol. 22 of *The Standard Edition of the Complete Psychological Works*, ed. and trans. J. Strachey (London: Hogarth, 1933), 116.

5. I discuss these issues in "Feminism, Femininity and Freud."

6. Freud, *New Introductory Lectures*, 118.

7. My account of dominant trends in the psychoanalytic psychology of gender draws from what we might call mainstream Freudian journals. I have mentioned the inbetween status of feminist psychoanalysts, prominent examples of whom include Carol Nadelson, Malkah Notman, and Ethel Person. These writers have led the feminist challenge from within psychoanalysis, focusing not only on deficiencies in psychoanalytic theory but also on the treatment of women in the profession and in society. Theoretically they seem closest either to object-relations or interpersonal psychoanalytic feminism. See, e.g., Malkah T. Notman and Carol C. Nadelson, eds., *The Woman Patient*, vols. 1–3, (New York: Plenum, 1978, 1982); Ethel Person, "Sexuality as a Mainstay of Identity," *SIGNS* 5 (1980): 605–30, and *Dreams of Love and Fateful Encounters: The Power of Romantic Passion* (New York: W.W. Norton, 1988). See also Tony Bernay and Dorothy W. Cantor, eds., *The Psychology of Today's Woman: New Psychoanalytic Visions* (Hillsdale, N.J.: Analytic, 1986); Judith L. Alpert, *Psychoanalysis and Women: Contemporary Reappraisals* (Hillsdale, N.J.: Analytic, 1986); two volumes edited by Martha Kirkpatrick: *Women's Sexual Development: Explorations of Inner Space* (New York: Plenum, 1980) and *Women's Sexual Experience: Explorations of the Dark Continent* (New York: Plenum, 1981).

8. See Herman Roiphe and Eleanor Galenson, *Infantile Origins of Sexual Identity* (New York: International Universities Press, 1981).

9. See, e.g., Janine Chasseguet-Smirgel, "The Consideration of Some Blind Spots in the Exploration of the Dark Continent," *International Journal of Psycho-Analysis* 57 (1976): 281; Judith Kestenberg, "Outside and Inside, Male and Female," *Journal of the American Psychoanalytic Association* 16 (1968): 457–520; idem, "The Inner-Genital Phase," in D. Mendel, ed., *Early Feminine Development: Contemporary Psychoanalytic Views* (New York: Spectrum, 1980); idem, "Maternity and Paternity in the Developmental Context," *Psychiatric Clinics of North America* 3 (1980): 61–79; James Kleeman, "Freud's Views on Early Female Sexuality in the Light of Direct Child Observation," *Journal of the American Psychoanalytic Association* 24/5 (1976): 3–28; Elizabeth Lloyd Mayer, "'Everybody Must Be Just like Me': Observations on Female Castration Anxiety," *International Journal of Psycho-Analysis* 66 (1985): 331–47.

10. See, e.g., Mayer, "'Everybody'"; Shahla Chehrazi, "Female Psychology: A Review," *Journal of the American Psychoanalytic Association*, 34 (1986): 141–62; and Phyllis Tyson, "A Developmental Line of Gender Identity, Gender Role, and Choice of Love Object," *Journal of the American Psychoanalytic Association* 30 (1982): 61–86.

11. Kleeman, "Freud's Views on Early Female Sexuality"; and various writings by Robert Stoller, including "A Contribution to the Study of Gender Identity," *International Journal of Psycho-Analysis* 45 (1964): 220–26, "The Sense of Maleness," *Psychoanalytic Quarterly* 34 (1965): 207–18, "The Sense of Femaleness," *Psychoanalytic Quarterly* 37

(1968): 42–45, "Primary Femininity," *Journal of the American Psychoanalytic Association* 24/5 (1976): 59–78.

12. The outlines of the object-relations perspective on feminine development and personality can be summarized in my own writing. I first argued in "Family Structure and Feminine Personality," in Michelle Z. Rosaldo and Louise Lamphere, eds., *Woman, Culture, and Society* (Stanford: Stanford University Press, 1974), 44, that "feminine personality comes to define itself in relation and connection to other people more than masculine personality. . . . For boys and men, both individuation and dependency issues become tied up with the sense of masculinity. . . . For girls and women, by contrast, issues of femininity, or feminine identity, are not problematic in the same way." I developed my argument more fully in *The Reproduction of Mothering* (Berkeley: University of California Press, 1978), and in "Difference, Relation and Gender in Psychoanalytic Perspective," in Hester Eisenstein and Alice Jardine, eds., *The Future of Difference* (Boston: G.K. Hall, 1980).

The term *object* in object-relations theory seems to be a holdover from a psychoanalytic theory centered on drives, which have, in Freud's view, "objects" and "aims." In this model the personhood of the object is not stressed, nor need the object be a person. By "object" object-relations theorists tend to mean "other," but it can be argued that the term "self-other relations" tends artificially to inflate the wholeness and overemphasize the sociological reality of such psychic representations.

13. Chodorow, *Reproduction*, 169.
14. Ibid., 209.
15. Ibid., 169.
16. Dorothy Dinnerstein, *The Mermaid and the Minotaur* (New York: Harper & Row, 1976). I stress differences in the way reactions to the mother are constituted in men and women more than Dinnerstein does, but such distinctions are not necessary for the purpose here.
17. See Jessica Benjamin, "The End of Internalization: Adorno's Social Psychology," *Telos* 32 (1977): 42–64, "Authority and the Family Revisited, or A World Without Fathers?" *New German Critique* 13 (1978): 35–57, and *The Bonds of Love: Psychoanalysis, Feminism and the Problem of Domination* (New York: Pantheon, 1988); Jane Flax, "Critical Theory as a Vocation," *Politics and Society* 8/2 (1978): 201–23, "Political Philosophy and the Patriarchal Unconscious," in Sandra Harding and Merrill B. Hintikka, eds., *Discovering Reality: Feminist Perspectives on Epistemology, Metaphysics, Methodology, and the Philosophy of Science* (Dordrecht: D. Reidel, 1983, and *Thinking Fragments: Psychoanalysis, Feminism, and Postmodernism in the Contemporary West* (Berkeley: University of California Press, 1989); and Evelyn Fox Keller, *Reflections on Gender and Science* (New Haven: Yale University Press, 1985). See also Isaac D. Balbus, *Marxism and Domination* (Princeton: Princeton University Press, 1982), and Nancy C. M. Hartsock, "The Feminist Standpoint: Developing the Grounds for a Specifically Feminist Historical Materialism," in Harding and Hintikka, *Discovering Reality.*
18. See Elizabeth Abel, ed., *Writing and Sexual Difference* (Chicago: The University of Chicago Press, 1980); and Elizabeth Abel, Marianne Hirsch, and Elizabeth Langland, *The Voyage In: Fictions of Female Development* (Hanover, N.H.: University Press of New England); Coppelia Kahn, "The Hand That Rocks the Cradle: Recent Gender Theories and Their Implications," in Shirley Nelson Garner, Claire Kahane, and Madelon Sprengnether, eds., *The (M)other Tongue: Essays in Feminist Psychoanalytic Interpretation* (Ithaca: Cornell University Press, 1985), 72–88; and Janet Adelman, "Born of Woman: Fantasies of Maternal Power in *Macbeth*," in Marjorie Garber, ed., *Cannibals, Witches and Divorce: Estranging the Renaissance*, Selected Papers from the English Institute, 1985 (Baltimore: Johns Hopkins University Press, 1987).

19. See on this Benjamin, "The End of Internalization"; Nancy Chodorow and Susan Contratto, "The Fantasy of the Perfect Mother," in Barrie Thorne, ed., with Marilyn Yalom, *Rethinking the Family: Some Feminist Questions,* (New York: Longman, 1982); Chodorow, *Reproduction;* "Difference"; and "Beyond Drive Theory: Object Relations and the Limits of Radical Individualism," *Theory and Society* 14 (1985): 271–319; and Keller, *Reflections,* pt. 2.

20. Jean Baker Miller, *Toward a New Psychology of Women* (Boston: Beacon, 1976), and Carol Gilligan, *In a Different Voice* (Cambridge: Harvard University Press, 1982). See also Janet L. Surrey, "Self-in-Relation: A Theory of Women's Development," Judith V. Jordan, "Empathy and Self Boundaries," and Jean Baker Miller, "The Development of Women's Sense of Self," all work in progress papers from the Stone Center for Developmental Services and Studies (Wellesley College, Wellesley, Mass.). Other papers from the Stone Center also address these issues. The firmly critical political stance and general critique of social inequality found in Miller's book and her later writings is not emphasized by her Stone Center colleagues, who stick more closely to psychological issues.

 The emphasis on women's relatedness found in Miller's work and my own, along with the work of Gilligan, has helped inspire a range of what are sometimes called feminist theories about women's special capacities and qualities. See, for instance, Sara Ruddick, "Maternal Thinking," in Thorne, with Yalom, *Rethinking;* Mary Field Belenky, Blythe McVicker Clinchy, Nancy Rule Goldberger, and Jill Mattuck Tarule, *Women's Ways of Knowing* (New York: Basic, 1987); and Nel Noddings, *Caring: A Feminine Approach to Ethics and Moral Education* (Berkeley: University of California Press, 1984).

21. See, e.g., Miller's *New Psychology,* also, "The Construction of Anger in Women and Men," Stone Center work in progress paper, "Women and Power," *Social Policy* 13/4 (1983): 3–6; and Carol C. Nadelson, Malkah T. Notman, Jean Baker Miller, and Joan Zilbach, "Aggression in Women: Conceptual Issues and Clinical Implications," in Notman and Nadelson, *Woman Patient,* vol. 3. See also Harriet Goldhor Lerner, *The Dance of Anger* (New York: Harper & Row, 1985).

22. See, e.g., Judith V. Jordan and Janet L. Surrey, "The Self-in-Relation: Empathy and the Mother-Daughter Relationship," in Bernay and Cantor, *Psychology,* which reproduces much of the account in Chodorow, *Reproduction.*

23. See Chodorow, *Reproduction;* Jane Flax, "The Conflict between Nurturance and Autonomy in Mother-Daughter Relationships and within Feminism," *Feminist Studies* 4 (1978): 171–89, and "Re-Membering the Selves: Is the Repressed Gendered?" in *Women and Memory,* special issue of *Michigan Quarterly Review* 26 (1987): 92–110; and Benjamin, *Bonds,* chap. 3. See also Susan Contratto, "Father Presence in Women's Psychological Development," in Rabow, Platt, and Goldman, eds., *Advances,* and Keller's discussion of "dynamic autonomy" in *Reflections.*

24. Paradigmatic Lacanian feminist statements can be found in Juliet Mitchell, *Psychoanalysis and Feminism* (New York: Pantheon, 1974), and in her *Women, the Longest Revolution* (New York: Pantheon, 1984); in Juliet Mitchell and Jacqueline Rose, "Introductions," in Jacques Lacan, *Feminine Sexuality* (New York: W.W. Norton, 1982); and in Jane Gallop, *The Daughter's Seduction* (Ithaca: Cornell University Press, 1982). Lacanian feminist literary criticism can be found in Garner, Kahane, and Sprengnether, *(M)other Tongue,* and in an extensive literature by Jane Gallop, Shoshana Felman, Toril Moi, Naomi Schor, and others. To my knowledge, Lacanian feminists do not discuss the work of the Jean Baker Miller group. The more literary proponents of Lacanian theory tend to engage with Lacan and Freud among psy-

choanalysts, with postmodernist French critics like Derrida, and otherwise with object-relations psychoanalytic feminists.

25. In one reading of Lacan, sexual constitution and subjectivity is different for him who possesses the phallus and her who does not. As this view is extended, the woman becomes not a subject in her own right—even one who can never have the phallus— but simply a symbol, or a symptom, or a "lack," in the masculine psyche.

Another reading (and some Lacanian feminists claim that the sexually critical and liberating potential of Lacan lies here) argues that although one sex has an anatomical penis, neither sex can finally possess the phallus: sexuality is incomplete and fractured for both. And as men and women line themselves up on one or the other side of the linguistic/sexual divide, they need not do so based on their anatomy.

26. Against Lacan's singling out of woman as the lack, or the Other, we find a French feminist anti-Lacanian revolt. In another version of the argument for primary femininity and for a genital awareness that does not hinge on perception and acceptance of unequal genital difference, Luce Irigaray, Hélène Cixous, and others reject male discourse and argue for women's reappropriation of their own unconscious, their body, and their genital configuration, for their being in themselves rather than being a lack in the male psyche. See Eisenstein and Jardine, *The Future of Difference*, pt. 2; Elaine Marks and Isabelle de Courtivron, *New French Feminisms* (New York: Schocken, 1981).

27. See Miriam Johnson, "The Reproduction of Male Dominance" in Rabow, Platt, and Goldman, ed., *Advances;* Johnson, *Strong Mothers, Weak Wives* (Berkeley: University of California Press, 1988); and Gayle Rubin, "The Traffic in Women," in Rayna Reiter, ed., *Toward an Anthropology of Women* (New York: Monthly Review Press, 1975).

28. On the issue of cross-gender transference, see Eva P. Lester, "The Female Analyst and the Erotized Transference," *International Journal of Psycho-Analysis* 66 (1985): 283–93; Marianne Goldberger and Dorothy Evans, "On Transference Manifestations in Male Patients with Female Analysts," *International Journal of Psycho-Analysis* 66 (1985): 295–309; Laila Karme, "The Analysis of a Male Patient by a Female Analyst: The Problem of the Negative Oedipal Transference," *International Journal of Psycho-Analysis* 60 (1979): 253–61; Phyllis Tyson, "The Gender of the Analyst," *Psychoanalytic Study of the Child* 35 (1980): 321–38; David L. Raphling and Judith F. Chused, "Transference across Gender Lines," *Journal of the American Psychoanalytic Association* 36 (1988): 77–104; and Ethel Person, "The Erotic Transference in Women and Men: Differences and Consequences," *Journal of the American Academy of Psychoanalysis* 13 (1985): 159–80.

29. This example is inspired by talks given back-to-back at "Women and Psychoanalysis: Today and Yesterday," a symposium celebrating the fiftieth anniversary of the Boston Psychoanalytic Society, February 1984. One of the talks was by Eleanor Galenson and the other by Jean Baker Miller, Carol Nadelson, Malkah Notman, and Joan Zilbach.

30. These points are discussed in Evelyn Fox Keller, "The Gender/Science System: Or, Is Sex to Gender as Nature Is to Science?" *Hypatia* 2 (1987): 37–49; and Jane Flax, "Postmodernism and Gender Relations in Feminist Theory," *SIGNS* 12 (1987): 621–43.

31. See Janet Malcolm, "Reflections: J'Appelle un Chat un Chat," *New Yorker* (April 20, 1987).

32. On gender salience, see Jane Atkinson, "Anthropology" review essay, *SIGNS* 8 (1982): 236–58. See also recent psychological work in gender schema theory, e.g.,

Sandra Lipsitz Bem, "Gender Schema Theory: A Cognitive Account of Sex Typing," *Psychological Review* 88 (1981): 354–64.

SYLVIA J. YANAGISAKO AND JANE F. COLLIER: THE MODE OF REPRODUCTION IN ANTHROPOLOGY

1. See, for example, Judith Shapiro, "Anthropology and the Study of Gender," *Soundings: An Interdisciplinary Journal* 64 (1981): 446–65.
2. In reviewing the work of feminist historians, Joan Scott, "Gender: A Useful Category for Historical Analysis," *American Historical Review* 91 (1986): 1054, notes that the use of *gender* emerged as a rejection of the biological determinism implicit in the use of such terms as *sex* and *sexual difference.*
3. See Evelyn Fox Keller, *Reflections on Gender and Science* (New Haven: Yale University Press, 1985); Donna Haraway, "In the Beginning Was the Word: The Genesis of Biological Theory," *SIGNS* 6 (1981): 469–81; and Ruth Hubbard's essay in this volume.
4. Sherry Ortner, "Is Female to Male as Nature Is to Culture?" in Michelle Z. Rosaldo and Louise Lamphere, eds., *Woman, Culture, and Society* (Stanford: Stanford University Press, 1974), 67–87.
5. Michelle Z. Rosaldo, "Woman, Culture, and Society: A Theoretical Overview," in Rosaldo and Lamphere, eds., *Woman, Culture, and Society,* 17–42.
6. Olivia Harris and Kate Young, "Engendered Structures: Some Problems in the Analysis of Reproduction," in Joel S. Kahn and Josep R. Llobera, eds., *The Anthropology of Pre-Capitalist Societies* (London: Macmillan, 1981), 109–47.
7. Pierre Bourdieu, *Outline of a Theory of Practice,* trans. Richard Nice (Cambridge: Cambridge University Press, 1977), and Sherry Ortner, "Theory in Anthropology since the Sixties," *Comparative Studies in Society and History* 26 (1984): 126–66.
8. Examples include Ruby Rohrlich-Leavitt, Barbara Sykes, and Elizabeth Weatherford, "Aboriginal Woman: Male and Female Anthropological Perspectives," in Rayna Reiter, ed., *Towards an Anthropology of Women* (New York: Monthly Review Press, 1975), 110–26; and Annette Weiner, *Women of Value, Men of Renown: New Perspectives on Trobriand Exchange* (Austin: University of Texas Press, 1976).
9. For an earlier version of this critique of analytical dichotomies, see Sylvia Yanagisako and Jane Collier, "Toward a Unified Analysis of Gender and Kinship," in Jane Collier and Sylvia Yanagisako, eds., *Gender and Kinship* (Stanford: Stanford University Press, 1987), 14–50.
10. Ortner, "Is Female to Male as Nature Is to Culture?"
11. Rosaldo, "Woman, Culture, and Society."
12. Carol MacCormack and Marilyn Strathern, eds., *Nature, Culture, and Gender* (Cambridge: Cambridge University Press, 1980).
13. Marilyn Strathern, "No Nature, No Culture: The Hagen Case," in MacCormack and Strathern, eds., *Nature, Culture, and Gender,* 174–222.
14. Maurice Bloch and Jean H. Bloch, "Woman and the Dialectics of Nature in Eighteenth-Century French Thought," in MacCormack and Strathern, eds., *Nature, Culture, and Gender,* 25–41.
15. Rosaldo, "Woman, Culture, and Society," 24.
16. Rayna Reiter, "Men and Women in the South of France: Public and Private Domains," in Reiter, ed., *Towards an Anthropology of Women,* 252–82.
17. Michelle Rosaldo, "The Use and Abuse of Anthropology," *SIGNS* 5 (1980): 404.
18. See John Comaroff, "*Sui Genderis:* Feminism, Kinship Theory, and Structural 'Domains,'" and Sylvia Yanagisako, "Mixed Metaphors: Native and Anthropological

Models of Gender and Kinship Domains," in Collier and Yanagisako, eds., *Gender and Kinship,* 53–85 and 86–118, respectively.

19. Rosaldo, "Woman, Culture, and Society," 23.

20. See, for example, Zillah Eisenstein, *Capitalist Patriarchy and the Case for Socialist Feminism* (New York: Monthly Review Press, 1979); Lourdes Beneria and Gita Sen, "Accumulation, Reproduction, and Women's Role in Economic Development: Boserup Revisited," *SIGNS* 7 (1981): 279–98; and Harris and Young, "Engendered Structures."

21. Harris and Young, "Engendered Structures," 110. For examples of the economistic versions of Marxism they criticize, see Barry Hindness and Paul Hirst, *Pre-Capitalist Modes of Production* (London: Routledge & Kegan Paul, 1975), and Jonathan Friedman, "Marxist Theory and Systems of Total Reproduction," *Critique of Anthropology* 7 (1976): 3–16.

22. Karl Marx, *Capital,* trans. Samuel Moore and Edward Aveling (New York: International Publishers, 1967), 3:566.

23. Friedrich Engels, ed. Eleanor Burke Leacock and trans. Alec West, *The Origin of the Family, Private Property and the State* (New York: International Publishers, 1972), 71.

24. Ester Boserup, *Woman's Role in Economic Development* (New York: St. Martin's Press, 1970).

25. Beneria and Sen, "Accumulation, Reproduction, and Women's Role."

26. Ibid., 290.

27. Ibid., 293.

28. Ibid., 291.

29. Louise Tilly and Joan W. Scott, *Women, Work, and Family* (New York: Holt, Rinehart and Winston, 1980), 6.

30. Harris and Young, "Engendered Structures," 113.

31. Ibid.

32. See Ortner, "Theory in Anthropology," 145.

33. Bourdieu, *Outline of a Theory of Practice.*

34. Ortner, "Theory in Anthropology," 127.

35. Bourdieu, *Outline,* 66.

36. Ibid., 213.

37. Ibid., 62.

38. *Webster's New World Dictionary of the American Language,* 2d college ed., s.v. "symbol."

39. Michelle Z. Rosaldo, *Knowledge and Passion* (New York: Cambridge University Press, 1980), 23.

40. Emile Durkheim, *Elementary Forms of the Religious Life* (New York: Macmillan, 1915).

41. See Sylvia Yanagisako, "Family and Household: The Analysis of Domestic Groups," *Annual Review of Anthropology* 8 (1979): 161–205; and Jane Collier, Michelle Z. Rosaldo, and Sylvia Yanagisako, "Is There a Family? New Anthropological Views," in Barrie Thorne, ed., *Rethinking the Family: Some Feminist Questions* (New York: Longman, 1982), 25–39.

42. See Jane Collier, "Women in Politics," in Rosaldo and Lamphere, eds., *Woman, Culture, and Society,* 89–96; Jane Collier, *Marriage and Inequality in Classless Societies* (Stanford: Stanford University Press, 1988); Louise Lamphere, "Strategies, Cooperation, and Conflict among Women in Domestic Groups," in Rosaldo and Lamphere, eds., *Woman, Culture, and Society,* 97–112; Olivia Harris, "Households as Natural Units," in Kate Young, Carol Wolkowitz, and Roslyn McCullagh, eds., *Of Marriage and the Market: Women's Subordination in International Perspective* (London: CSE Books, 1981), 49–68; Margery Wolf, *Women and the Family in Rural Taiwan* (Stanford:

Stanford University Press, 1972); and Sylvia Yanagisako, *Transforming the Past: Tradition and Kinship among Japanese Americans* (Stanford: Stanford University Press, 1985).

43. Carol Gilligan, *In a Different Voice* (Cambridge: Harvard University Press, 1982).

44. See Marilyn Strathern, "Culture in a Netbag: The Manufacture of a Subdiscipline in Anthropology," *Man* 16 (1981): 665–88.

45. See, for example, Edwin Ardener, "Belief and the Problem of Women," in Jean LaFontaine, ed., *The Interpretation of Ritual* (London: Tavistock, 1972), 135–58.

46. Sherry Ortner and Harriet Whitehead, "Introduction: Accounting for Sexual Meanings," in Sherry Ortner and Harriet Whitehead, eds., *Sexual Meanings* (New York: Cambridge University Press, 1981), 12.

47. Ortner and Whitehead, preface to *Sexual Meanings*, x.

48. See, for example, Sylvia Yanagisako, "Mixed Metaphors."

49. Ortner, "Theory in Anthropology," 156–57.

50. Rosaldo, "The Use and Abuse of Anthropology."

51. Judith Shapiro, "Anthropology and the Study of Gender," 449 (our emphasis).

52. Harris and Young, "Engendered Structures."

53. Emile Durkheim, *Elementary Forms*.

54. Several authors have begun this work. See Carol Delaney, "The Meaning of Paternity and the Virgin Birth Debate," *Man* 21 (1986): 494–513; Emily Martin, *The Woman in the Body* (Boston: Beacon, 1987); and Rayna Rapp, "Constructing Amniocentesis: Maternal and Medical Discourses," in Anna Ising and Faye Ginsburg, eds., *Negotiating Gender in American Culture* (Boston: Beacon, forthcoming). All offer feminist analyses of discourses on reproduction in American society. Their works reveal how the form, consequences, and meanings of conception, pregnancy, and parturition are culturally constructed, just as are mothering, fathering, judging, ruling, and talking with the gods. What American culture presents to us as biological facts are themselves cultural interpretations that assign meaning and social consequences to acts and processes, just as in the case of our ideas about physical force, the ownership of the means of production, and the contribution of labor to production.

SUSAN MOLLER OKIN: THINKING LIKE A WOMAN

1. See Terence Ball, "Utilitarianism, Feminism and the Franchise: James Mill and His Critics," *History of Political Thought* 1 (1980): 91–115, on Bentham; Nannerl O. Keohane, "Female Citizenship: 'The Monstrous Regiment of Women'" (paper presented at the annual meeting of the Conference for the Study of Political Thought, April 6–8, 1979), on Bodin, John Knox, and Rousseau; Carole Pateman, "The 'Disorder of Women': Women, Love, and the Sense of Justice," *Ethics* 91 (1980): 20–34, on Rousseau.

2. Plato, *Republic,* 548a, trans. Allan Bloom (New York: Basic, 1968), 225.

3. Plato, *Republic,* 549c–550b (227).

4. Plato, *Laws,* 781a–b.

5. For an illuminating discussion and critique of the influence of this way of thinking in modern social theory, see Michelle Z. Rosaldo, "The Use and Abuse of Anthropology: Reflections on Feminism and Cross-Cultural Understanding," *SIGNS* 5 (1980): 401–09.

6. For a very good discussion of Hegel in this context, see Genevieve Lloyd, "Public Reason and Private Passion," *Politics* (Australasian Political Studies Association Journal) 18 (1983): 27–35.

7. G. W. F. Hegel, *Phenomenology of Spirit,* trans. A. V. Miller (Oxford: Clarendon, 1977), 280 (para. 465); also 268 (para. 450).

8. Hegel, *Phenomenology,* 276 (para. 460).

9. Hegel, *The Philosophy of Right,* trans. T. M. Knox (Oxford: Clarendon, 1952), 114 (para. 166).

10. Hegel, *Phenomenology,* 288 (para. 475).

11. Hegel, *Phenomenology,* 288–89 (para. 475).

12. Hegel, *Philosophy of Right,* 263–64 (addition to para. 166).

13. Jeremy Bentham, *Introduction to the Principles of Morals and Legislation,* ed. J. H. Burns and H. L. A. Hart (London: Athlone, 1970), 64; Ball, "Utilitarianism," 100–01.

14. Sigmund Freud, *Civilization and Its Discontents,* vol. 21 of *The Standard Edition of the Complete Psychological Works,* ed. and trans. James Strachey and Anna Freud (London: Hogarth, 1961), 95.

15. Ibid., 103.

16. Freud, "Some Psychical Consequences of the Anatomical Distinction between the Sexes" (1925) *Standard Edition,* 19:257–58.

17. Lawrence Kohlberg, *The Philosophy of Moral Development: Moral Stages and the Idea of Justice* (San Francisco: Harper & Row, 1981); Lawrence Kohlberg and R. Kramer, "Continuities and Discontinuities in Childhood and Adult Moral Development," *Human Development* 12 (1969): 93–120.

18. Kohlberg, *Philosophy of Moral Development,* 18; see also 147–68 for more detailed descriptions of the stages.

19. Ibid., 19.

20. Ibid., 150.

21. W. P. Alston, "Comments on Kohlberg's 'From *Is* to *Ought,*' " and R. S. Peters, "Moral Development: A Plea for Pluralism," in T. Mischel, ed., *Cognitive Development and Epistemology* (New York: Academic, 1971). Kohlberg's philosophical defense of his scale forms a major part of *The Philosophy of Moral Development.*

22. Carol Gilligan, *In a Different Voice* (Cambridge: Harvard University Press, 1982); see also Gilligan, "In a Different Voice: Women's Conceptions of Self and of Morality," *Harvard Educational Review* 47 (1977): 481–517; and "Women's Place in Man's Life Cycle," *Harvard Educational Review* 49 (1979): 431–46; Constance Boucher Holstein, "Irreversible, Stepwise Sequence in the Development of Moral Judgment: A Longitudinal Study of Males and Females," *Child Development* 47 (1976): 51–61.

23. Kohlberg and Kramer, "Continuities and Discontinuities," 108, and references cited there.

24. Kohlberg, *Philosophy of Moral Development,* 231–42.

25. Ibid., 353–54.

26. J. S. Mill, "The Subjection of Women" (1869), in Alice S. Rossi, ed., *Essays on Sex Equality* (Chicago: University of Chicago Press, 1970); Simone de Beauvoir, *The Second Sex* (1949), trans. H. M. Parshley (New York: Vintage, 1974).

27. Mill, "Subjection of Women," 226. See also 141, 168.

28. De Beauvoir, *The Second Sex,* 375–76, 480–81, 517–25, 572–75.

29. De Beauvoir, interview with Alice Schwarzer in *Ms.,* July 1972; reprinted in Elaine Marks and Isabelle de Courtivron, eds., *New French Feminisms* (New York: Schocken, 1981), 145.

30. Mary Daly, *Gyn/Ecology: The Metaethics of Radical Feminism* (Boston: Beacon, 1978); Susan Griffin, *Woman and Nature: The Roaring inside Her* (New York: Harper & Row, 1978); Mary O'Brien, *The Politics of Reproduction* (London: Routledge & Kegan Paul, 1981).

31. Clear expressions of such views in the works of those writers appear in translation in Marks and de Courtivron, eds., *New French Feminisms.* See especially 79–110, 161–64.

32. Xavière Gauthier, "Existe-t-il une écriture de femme?" (1974) in Marks and de Courtivron, eds., *New French Feminisms*, 164.
33. Marks and de Courtivron, *New French Feminisms*, 132–36, 153.
34. Jean Baker Miller, *Toward a New Psychology of Women* (Boston: Beacon, 1976), 7.
35. Inge K. Broverman et al., "Sex-Role Stereotypes: A Current Appraisal," *Journal of Social Issues* 28/2 (1972): 59–78.
36. See Jean Grimshaw, *Philosophy and Feminist Thinking* (Minneapolis: University of Minnesota Press, 1986), chap. 7, and Joan Tronto, "'Women's Morality': Beyond Gender Difference to a Theory of Care," *SIGNS* 12 (1987): 644–63, for good discussions of the implications of sex stereotyping for the idea of a female ethic.
37. Dorothy Dinnerstein, *The Mermaid and the Minotaur* (New York: Harper & Row, 1977); Nancy Chodorow, *The Reproduction of Mothering* (Berkeley: University of California Press, 1978); Jane Flax, "The Conflict between Nurturance and Autonomy in Mother-Daughter Relationships and within Feminism," *Feminist Studies* 4 (1978): 171–92; Sara Ruddick, "Maternal Thinking," *Feminist Studies* 6 (1980): 342–67.
38. Holstein, "Irreversible, Stepwise Sequence," 59.
39. Ibid., 61.
40. Gilligan, *In a Different Voice*, 18.
41. Ibid., 19.
42. Gilligan, *In a Different Voice*. Compare, for example, (1) the paragraph beginning "The different voice I describe is characterized not by gender but by theme" with (2) the paragraph on page 105 that begins "The abortion study suggests that women impose a distinctive construction on moral problems." Cf. Nona Plessner Lyons, "Two Perspectives: On Self, Relationships, and Morality," *Harvard Educational Review* 55 (1983): 127–45. Lyons finds a relationship between gender and the "two different orientations to morality" based on an empirical study, but she states clearly that this finding "is not absolute since individual men and women use both types of considerations" (140).
43. See, for example, John M. Broughton, "Women's Rationality and Men's Virtues: A Critique of Gender Dualism in Gilligan's Theory of Moral Development," *Social Research* 50 (1983): 597–642; Catherine G. Greeno and Eleanor E. Maccoby, "How Different Is the 'Different Voice'?" *SIGNS* 11 (1986): 310–16; Debra Nails, "Social-Scientific Sexism: Gilligan's Mismeasure of Man," *Social Research* 50 (1983): 643–64; Lawrence J. Walker, "Sex Differences in the Development of Moral Reasoning: A Critical Review," *Child Development* 55 (1984): 677–91. Kohlberg has recently stressed that the initial differences found in studies using his scale and methodology were differences of role, not sex differences per se. See Lawrence Kohlberg with Charles Levine and Alexandra Hewer, "Synopses and Detailed Replies to Critics," in Lawrence Kohlberg, ed., *The Psychology of Moral Development: Essays on Moral Development* (San Francisco: Harper & Row, 1984), 2:345–61.
44. Gilligan, *In a Different Voice*. This problem applies particularly to pages 25–39 (on Amy and Jake). See Broughton, "Women's Rationality," 603–09.
45. First and most obviously, abortion is the one major moral dilemma that men are biologically incapable of ever having to face in the same sense that a woman faces it. Second, a woman's thinking about having an abortion and her thinking about other moral issues at that time may not be representative of her moral thinking in general. As Gilligan says, because pregnancy is a state of extreme connectedness and responsibility, "the abortion dilemma *magnifies* the issues of responsibility and care that derive from the fact of relationship" (*In a Different Voice*, 108; my emphasis). But since this is clearly so—any woman considering an abortion is more connected with

and more solely responsible for the fate of another potential human being than at any other time—it seems that her moral thinking at this time may be far more likely to center around issues of connectedness and responsibility for others. It seems unwarranted to generalize, as Gilligan clearly does (72 and 105) from the findings of the abortion study to women's thinking about moral dilemmas in general. The third problem arising from the use of the abortion study is due to the fact, acknowledged but not regarded as a problem by Gilligan, that the women interviewed were probably more conflicted than average about the abortion decision. This is a real problem when one is discussing whether women are more prone than men to think in terms of abstract rights or of contractual responsibilities. Presumably those who think about abortion in terms of abstract or absolute rights—whether the fetus's right to life or the woman's right to control her own body—are more likely to have escaped the sample population. Those who feel strongly about the fetus's rights are in theory more likely to carry their pregnancies to term; those whose principal focus is their right to control their own bodies, being unconflicted about having an abortion, may be less likely to seek counseling or to wish to participate in such a study. For these reasons, the findings of the abortion decision study are probably less than ideal for investigating the modes of women's moral thinking.

46. Gilligan, *In a Different Voice.* For the identification of rights with selfishness, lack of responsibility, and noninterference see, for example, pages 22, 136. Gilligan tends to interpret male respondents' talk of rights in accordance with this conception. I was helped much on this issue by comments from Bob Keohane and Iris Young.

47. For example, Henry Shue, *Basic Rights: Subsistence, Affluence and U.S. Foreign Policy* (Princeton: Princeton University Press, 1980); James Nickel, "Is There a Human Right to Employment?" *Philosophical Forum* 10 (1978–79): 149–70.

48. On this see Holstein, "Irreversible, Stepwise Sequence," 60.

49. Kohlberg, *Philosophy of Moral Development,* 150.

50. Gilligan, *In a Different Voice,* 135, 21, 139.

51. Ibid., 57, 160.

52. Ibid., 100.

53. See Grimshaw, *Philosophy and Feminist Thinking,* 164, and chaps. 7 and 8; and Tronto, " 'Women's Morality,' " for good discussions of the importance of this issue in developing a morality of care.

54. Kohlberg, "The Current Formulation of the Theory," in *Essays in Moral Development,* 2:229.

NEL NODDINGS: ETHICS FROM THE STANDPOINT OF WOMEN

1. See Jean Grimshaw, *Philosophy and Feminist Thinking* (Minneapolis: University of Minnesota Press, 1986).

2. See Rosemary Radford Ruether, "Misogynism and Virginal Feminism in the Fathers of the Church," and Eleanor Commo McLaughlin, "Equality of Souls, Inequality of Sexes: Woman in Medieval Theology," both in Rosemary Radford Ruether, ed., *Religion and Sexism* (New York: Simon and Schuster, 1974).

3. This view may be traced to Thomas Aquinas, *Summa Theologica,* and before him to Aristotle, *Politics.*

4. See Judith Hauptman, "Images of Women in the Talmud," in Ruether, ed., *Religion and Sexism.*

5. See Larry Blum, Marcia Homiak, Judy Housman, and Naomi Scheman, "Altruism and Women's Oppression," *Philosophical Forum* 5 (1973–74): 222–47; also Barbara Houston, "Prolegomena to Future Caring" (paper presented at the annual meeting

of the Association for Moral Education, Toronto, September 1985; also in *Hypatia*, forthcoming).

6. Grimshaw, *Philosophy and Feminist Thinking*, 36.
7. Ibid.; also Mary Briody Mahowald, ed., *Philosophy of Women* (Indianapolis: Hackett, 1983).
8. Kant, "Of the Distinction between the Beautiful and Sublime in the Interrelations of the Two Sexes," in Mahowald, ed., *Philosophy of Women*, 194.
9. Grimshaw, *Philosophy and Feminist Thinking*, 49.
10. Joan Tronto, "Beyond Gender Difference to a Theory of Care," *SIGNS* 12 (1987): 646.
11. The response to Gilligan's work (Carol Gilligan, *In a Different Voice* [Cambridge: Harvard University Press, 1982]) has been tremendous. Several writers have argued that the response itself is a phenomenon of importance. See, for example, Betty Sichel, *Moral Education* (Philadelphia: Temple University Press, 1988), chap. 6.
12. Friedrich Nietzsche, *Beyond Good and Evil*, trans. R. J. Hollingdale (1886; Harmondsworth, Middlesex, England: Penguin, 1973), 70.
13. Some of these insights are noted, for example, in Mary Daly, *Beyond God the Father* (Boston: Beacon, 1973).
14. Otto Weininger, *Sex and Character* (Vienna: W. Braumueller, 1903), 186.
15. Ibid., 161. Quoted in Bram Dijkstra, *Idols of Perversity* (New York: Oxford University Press, 1986), 219.
16. William James, *The Varieties of Religious Experience* (New York: Mentor, 1958), 284.
17. Ibid., 282.
18. Ibid., 285.
19. Nel Noddings, *Caring: A Feminine Approach to Ethics and Moral Education* (Berkeley: University of California Press, 1984).
20. See, for example, Jane Roland Martin, *Reclaiming a Conversation* (New Haven: Yale University Press, 1985); also Barbara Hilkert Andolsen, Christine E. Gudorf, and Mary D. Pellauer, eds., *Women's Consciousness, Women's Conscience* (Minneapolis: Winston, 1985).
21. See Mary O'Brien, *The Politics of Reproduction* (London: Routledge & Kegan Paul, 1981).
22. See, for example, Paula M. Cooey, Sharon A. Farmer, and Mary Ellen Ross, eds., *Embodied Love* (San Francisco: Harper & Row, 1987); Daly, *Beyond God the Father;* Elisabeth Schussler Fiorenza, *In Memory of Her* (New York: Crossroads, 1983); Beverly Wildung Harrison, *Our Right to Choose* (Boston: Beacon, 1983); Catherine Keller, *From a Broken Web* (Boston: Beacon, 1986); and Sharon D. Welch, *Communities of Resistance and Solidarity* (Maryknoll, N.Y.: Orbis, 1985).
23. Sara Ruddick, "Maternal Thinking," *Feminist Studies* 6 (1980): 342–67.
24. See the discussion in Owen Flanagan and Kathryn Jackson, "Justice, Care, and Gender: The Kohlberg-Gilligan Debate Revisited," *Ethics* 97 (1987): 622–37.
25. This is one of Tronto's ("Beyond Gender Difference") points. It is also a point well made by Deborah L. Rhode, "The 'Woman's Point of View,'" *Journal of Legal Education* 38 (1988): 39–46.
26. Charlotte Perkins Gilman, *Woman and Economics*, ed. Carl N. Degler (New York: Harper & Row, 1966); see also the account in Page Smith, *Daughters of the Promised Land* (Boston: Little, Brown, 1970), 245–51.
27. Shulamith Firestone, *The Dialectic of Sex* (London: Women's, 1970).
28. A wonderful source for these stories is cookbooks. See, for example, Jean Anderson, *The Grass Roots Cookbook* (New York: Times Books, 1977).
29. Martin, *Reclaiming a Conversation*, 197.

30. Jean Watson, *Nursing: Human Science and Human Care* (Norwalk, Conn.: Appleton-Century-Crofts, 1985).
31. See Mark Timmons, "Foundationalism and the Structure of Ethical Justification," *Ethics* 97 (1987): 595–609.
32. See Gilligan, *In a Different Voice.*
33. See Muriel J. Bebeau and Mary M. Brabeck, "Integrating Care and Justice Issues in Professional Moral Education: A Gender Perspective," *Journal of Moral Education* 16 (1987): 189–203.
34. See Susan Moller Okin, "Thinking like a Woman," in this volume.
35. See, for example, G. E. M. Anscombe, "Modern Moral Philosophy," *Ethics, Religion and Politics*, vol. 3 of *Collected Philosophical Papers of G. E. M. Anscombe* (Minneapolis: University of Minnesota Press, 1981), 26–42; also Alasdair MacIntyre, *After Virtue* (Notre Dame: University of Notre Dame Press, 1984).
36. MacIntyre, *After Virtue*, 187–203, 29–32.
37. Grimshaw, *Philosophy and Feminist Thinking*, 99.
38. Houston, "Prolegomena to Future Caring," 7.
39. Kari Waerness, "The Rationality of Caring," *Economic and Industrial Democracy* 5 (1984): 185–211.
40. Ibid., 188.
41. See Allen Buchanan, "Justice and Charity," *Ethics* 97 (1987): 558–75.
42. See Martin's *Reclaiming a Conversation*, also her "Bringing Women into Educational Thought," *Educational Theory* 34 (1984): 341–54, and "Transforming Moral Education," *Journal of Moral Education* 16 (1987): 204–13.
43. See Robert N. Bellah, Richard Madsen, William M. Sullivan, Ann Swidler, and Steven M. Tipton, *Habits of the Heart* (Berkeley: University of California Press, 1985).
44. Houston, "Prolegomena to Future Caring," 8.
45. Noddings, *Caring*, 69.
46. For a view that restricts rights bearing to duty bearers, see A. I. Melden, *Rights and Persons* (Oxford: Oxford University Press, 1977); for a more generous view, see L. Wayne Sumner, "Abortion: A Third Way," in Jan Narveson, ed., *Moral Issues* (Toronto: Oxford University Press, 1983), 194–214.

MARILYN FRYE: THE POSSIBILITY OF FEMINIST THEORY

1. Deborah Rhode suggested that what I am saying here is simply that women's experience appears to be "different." But in the current lingo, influenced by the French, "difference" is an abstract and generic term. What I am referring to here is two quite specific things—that which is flat-out unintelligible (which is not quite what the French, following Derrida and in the shadow of Lacan, mean by "difference"), and that which is specifically and concretely "different" in that it is abnormal, in the negatively charged sense of that concept. I am talking here from the experience of women. We do not experience ourselves, under the conceptual net of patriarchal forms, as abstractly and semantically "different," but as unintelligible or abnormal. So also do men commonly experience women.
2. My use of *we, our, feminist theorists*, and *feminist theory* is and will remain problematic. I know I am not the only one engaged in the pilgrimage described here, but I could not and would not pretend to say who else this speaks for. For those who do not identify with this *we*, I think the essay can be read as a record of what *some* women who have called themselves feminists and theorists have thought and done.
3. This approach is perhaps the general tendency of which the "feminist empiricism" described by Sandra Harding is a more specific instance. See Harding, *The Science Question in Feminism* (Ithaca: Cornell University Press, 1986), 24–25.

4. This dogma has been questioned within that same tradition, but it still has power in contemporary thinking. The "postmodern" critique of this tradition's concepts of truth, reality, and knowledge is by no means universally acknowledged as sound, and furthermore the transformation of worldview that would be involved in actually abandoning those concepts is more profound than most of us can manage in less than a decade or so.

5. Cf. Maria Lugones, "Playfulness, 'World'-Travelling, and Loving Perception," *Hypatia* 2 (1987): 3–19.

6. This phrase was coined by Nelle Morton in a talk given at an American Academy of Religion Workshop, December 28, 1977 (cited in Mary Daly, *Gyn/Ecology: The Metaethics of Radical Feminism* [Boston: Beacon, 1978], 313).

7. For some elaboration of this point see the introduction to my book *The Politics of Reality: Essays in Feminist Theory* (Trumansburg, N.Y.: Crossing, 1983), xii–xiv.

8. The term comes from Ruth Ginsberg (conversation).

9. The phrase as used in this context is due to Alison Jaggar.

10. The centering of a Black woman's voice and views as accomplished in Bell Hooks's *Feminist Theory: From Margin to Center* (Boston: South End, 1984) is a good example of this. The entire phenomenon of U.S. feminism looks very different when cast as relatively marginal to the lives and interests of Black and poor women than when cast as central to history.

BELL HOOKS: FEMINISM: A TRANSFORMATIONAL POLITIC

1. Vivian Gordon, *Black Women, Feminism, and Black Liberation: Which Way?* (Chicago: Third World, 1987).

2. Charlotte Bunch, *Passionate Politics* (New York: St. Martin's, 1987).

3. Paulo Freire, *Pedagogy of the Oppressed* (New York: Seabury, 1970).

DEBORAH L. RHODE: DEFINITIONS OF DIFFERENCE

1. For example, 85 percent of all elective officeholders are male, and two-thirds of all indigent adults are female. See Janice Peterson, "The Feminization of Poverty," *Journal of Economic Issues* 21 (1987): 329; Ruth B. Mandel, "The Political Woman," in Sara E. Rix, ed., *The American Woman, 1988–89* (New York: W.W. Norton, 1988), 78; "Women in Politics," *Los Angeles Times*, November 30, 1987, sec. 3, p. 6. For salary disparities among full-time workers, see the discussion in part 4.

2. Quong Wing v. Kirkendall, 223 U.S. 59, 63 (1929).

3. Platt v. Commonwealth, 256 Mass. 539, 52 N.E. 914, 915 (1926); Salt Lake City v. Wilson, 46 Utah 60, 63 (1915).

4. State v. Heitzman, 105 Kan. 139, 146–47, 181 P. 630, 634 (1919).

5. Bradwell v. State, 83 U.S. 130, 137 (1872) (Bradley, J., concurring).

6. In the matter of Goodell, 39 Wis. 232, 244 (1875). See also *In re* Kilgore, 17 Phila. 192, 193 (1884); Lockwood v. United States, 9 Ct. Claims 346, 348, 355 (1873).

7. Judith Baer, *The Chains of Protection* (Westport, Connecticut: Greenwood, 1978), 31; Comment, "Are Sex Based Classifications Constitutionally Suspect?" *Northwestern University Law Review* 66 (1969): 481, 490.

8. Hoyt v. Florida, 368 U.S. 57 (1961).

9. Arends v. Arends, 30 Utah 2d 328, 517 P.2d 1019, *cert. denied*, 419 U.S. 881 (1974).

10. Martin Binken and Shirley J. Bach, *Women and the Military* (Washington: Brookings, 1977); United States v. St. Clair, 291 F. Supp. 122, 125 (S.D.N.Y. 1968).

11. Jill Laurie Goodman, "Women, War, and Equality: An Examination of Sex Discrimination in the Military," *Women's Rights Law Reporter* 5 (1979): 243; Lisa Kornblum,

"Women Warriors in a Man's World: The Combat Exclusion," *Law and Inequality* 2 (1984): 351.

12. General Robert Barrow, quoted in Genevieve Lloyd, "Selfhood, War and Masculinity," in Carole Pateman and Elizabeth Gross, *Feminist Challenges: Social and Political Theory* (Boston: Northeastern University Press, 1986), 63. See also William Westmoreland, quoted in Sara Ruddick, "Women in the Military," *Report from the Center for Philosophy and Public Policy* 4 (College Park, Md.) (1984): 3; testimony summarized in Goodman, "Women, War, and Equality"; and Deborah L. Rhode, "Equal Rights in Retrospect," *Law and Inequality* 1 (1983): 1, and *Justice and Gender* (Cambridge: Harvard University Press, 1989).

13. Rostker v. Goldberg, 453 U.S. 57 (1981).

14. Adams v. Cronin, 29 Colo. 448, 69 P. 590, 593 (1902), *aff'd,* 192 U.S. 108 (1904); People v. Case, 153 Mich. 98, 100, 116 N.W. 558, 560 (1908); *Ex parte* Hayes, 98 Cal. 555, 33 P. 337, 338 (1893); Commonwealth v. Price, 123 Ky. 163, 164–65, 94 S.W. 32, 33 (1906); John D. Johnston, Jr., and Charles L. Knapp, "Sex Discrimination by Law: A Study in Judicial Perspective," *New York University Law Review* 46 (1971): 675.

15. Johnston and Knapp, "Sex Discrimination" (discussing Eve/Eva), 704–05; Goesaert v. Cleary, 335 U.S. 464, 465–67 (1948); Goesaert v. Cleary, Brief of Appellants, 23; Goesaert v. Cleary, Transcript of Records, 19–42.

16. Diaz v. Pan American World Airways, 442 F.2d 385 (5th Cir. 1971); Wilson v. Southwest Airlines, 517 F. Supp. 292 (N.D. Tex. 1981).

17. Susan B. Anthony and Ida Husted Harper, eds., *History of Woman Suffrage* (Indianapolis: Hallenbach, 1902), 4:39.

18. Bradwell v. State, 83 U.S. 130, 137 (1872) (Bradley, J., concurring); *In the matter of* Goodell, 39 Wis. 232, 244 (1875), Bailey v. State, 215 Ark. 53, 61, 219 S.W.2d 424, 428 (1929).

19. *In the matter of* Goodell, 39 Wis. 232, 237, 238 (1875); Matthew Carpenter, Brief for the Plaintiffs in Error in Bradwell v. State, 83 U.S. 130 (1872), 2, quoted in Albie Sachs and Joan H. Wilson, *Sexism and the Law* (London: Robertson, 1978), 100.

20. Jennie Latman Barron, "Jury Service for Women," in Marlene Stein Wortman, *Women in American Law* (New York: Holmes and Meier, 1985), 1:330; Brief for Appellant in Hoyt v. Florida, 368 U.S. 57 (1961), 19–20.

21. Goesaert v. Cleary, 335 U.S. 464 (1948); Brief of Appellants, 23; Goesaert v. Cleary, Transcript of Records, 19–42. See Wendy Williams, "The Equality Crisis," *Women's Rights Law Reporter* 7 (1982): 189; Mary Eastwood, "The Double Standard of Justice," *Valparaiso Law Review* 5 (1971): 308; Ruddick, *"Women in the Military,"* 3; and Kornblum, "Women Warriors," 383–85.

22. Compare *ex parte* Gosselin, 141 Me. 412, 442, 44 A.2d 882, 886 (1945); Territory v. Armstrong, 28 Hawaii 88 (1924); Commonwealth v. Daniels, 210 Pa. Super. 156, 232 A.2d 247 (1967), *rev'd,* 430 Pa. 642, 243 A.2d 400 (1968); Wark v. State, 226 A.2d 62 (Maine Sup. Ct.), *cert denied,* 400 U.S. 952 (1970).

23. Lochner v. New York, 195 U.S. 45 (1905).

24. New York v. Williams, 189 N.Y. 131 (1907); People v. Ritchie, 155 Ill. 98, 116; 40 N.E. 454 (1895); Adkins v. Children's Hospital, 261 U.S. 525, 546–53 (1922).

25. The combination of domestic burdens and working hours is reviewed in Elizabeth Baker, *Protective Labor Legislation*, rev. ed. (New York: AMS, 1969), 207–10; Alice Kessler-Harris, *Women Have Always Worked* (Old Westbury, N.Y.: Feminist, 1981), 189, 191. According to Kessler-Harris, estimates suggest that during the early twentieth century about one in nine male workers but only one in thirty-four female workers was unionized; and Alice Kessler-Harris, "Where are the Organized Women

Workers?" in Nancy Cott and Elizabeth Pleck, eds., *A Heritage of Her Own* (New York: Simon and Schuster, 1979), 348.

26. See John R. Commons et al., eds., *A Documentary History of American Industrial Society* (New York: Russell & Russell, 1958), 6:1955; Emile Josephine Hutchin, *Women's Wages: A Study of the Wages of Industrial Women and Measures Suggested to Increase Them* (Providence: American Mathematical Society, 1968), 24–25.

27. Muller v. Oregon, 208 U.S. 412, (1908); Facts of Knowledge Submitted on Behalf of the People, People v. Charles Schweiner Press (quoted in Baer, *The Chains of Protection*), 84.

28. See Baker, *Protective Labor Legislation*, 351–53; U.S. Women's Bureau, bulletin no. 65, "The Effects of Labor Legislation on the Employment Opportunities of Women," (Washington: U.S. Government Printing Office, 1928); Alice Kessler-Harris, *Out to Work: A History of Wage-Earning Women in the United States* (New York: Oxford University Press, 1982).

29. Elisabeth M. Landes, "The Effect of State Maximum Hours Laws on the Employment of Women in 1920," *Journal of Political Economy* 88 (1980): 476. William Chafe, *The American Woman* (New York: Oxford University Press, 1972), 124–28.

30. See Kessler-Harris, *Out to Work*, 196, 211; Susan Deller Ross, "Sex Discrimination and 'Protective' Labor Legislation," reprinted in "The Equal Rights Amendment, Hearings before the Subcommittee on Constitutional Amendments of the Committee on the Judiciary, United States Senate," 91st Congress, 2d session, May 5, 6, and 7, 1970, 392–411; U.S. Women's Bureau, bulletin no. 66-I; *History of Labor Legislation for Women in Three States* (Washington: U.S. Government Printing Office, 1929); U.S. Women's Bureau, *Effects of Labor Legislation*, 172–73, 247–67; Chafe, *The American Woman*, 124–28; Nancy Woloch, *Women and the American Experience* (New York: Alfred A. Knopf, 1984), 448. See also "The Night Shift," in Rosalyn Baxandall, Linda Gordon, Susan Reverby, eds., *America's Working Women* (New York: Vintage, 1976), 160.

31. See Wendy Williams, "Equality's Riddle: Pregnancy and the Equal Treatment/ Special Treatment Debate," *New York University Review of Law and Social Change* 13 (1985): 325; Frances Olsen, "From False Paternalism to False Equality: Judicial Assaults on Feminist Community, Illinois, 1869–1895," *University of Michigan Law Journal* 84 (1986): 1518.

32. Fair Labor Standards Act, 29USC201; E.E.O.C. Guidelines, 34 *Fed. Reg.* 13367 (1969).

33. Geduldig v. Aiello, 417 U.S. 484, n. 21 (1974); General Electric Company v. Gilbert, 429 U.S. 125 (1976). See generally Katherine Bartlett, "Pregnancy and the Constitution: The Uniqueness Trap," *California Law Review* 62 (1974): 1532.

34. 42 U.S.C. 2000e (K).

35. Anne L. Radigan, *Concept and Compromise: The Evolution of Family Leave Legislation in the U.S. Congress* (Washington: Women's Research and Education Institute, 1988), 9; Sheila B. Kamerman and Alfred Kahn, *The Responsive Workplace: Employers in a Changing Labor Force* (New York: Columbia University Press, 1987), 15, 56; Sheila Kamerman, Alfred Kahn, and Paul Kingston, *Maternity Policies and Working Women* (New York: Columbia University Press, 1983).

36. California Federal Savings and Loan Association v. Guerra, 479 U.S. 272 (1987); Radigan, *Concept and Compromise*.

37. Lucinda M. Finley, "Transcending Equality Theory: A Way out of the Maternity and the Workplace Debate," *Columbia Law Review* 86 (1986): 1118; Herma Hill Kay, "Equality and Difference: The Case of Pregnancy," *Berkeley Women's Law Journal* 1

(1985): 1; Sylvia Law, "Rethinking Sex and the Constitution," *University of Pennsylvania Law Review* 132 (1984); Christine Littleton, "Reconstructing Sexual Equality," *University of California Law Review* 75 (1987): 1279; Reva B. Siegel, Note, "Employment Equality under the Pregnancy Discrimination Act of 1978," *Yale Law Journal* 94 (1985): 929, 942–44.

38. See Williams, "Equality's Riddle"; Nadine Taub, "From Parental Leaves to Nurturing Leaves," *New York University Review of Law and Social Change* 13 (1985): 381.

39. See Congressional Caucus for Women's Issues, "Fact Sheet on Parental Leave Legislation" (Washington, 1985); Catalyst, Inc., "Report on a National Study of Parental Leaves" (New York: Catalyst, Inc., 1986); David Wessel, "Working Fathers Feel New Pressures Arising From Child-Rearing Duties," *Wall Street Journal*, September 7, 1984, sec. 2, p. 29, reporting, e.g., that of Prudential Life Insurance Company's 60,000 employees about a dozen men had taken paternity leave over five years; "Dads Ignore Paternity Leave," *San Francisco Examiner*, June 14, 1984, C-12; Patricia Schroeder, "Should Leaves for New Parents Be Mandatory?" *New York Times*, December 29, 1985, 16e; Gail Gregg, "Putting Kids First," *New York Times Magazine*, April 13, 1986, 46.

40. For psychoanalytic theories, see Nancy Chodorow, *The Reproduction of Mothering: Psychoanalysis and the Sociology of Gender* (Berkeley: University of California Press, 1978); Dorothy Dinnerstein, *The Mermaid and the Minotaur* (New York: Harper & Row, 1976).

41. For an example of proposed federal legislation that would have provided limited coverage for both parents, see Parental and Disability Leave Act, H.R. 2020, 99th Congress, 131 *Congressional Record* H 1942 (1985), discussed in Radigan, *Concept and Compromise*. See Roberta M. Spalter-Roth, *Unnecessary Losses: Costs to Americans of the Lack of Family and Medical Leave* (Washington: Institute for Women's Policy Research, 1988); Rhode, *Justice and Gender,* 120–25.

42. Kamerman and Kahn, *The Responsive Workplace;* Finley, "Equality Theory"; Taub, "Nurturing Leaves"; For discussion of infant needs, see Edward F. Zigler and Meryl Frank, eds., *The Parental Leave Crisis: Toward A National Policy* (New Haven: Yale University Press, 1988), 44–45, 161–62, 36–51.

43. Heidi Hartmann, ed., *Comparable Worth: New Directions for Research* (Washington: National Academy Press, 1985); Heidi Hartmann and Barbara Reskin, eds., *Women's Work, Men's Work: Sex Segregation on the Job* (Washington: National Academy Press, 1986); National Committee on Pay Equity, "Briefing Paper on the Wage Gap" (Washington, September 18, 1987).

44. Lenore J. Weitzman, *The Divorce Revolution* (New York: Free Press, 1985); Ruth Sidel, *Women and Children Last: The Plight of Poor Women in Affluent America* (New York: Viking, 1986).

45. Congressional Caucus for Women's Issues, *The American Woman: A Report in Depth* (1987) and "Fact Sheet" (1987), 4; Peterson, "The Feminization of Poverty." See Sidel, *Women and Children Last;* Irwin Garfinkel and Sara S. McLanahan, *Single Mothers and Their Children: A New American Dilemma* (Washington: Urban Institute Press, 1986), 91–94.

46. Julianne Malveaux, *No Images* (1990); Margaret C. Simms and Julianne Malveaux, *Slipping through the Cracks: The Status of Black Women* (New Brunswick, N.J.: Transaction, 1986); Peterson, "The Feminization of Poverty."

47. Weitzman, *Divorce Revolution;* Peterson, "The Feminization of Poverty"; Congressional Caucus for Women's Issues, *The American Woman; The Road to Poverty: A Report on the Economic Status of Midlife and Older Women in America* (Washington: Older Women's

League, 1988); U.S. Senate Special Committee on Aging, *Women in Our Aging Society* (Washington: U.S. Government Printing Office, 1985).

48. For decisions denying the right to public funding for abortion, see Maher v. Roe, 432 U.S. 464 (1977) and Harris v. McRae, 448 U.S. 297, 316 (1980). For discussion of the inadequacy of abortion, health, and contraceptive services, see sources cited in "Brief for the National Abortion Registration League et al." in Thornburgh v. American College of Obstetricians and Gynecologists, 106 S. Ct. 2169 (1986); Panel on Adolescent Pregnancy and Childbirth of the National Research Council, *Final Report* (Washington: National Academy Press, 1986); Sherrell Cohen and Nadine Taub, eds., *Reproductive Law for the 1990's* (Clifton, N.J.: Humana Press, 1988).

CATHARINE A. MACKINNON: LEGAL PERSPECTIVES ON SEXUAL DIFFERENCE

1. Jean Harris, quoted by Shana Alexander in *Very Much a Lady* (from a review by Anne Bernays, *New York Times Book Review*, March 27, 1983, p. 13).

2. J. Tussman and J. tenBroek, "The Equal Protection of the Laws" (*California Law Review* 37 [1949]) were the first to use the term *fit* to characterize the necessary relation between a valid equality rule and the world to which it refers.

3. Royster Guano Co. v. Virginia, 253 U.S. 412, 415 (1920).

4. Craig v. Boren, 429 U.S. 190 (1976).

5. Barbara Brown et al., "The Equal Rights Amendment: A Constitutional Basis for Equal Rights for Women," *Yale Law Journal* 80 (1971). Seen on this doctrinal continuum, the ERA was not a new departure but a proposal to take the standard equal protection approach to its extreme.

6. "Regardless of their sex, persons within any one of the enumerated classes . . . are similarly situated. . . . By providing dissimilar treatment for men and women who are thus similarly situated, the challenged section violates the Equal Protection Clause" (Reed v. Reed, 404 U.S. 71, 76 [1971]); Rostker v. Goldberg, 453 U.S. 57 (1981) (women differentially situated for combat by legislation, therefore male-only registration for draft does not violate equal protection clause). See also Califano v. Webster, 430 U.S. 313 (1977); Parham v. Hughes, 441 U.S. 346, 355 (1979) (mothers not similarly situated with fathers for purposes of legitimizing children because only fathers have legal power to do so); Schlesinger v. Ballard, 419 U.S. 498 (1975); Michael M. v. Superior Court of Sonoma County, 450 U.S. 464 (1981) (women dissimilarly situated from men "with respect to the problems and risks of sexual intercourse," meaning pregnancy).

7. G. Rutherglen, "Sexual Equality in Fringe-Benefit Plans," *Virginia Law Review* 65 (1979): 206. The proposed federal ERA's otherwise uncompromising prohibition on sex-based distinctions provides parallel exceptions for "unique physical characteristics" and "personal privacy." Brown et al., "Equal Rights Amendment."

8. Nadine Taub, "Keeping Women in Their Place: Stereotyping Per Se as a Form of Sex Discrimination," *Boston College Law Review* 21 (1980). See also Barbara Kirk Cavanaugh, "A Little Dearer Than His Horse: Legal Stereotypes and the Feminine Personality," *Harvard Civil Rights Civil Liberties Law Review* 6 (1970): 260–87.

9. The Bona Fide Occupational Qualification exception to Title VII of the Civil Rights Act of 1964, 42 U.S.C. § 2000 e-(2) (e) permits sex to be a job qualification when it is a valid one. For ERA theory, see n. 4, supra.

10. For examples, see Wendy Williams, "The Equality Crisis: Some Reflections on Culture, Courts, and Feminism," *Women's Rights Law Reporter* 7 (1982); Herma Kay, "Models of Equality," *University of Illinois Law Review* 1985; Fran Olsen, "Statutory Rape: A Feminist Critique of Rights Analysis," *Texas Law Review* 63 (1984); Wendy Williams, "Equality's Riddle: Pregnancy and the Equal Treatment/Special Treat-

ment Debate," *New York University Review of Law and Social Change* 13 (1985); Sylvia Law, "Rethinking Sex and the Constitution," *University of Pennsylvania Law Review* 132 (1984); Stephanie Wildman, "The Legitimation of Sex Discrimination: A Critical Response to Supreme Court Jurisprudence," *Oregon Law Review* 63 (1984); Herma Kay, "Equality and Difference: The Case of Pregnancy," *Berkeley Women's Law Journal* 1 (1985); Nancy E. Dowd, "Maternity Leave: Taking Sex Differences into Account," *Fordham Law Review* 54 (1986); Frances Olsen, "From False Paternalism to False Equality: Judicial Assaults on Feminist Community, Illinois 1869–1895," *Michigan Law Review* 84 (1986), sees the definition of the issues as limiting.

11. Illustrations in employment: Title VII of the Civil Rights Act of 1964, 42 U.S.C. § 2000e; Phillips v. Martin-Marietta, 400 U.S. 542 (1971). Education: Title IX of the Civil Rights Act of 1964, 20 U.S.C. § 1681; Cannon v. University of Chicago, 441 U.S. 677 (1981); DeLaCruz v. Tormey, 582 F.2d 45 (9th cir. 1978). Academic employment: Women appear to lose most of the cases that go to trial, but cf. Sweeney v. Board of Trustees of Keene State College, 604 F.2d 106 (1st cir. 1979). Professional employment: Hishon v. King & Spaulding, 467 U.S. 69 (1984). Blue-collar employment: Vanguard Justice v. Hughes, 471 F. Supp. 670 (D. Md. 1979); Meyer v. Missouri State Highway Commission, 567 F.2d 804, 891 (8th cir. 1977); Payne v. Travenol Laboratories Inc., 416 F. Supp. 248 (N.D. Mass. 1976). See also Dothard v. Rawlinson, 433 U.S. 321 (1977) (height and weight requirements invalidated for prison guard positions because of disparate impact on the basis of sex). Military: Frontiero v. Richardson, 411 U.S. 484 (1974); Schlesinger v. Ballard, 419 U.S. 498 (1975). Athletics: This situation is relatively complex. See Gomes v. R.I. Interscholastic League, 469 F. Supp. 659 (D. R.I. 1979); Brenden v. Independent School District, 477 F.2d 1292 (8th cir. 1973); O'Connor v. Board of Education of School District No. 23, 645 F.2d 578 (7th cir. 1981); Cape v. Tennessee Secondary School Athletic Association, 424 F. Supp. 732 (E.D. Tenn. 1976), *rev'd*, 563 F.2d 793 (6th cir. 1977); Yellow Springs Exempted Village School District Board of Education v. Ohio High School Athletic Association, 443 F. Supp. 753 (S.D. Ohio 1978); Aiken v. Lieuallen, 593 P.2d 1243 (Or. App. 1979).

12. Rostker v. Goldberg, 453 U.S. 57 (1981). See also Lori S. Kornblum, "Women Warriors in a Men's World: The Combat Exclusion," *Law and Inequality: A Journal of Theory and Practice* 2 (1984).

13. On alimony and other economic factors, see L. Weitzman, "The Economics of Divorce: Social and Economic Consequences of Property, Alimony and Child Support Awards," *U.C.L.A. Law Review* 28 (1982): 1251, which documents a decline in women's standard of living of 73 percent and an increase in men's of 42 percent within a year after no-fault divorce in California. I think Weitzman attributes to no-fault what should be attributed to gender neutrality. On custody, see Phyllis Chesler, *Mothers on Trial* (New York: McGraw-Hill, 1986).

14. Comparing the median income of the sexes from 25 to 50 years of age, 1975 to 1983, the U.S. Department of Labor Women's Bureau reports that women in 1975 made about $8,000 to men's $14,000; in 1983 women made $15,000 to men's $24,000. U.S. Department of Labor Women's Bureau, *Time of Change: 1983 Handbook of Women Workers*, Bulletin 298 (1983): 456. The Equal Pay Act was passed in 1963. On equal pay for equal work, see Christenson v. State of Iowa, 563 F.2d 353 (8th cir. 1977); Gerlach v. Michigan Bell Tel. Co., 501 F. Supp. 1300 (E.D. Mich. 1980); Odomes v. Nucare, Inc., 653 F.2d 246 (6th cir. 1981); Power v. Barry County, Michigan, 539 F. Supp. 721 (W.D. Mich. 1982); Lemons v. City and County of Denver, 17 FEP Cases 910 (D. Colo. 1978) *aff'd* 620 F.2d 228 (10th cir. 1977), *cert. denied*, 449 U.S. 888 (1980). See also Carol Jean Pint, "Value, Work and Women,"

Law and Inequality: A Journal of Theory and Practice (1983). To see the demise of women's schools on the horizon, combine the result of Bob Jones University v. United States, 461 U.S. 547 (1983) (private university loses tax exemption because internal racial segregation violates public policy) with Mississippi University of Women v. Hogan, 458 U.S. 718 (1982) (all-women public nursing school is sex discrimination).

15. A recent disgraceful example is the litigation in California Federal Savings and Loan Assn. v. Guerra, 479 U.S. 272 (1987), concerning statutory maternity leave. No feminist group supported the position the Supreme Court ultimately adopted that it was not sex discrimination for a state legislature to require maternity leaves and job security for pregnant women, and all but one (who argued that reproduction is a fundamental right) argued that it was. The Supreme Court figures out this women's rights issue better than the advocates for the women's movement.

16. Lemons v. City and County of Denver, 17 FEP Cases 910 (D. Colo. 1978).

17. E.E.O.C. v. Sears, Roebuck and Co., Civil Action No. 79-C-4373 (N.D. Ill. 1986), "Offer of Proof Concerning the Testimony of Dr. Rosalind Rosenberg," "Written Testimony of Alice Kessler Harris," "Written Rebuttal Testimony of Dr. Rosalind Rosenberg"; Rosalind Rosenberg, "The Sears Case: An Historical Overview," (mimeograph, November 25, 1985); Rosalind Rosenberg, "Women and Society Seminar: The Sears Case" (paper, December 16, 1985); Jon Weiner, "The Sears Case: Women's History on Trial," *The Nation*, September 7, 1985, pp. 1, 176–80; Alice Kessler-Harris, "Equal Employment Opportunity Commission v. Sears, Roebuck and Company: A Personal Account," *Radical History Review* (1986): 57–59. On February 3, 1986, the U.S. district judge ruled that the E.E.O.C. had failed to show that Sears discriminated against women.

18. Phillips v. Martin-Marietta, 400 U.S. 542 (1971).

19. Reed v. Reed, 404 U.S. 71 (1971).

20. City of Los Angeles v. Manhart, 435 U.S. 702 (1978) (fact women live longer does not justify sex discrimination in pension plans; but note that relief was not retroactive).

21. Aristotle, *Politics: A Treatise on Government,* trans. A. D. Lindsay (New York: E.P. Dutton, 1912), bk. 3, chap. 16: "Nature requires that the same right and the same rank should necessarily take place amongst all those who are equal by nature" (p. 101); idem, Ethica Nichomachea, trans. W. Ross (London: Oxford University Press, 1972), bk. 13, 1131a–b: "Things that are alike should be treated alike, while things that are unalike should be treated unalike in proportion to their unlikeness."

22. On women's nature: "Although moral virtue is common to all . . . yet the temperance of a man and a woman are not the same, nor their courage, nor their justice . . . for the courage of the man consists in commanding, the woman's in obeying" Aristotle, *Politics,* p. 24.

23. Kahn v. Shevin, 416 U.S. 351, 353 (1974).

24. Schlesinger v. Ballard, 419 U.S. 498 (1975).

25. Dothard v. Rawlinson, 433 U.S. 321 (1977).

26. Doerr v. B.F. Goodrich, 484 F. Supp. 320 (N.D. Ohio 1979); Hayes v. Shelby Memorial Hospital, 546 F. Supp. 259 (N.D. Ala. 1982); Wright v. Olin Corp., 697 F.2d 1172 (4th cir. 1982).

27. Meritor Savings Bank, FSB v. Vinson, 477 U.S. 57 (1986), includes a complaint for sexual harassment based on two-and-one-half years of rape by a bank supervisor.

28. David Cole, "Strategies of Difference: Litigating for Women's Rights in a Man's World," *Law and Inequality: A Journal of Theory and Practice* 2 (1984): 34, n. 4 (collecting cases).

29. One striking example is American Booksellers v. Hudnut, 771 F.2d 323 (7th cir.

1985) which held an ordinance to make pornography actionable as sex discrimination invalid under the First Amendment. The Supreme Court summarily affirmed, 106 S.Ct. 1172 (February 24, 1986), giving the City of Indianapolis no opportunity to argue the point on women's behalf.

30. Michael M. v. Superior Court of Sonoma County, 450 U.S. 464 (1981).

31. Rostker v. Goldberg, 453 U.S. 57 (1981).

32. The classic articulation of "neutral principles in constitutional adjudication" is by Herbert Wechsler in his attack on the Supreme Court for deinstitutionalizing racial segregation by law in Brown v. Board of Education (1954). "Toward Neutral Principles of Constitutional Law," *Harvard Law Review* 73 (1959).

JULIANNE MALVEAUX: GENDER DIFFERENCE AND BEYOND: AN ECONOMIC PERSPECTIVE ON DIVERSITY AND COMMONALITY AMONG WOMEN

1. In 1984, Black families had a median income of $15,432, just a few thousand dollars more than the poverty line, and 55.7% of white median family income. Though the ratio of Black family income to white rose among married-couple families (77.9%) and among families with wives in the labor force (81.8%), for families at the lower end of the economic spectrum two workers made the difference whether a family lived in poverty or not. See U.S. Department of Commerce, Bureau of the Census, *Money Income and Poverty Status of Families and Persons in the United States: 1984*, Current Populations Reports, Series P-60, No. 149 (Washington: U.S. Government Printing Office, 1985).

2. Julianne Malveaux, "Similarities and Differences in the Economic Interests of Black and White Women," *Review of Black Political Economy* 14/1 (Summer 1985). Data from this article, which is referenced extensively for this essay, come from published and unpublished Bureau of Labor Statistics sources. Data on detailed occupation and earnings in particular come from unpublished sources.

3. For information on the historically high level of Black women's participation in the labor force, see Julianne Malveaux, "Shifts in the Occupational and Employment Status of Black Women: Current Trends and Future Implications" in *Black Working Women: Debunking the Myths* (Berkeley: Center for the Study, Education and Advancement of Women, 1981).

4. Audre Lorde, "The Master's Tools Will Never Dismantle the Master's House," in *Sister Outsider* (New York: Crossing, 1984).

5. Julianne Malveaux, "From Domestic Worker to Household Technician: Black Women in a Changing Occupation," in Phyllis Wallace, *Black Women in the Labor Force* (Cambridge: MIT Press, 1980).

6. Julianne Malveaux and Susan Englander, "Race and Class in Nursing Occupations," *Sage Journal of Black Women's Studies* 3 (1987).

7. The term *labor market status* is used instead of *economic status* because labor status may be the most important determinant of black economic status. Still, there are more Blacks than whites with zero earnings. Of 11.1 million Black women, 1.6 million had no income. While 15 percent of Black women and 14 percent of Black men had no income, only 9.3 percent of white women and 4.4 percent of white men were in the same position. See U.S. Department of Commerce, Bureau of the Census, *"Money Income of Households, Families, and Persons in the United States, 1984* (Washington: U.S. Government Printing Office, 1986).

8. U.S. Department of Labor, Bureau of Labor Statistics, *Employment and Earnings* 34 (January 1987).

9. See Julianne Malveaux, "Economic Interests."

10. U.S. Bureau of Labor Statistics, *Employment and Earnings* 34.

11. Julianne Malveaux, "Black Women's Employment in Recession and Recovery," American Economics Association meetings, New York, December 1985.
12. Julianne Malveaux, "The Economic Interests of Black and White Women."
13. Ibid. See also Julianne Malveaux, *Low Wage Black Women: Occupational Descriptions, Strategies for Change* (New York: NAACP Legal Defense and Education Fund, 1984).
14. Julianne Malveaux, "The Economic Interests of Black and White Women."
15. Ibid.
16. Ibid.
17. Ibid.
18. Ibid.
19. Bureau of Labor Statistics, *Employment and Earnings* 34.
20. These differences are detailed in Julianne Malveaux "The Economic Interests of Black and White Women."
21. Julianne Malveaux, *No Images: Contemporary Black Women in the Workplace* (forthcoming). See chap. 6, "Daughters of Madame C. J. Walker: Black Women Entrepreneurs." See also U.S. Department of Commerce, *1982 Survey of Minority-Owned Business Enterprises* and *1982 Survey of Women-Owned Business Enterprises* (Washington: U.S. Government Printing Office, 1985).
22. Andrew Brimmer, "Prosperity among Black Women," *Black Enterprise Magazine* (December 1984).
23. Andrew Hacker, "Women and Work," *New York Review of Books*, August 14, 1986.
24. Bureau of Labor Statistics, unpublished data, 1986.
25. Bill Moyers, "The Vanishing Black Family: Crisis in the Black Community," *CBS Special Report*, January 1986.
26. William Wilbanks, *The Myth of a Racist Criminal Justice System* (Monterey, Calif.: Brooks/Cole, 1985), tables 3–7. Although the author argues that the criminal justice system is not racist, the data he presents suggest the opposite, that Black men are more likely to be arrested and convicted than are white men.
27. Bebe Moore Campbell, *Angry Men, Successful Women: Backlash in Two-Career Marriages* (New York: Random House, 1985).
28. Paula Giddings, *When and Where I Enter: The Impact of Black Women on Race and Sex in America* (New York: William Morrow, 1982).
29. Julianne Malveaux, "The Political Economy of Black Women," in Manning Marable, *The Year Left* (London: Verso, 1987).
30. Julianne Malveaux, "Comparable Worth and Its Impact on Black Women," (*Review of Black Political Economy*; reprinted in Margaret Simms and Julianne Malveaux, eds., *Slipping through the Cracks: The Status of Black Women* (New Brunswick, N.J.: Transactions, 1986).

ALISON M. JAGGAR: SEXUAL DIFFERENCE AND SEXUAL EQUALITY

1. Estelle Freedman, "Separatism as Strategy: Female Institution Building and American Feminism, 1870–1930," *Feminist Studies* (1979): 512–29.
2. Rosalind Rosenberg, *Beyond Separate Spheres: Intellectual Roots of Modern Feminism* (New Haven: Yale University Press, 1982).
3. Mary Wollstonecraft, *The Rights of Woman* (London: Dent, 1965); John Stuart Mill, *The Subjection of Women* (London: Dent, 1965).
4. Carolyn G. Heilbrun, *Toward a Recognition of Androgyny* (New York: Alfred A. Knopf, 1973).
5. Lenore J. Weitzman, *The Divorce Revolution* (New York: Free Press, 1985).
6. Katharine T. Bartlett and Carol B. Stack, "Joint Custody, Feminism, and the Dependency Dilemma," *Berkeley Women's Law Journal* (Winter 1986–87).

7. Linda J. Krieger, "Through a Glass Darkly: Paradigms of Equality and the Search for a Woman's Jurisprudence," *Hypatia* 2 (1987).

8. Hilary Allen, "At the Mercy of Her Hormones: Premenstrual Tension and the Law," *m/f* 9 (1984).

9. Cynthia Gillespie, *Justifiable Homicide: Battered Women's Self Defense and the Law* (Columbus: Ohio State University Press, 1989).

10. Mary K. Blakely, "Is One Woman's Sexuality Another Woman's Pornography?" *Ms.* (April 1985): 46–47.

11. Wendy Williams, "The Equality Crisis: Some Reflections on Culture, Courts, and Feminism," *Women's Rights Law Reporter* 7 (1982): 196, n. 114.

12. Ibid., 188, n. 75.

13. Ynestra King, private conversation, 1985.

14. Elizabeth V. Spelman, *Inessential Woman: Problems of Exclusion in Feminist Thought* (Boston: Beacon, 1988).

15. Alison M. Jaggar, "Human Biology in Feminist Theory," in *Beyond Domination: New Perspectives on Women and Philosophy*, ed. Carol C. Gould (Totowa, N.J.: Rowman and Allanheld, 1984).

16. Alison M. Jaggar, "Sex Inequality and Bias in Sex Differences Research," *Canadian Journal of Philosophy*, suppl. 13 (1987).

17. Nancy Hartsock, *Money, Sex and Power: Toward a Feminist Historical Materialism* (New York: Longman, 1983), 23.

18. Sara Ruddick, "Remarks on the Sexual Politics of Reason," in Eva Feder Kittay and Diana Meyers, eds., *Women and Moral Theory* (Totowa, N.J.: Rowman and Allanheld, 1987).

19. Carol Gilligan, *In a Different Voice: Psychological Theory and Women's Development* (Cambridge: Harvard University Press, 1982).

20. Idem, "Reply," *SIGNS* 11 (1986).

21. See, for example, Sheila Mullett, "Only Connect: The Place of Self-Knowledge in Ethics," *Canadian Journal of Philosophy*, suppl. 13 (1987).

22. Ruddick, "Sexual Politics," 252.

23. Seyla Benhabib, "The Generalized and the Concrete Other: The Kohlberg-Gilligan Controversy and Feminist Theory," *Praxis International* 5 (1986).

24. Nel Noddings, *Caring: A Feminine Approach to Ethics and Moral Education* (Berkeley: University of California Press, 1984).

25. Karl Marx, *Critique of the Gotha Programme*, in *Selected Works of Karl Marx and Frederick Engels* (New York: International, 1968), 328.

26. Kai Nielsen, *Equality and Liberty: A Defense of Radical Egalitarianism* (Totowa, N.J.: Rowman and Allanheld, 1985).

27. Ynestra King, "Postscript," in Adrienne Harris and Ynestra King, eds., *Rocking the Ship of State: Towards a Feminist Peace Politics* (Boulder, Colo.: Westview, 1989).

28. John Rawls, *A Theory of Justice* (Cambridge: Harvard University Press, 1971), 3.

29. Barbara Ehrenreich and Deirdre English, *For Her Own Good: 150 Years of the Experts' Advice to Women* (New York: Anchor, 1979).

ESTELLE B. FREEDMAN: THEORETICAL PERSPECTIVES ON SEXUAL DIFFERENCE: AN OVERVIEW

1. Rosalind Rosenberg, *Beyond Separate Spheres: Intellectual Roots of Modern Feminism* (New Haven: Yale University Press, 1982), 5–12.

2. Rossi's essay appears in *Daedalus* 106 (Spring 1977): 1–31.

3. Carol Gilligan, *In a Different Voice: Psychological Theory and Women's Development* (Cambridge: Harvard University Press, 1982).

4. Michelle Z. Rosaldo, "Theoretical Overview," in Michelle Zimbalist Rosaldo and Louise Lamphere, *Woman, Culture and Society* (Stanford: Stanford University Press, 1974), 17–42; and "The Use and Abuse of Anthropology: Reflections on Feminism and Cross-Cultural Understanding," *SIGNS* (1980): 389–417.

5. Cherrie Moraga and Gloria Anzaldua, *This Bridge Called My Back: Writings by Radical Women of Color* (Watertown, Mass.: Persephone, 1981); Barbara Smith, ed., *Home Girls: A Black Feminist Anthology* (New York: Kitchen Table—Women of Color, 1983); Evelyn Torton Beck, ed., *Nice Jewish Girls: A Lesbian Anthology* (Watertown, Mass: Persephone, 1982); Marsha Saxton and Florence Howe, eds., *With Wings: An Anthology of Literature by and about Women with Disabilities* (New York: Feminist, 1987). See also Bonnie Zimmerman, "The Politics of Transliteration: Lesbian Personal Narratives," in Estelle B. Freedman et al., *The Lesbian Issue: Essays from SIGNS* (Chicago: University of Chicago Press, 1985), 251–70; and Adrienne Rich, "Notes Towards a Politics of Location," in *Blood, Bread, and Poetry: Selected Prose, 1979–1985* (New York: W. W. Norton, 1986), 210–31. See also the essay by Bell Hooks in this collection.

6. Bernice Johnson Reagon, "Coalition Politics: Turning the Century," in Smith, *Home Girls,* 360–61.

7. For an excellent critique of the use of deconstruction in feminist theory, see Barbara Christian, "The Race for Theory," *Feminist Studies* 14 (1988): 67–79.

8. I have made this argument in "Separatism as Strategy: Female Institution Building and American Feminism, 1870–1930," *Feminist Studies* 5 (1979): 512–29.

Contributors

Nancy J. Chodorow is the author of *The Reproduction of Mothering: Psychoanalysis and the Sociology of Gender* (1978) and *Feminism and Psychoanalytic Theory* (1989). She teaches sociology and women's studies at the University of California, Berkeley, and has a psychoanalytic clinical practice.

Jane F. Collier is associate professor of anthropology at Stanford University. She received her Ph.D. from Tulane University and has coedited, with Sylvia Yanagisako, *Gender and Kinship: Essays Toward a Unified Analysis* (1987). She is completing a book on changing family patterns in southern Spain.

Kay Deaux is professor and head of the Social-Personality Psychology Program at the Graduate Center of the City University of New York. She is the author of *The Behavior of Women and Men* (1976), *Women of Steel* (1983), and numerous articles and chapters on gender.

Carl N. Degler is Margaret Byrne Professor of American History at Stanford University. He is the author of *At Odds: Women and the Family from the Revolution to the Present* (1980), and other works on the history of women. Presently he is completing a history of the use of biological ideas in the social sciences from 1900 to the present.

John Dupré, associate professor of philosophy, has taught at Stanford since 1982. In addition to his work on feminist philosophy, he has published on metaphysics and the philosophy of science, especially biology, in journals including *Philosophical Review, Mind,* and *Philosophy of Science.* He is also the editor of *The Latest on the Best: Essays on Evolution and Optimality* (1987).

Estelle B. Freedman is professor of history at Stanford University, where she teaches women's and social history and feminist studies. She is the coauthor with John D'Emilio of *Intimate Matters: A History of Sexuality in America* (1988) and the author of *Their Sisters' Keepers: Women's Prison Reform in America, 1830–1930* (1981).

Marilyn Frye is a professor of philosophy and affiliate of the Women's Studies Program at Michigan State University. Her theorizing is rooted both in philosophy and in her participation in an activist lesbian/feminist community. She is author of *The Politics of Reality* (1983).

Regenia Gagnier is an associate professor of English and a member of the Feminist Studies Committee, the Institute for Research on Women and Gender, and the Cultural Studies Group at Stanford. Her publications include *Subjectivities*, a comparative analysis of subjectivity and value across gender and socioeconomic class in Victorian and early twentieth-century Britain (1991), *Idylls of the Marketplace: Oscar Wilde and the Victorian Public* (1986), and articles on feminist, social, and cultural theory.

Bell Hooks (Gloria Watkins) is a writer, feminist theorist, cultural critic, and associate professor of English and women's studies at Oberlin College. She is the author of *Ain't I a Woman: Black Women and Feminism* (1981), *Feminist Theory: From Margins to Center* (1984), and a recent collection of essays, *Talking Back* (1988).

Ruth Hubbard is professor of biology at Harvard University, where she teaches courses on the interrelationship of science and society, particularly as it affects women. She has written numerous articles and edited several books on women's biology and health. Her latest book is *The Politics of Women's Biology* (1990), and she is currently working on a book for nonscientists about the new genetic technologies.

Alison M. Jaggar is Obed J. Wilson Professor of Ethics and professor of philosophy at the University of Cincinnati. Her work has been primarily in social, political, and moral philosophy, including philosophy of education, and in feminist philosophy. Her books include: *Feminist Frameworks*, coedited with Paula Rothenberg (1978, 1984), *Feminist Politics and Human Nature* (1983), and *Gender/Body/Knowledge: Feminist Reconstructions of Being and Knowing*, coedited with Susan R. Bordo (1989). At present she is working on feminism and moral theory with the support of a grant from the Rockefeller Foundation. Jaggar was a founder of the Society for Women in Philosophy, serves on the editorial board of several journals, and chairs the American Philosophical Association Committee on the Status of Women.

Herma Hill Kay has been professor of law at the University of California, Berkeley, since 1960. Her specialties include sex-based discrimination, family law, and the conflict of laws. She is particularly interested in the social and behavioral implications of the legal concept of equality between women and men.

Catharine A. MacKinnon is a feminist lawyer, teacher, writer, and activist. She designed the legal claim for sexual harassment and, with Andrea Dworkin, ordinances defining pornography as a violation of women's civil rights. Her books include *Sexual Harassment of Working Women* (1979), *Feminism Unmodified* (1987), and *Toward a Feminist Theory of the State* (1989).

Brenda Major is professor of psychology at the State University of New York at Buffalo. She is a corecipient of the 1988 Gordon Allport Intergroup Relations Prize from SPSSI and of the 1985 Distinguished Publication Award from the Association for Women in Psychology. Her research focuses on social comparison processes and coping and on the consequences of social stigma for self-esteem.

Julianne Malveaux is an independent scholar-activist whose economic research focuses on labor-market and social policy issues, especially their impact on African-Americans, other ethnic minorities, and women. She has most recently been affiliated with the Economics Department at the University of California, Berkeley, and the Institute for Research on Women and Gender at Stanford University. Her publications include *Slipping through the Cracks: The Status of Black Women* (with Margaret Simms) (1986), *No Images: Contemporary Black Women in the Labor Market* (forthcoming), and "Transitions: The Black Adolescent in the Labor Market," in Reginald Jones ed., *The Black Adolescent* (1989).

Nel Noddings is professor of education at Stanford University, where she teaches courses in ethics, moral education, and feminist studies. She is author of *Caring* (1984) and *Women and Evil* (1989).

Karen Offen is a historian and independent scholar affiliated with the Institute for Research on Women and Gender at Stanford University. Her training is in modern European history with an emphasis on France, and she is currently publishing on European women's history and the comparative history of feminism.

Susan Moller Okin is professor of politics at Brandeis University. She is the author of *Women in Western Political Thought* (1979) and *Justice, Gender, and the Family* (1989).

Deborah L. Rhode is a professor of law and director of the Institute for Research on Women and Gender at Stanford University. She teaches and writes on sex-based discrimination and legal ethics. Her most recent work is *Justice and Gender* (1989).

Barrie Thorne is the Streisand Professor in the Program for the Study of Women and Men in Society and in the Sociology Department at the University of Southern California. She coedited *Language, Gender and Society* (1983) and *Rethinking the Family: Some Feminist Questions* (1982).

Sylvia J. Yanagisako is associate professor of anthropology and chair of the program in Feminist Studies at Stanford University. She has done research on kinship and gender among Japanese-Americans and entrepreneurial families in northern Italy. Her publications include *Transforming the Past: Kinship and Tradition among Japanese Americans* (1985) and (with Jane Collier) *Gender and Kinship: Essays Toward a Unified Analysis* (1987).

Index